Landscape Techniques

Incorporating

Techniques of

Landscape Architecture

Landscape Techniques

incorporating

*Techniques of
Landscape Architecture*

Edited for the Landscape Institute by

A. E. WEDDLE

VNR VAN NOSTRAND REINHOLD COMPANY
NEW YORK   CINCINNATI   TORONTO   LONDON   MELBOURNE

opposite Beech trees in Savernake Forest

Copyright © 1979 by Landscape Institute

Library of Congress Catalog Card Number 79–65684

ISBN O–442–25627–2

First published 1979 in Great Britain
by William Heinemann Ltd.

Printed in Great Britain

Published in 1979 by Van Nostrand Reinhold Company
A division of Litton Educational Publishing, Inc.
135 West 50th Street, New York, NY 10020, U.S.A.

Van Nostrand Reinhold Limited
1410 Birchmount Road
Scarborough, Ontario M1P 2E7, Canada

16 15 14 13 12 11 10 9 8 7 6 5 4 3 2 1

Introduction

This book is a complete revision of the original *Techniques of Landscape Architecture* first published in 1967. Three chapters are entirely new and by new authors. Other chapters have been fully revised and brought up to date by their original authors. The new chapters are SURVEY AND ANALYSIS – Gorden Hyden, WATER – D.G. Thornley, and MAINTENANCE AND CONSERVATION – Tom Wright and John Parker. A recasting of chapter sequence brings Gordon Hyden's chapter on survey work to the beginning of the book to precede that by Dame Sylvia Crowe on site planning. D.G. Thornley's chapter deals more extensively with water as a larger element in the landscape than was previously the case in the original chapter by G.A. Jellicoe, whilst some of the original material is still retained. The chapter on management now covers conservation and broad-scale landscape management in replacement of the previous treatment of administration and maintenance. This recasting has also made it logical to move Geoffrey Collens' revised chapter on professional practice to the end of the book.

In the decade which has elapsed since the preparation of the original book a great deal has happened in the landscape profession. There are now more landscape architects in total and much of the increase is in areas where individual involvement comes earlier in the planning process and at a more senior level than previously. In common with members of other environmental professions landscape architects find their services in great demand. They also find the need for increased expertise and professionalism in the application of their skills. This has been recognised by the landscape profession which has recently resolved to incorporate the land sciences and landscape management within an expanded LANDSCAPE INSTITUTE.

Contents

1967 – Tree and Woodland grants – National Parks Acts – Control of
caravan and camp sites – Reclamation of derelict land – Agriculture Act,
1947 – Recent legislation and taxation

Appendix

Authors

MRS PATRICIA BOOTH, B.Sc.(Hort), F.L.I. Landscape Architect in private practice.

TIMOTHY COCHRANE, M.L.A.(Pennsylvania), Dip.L.D.(Dunelm) R.I.B.A., F.L.I., Architect and Landscape Architect in private practice.

GEOFFREY A. COLLENS, M.L.A.(Pennsylvania), R.I.B.A., F.L.I., Architect and Landscape Architect, Senior Associate, Derek Lovejoy and Partners, London. Editor of *Landscape Design*.

MISS BRENDA COLVIN, C.B.E., P.P.I.L.A., Landscape Consultant to Department of the Environment, Central Electricity Generating Board, etc. Author of *Land and Landscape*, Murray, and *Trees for Town and Country*.

DAME SYLVIA CROWE, D.B.E., P.P.I.L.A., Hon.F.R.I.B.A., Hon.M.R.T.P.I., Lately Landscape Consultant to the Forestry Commission, C.E.G.B., Harlow and Washington New Towns, etc. Author of *Tomorrow's Landscape*, *Landscape of Power*, *Landscape of Roads* and *Garden Design*.

FREDERICK GIBBERD, K.B., C.B.E., R.A., F.R.I.B.A., M.T.P.I., F.L.I., Architect, planner and landscape consultant. Author of *Town Design*, *Architecture of England*, *Modern Flats* (with F. R. S. Yorke), *Design in Town and Village* (with Sharp and Holford).

IAN GREENFIELD, B.Sc.(Agric.), M.I.Biol. Turf grass consultant, director of the Cayford Technical Service. Talks and broadcasts. Author of *Turf Culture*.

BRIAN HACKETT, M.A., P.P.I.L.A., R.I.B.A., M.T.P.I., Professor of Landscape Architecture, University of Newcastle-upon-Tyne (to 1977) Visiting Professor of Landscape Architecture, University of Illinois, U.S.A. 1960–62. Author of *Man, Society and Environment*, and *Landscape Planning*.

GORDON HYDEN, Dip. L.A.(Birmingham), A.L.I. Head of Department of Landscape Architecture, Gloucestershire College of Art and Design, Cheltenham.

JOHN C. PARKER, B.Sc.(Hort), Principal Assistant (Landscape Maintenance), Estates and Valuation Department, Kent County Council.

IAN PURDY, R.I.B.A., Dip.T.P.(Lond.). M.R.T.P.I., County Planning Officer, Cambridgeshire County Council.

DENIS G. THORNLEY, B.A., F.R.I.B.A. Reader in Architecture, University of Manchester. Architect and Landscape Consultant.

TOM W. J. WRIGHT, B.Sc.(Hort), Senior Lecturer in Landscape and Amenity Horticulture, Wye College (University of London).

OTHER CONTRIBUTORS:

G. A. BASS, Dip.Arch.(Leicester), R.I.B.A., A.L.I. Partner, G. Alan Burnett & Partners, Chartered Architects, Structural Engineers, Landscape Architects, Planning Consultants.

E. BRENT JONES, Civic Trust.

G. V. DARRAH, B.A.(Nat. Sc.), B.A.(For.), South-Western Woodlands Association Ltd.

O. L. GILBERT, B.Sc.(Bot), D.I.C.(Plant Path), Ph.D., Ecologist, Lecturer in Landscape Architecture, University of Sheffield.

D. J. GREIG, B.Sc.(Agric), M.Sc.(Agric. Eng.), A.M.I.Agr.E., Lecturer in Farm Mechanisation, University of Newcastle-upon-Tyne.

Plates

Acknowledgements

Contributors

Many landscape architects and members of allied professions have been consulted and have given advice or commented on the preparation and revision of this book. Their help is gratefully acknowledged. In the original version it was possible to mention some by name but the list would now be difficult to make up especially to give due credit to those who drew attention to important points soon after publication as well as to those who have kindly helped individual chapter authors with recent revisions. The editor wishes to express appreciation for all that has been done to add to the usefulness of *Landscape Techniques*.

Photographs

J. Allan Cash, *frontispiece:*

Lawrence Halprin, Plate 2.1; H. S. Howgrave-Graham, 2.2; Derek Lovejoy and Partners, 2.3; Craigavon Planning Executive, 2.4; Harlow Development Corporation, 2.6; *Country Life*, 2.8; Handford Photography, 2.10; Michael Porter, 2.11; Caterpillar Tractor Co. Ltd., 3.1, 3.2, 3.3, 3.4, 3.5, 3.6; N.C.K. Rapier Ltd., 3.7, 3.8, 3.9, 3.10, 3.11, 3.12, 3.13; Architectural Press, 4.1, 4.4, 8.4; Cement and Concrete Association, 4.2, 4.9, 4.10; C. R. V. Tandy, 4.5, 9.5, 9.7, 9.8, 9.9, 10.13; Michael Brown, 4.6; Basildon Development Corporation, 4.8; G. S. Thomas, 5.5; Frederick Gibberd and Partners, 6.1; John Donat, 6.2; Richard Sheppard, Robson and Partners, 6.3; Neptune Concrete Ltd., 6.4; Building Design Partnership, 6.5; Stevenage Development Corporation, 6.6; Colin Westwood, 6.7; Abacus Municipal Ltd., 6.8; Atlas Lighting Ltd., 6.9; Elton Civic Supplies Ltd., 6.11; Burnham and Co. Ltd., 6.13; Mono Concrete Ltd., 6.14; Aerofilms Ltd., 7.1, 7.2, 7.5, 7.18; Brenda Colvin 7.3, 10.1, 10.3; Jellicoe and Coleridge, 7.4; Airviews Ltd., 7.13; Meridian Airmaps Ltd., 7.14; John Brooks, 8.2, 8.3, 8.4, 8.6; Sisis Equipment Ltd., 9.3; Ransomes Sims and Jefferies Ltd., 9.4, 9.5, 9.7, 9.8; H. Pattisson and Co. Ltd., 9.6; Forestry Commission, 10.2, 10.4, 10.6; Geigy Agricultural Chemicals, 11.16, 11.17.

Note on Metrication

Since first publication of the original *Techniques of Landscape Architecture* the development and construction industries in Britain have adopted metric measure. This has now been used in the present publication. Metric dimensions are given in the text and tables and wherever possible they have been followed by Imperial measure in brackets for the benefit of those who still use, or think in terms of, the old quantities. The principle adopted has been to give sensible metric dimensions of the kind necessary to describe or specify landscape work with an *approximate* indication of the nearest dimension which would be used in Imperial measure, rather than the exact equivalent used in conversion from one to the other.

It is hoped that readers will find this translation helpful to grasp the quantities involved, especially where order of magnitude measures rather than precise dimensions are required in both the metric and Imperial measures. Neither the British Standard version of metric nor the British Standard code of practice for conversions are especially helpful in this respect. Anyone familiar with Continental metric usage which for example employs the centimetre will still find the millimetre, as used in British practice, a unit too small to deal with the bulky items measured for landscape work, and the empirical rates of oz per sq yd, cwt per acre will after a transition period give way to similarly broad approximate rates in metric. Familiarity with quantities such as 2–3 oz per sq yd and $1\frac{1}{2}$–2 cwt per acre will find their rounded off equivalent rather than their converted rates in g per m^2 and kg per hectare irrespective of the rates which might be needed for accurate conversion. Some examples of broad approximations are as follows.

In Chapter 10 the author refers to 1500 ft as the generally accepted upper limit of conifer planting in Britain. Use of the precise metric conversion would be silly when we are describing an arbitrary limit which lies between 450 and 500 m. The same author prescribes soil depth of *about 18 in* after talking of 9–18 in depths and going on to say that much depends on local conditions and suggesting that no hard and fast rules apply; thus up to 'half a metre' will be a more helpful translation than the precise conversions in millimetres.

In the chapter on grasses the precise conversion of appropriate grass heights, width of mowing machines, seed in lb per sq yd, fertiliser in cwt per acre has needed sensible translation from time to time, rounded off more roundly than the direct conversion figures. In the same chapter some further rounding off has been done, especially in tables, to ensure that separately the rates in kg/100 m^2 and lbs per 100 sq yd give sensible quantities which will be readily grasped by anyone used to either metric or Imperial measures.

A. E. W.

1 Site Survey and Analysis

G. W. HYDEN

1.1 Introduction

1.1.1 The survey

A landscape survey will consist of a collation of the measurable quantities and qualities of a site. The amount, type and quantity of material collected will to a large extent be dependent upon the purpose for which the survey is being undertaken. The procedure adopted for the production of the survey will fall into three primary areas:

The collection of data previously recorded, which is available and is relevant to the site under investigation and to the aims of the survey.

The site survey, which will consist of the measurement of the physical characteristics of the site by means of instruments of various types.

The visual and qualitative characteristics of the site, which will be dependent upon the observations of the surveyor. In the case of landscape surveys this can only be carried out successfully by a person trained to take note of the biotic and visual qualities of a site and its surroundings.

The information, when gathered, should be subjected to careful collation, finally producing in the most concise manner a record of the information collected. This may be presented in the form of drawings, photographs, written documents and in some cases by three-dimensional models, according to the demands the survey must satisfy.

1.1.2 Analysis

The analysis of the information gathered at the landscape survey stage will consist of the breaking down of the available matter into its component parts. The components may vary in accordance with the proposed or potential use of the area. At this stage it may be important to consider the reasons which generated the need for the survey and analysis. The objective may be to produce as much information as is possible, to assist in the successful completion of an established aim. For example, to provide the basic site data which will enable a housing project to go forward in the best relationship to the site possible.

On the other hand the objective of the survey and analysis may be to identify the most suitable use for the site, or to provide data which will enable several sites to be compared, in relation to several alternative uses. For example, to select sites most suitable for housing within a potential development area.

1.2 Data collection

1.2.1 Maps

Vast quantities of previously collected and recorded information are available for the majority of sites in Great Britain. The Ordnance Survey has been responsible for the surveying and mapping of Great Britain since the end of the eighteenth century. A wide variety of scales are used and many discontinued scales may be encountered. The principal scales in use at present are as follows.

Larger scale maps. $1:1,250$ (50in) $50\cdot688$ in to 1 mile covers 500×500 m of some urban areas only. Bench marks and spot heights are shown.

$1:2,500$ (25 in) $25\cdot344$ in to 1 mile, covers 1 sq km (published in pairs) of the whole country. Bench marks and spot heights are shown.

$1:10,560$ (6 in) 6 in to 1 mile, covers 5×5 km of the whole country. Contours drawn at 25 ft ($7\cdot62$ m) vertical intervals. Being systematically replaced by $1:10,000$.

Small scale maps. $1:25,000$ ($2\frac{1}{2}$ in) Approximately $2\frac{1}{2}$ in to 1 mile covers 10×10 km of the whole country. Contours drawn at 25 ft ($7\cdot62$ m) vertical intervals.

$1:50,000$ Approximately $1\frac{1}{4}$ in to 1 mile, covers the whole of the country.

Other small scale maps. $1:1,000,000$; $1:250,000$; $1:625,000$; $1:100,000$; $1:1,125,000$; and $1:63,360$. These are often used for specialist purposes. O.S. publications will give details.

1

Maps are produced to record the currently available data of the following:

Geological Survey maps now cover most of the country to scales of 1:250,000 ($\frac{1}{4}$ in) and 1:50,000 or 1:63,360 (1 in). With the exception of a few areas where combined editions are produced the solid and drift geology are shown separately.

Land Classification maps are published by the Ministry of Agriculture, Fisheries and Food, overprinted on to the 1:63,360 O.S. maps. These are agricultural classifications, giving information on a broad basis of land quality related to cultivable crops.

The Soil Survey of England and Wales has begun to produce information on the soils of some districts. These are also produced to a scale of 1:63,360 on an O.S. base.

The Climatological Atlas of the British Isles produced by the Meteorological Office shows a collection of climatic data.

1.2.2 Photographic survey

Information relative to a particular site may be available in the form of photographic records. These will be one or a combination of the following types:

(a) Terrestrial photographs, taken from the ground with the camera axis horizontal. These photographs may be invaluable later as a base for photomontage impressions of changes which may be created by development.

(b) Aerial oblique photographs are usually taken from an aircraft with the axis of the camera inclined to the vertical, giving a bird's eye view of the site.

(c) Vertical photographs are taken from an aircraft in level flight, with the axis of the camera vertical. These photographs can be assembled as a mosaic and printed to a scale which will coincide with maps being used on a project.

A pair of overlapping photographs (60% overlap is usual) will permit stereoscopic viewing of an area and can provide the data necessary for a visual reconstruction of the three-dimensional image. Maps can then be made with the heights measured from the photographs, or a pair of prints may be viewed with a stereoscope, simply to get a three-dimensional impression of the site. False colour film can be used, presenting areas normally green in shades of pink. Variations in the tone can indicate differences in species and in the condition of the vegetation.

Plate 1.1. An oblique aerial photograph used for landscape survey work on the Heriot-Watt University site at Riccarton. Landscape consultant A. E. Weddle.

Information may be available from sensing equipment other than the conventional camera and invisible information may be obtained by means of thermal change, differential gravitation and electromagnetic variation. These more sophisticated techniques will usually be associated with larger surveys and in exploration surveys associated with Landscape Planning and Resource Development.

1.2.3 Recorded data

Additional data regarding the site may be obtained from various sources. Information referring to climate can be obtained from the Meteorological Office. This is a summary of the information provided by the Regional Meteorological Stations. Information from local stations, universities and research establishments is available in certain parts of the country. The most common information will include, rainfall, temperature, hours of sunshine, wind speed and direction. In larger urban areas it may also be possible to obtain air pollution statistics from the local authority. Obtaining the number of readings necessary to give a useful set of results can take many years, and short-term results should be treated with great caution, particularly with regard to details.

1.2.4 Restraints

It is important to ascertain the existence of all restrictions which may influence possible development of the site under scrutiny. These may take the form of administrative restrictions, or may be the result of existing land use or services. Planning restrictions will be obtainable from the District Office of the Local Planning Authority. Existing or proposed uses should be checked to ascertain any possible effect on the site potential; these may include the following: ownership; rights of way; easements and holders of wayleaves. It may be necessary to consult adjoining owners. Gas, water and electricity boards, the post office for telecommunications, oil companies and the Coal Board and the Ministry of Defence may be among many others who will have rights and interests in the site.

1.3 Site survey

1.3.1 Field surveying

The scope of this chapter is confined to the site surveying which a landscape architect might be expected to carry out himself and deals only with the equipment one would expect to find in a medium size office, which did not employ a specialist surveyor. Survey work is now most commonly completed in metric units and for all practical purposes the kilometre, the metre and the millimetre only should be used for linear measurement.

1 km = 1,000 m
1 m = 1,000 mm

Normally only the metre and millimetre will be used in the field book, and to avoid writing m or mm after each entry and on drawings the convention is to show metres with a decimal marker (25·0) but to show millimetres to the nearest whole millimetre without a decimal marker (250). The kilometre will not be used very frequently in field work but when it is used, km is inserted after the figures. Heights are expressed in metres normally to a precision of one millimetre (0·001 m). The units of area normally accepted are the square kilometre, the hectare and the square metre.

1 km² = 100 ha
1 ha = 10,000 m²

Volume is expressed in cubic metres (m³) and liquid volumes in litres (l).

Almost every survey method is based upon triangulation and the basic triangle can be obtained in one of three ways by establishing:

The lengths of all three sides;
The lengths of two sides and one angle;
The length of one side and two angles.

The first of the three methods is usually achieved by a chain survey. The measurement of the sides is made by the use of a steel chain, linen or glass-fibre tapes. The metric chain is made in a variety of lengths (50, 30, 25 or 20 m), the 20 m length being preferred for tapes. Steel tapes and steel bound chains are subject to easy damage and the linen tape is subject to stretching, particularly when wet.

The corners of the triangles are marked with ranging rods 2, 2·5 or 3 m long with 0·2 or 0·5 m bands in red, white and black. From known points on the main chain lines, offsets are taken to pick up detail. The offsets are obtained by steel rule, a short steel tape or with a 2 m surveyor's folding rod. Having sketched the basic framework of the survey identifying letters should be added. The chain distance along the chain line is written between the centre lines of the field book and the offset with detail sketches are placed on the appropriate side of the lines. The book is commenced at the last page and filled in from bottom to top.

In addition to the plane survey it will be necessary to establish the relative height of points on the survey. This is done by levelling. The Ordnance Survey use Mean Sea Level at Newlyn in Cornwall as a datum throughout the United Kingdom and refer to this as Ordnance Datum (OD). Bench Marks (BM) are set up throughout the country as fixed points of known height above OD. From

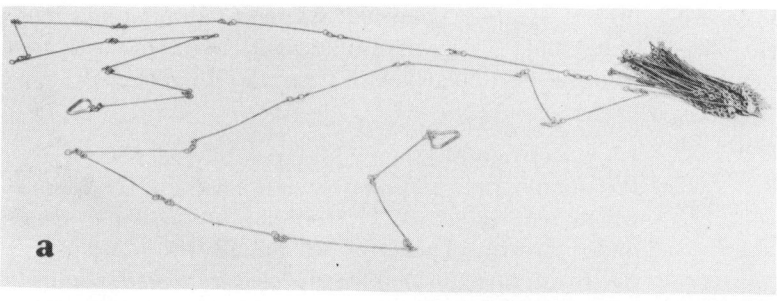

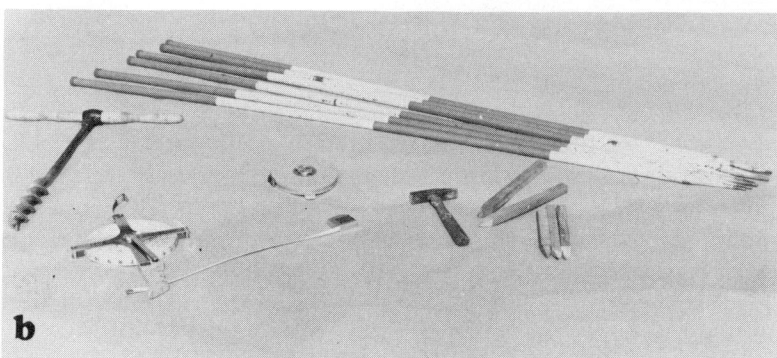

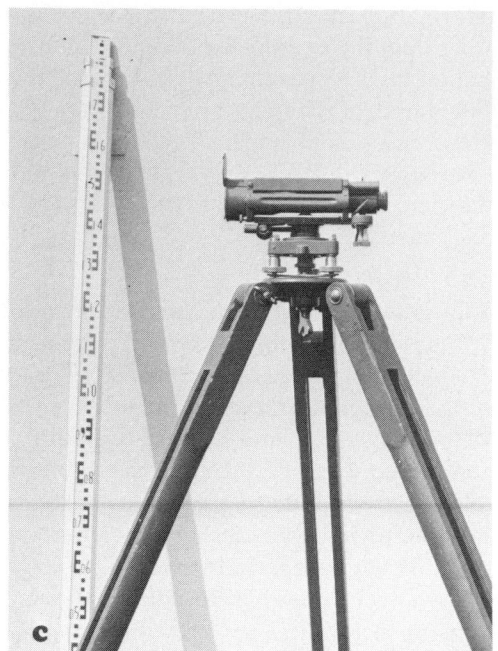

Plate 1.2. SURVEY EQUIPMENT – (*a*) The chain (*b*) Surveying equipment (*c*) Tilting level and staff.

these the level of other points may be established.

The most common instrument in use for levelling is the dumpy level which is a simple telescope with a levelling bubble tube attached. This is supported by a plate adjusted by three foot-screws and all attached to a tripod. The tilting level is similar to the dumpy in all but its support system, in which usually a ball and socket replaces the screws, but a pivot is placed between the support and the telescope which requires a slight readjustment before each reading is taken, unlike the dumpy, which once set up requires no resetting. Automatic levels are now in use: these require only rough levelling up; the fine adjustment is catered for within the instrument itself.

Once a level is set up the telescope will sweep a horizontal plane of a constant height. The vertical distance to the ground is then measured by means of a graduated levelling staff, observed through the level. Levelling staffs can be metal or wood and may be of telescopic, sectional or folding construction to facilitate transport, giving open lengths of 2, 3, 4 or 5 m. Graduations are in multiples of 10 mm and the final place can be estimated if a more accurate reading is required. A single position for the level is often inadequate to cover the whole of the survey area. When all the required levels have been taken, a fore sight is taken on to a change point, the level is then moved and a back sight on to the same change point is taken before starting a new series of intermediate sights. The process is repeated, giving a process known as series levelling. Observations are recorded in a level book, of which there are two types in common use:

The rise and fall method which relates each reading to the previous one, recording its rise above or fall below the previous entry.

The collimation, in which each reading is related to the height of the instrument.

In both cases remarks are placed on the right-hand side of the page and levels are reduced to a common datum level, usually the OD on a BM.

On occasions when the chain-survey method may be inadequate, a combination of angular and linear measurement may be necessary. Combine with this the need to establish levels and the theodolite becomes the obvious choice of instrument. In principle the instrument is simple. It is however a most versatile survey instrument that is designed to measure horizontal and vertical angles. Calculations based upon the readings require mathematical tables or calculating machines and are beyond the scope of this chapter. This takes us into the field of more sophisticated survey methods and instruments which are used for larger and more complex surveys and are the concern of specialist surveyors rather than the practising landscape architect.

1.3.2 Visual survey

A visual survey of the site and its surroundings forms a most important part of the landscape survey. The concern of the landscape architect with the visual characteristics of the landscape makes this part of the survey particularly relevant to him. Many details will be recorded on

4

Fig. 1.1. LEVEL AND FIELD BOOK NOTES – (*a*) Field sketch; (*b*) Field book; (*c*) Level book, rise and fall; (*d*) Level book, collimation.

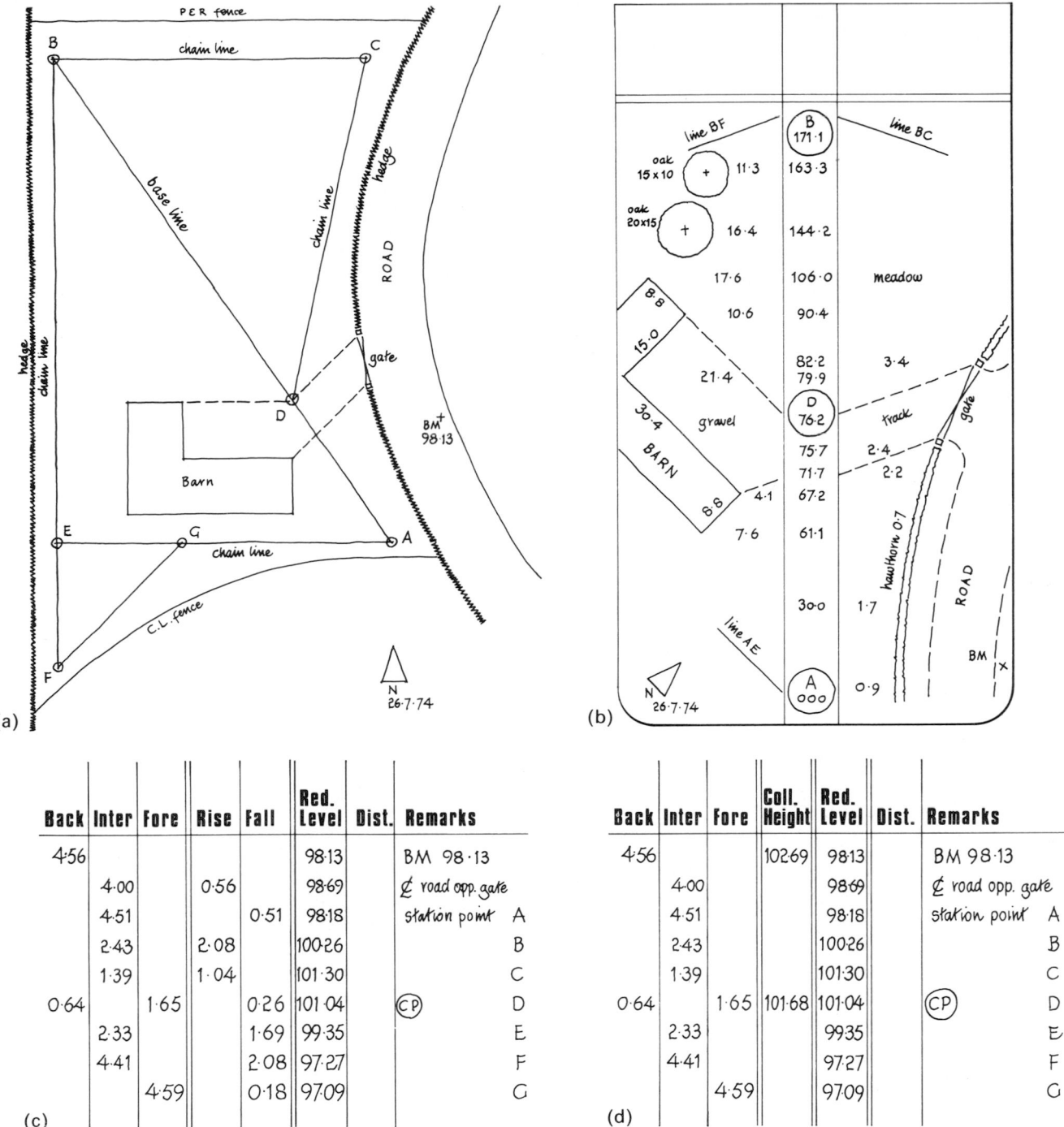

(a)

(b)

(c)

Back	Inter	Fore	Rise	Fall	Red. Level	Dist.	Remarks	
4·56					98·13		BM 98·13	
	4·00		0·56		98·69		₵ road opp. gate	
	4·51			0·51	98·18		station point	A
	2·43		2·08		100·26			B
	1·39		1·04		101·30			C
0·64		1·65		0·26	101·04		(CP)	D
	2·33			1·69	99·35			E
	4·41			2·08	97·27			F
		4·59		0·18	97·09			G

(d)

Back	Inter	Fore	Coll. Height	Red. Level	Dist.	Remarks	
4·56			102·69	98·13		BM 98·13	
	4·00			98·69		₵ road opp. gate	
	4·51			98·18		station point	A
	2·43			100·26			B
	1·39			101·30			C
0·64		1·65	101·68	101·04		(CP)	D
	2·33			99·35			E
	4·41			97·27			F
		4·59		97·09			G

the basis of subjective judgements, but the essence of the spacial organisation can be recorded to include generally recognised qualities. Such a system will be concerned with visual horizons, views out of site, enclosure, visual watersheds and dead ground. Visual intrusions and views beyond the site which are attractive or detrimental to the site should be recorded together with the effect of the site on the surrounding landscape. The information can be marked on a plan with additional notes or with the help of a pocket tape recorder. It is important to make a precise record of the position from which views are observed throughout this part of the survey. Sketches are especially useful, allowing the major elements to be emphasised and insignificant or transitory elements to be

5

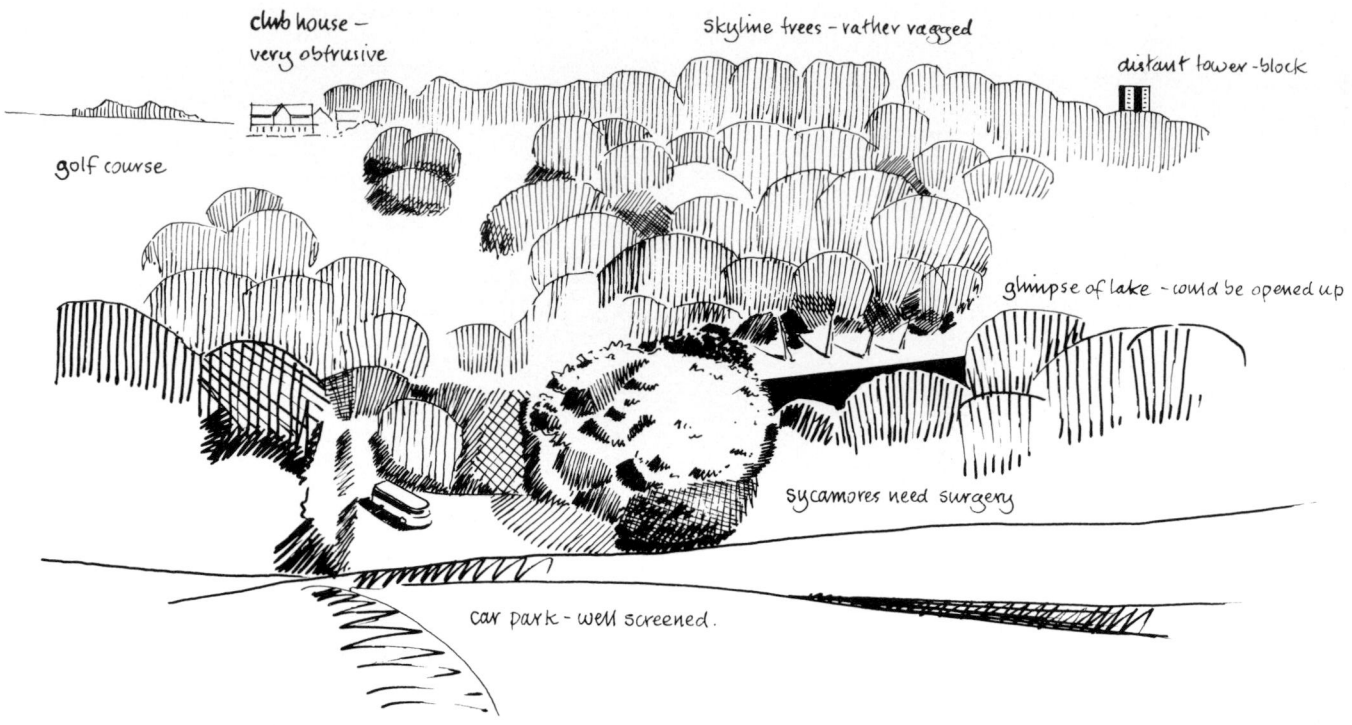

club house – very obtrusive

skyline trees – rather ragged

distant tower-block

golf course

glimpse of lake – could be opened up

sycamores need surgery

car park – well screened.

Fig. 1.2. SITE SKETCHES WITH NOTES – These are especially useful, allowing the major elements to be emphasised.

omitted. The discipline of making the sketches will be of assistance in concentrating the observer's attention upon the scenic character of the area. Photography is quick and can be useful for later reference. Both colour and black and white prints can be obtained and in conjunction with wide angle lenses and panoramic cameras, useful strip panoramas can be obtained, without the necessity of cutting and patching series photographs which can lead to distortion.

1.3.3 Ecological survey

A complete ecological survey would provide a complete record of all flora and fauna related to a site but this is usually out of the question and an outline of plant communities with recording of quality where necessary is all that is possible. In straightforward cases a system of quadrats or squares can be used, within each of which a record of species is taken divided, by frequency into (do.) dominant, (co.) co-dominant, (va.) very abundant, (a.) abundant, (f.) frequent, (o.) occasional, (r.) rare and (vr.) very rare with (l.) local, used as a prefix where necessary. Other systems involve line transects which record only plants which occur at fixed distances along a line but this particular system seems to have little to offer as part of

the landscape survey. A belt transect, usually 1 m wide, with divisions along its length, is in effect a series of quadrats, the percentage of each square occupied by each species being the recorded measurement. On sites which are known to be due for radical development identification of the tree and shrub layer may be all that is of practical use. Trees and larger shrubs including hedgerows should be recorded by species, height, spread, girth or diameter of trunk together with notes on condition. It is advisable to reduce the qualitative notes to a minimum, perhaps four categories:

those it is essential to keep;
those it is desirable to keep;
those which will require extensive treatment;
those which for one reason or another should be removed.

A more detailed survey may be required by an arboriculturist or tree surgeon where work is required to improve the condition of trees or shrubs. Much more attention is required when mature trees are on a site to be used by large numbers of people than when they are in open countryside.

6

1.3.4 Soil survey

Some of the engineering qualities of topsoil and substrata will be important to the landscape survey. It is, however, the biological qualities with which we are most concerned. Preliminary indications will be available by observation of local plant communities, which will contain indicators of soil type, fertility and moisture content. Outcrops of rock, and colour of the soil where exposed will also give a good indication of what to expect. Borehole information may be necessary on a site but usually shallow trial holes will be adequate not often exceeding 1 m in depth but on occasions 2 m may be required particularly if one is investigating an area with a fluctuating water table. The samples from the trial holes or obtained by a hand auger must be carefully handled to keep topsoil and subsoil separate. Accurate plotting of the trial holes or sample positions should be made on the survey plan. Various tests can be made on the soil samples, some requiring simple chemical tests which can be carried out on site to give very approximate results whilst others will require more specialist equipment used in a laboratory by an expert.

Information about soil. This will include:

the depth of topsoil and other horizons;
the texture of the topsoil;
stone content;
chemical reaction (pH);
soil type (gravel, sand, silt, clay);
moisture content and water table.

The last item, water table, may require a long period of time to establish, with a trial hole being observed regularly over a period of at least 1 year together with careful weather records. Further information including available nutrients can be obtained and more extensive tests may be thought necessary to establish the existence of toxic chemicals, heavy metal residue or detrimental waste material. Subsoil water movement may also be established at this stage if this is relevant to the project.

1.4 Presentation of information

1.4.1 Location plans

It is often necessary to produce a plan or map, which will locate the area of study, for the benefit of those who are not conversant with its location either at local or even regional level. This plan can be at a small scale and may simply show the site as a block with major communication links, geographical features, a north point and a scale. All the information required should be available from appropriate Ordnance Survey maps.

1.4.2 The base plan

A useful technique in the presentation of survey material is to provide a base plan which is a selection of information which will be constant whatever special aspect of the survey information is to be studied and represented cartographically. This plan can often be appropriately based upon information obtained from Ordnance Survey maps. The Base Plan should record the following information:

Scale – which should be shown as a linear scale drawn on the plan and divided into appropriate sub-divisions. This has the advantage over a written scale (1:1,000) of allowing reduction or enlargement without the need for change. However, a written scale can be added if the drawing is not expected to be reproduced to a different size.

Orientation – three different orientations of North are used: True North which speaks for itself, Magnetic North which varies approximately $\frac{1}{2}°$ in eight years and Grid North, upon which Ordnance sheets are based. A careful note of which is being used may be necessary.

Communication routes – roads, railways and canals should be shown in such a way as to avoid confusion with each other. Footpaths, particularly established rights of way, should be drawn on. This information should not be restricted to within the site boundary but should extend a reasonable distance into surrounding areas.

Artifacts – permanent buildings and man-made features, such as power lines or towers should appear.

Natural features – only major and permanent features should be recorded at this stage. Large areas of woodland, water courses and significant geological features are all that will be necessary.

Site boundary – if the site boundary is established at this stage it can be recorded, but should not be allowed to become dominant or restrictive to the recording of information outside the site limits, which may be vital at a later stage.

This base information can now be used in conjunction with a series of transparent overlays upon which more specialist information can be recorded. An alternative is to have the information reproduced on a series of transparent copies upon which further information can be drawn direct and subsequently reproduced. It is worth repeating that it can be of great importance to show information beyond the site boundary. This can be

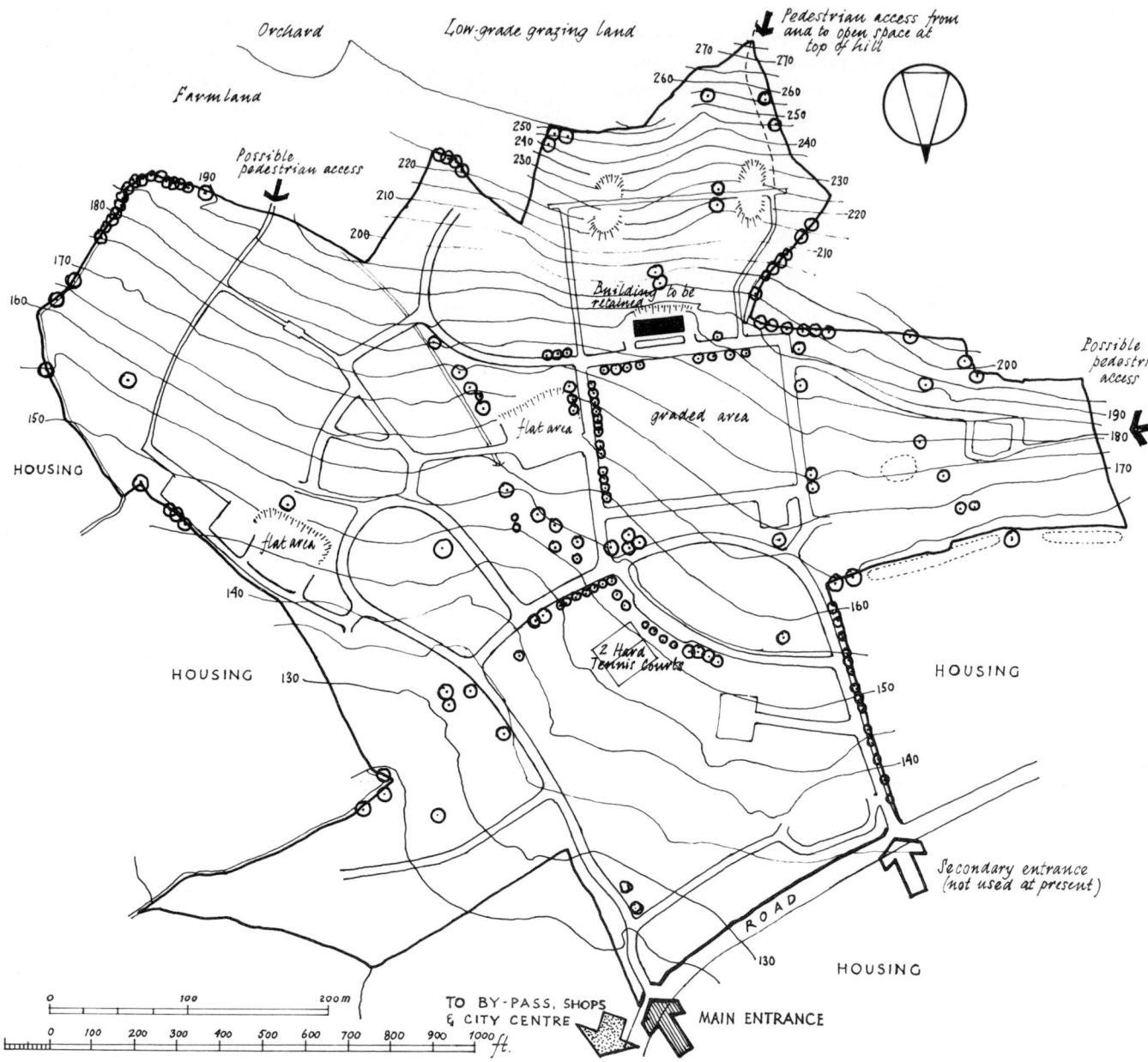

Fig. 1.3. TOPOGRAPHY – Survey plan showing topography and access.

1.4.3 Topography

The information related to the topography of an area may be expressed in various ways. Simple spot heights marked on the plan may be sufficient. These can be related to a false datum set up within the site but this can lead to confusion and wherever possible an Ordnance Datum should be used.

A contour plan shows lines representing all points of the same level. Contour lines are usually arrived at by interpolation between spot levels related to the datum. The vertical intervals between contours will be determined by need and the degree of accuracy obtained from the information taken on site. Very steep slopes may not lend themselves to illustration by contours and in these cases a convention of hatching is used with the wider end of the lines at the top of the slope.

encouraged or restricted by the form and size chosen for the base plan. Such information may eventually result in major modification to decisions which would be made based only upon material contained within the site itself.

8

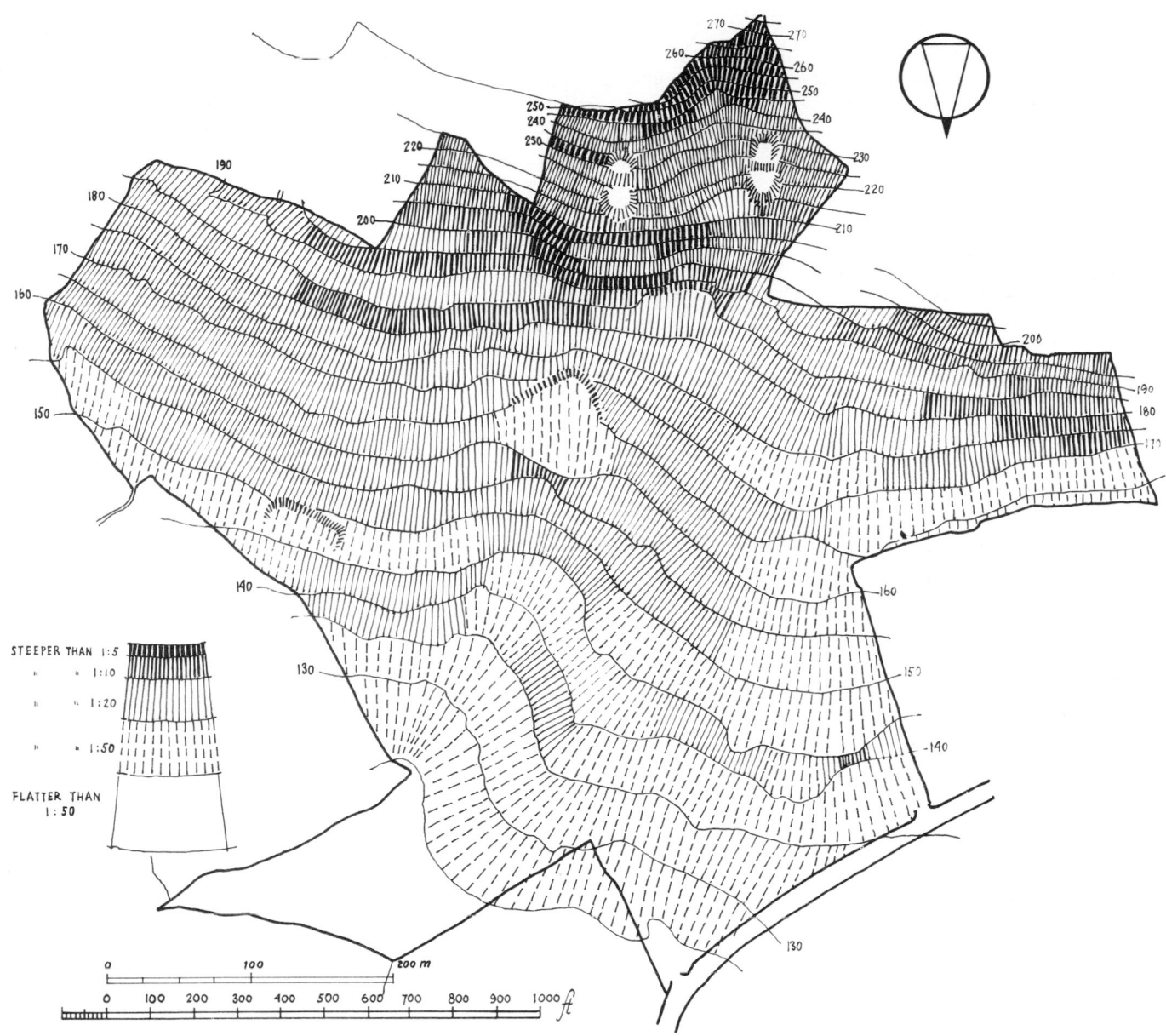

Fig. 1.4. SLOPE ANALYSIS – Shaded diagram illustrating slope analysis of site.

A slope analysis may be required to show clearly which areas are within acceptable limits for development without regrading. A simple technique involves hatching between contour lines. The closer the hatching the steeper will be the slope. The requirements of the project may determine the choice of slope limits but a range of:

steeper than 1 in 5
steeper than 1 in 10
steeper than 1 in 20
steeper than 1 in 50
and flatter than 1 in 50

is commonly used. In cases where colour is available this may be used or a grading from dark grey on steep slopes to white on flat areas may be acceptable. Sections drawn through the site should be considered as these may provide ready information if earthwork calculations or visibility limits are to be used. An exaggerated vertical scale is frequently used. Depending upon the configuration of the land and the scale of the plan it may be $\times 2$, $\times 2\frac{1}{2}$ or $\times 5$ the horizontal scale. A clear note of any change in vertical scale should be made on drawings to avoid any possible confusion. Topographical or contour models can be of value, and these are often built with

9

sheets of card or expanded polystyrene of appropriate thickness to suit the vertical contour intervals. However, other techniques include sand tables and the moulding of plaster or plastic sheet.

It may be appropriate to show surface water drainage patterns, water courses, and standing water at this stage.

1.4.4 Geology and soils

Geological information may be recorded in various forms of hatching or by colour and the basis of the information will come directly from the published solid and drift maps. Further, detailed information may be revealed by the results of bore holes taken on the site which are often required for engineering purposes and may already have been called for by architects or engineers. Soil and geology can be conveniently recorded together, since they are often interdependent. Trial holes should be plotted and profile sections may be set out at the side of this drawing with other relevant information on water table, pH, texture and quality of topsoil. Marsh

land, water courses and standing water may be appropriately recorded here instead of on the topographical plan.

1.4.5 Services

Services being available on a site may give it great potential but on the other hand they may impose severe restrictions on possible future use. All services should be plotted, both above and below ground. They will include:

(a) Drainage, with depth to invert, and size. Land drains, storm water drains or foul drains should be identified.
(b) Underground pipes with depth and size. Gas, oil and water, etc., are to be identified.
(c) Underground cables with depth, for example, electricity and telephone.
(d) Above ground services with towers and pylons, for example, electricity and telephone.

Fig. 1.5. GEOLOGY AND SOIL – A simplified presentation of the geological map (drift) which includes information from soil test reports.

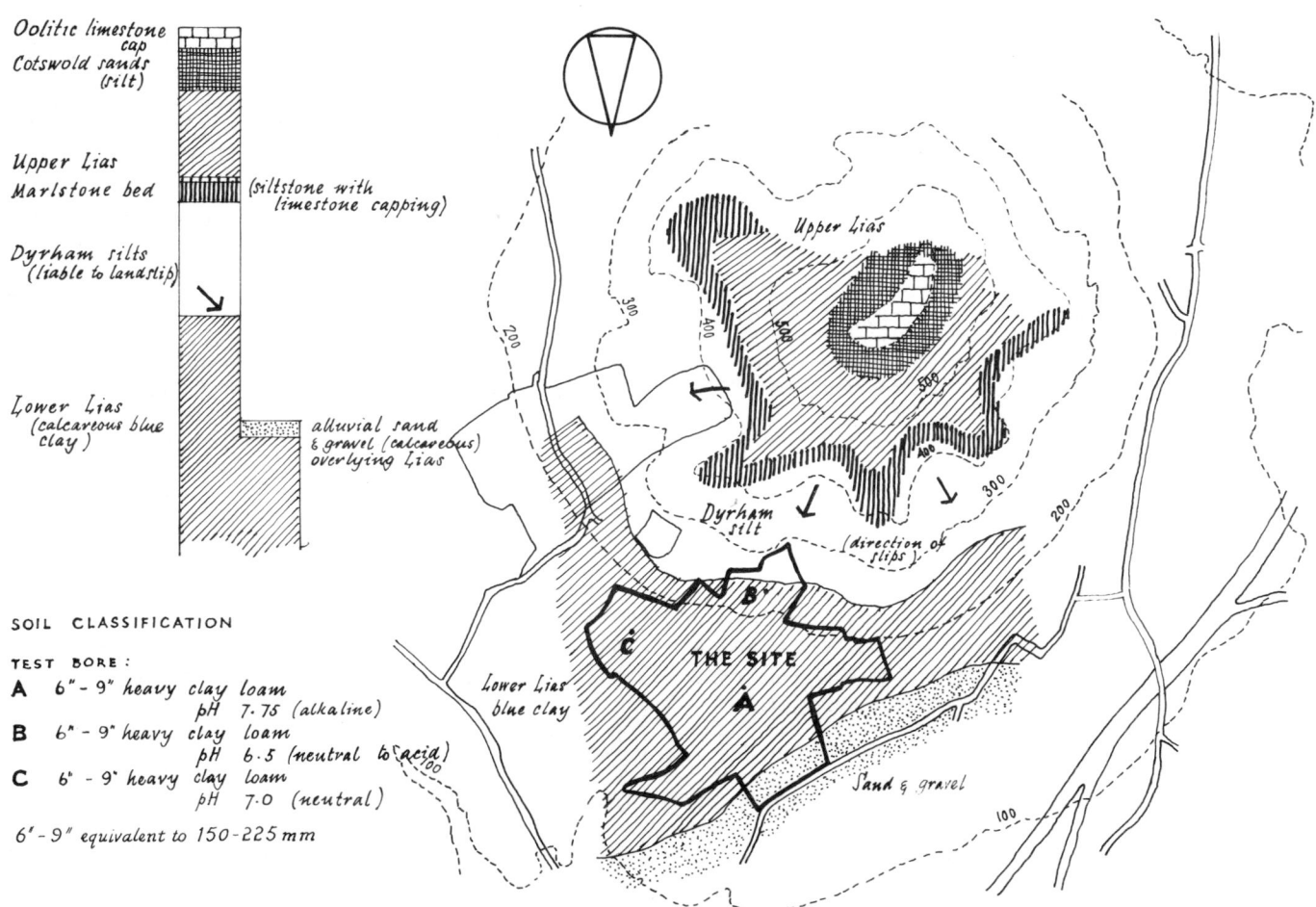

SOIL CLASSIFICATION

TEST BORE :
A 6" – 9" heavy clay loam
        pH 7.75 (alkaline)
B 6" – 9" heavy clay loam
        pH 6.5 (neutral to acid)
C 6" – 9" heavy clay loam
        pH 7.0 (neutral)

6" – 9" equivalent to 150–225 mm

10

When plotted, this information should be checked with the appropriate statutory or local authority. It must be remembered and if possible drawn on the plan that some services will prevent the development of land above, below and on either side of the service run itself. Over-head electricity service cables will require clearance for safety and not only below to allow for sag but on each side to allow swing in winds.

Definitive proposals for service runs should also be shown. These may have serious effects on the possibilities for development, so equal account of their implications will have to be taken.

1.4.6 Access and circulation

Access to a site may well determine the basic form of a development. Roads and paths should be clearly marked particularly where they come into contact with the edge of the site. Their type, size, possible capacity and not least character should be clearly indicated. Possible access points to the site should be indicated, referring clearly to the type of traffic for which the access can be used. Existing circulation patterns within the site should be established and records of 'rights of way' and public foot-paths should be made. It will require a lengthy procedure to be completed before these can be repositioned or closed. Departure and destination points should be established on the plan with diagrammatic links. Predict-able additional requirements should also be inserted.

1.4.7 Microclimate

Microclimate is used in this context to describe the cli-matic conditions within defined spatial units of the site and the information recorded on the plan will be that which is different to the average for the region within which the site exists. Data on such a small scale is not readily available and the collection of relevant informa-tion can only be obtained by prolonged observation extending over several years. In many cases direct read-ings will not be possible and informed expert judgement may be required, which coupled with local knowledge will provide a reasonable indication of the microclimatic character of the site. The plan will record shade and exposure to sun and wind, sheltered areas and localities which will suffer from accelerated wind speed due to topography or vegetation. Frost pockets and air drainage may be predictable and wind-borne salt spray in coastal conditions should be recorded. This plan will also be appropriate for showing areas subjected to pollution in-cluding fumes, smoke and noise.

General climatic information can be added to this drawing. A wind rose recording frequency and intensity, general temperature, rainfall and sunlight graphs can be shown if the information is likely to be of use.

1.4.8 Ecology

The available ecological information may be recorded in several ways. In so far as the fauna is concerned it may be necessary simply to write notes on the plan. It may be useful to consider plants as if they were arranged in distinct layers.

(a) Tree layer: comprising dominant and all other tall trees;
(b) Second tree layer: trees between 5 and 15 m, whose crowns are below those of the tree layer. It will also contain young trees which on maturity will occupy a place in the upper tree layer.
(c) Shrub layer: all woody perennials;
(d) Field layer: non-woody plants usually less than 1 m high;
(e) Ground layer: mosses, liverworts and ferns.

Fig. 1.6. VEGETATION – A tree survey with trees graded by size and quality. Each tree is numbered and information is scheduled.

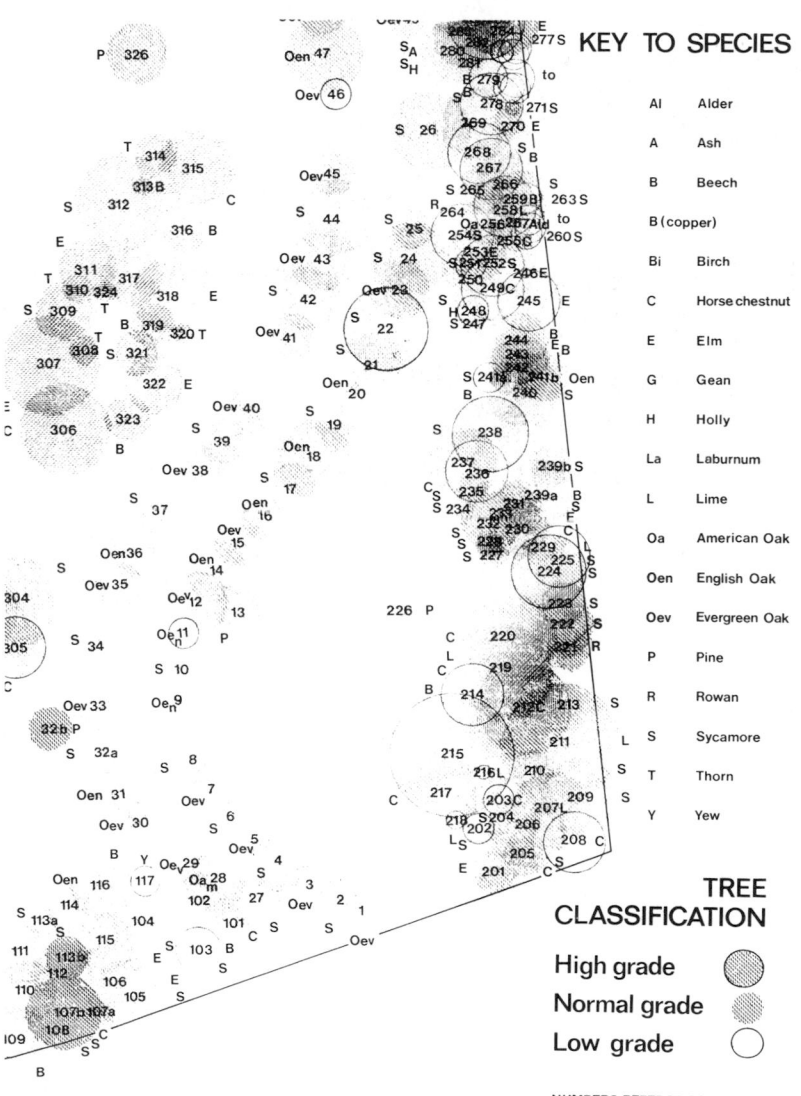

KEY TO SPECIES

Al	Alder
A	Ash
B	Beech
B (copper)	
Bi	Birch
C	Horse chestnut
E	Elm
G	Gean
H	Holly
La	Laburnum
L	Lime
Oa	American Oak
Oen	English Oak
Oev	Evergreen Oak
P	Pine
R	Rowan
S	Sycamore
T	Thorn
Y	Yew

TREE CLASSIFICATION

High grade
Normal grade
Low grade

NUMBERS REFER TO SCHEDULE

11

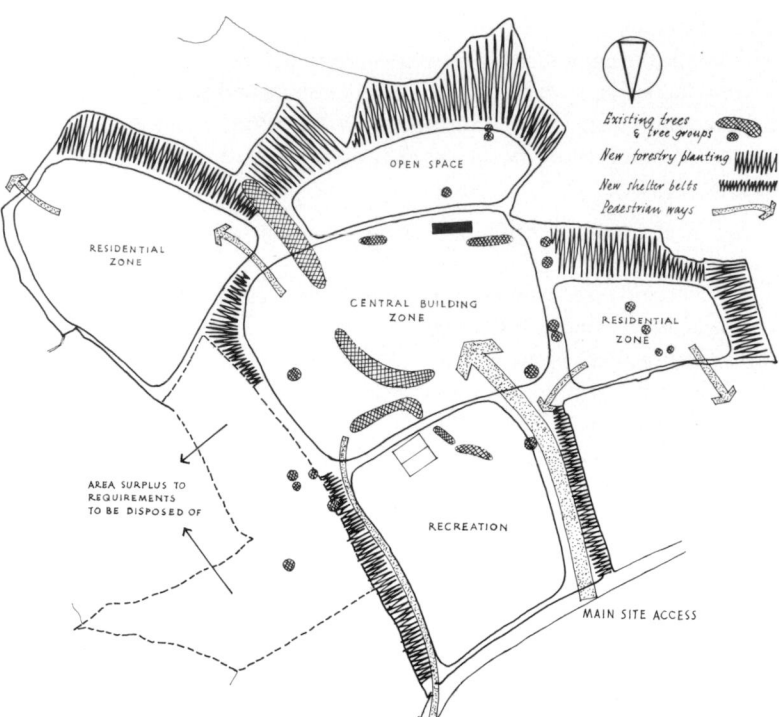

Existing trees & tree groups
New forestry planting
New shelter belts
Pedestrian ways

OPEN SPACE

RESIDENTIAL ZONE

CENTRAL BUILDING ZONE

RESIDENTIAL ZONE

AREA SURPLUS TO REQUIREMENTS TO BE DISPOSED OF

RECREATION

MAIN SITE ACCESS

Fig. 1.7. VISUAL ANALYSIS – Diagram analysing main visual features within the site and indicating the main prospects afforded over the surrounding landscape.

These layers may be shown as overlays to each other. Plant association plots may also be used, the type of presentation depending largely upon the use to which the information is to be put. In any case which is even slightly complex, the services of an ecologist should be used. Some trees may have Tree Preservation Orders (T.P.O.s) placed upon them by the local planning authority. These must be recorded together with all information previously collected about individual trees, i.e. height × spread × girth or diameter of trunk 1·5 m above ground together with a note or key representing quality.

1.4.9 Visual character

The presentation of the information obtained during the visual survey has led to numerous techniques being developed. It should be possible to present the major visual features by means of diagrammatic hatching, lines and symbols. Skylines as seen from the site will indicate the larger enclosures and where wider views from the site will be possible. Internal visual links and local interruptions to the overall pattern can then be superimposed. Intrusive elements both on and off site should with some sort of emphasis indicate the quality of the object. Sketches can be included to supplement the diagrammatic information drawn on the plan. The position from which views are observed, with their extent and direction, must be clearly marked on the plan. A 'bird's-eye' view may be constructed which will help, but it must be remembered that the view is an unnatural one which probably will never be seen. Photographs are frequently used to amplify the information in this section. They may be mounted on or alongside the plan with cross-reference and links. Information can be conveniently written above or on the photographic views to emphasise or simply to facilitate understanding.

1.4.10 Reports

With carefully presented drawings a great deal of information can be quickly communicated. There is however a body of information which should be readily available, which can only be recorded in written form. This information will be presented as a site report. It may contain any supplementary information related to the previously mentioned drawings. The report may in fact be the major document, into which suitably reduced or folded drawings will be inserted. It is essential that clear and concise language should be used and that the document has a comprehensive index. Detailed supplementary or back-up information may be included as an appendix and drawings which cannot be conveniently bound into the report may be placed in a pocket at the back of the document.

1.5 Analysis

1.5.1 Information evaluation

The survey material can be regarded as factual information with a few obvious qualitative decisions added. However the collation of the survey material and its presentation does nothing in itself towards establishing either the suitability of the site for a predetermined purpose or its development potential in landscape terms. The application to which the survey material is to be put should be established before the next stage – analysis of the data – is commenced. If a defined proposal has generated the need for the analysis, it will be possible for the effect of such a proposal to be predicted and an evaluation made of this on the site itself and the surrounding landscape. Establishment of landscape potential may be the object of the exercise, in which case some parts of the survey information will have to be carefully weighed against the remainder, coupled with assessment of possible future demands upon the landscape under scrutiny. The landscape analysis should interpret the information provided on the survey drawings or the data contained within the site report, for the benefit of client, or to assist the design team which will be required to de-

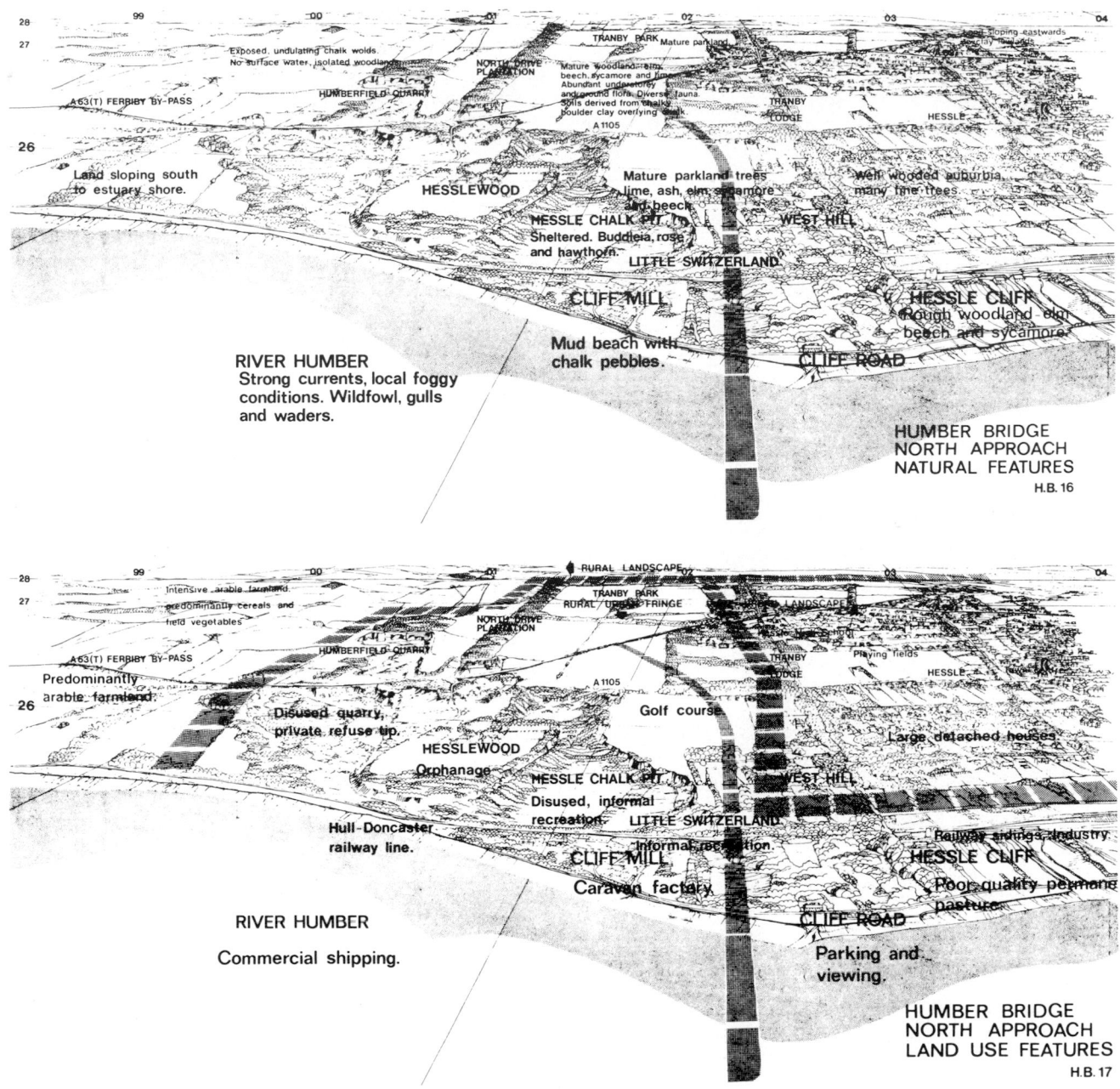

Mature woodland—elm, beech, sycamore and fir. Abundant understorey and ground flora. Diverse fauna. Soils derived from chalky boulder clay overlying chalk.

A 1105

TRANBY PARK Mature parkland

Exposed, undulating chalk wolds. No surface water, isolated woodland.

NORTH DRIVE PLANTATION

HUMBERFIELD QUARRY

A63(T) FERRIBY BY-PASS

Land sloping south to estuary shore.

HESSLEWOOD

Mature parkland trees—lime, ash, elm, sycamore and beech.

HESSLE CHALK PIT Sheltered. Buddleia, rose and hawthorn.

LITTLE SWITZERLAND

CLIFF MILL

RIVER HUMBER Strong currents, local foggy conditions. Wildfowl, gulls and waders.

Mud beach with chalk pebbles.

TRANBY LODGE

HESSLE

WEST HILL

Well wooded suburbia, many fine trees.

sloping eastwards

HESSLE CLIFF Rough woodland—elm, beech and sycamore.

CLIFF ROAD

HUMBER BRIDGE NORTH APPROACH NATURAL FEATURES H.B. 16

RURAL LANDSCAPE

Intensive arable farmland, predominantly cereals and field vegetables.

A63(T) FERRIBY BY-PASS

Predominantly arable farmland.

HUMBERFIELD QUARRY

TRANBY PARK RURAL/URBAN FRINGE

A 1105

NORTH DRIVE PLANTATION

LANDSCAPE

Playing fields

Disused quarry, private refuse tip.

HESSLEWOOD Orphanage

HESSLE CHALK PIT Disused, informal recreation.

LITTLE SWITZERLAND

Golf course

TRANBY LODGE

HESSLE

WEST HILL

Large detached houses

Hull-Doncaster railway line.

CLIFF MILL

Caravan factory.

Informal recreation.

RIVER HUMBER Commercial shipping.

Railway sidings, industry.

HESSLE CLIFF Poor quality permanent pasture.

CLIFF ROAD

Parking and viewing.

HUMBER BRIDGE NORTH APPROACH LAND USE FEATURES H.B. 17

Fig. 1.8(a) & (b) BIRD'S EYE VIEWS – This may be constructed to help the designer appreciate the overall characteristics of a large or complex site and to convey site problems and possibilities to clients and to other members of a design team. Humber Bridge North Approach. Landscape Architect: A. E. Weddle.

velop the design potential of the site. A series of maps may be produced to emphasise a particular development potential or restraint element. When all the plans have been completed they can be combined, possibly by creating overlays, thus showing areas which will satisfy all or many of the design criteria. This is known as a sieve map technique.

1.5.2 Analytical techniques
Analytical techniques are continually being updated and refined. Complex network techniques demand extensive calculations and graphic sorting, being facilitated by or in some cases dependent upon the use of computer programmes. Numerical evaluation of the landscape is a tool which is in great demand. Numerous methods are being

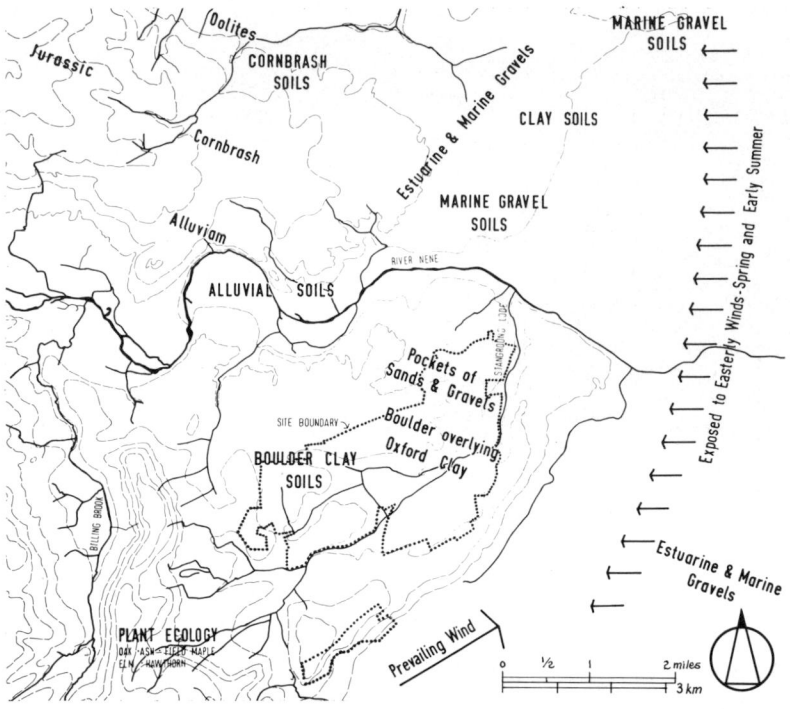

Fig. 1.9. LANDSCAPE ANALYSIS – NATURAL FACTORS. A first-stage analysis picking out natural conditions over which the designer has little control. Survey at Peterborough. Landscape Architect: A. E. Weddle.

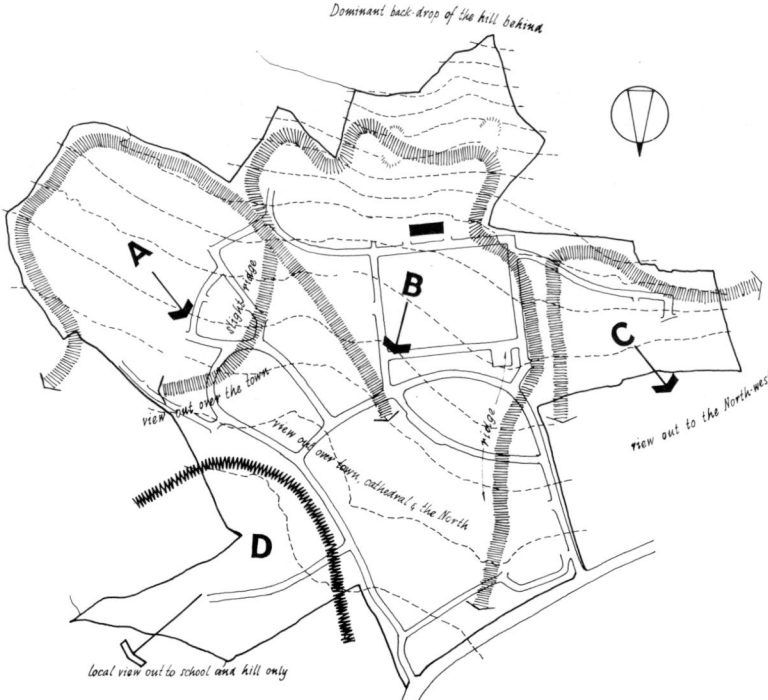

Fig. 1.10. LANDSCAPE APPRAISAL – Preliminary recommendations and zoning expressing broad principals of design which arise out of analysis of the survey.

developed, but are beyond the scope of this chapter, their application being more often used in regional landscape planning projects. These more sophisticated evaluation techniques may be required if zoning of an area for suitable land use is to be achieved.

1.5.3 Regional evaluation
For larger areas of regional or sub-regional scale square grids may be used, each square being valued against various criteria. Whilst a kilometre square has been the basis of some studies, this basic grid can be subdivided down to a finer grid, thus allowing an evaluation of whatever detail is required. At any level and at whatever scale the techniques used are only capable of producing results commensurate with the quantity and quality of the data introduced.

Bibliography

Basic Metric Surveying, W. Whyte, Butterworth.

Climate and the British Scene, G. Manley, Collins and Fontana.

Climatological Atlas of the British Isles, Met. Office, H.M.S.O.

Geology and Scenery in England and Wales, A. Trueman, Penguin.

Handbook of Urban Landscape, C. Tandy, Architectural Press.

Introduction to Plant Ecology, A. Tansley, Allen and Unwin.

Landscape Planning, B. Hackett, Oriel Press.

Land Use and Landscape Planning, D. Lovejoy, Leonard Hill.

Ordnance Survey Maps: a descriptive manual, J. B. Harley, Ordnance Survey.

Practical Field Ecology, R. McLean and W. R. Ivimey-Cook, Allen and Unwin.

Site Planning, K. Lynch, M.I.T., Cambridge, Mass.

2 Site Planning

SYLVIA CROWE

2.1 Introduction

The service which a landscape architect can render his client rests on his ability to apply the principles of sound design to the use of open spaces. This entails, in addition to basic design ability, a knowledge of the materials of landscape, that is land, water and organic life. He must also understand the interaction between these materials, the climate in which they function and the human use to which they are being adapted. These factors together determine the ecological situation of a landscape and it is the landscape architect's function to arrange, develop and adapt them to serve the particular use for which the land space is designed. The extent of this field of work ranges from the smallest open space within urban development to national parks and the countryside as a whole.

The means by which a landscape architect will carry out his work are:

An assessment of the site and its surroundings.
A compilation and understanding of the required land use and functions of the proposed development.
The preparation of plans by which his ideas may first be conveyed to his client and then be translated to the ground.
Such supervision of the implementation of the plans as may be necessary to ensure their functioning.
The laying down of a maintenance programme.

2.1.1 Types of landscape site plans

The function of all site plans is to state how a given project is to be translated into good landscape. That is, a landscape which will fulfil its functions with efficiency, can be maintained in a viable condition and contributes to the welfare and good appearance of the environment both in long and short terms. The scope and degree of detail of the plans will in each case depend on the nature of the project and the stage of development for which the landscape plan is prepared.

Master plans. These lay down the essential principles to be followed in the development and the broad lines of the design. They are not detailed. They are flexible within the limits of the basic principles and broad conception and will be subject to revision by the landscape architect as the detailing of the project proceeds. The landscape master plan may form one element within a town planning, engineering or architectural project. In this case it may either take the form of a report and of principles diagrammatically expressed which will be incorporated into a comprehensive master plan prepared by the planning team, or it may be produced as a separate plan in consultation with the team. Alternatively, the project may be a predominantly landscape problem, entirely within the province of the landscape architect, or (more often) carried out in consultation with other professions involved, but remaining solely a landscape plan. From the master plan will evolve definitive plans for different sections of the project as they develop.

On long-term projects the plan may not be developed beyond the master plan stage, while on projects for more immediate realisation, the master plan stage will be developed, after agreement and adjustment, into working plans.

Site plans for existing projects. Ideally any landscape plan will follow early consultations with those responsible for other elements in the project. But in practice it will often be required for projects in which other elements are already completed, or planned beyond the possibilities of major adjustment. A site plan for a completed or completely planned project will usually be more rigid and detailed than those referred to in section 2.1.1, and will often be developed, with only minor revisions, directly into working plans. All site plans and master plans should be accompanied by reports. At the master plan stage these can be of greater importance than the plans. The material required for the presentation of a site plan may include:

Plans – Site analysis, use analysis. Small-scale location plan showing the influence of the environment on the new project, and the project's influence on the environment. Contoured site plan showing design solution.

Illustrations, sections, model – (For details of the various types of plan and presentation see Chapter 11.)

Report – The report will state the problem, the reasons for the solution, the phasing, the costs and the means of maintenance.

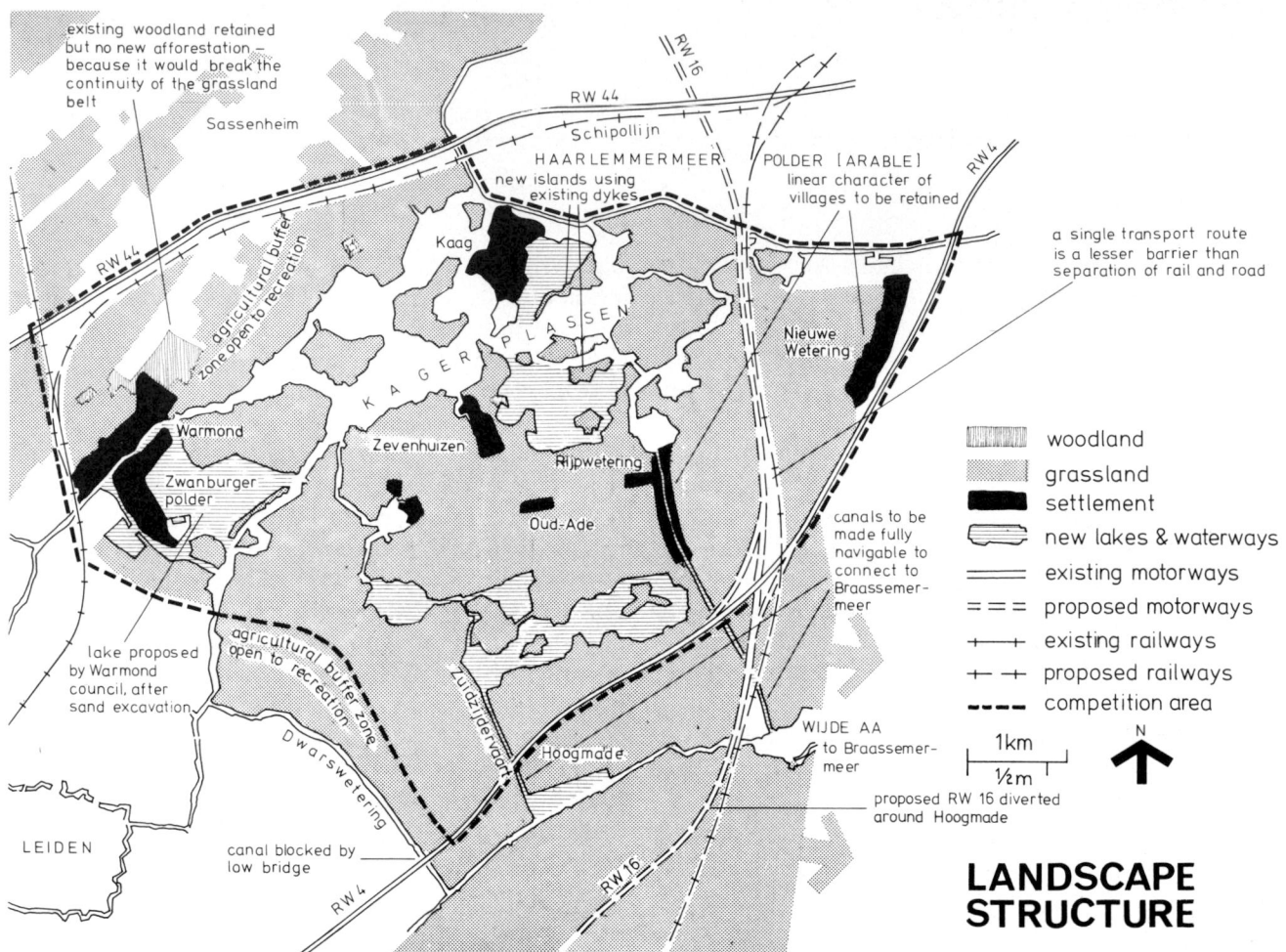

Fig. 2.1. The broad lines of a new landscape based on physical factors and future uses (Chris Blandford, Robert Holden and Xavier Monbaillou).

2.2 The basis of the site plan

The landscape plan evolves from two sets of factors:

(*a*) The site.
(*b*) The function.

2.2.1 The site factors (see also Chapter 1 – Survey and Analysis). These apply not only to the site but also to its surroundings. The relevant minimum extent of these is the visual limit into and out from the site and the character of adjacent though unseen landscape. This will influence:

Kinetic experience (e.g. passing from one urban square to another).
Use requirements (e.g. proximity of city, coast).

Ecological and climatic factors (e.g. the presence of some distant windbreak).

2.2.2 Use factors
These comprise the following:

The primary function of the site.
Subsidiary functions or multiple use.
Density of use.
Access and traffic requirements.
The appearance and well-being of the landscape both within the site and beyond it.
Capital and maintenance cost (see also Chapter 11 – Conservation and Management).
Planning and legal requirements (see also Chapter 12 – Professional Practice).

16

2.3 Information needed for preparation of site plan

2.3.1 Contoured surveys (of site and surroundings to the scope and scale appropriate to the project)

Complete details of existing and proposed buildings, with differentiation, in the case of buildings planned and not yet built, between essential features and variable ones. There may for instance be latitude in the siting or in the arrangement of some structures, while others are inexorably fixed by necessity of their particular functions. This should be ascertained from the architects or engineers.

2.3.2 Site appreciation

Climatic, soil and ecological reports are needed and the visual character and potential of the site must be assessed (see also Chapter 1).

2.3.3 Planning implications

These include the influence of the project on its environment; its relationship to other proposed developments; legal and planning restrictions; its possible influence on traffic problems. Consultations will usually be required on these points with the relevant bodies, e.g. the local planning authority, the Nature Conservancy Council, etc. (see also Chapter 11). The client should be informed of the proposed consultations.

2.3.4 Client requirements

To discover the client's true requirements is a matter first of asking the right questions, and then of separating the essential from the inessential and establishing the priorities of needs and desires. Where the client is an individual it is comparatively easy to ascertain the requirements, but in the case of a multiple body it may be more difficult and most difficult of all is the case of unknown, future users, such as the inhabitants of a new town. Full use of research and the application of common sense must be made in these cases.

Existing examples of similar or relevant projects should be studied and their failures and successes noted. Judgment must then be used to decide how far the lessons of other projects are applicable. Allowance must be made for different soil and climatic factors and for social conditions. This is particularly important when studying examples from other countries. In all cases where uncertainty exists, the plan should allow for maximum flexibility. For instance, in planning for recreation changing habits must be taken into account, and it should be realised that further and unexpected trends may develop, and wherever possible, plans should be sufficiently flexible to allow for future adjustment. Specialist bodies should be consulted on all subjects in which the landscape architect is not himself an expert.

Function. Where the primary function of the site lies outside the technical knowledge of the landscape architect he must acquaint himself with the factors of those functions which might influence his design of the landscape. For instance if he is dealing with a reservoir he must find out the requirements to avoid pollution, or in the case of a mineral working he must discover the working process and programme. No landscape architect can be expert in all the matters he must deal with but he can acquire the skills to extract the data essential for his purpose.

Density of use. This includes traffic density, static and in passage, residential density and visitor density.

2.3.5 Timing

The designer will be concerned with two time scales, first the period of development, which may be in phases, and second the life or expected duration of the completed project.

2.3.6 Costs

These are in two simple categories; capital costs and maintenance costs.

2.3.7 Means of maintenance

These are dealt with in detail in Chapter 11. They are fundamental and must be considered in parallel with design for function.

2.4 Site factors

2.4.1 Climate

The creation of a favourable micro-climate is one of the basic reasons for site manipulation and in attaining this the placing of shelter belts is often the first step in preparing the plan. Since a certain minimum width is required according to site conditions (see also Chapter 10 – Tree Planting) they may influence all other elements of the plan including the siting of buildings. The basic pattern of the plan will also be influenced by the need for maximum sun in cool climates and shade in hot ones.

2.4.2 Site contours

The contours of a site may provide the first line of thought on how a site should be developed. They will suggest the best positions for buildings, for views, for shelter and for large level elements such as playing fields.

The siting of roads will depend on their gradient in relation to the site gradients. If traffic separation is to be achieved by over- and under-passes the site contours will suggest the most economic siting for these. A road sited side-long to the contours will give an opportunity to run the road and footpath at different levels. If the required maximum road gradient is less than the site gradient between the road's point of entry and destination, the road will have to take a suitably extended course.

Elements such as car parks, which it is desirable to conceal should usually be sited on the lower contours. Normally tree-screens will be sited on the higher contours often on the brow of hills. From the first tentative sketch onwards all design should be carried out on a contoured plan.

2.4.3 Existing vegetation

Where any part of the site can remain undisturbed the existing ground cover should be examined to see if it is suitable for retention. If so it must be both protected and maintained for the duration of site works. Hedges and bushes may sometimes be used in the new development and particularly on exposed sites their value as shelter for new planting may be considerable. Healthy trees should always be preserved where possible. Their position, spread and the ground level at their base must be shown on the surveys, as the need to retain approximately the same level over their root area may determine the shaping and levelling of the site. Any existing features which are to be kept must be protected by fencing before the first construction machinery reaches the site.

2.4.4 Water (see also Chapter 7 – Water)

Early site investigation should ascertain whether water is available from natural sources. If it is it may form an important element in the site plan. Before including existing water, either in the form of a pond or a stream, in the new development, its seasonal variations and purity must be discovered, also whether its volume is likely to be decreased as a result of site development. This often occurs when surface water is drained off in urban development. There may also be opportunities for augmenting the supply or for creating new lakes by damming or excavation. The latter possibility will depend on the water retention quality of the subsoil.

2.4.5 Soil conditions

In some cases there may be a determining factor. Overall lack of soil may dictate the same type of pattern which would result from extreme aridity, that is, a pattern of localised areas where growing conditions are artificially induced, on a background of inert material or of poverty plants.

Modern techniques of soil improvement have made it possible to obtain growth on areas which would at one time have been considered infertile. The possibilities and cost of this should be ascertained in difficult cases, before the plan is evolved. But in normal cases the soil conditions should be reflected in the plan and marked differentiation of soil quality within the site will influence the siting of different elements.

The nature of the subsoil will also influence the site plan from the first. In projects where there is any question of undergrounding structures or putting roads in cutting the nature of the subsoil may be decisive. The practicability and cost of contouring and levelling will equally be affected. In considering both these operations the level of the water-table must also be ascertained.

2.4.6 Site surroundings

These will influence the visual pattern of the development which must relate the site to the surroundings. The position of screen planting will be influenced by the need to exclude unpleasant views, reduce noise, or mitigate pollution emanating from adjacent sites (see also Chapter 10); the access or prevention of access – for instance adjacent areas of public resort, such as commons, should influence the pedestrian way system in urban development, and equally fast traffic roads should be insulated from uncontrolled pedestrian access.

Views seen from the site will influence the siting of buildings, and the arrangement of plantings. Views into the site may have to be considered from view points some distance from the site. The importance of these will depend on distance, which will determine not only whether an object is seen at all, but also whether it is identifiable, or blurred by atmospheric perspective, or contours, or by intervening objects such as trees. The effect of new structures on distant views should be ascertained by taking out sections along a number of sight lines.

Montage on photographs, or a scale study model may also be used. In using the latter, the view point, even if some miles away can be scaled out and fixed at the correct level. The visibility of proposed structures on the model can then be ascertained. Contoured ordnance maps to a scale of $1:25,000$ ($2\frac{1}{2}$ in to 1 mile) will be found useful in assessing the interplay between a site and its surroundings. From these, probable view points can be picked out and then checked on site.

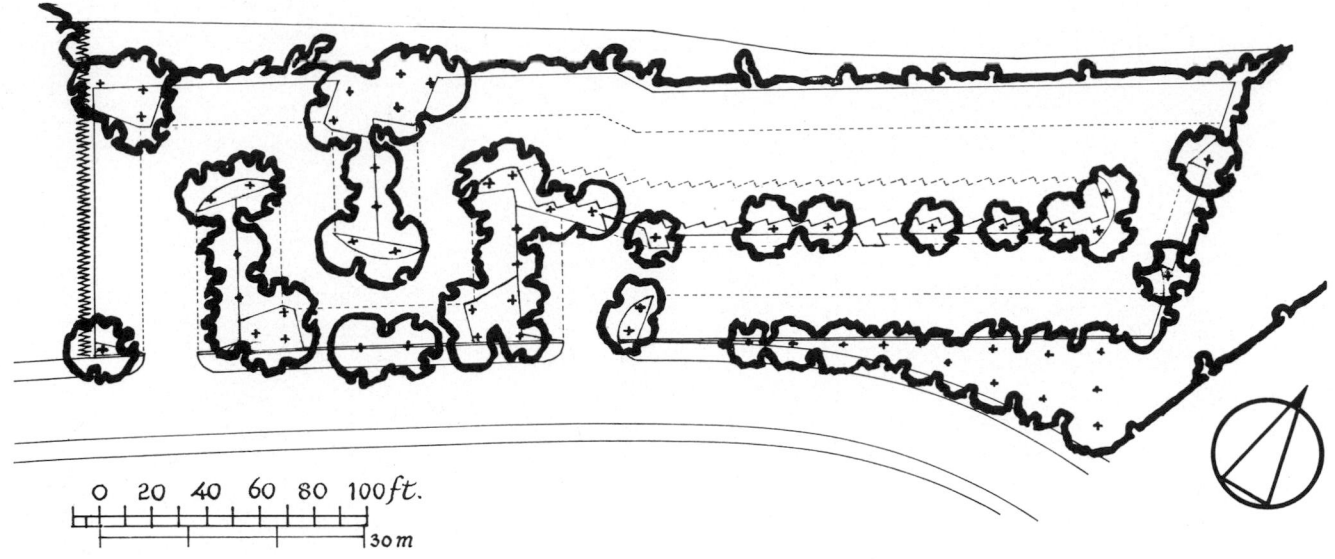

Fig. 2.2. Tree screened car park, Aldershot. Landscape Architect: Brenda Colvin.

2.5 Use factors

These must be ascertained from the client and from those concerned with the particular use to which the site is to be put.

2.5.1 Traffic
Access for traffic and parking is now often a major site use. Requirements must be ascertained for:

Access to public road with requisite sight lines.
Access points for each type of traffic within the site. This will cover loading bays for lorries, workers' cars, residents' cars, visitors' cars.
Turning spaces appropriate to each type of vehicle.
Parking requirements.

Peripheral screening and/or trees within the car parks is desirable, as cars are a restless element in any landscape. It can be achieved with little or no loss of parking space. Screening is especially necessary for projects in the countryside (Fig. 2.2). Car parks for occasional or seasonal use need not always be hard surfaced. The site plan should differentiate between hard surfaced and green car parks. Approach roads should normally take the shortest route compatible with contours and a pleasant line. But easy deviations may be justified to avoid severing land, since land cut off by a traffic route is largely wasted.

Whether or not cycle traffic should be segregated from motor traffic and/or pedestrians depends on the amount of cycle traffic expected. On the approaches to some industrial sites it may be heavy and will justify separate cycle tracks. Cycle parking should be provided even for small numbers, otherwise cycles will be leant against windows and plants.

Pleasant conditions for pedestrians should be assured along any public footpaths through or adjacent to the site. Segregation of pedestrians and vehicles is desirable for all areas of fast or heavy traffic, and where children are concerned, even in the case of light traffic. Where possible, traffic and pedestrians should take different routes. The pedestrian routes should be more direct, but can have steeper gradients. Approaches to either underpasses or foot-bridges should be made to appear the natural and easiest route for the pedestrian by making them pleasant and gradual, with a maximum gradient of 1:10 which is negotiable by perambulators. In all cases there should be protection from noise and fumes between cars and pedestrians. Where the routes run roughly parallel, grade separation is helpful in giving protection with economy of land use.

2.5.2 Density
Density is a factor in all planning from the simple case of the size of a family in a dwelling to the number of visitors to a National Park. There is an appropriate ecological design for every density, which the site plan must evolve. In high density housing small public open spaces must be conceived as hard wearing surfaces. In a heavily used town centre for instance the whole surface is an open air floor, furnished, if at all, with well-protected trees or plants. The more difficult problems arise in housing areas with nett residential densities of 240 persons per hectare where some grass surface is desired, but will only survive if sited off the main lines of access, or if protected.

The minimum viable size of grass areas is influenced by climatic and soil conditions as well as by density and siting. This factor of wear and density should influence

Plate 2.1. A pattern where the background is hard wearing surface with plant groups superimposed. House in California. Landscape Architect: Lawrence Halprin.

Plate 2.2. Protection of growing material in a high density area by the use of cobbles and changed level. Gossops Green. Crawley New Town.

the whole development, from the master plan onwards, since it requires a differentiation of open space into large areas not cut up with access roads and paths, where green landscape can flourish, and into small, densely used areas of hard wearing surfaces and intermediate areas where elements of green landscape are possible if incorporated within a design which provides protection for them within areas of access (Fig. 2.2).

There is a basic division in design between a density which requires a background of wearing surface, on which living material is imposed (Plate 2.1), and a density which allows a background of living material on which a pattern of wearing surface is imposed (Plate 2.5).

Detail design can reduce the wear/density ratio by such devices as change of level or use of deterrents such as cobbles and hazards (Plates 2.2, 2.3, 2.4).

But the greatest prevention of wear results from providing adequate paths in the direction in which they are needed. The most direct desire routes may sometimes have to be modified but they must always form the basis of the design and any deviations must be made to appear natural and inevitable.

Plans for rural projects, e.g. camp sites, must take account of the probable increase in density not only of

Fig. 2.3. A residential area, where high density dwellings opening on to paved ways contrast with wedges of unbroken grass. Harlow. Architect: Michael Neylan, A.R.I.B.A. Landscape Architect: Sylvia Crowe.

the site itself but of its surroundings, and devise any necessary protection or modification of the ecology to deal with this. Methods of doing this are:

Protective planting of thickets to prevent access to certain areas.

Provision of paths.

Use of change of level, or ditches, to discourage straying.

Change or modification of vegetation.

Reduction of density by difficulty of access, e.g. allowing only rough tracks past certain points, thereby discouraging vehicle access.

In the vicinity of a camp or a car park, a buffer zone must be planned for, to allow people to fan out from the access point for picnics and short walks. Particular care must be taken on geological formations liable to erosion, e.g. sand dunes.

2.5.3 Safety factors

Safety precautions will often influence and may sometimes inhibit the design. Serious physical hazards should be foreseen by the landscape architect and guarded against in the site plan. Subsequent emergency measures can ruin the design. Examples of genuine hazards are:

Plate 2.3. Strong simple protection enabling plants to give relief to an area which without them would appear bleak. Craigavon Planning Executive.

21

Plate 2.4. Planting in hard surface, protected by change of level. Islamabad Government Hostel, Derek Lovejoy and Partners.

Access to fast traffic roads by pedestrians and especially children.
High unprotected retaining walls.
Deep water accessible to children.

Other hazards, not serious in themselves may involve legal liability. These may sometimes be dealt with by insurance.

2.5.4 Special functions

Residential. The functions of residential open space are (*a*) to give access and (*b*) to provide for outdoor living.

In (*a*) the needs of vehicle/pedestrian segregation must be combined with providing both forms of access to the dwellings. In (*b*) an important factor is whether the use of the open space is to be for privacy or sociability. Complete privacy is usually required in at least one section of private gardens. The provision of this is more important than size. Some degree of privacy is also desirable in the gardens of flats and in communal gardens, which should be designed to provide secluded sitting places.

Sociability is required in the public open space which will comprise residential courts, playgrounds and town

Plate 2.5. The direction of the path is guided by land-shaping.

22

squares, each designed for its appropriate density of use. Pedestrian ways should link the public open spaces into a connected system, to which private houses will have easy access and which will lead to the schools, the shopping centres and the recreation areas. All paths in the pedestrian system must be wide enough for two perambulators abreast (minimum 1,400 mm approx. 4 ft 6 in) and the main paths will be wider.

One of the basic patterns for pedestrian/vehicle separation is the Radburn system. Many variations on this have recently been evolved.

It must be ascertained in consultation with the architects, whether the architectural elements of the plan will themselves provide an interesting setting for the pedestrian way or whether space must be provided to establish planting beside the paths. Normally both methods will be combined to give variations between one section and another. To achieve this change of pattern the width left between buildings for the path must vary. Where planting is required, ample space for whatever type is intended must be provided, both above and below ground and kept free from services.

Paths must be direct in their general line. In their minor deviations, devices such as changes of level and hazards must make them appear as the natural course and discourage short-cutting, which is a sign that the static and passage elements of the system have been confused (see p. 33). Steps, unless very shallow, should have a ramped alternative for perambulators and wheelchairs.

Childrens' playgrounds of all types should be located at an early stage of the plan and linked into the pedestrian system. Similarly resting places with provision for sitting in both sun and shade should be related to shopping centres, old peoples' dwellings and to any features likely to attract onlookers.

Private gardens. The basic function of a private garden is the provision of open-air living for the inhabitants. To this may be added the client's special requirements, such as space for growing trees, fruit, flowers or vegetables, the provision of a swimming pool, tennis courts or other special features. The open-air room will require privacy, a view either looking out from the site or created within the site and direct access from the appropriate part of the house. Some form of terrace is usually required. If the terrace looks on to rising ground, sufficient space must be levelled to avoid an appearance of oppression, and drainage must be arranged to prevent water flooding into the house. There must be co-ordination between the levels of the damp-proof course (d.p.c.) and facing bricks, and of manhole covers with the finished ground level.

In all but the smallest gardens provision must be made for tool and potting sheds, compost heaps and their access paths. The need for stand-pipes must also be considered. In country house gardens and estates the client will often require only a small area which needs garden maintenance, but will wish to develop additional land as amenity woodland, or grazed park. Success here will require a solution to the problems of maintenance by farm and forest methods. (See also Chapter 11 – Conservation and Management.)

Hospitals. The use of hospital grounds will be for access and car parks, patients, visitors and staff.

Patients – These need a pleasant outlook from windows, and easy attractive walks to take them out-of-doors in convalescence. Special requirements for geriatric and long-term patients include sunny terraces on which to sit. Wind shelter is essential. For mental patients small plots for gardening may be needed and safe boundaries which do not appear restrictive must be provided.

Visitors – Seating in pleasant surroundings should be provided where visitors and patients can sit together.

Staff – The needs and composition of the staff must be ascertained. Possible requirements are tennis and squash courts, private gardens for resident medical staff and study gardens for resident student nurses. Hospitals with large grounds may require kitchen gardens for vegetables and cut flowers.

Access – Separate car parks are likely to be required for staff and visitors, the former probably including coaches. Separate access may be required for ambulances and mortuary vans.

Parks. An exact client's brief is essential in designing public parks. Their proposed use may range from the grounds of an old country house in the green belt intended only as a place for walks and views, to a multi-use park in a high density area, which will be subject to heavy use and required for a wide range of activity.

In either case the plan must ensure that all the proposed activities will be welded into an overall landscape, with maximum opportunities for pleasant walks, views and relief from the noise and congestion of the city. The necessary provision for car parking should be included in the overall scheme. Otherwise the intention of the plan will be nullified by unplanned car parking. The car park may, however, be sited outside but adjacent to the park. Requirement for glasshouses, maintenance yards, access for lorries and lavatories must also be ascertained. Noisy activities should be segregated from quiet areas.

Educational buildings. The major land use around schools and colleges will be for recreation.

Plate 2.6 A tree planted car park. Harlow Town Centre.

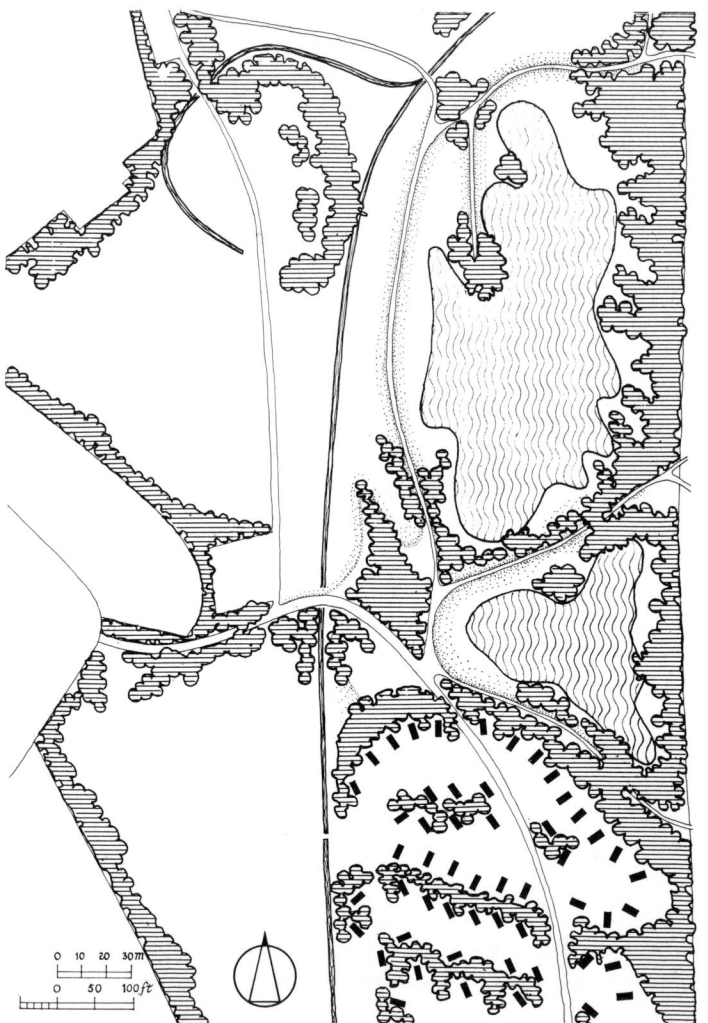

Fig. 2.4. Planted banks are used to divide the caravan camp into secluded enclosures, and to screen them from view. Landscape Architect: Sylvia Crowe.

Many schools now use open-air class rooms. These require sheltered positions and insulation from noise, which may be provided by planting, by baffle walls or by ground shaping. For primary schools safe pedestrian access is essential. Safe cycle access is required for almost all academic buildings. The grounds of colleges and universities should provide space for open-air study and opportunities for students to congregate and talk. It must be ascertained by consultations with the architects and clients whether the concept is to be that of a campus on the American pattern, where a large open space will cater for great numbers and for varied activities, or whether a more domestic scale is visualised. In any case the plan will need to cater for sports activities, spaces for open-air congregation, strolling and sitting, quiet areas for study, and fellows' or staff gardens. The two landscape elements of the plan will be the large area of the playing fields and the more intimate areas associated with the buildings. Car parks should be excluded from the internal landscape. Their siting, and that of the cycle parks, must be an early decision in evolving the plan. Collegiate discipline may make it possible to use grass as a ground covering under far higher density than would be possible in public schemes.

Industry. The major function is always production – with this should be combined considerations for the surrounding landscape and good working conditions for the staff. To carry out the functions, good access, adequate storage space, and usually space for future development are essential.

Consideration for environment entails prevention of pollution or noise. While the care for this lies primarily within the industry, landscape treatment can help by planting wide tree screens and/or building baffles of soil. Screening is always required for storage yards, car parks, etc. It may or may not be required for the main building. Expansion areas may also need grassing and screening.

Pleasant working conditions are primarily achieved by good appearance. In addition the following may be desirable:

Tree planting to give shade or shelter or to cut out noise.
Provision of out-door sitting areas. This is particularly appreciated by women workers.
Provision of recreation. Male workers appreciate a kick-about space.

There may in addition to these provisions for lunch-break, be wider sports facilities provided for after work and weekends.

Access will usually be required for staff and visitors' cars, workers' cars, works buses, bicycles, pedestrians and loading lorries. The various points of access, the expected volume and the required parking space for each must be ascertained or assessed.

Special requirements by different types of industry

Industrial estates – In these the individual requirements of each factory must be fitted into and reconciled with the overall landscape of the estate.

Space for large trees, which are the best foil for the buildings, will have to be found either within the industrial sites, or on ground reserved to the estate as a whole. This point must be settled before the individual sites are let. A policy must also be agreed on fencing along road frontages, to ensure either a good looking type of fencing, or to reserve space for planting between boundary fences and frontages and to ensure that it is planted. Similarly a policy must be agreed for screening storage yards and for the treatment of areas for future expansion.

The estate may include common open space and recreational facilities, or individual firms may require their own. Convenient access by bus, car, cycle and foot will be required and separation of the foot and cycle from motor traffic is desirable. Foot and cycle tracks must be made direct and attractive if they are to be used.

Isolated industry and public utilities – Where siting requirements take certain undertakings out of industrial areas into the countryside, or into residential areas, the landscape architect will be chiefly concerned with making them acceptable in their surroundings, while maintaining their working efficiency.

To do this he must find out their essential working conditions, which may not always be the same as their tradi-

Plate 2.7. Trees give welcome shade in an otherwise open landscape.

tional requirements. Often, the traditional solution to a certain problem is not the best for the landscape. It is for the landscape architect to grasp the problem, and to think out afresh what the acceptable solution might be. Any fresh solution must however be carefully cleared with the technicians involved to make sure that there are no hidden snags.

Particular points on which the landscape architect should be able to contribute ideas are:

The disposal of waste and spoil.
Treatment of site boundaries (see p. 34, Chapter 2, and Chapter 5).
Multi-purpose use, such as recreation and nature conservation in conjunction with reservoirs.
Protection of surrounding country, visually and ecologically.

Information which he will need will include:

Life and phasing of project. This is particularly relevant to mineral workings.
Amount, type and speed of accretion of waste materials, e.g. ash from power stations.
Amount and type of industrial material to be stored, e.g. coal for power stations.

Pollution – Fumes from chemical works or dust from quarries may inhibit plant growth, but planting may be needed to check dust or smell from causing annoyance outside the site. Amelioration by planting is usually only partially successful, and every possible step should be taken to ensure prevention of pollution at source. The landscape architect can contribute to this by foreseeing and pointing out the harmful effects on surroundings and vegetation and wild life.

Expected traffic – This will not only affect the amount of car parking and road use on site, but may necessitate road widening on site approaches.

25

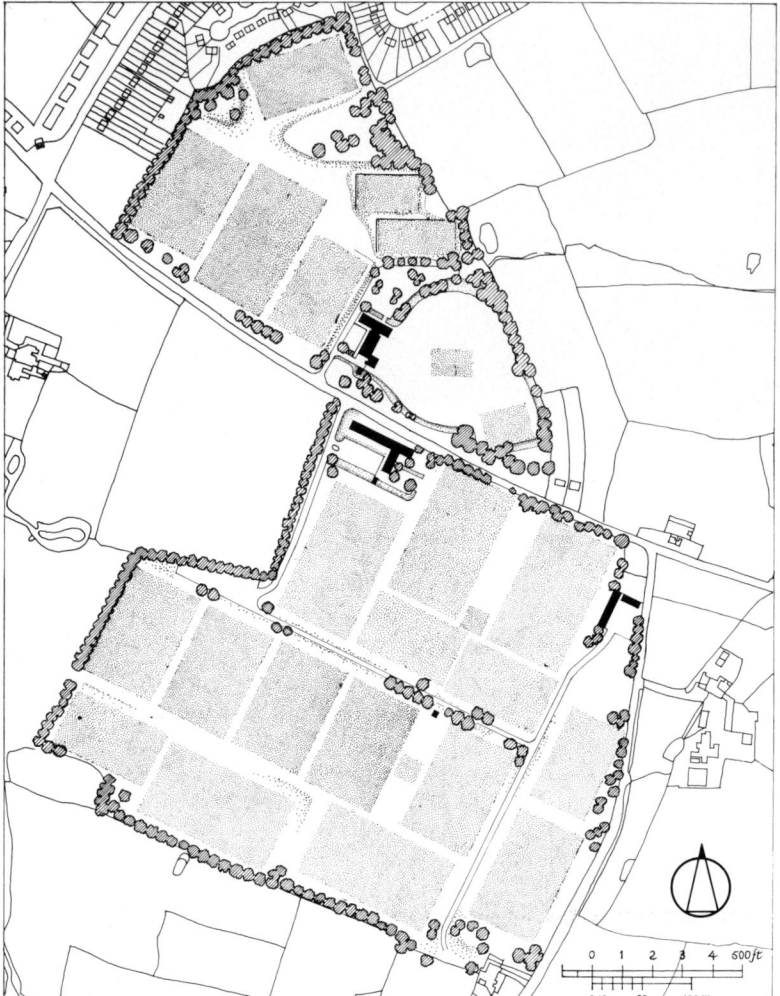

Fig. 2.5. Wast Hills Playing Fields, University of Birmingham, showing comprehensive arrangements for tree planting, car parking, Clubhouse and other facilities. Landscape Architect: R. Frank Marshall.

Number of workers, and whether new housing will be required – A reservoir for instance may require on-site housing, and this must be integrated with the proposed multi-use of the site.

Degree of security necessary – This may often be exaggerated by clients, and tactful probing may be needed to find out the true position. This is very relevant where it is hoped to combine recreation with the primary site use.

Roads. Where the landscape architect is also qualified in road engineering, the aligning of roads and treatment of their boundaries and the intersections may be his responsibility solely. Where he is not so qualified, ideally he should work in collaboration with the road engineers. If his advice is sought at the earliest stages, his concern will be:

To bring full consideration of the landscape into the choice of route.
To ensure that in detail routeing the road preserves features of landscape value wherever possible.
To reconcile the grading required for traffic with the best interests of the landscape.

In cases where the route and gradient of the road is already settled, his contribution will be the grading of cuttings and embankments and roadside planting.
Information required for the compilation of road plans, includes:

Type and speed of traffic for which road is designed.
Sight lines.
Requirements for parking and lay-bys.

Landscape plans for roads must include sufficient widths of land beyond the road curtilage on each side to ensure that the road landscape relates to its surroundings. In some cases a small-scale plan will also be needed to show views to distant points of interest.

Recreation. Recreational requirements may be divided into informal pursuits which may function within an infinite variety of areas and types of landscape, and organised games which require specific sizes and conditions for their grounds.

Informal recreation

Water sports – Reservoirs and wet gravel pits are increasingly being used for water sports of various kinds. The possibility of catering for these sports should be considered wherever the opportunity arises. Decisions to be made are:

Which sports are compatible and which must be kept separate. Separation can be either by zoning or by season. For instance a reservoir may be used for fishing in summer and sailing in winter.
The effect of certain sports, e.g. water skiing and speed boats on bank erosion.
The suitability of the water for public access as regards purity and safety.
Any steps which must be taken to prevent bank erosion or water fouling caused by public access.
The effect of any recreational use on nature conservation. Bird-watching is an important recreation in itself.

Caravanning and camping – Sites laid out as recognized camps require sanitation, water supply and usually a warden's accommodation (for space standards see p. 248). These are recognised as minimum space standards, but additional space for providing privacy for campers and screening from surroundings should be allowed (Fig. 2.3).

The minimum number of vans required to make the camp financially viable may vary according to circumstances, and should be ascertained. Firm standing for the vans and approach roads is required, but this need not always entail exposed hard surface except for the main access routes (see p. 24). Sites should be well drained. Wherever possible sites should be screened from surrounding view points. Thinned woodland forms one of the best sites but precautions must be taken to avoid damage to the trees by soil compaction over their roots. Safe access to the highway must be assured and this point must be cleared with the Highway Authority.

Riding, walking and cycling – All landscape planning projects should consider the needs of these users. Any or all of the three may follow the same general line, but cycles cannot share the same surface as the others. If walkers and riders share a ride it must be sufficiently wide and well drained to prevent winter ponding. In areas of heavy use it is better to separate the paths from the rides. All these routes require separation from motor traffic, a pleasant setting and continuity.

Organised games – Playing fields for football, cricket and hockey require large, level open spaces, and are therefore some of the first open-air uses to be settled on the site plan. One in 40 is usually considered the maximum acceptable slope for football pitches (other than first-class pitches).

Current minimum space requirements are:

	hectares	acres
Primary schools (excluding infants)		
Playing fields for up to 50 pupils	0·2	0·5
Secondary schools		
Boys only		
Playing fields for up to 150 pupils	1·8	4·5
Girls only		
Playing fields for up to 150 pupils	1·6	4·0
Boys and girls		
Playing fields for up to 150 pupils	1·8	4·5
(For detailed requirements relative to increased pupillage, see *Department of Education and Science Regulations*)		
Universities		
Playing fields for 5,000 students	11·3	28·25
Large towns		
Per 1,000 population	1·6	4·0

These allowances are all for grass pitches. All-weather pitches permit 4 times the amount of play, and if one or more such pitch is included a proportionate reduction in playing acreage can be made.

Additional land up to 30% should always be allowed for tree planting, car parks, pavilions, etc. (Fig. 2.5).

The setting out of the pitches should give latitude to change the position of goalmouths, thus equalising wear.

This means that for economy of space several pitches should be grouped together, on one level. For public recreation grounds minimum areas of 4 ha (approx. 10 acres) of grouped facilities are desirable; smaller areas tend to be uneconomic in upkeep.

There is a growing demand for a proportion of hard pitches for all-weather use. These must be visualised as interruptions to the green expanse traditionally formed by sports areas, and means devised of making them visually acceptable, or screening them on the same principle as car parks.

Public playing pitches can be left visually open, but private clubs usually require seclusion, and this again must be visualised as a break in the landscape. Unless the pitches are near a related building, a pavilion with changing accommodation is needed. This should be associated with the car park, and usually set in trees.

Sports stadia – These may be classed as buildings rather than open space. The requirement of a 'gate' means that they must be screened from their surroundings, and the stands, car parks and usually flood-lights, constitute a large urban unit. Their siting should therefore be regarded as a subtraction from and not an addition to, the visually open space system. The same applies to squash courts, indoor swimming pools, hard tennis courts and sports halls. All these uses, with their access roads and car parks, should be classed as urban buildings rather than landscape – although they may reasonably be sited in close relationship to open recreation areas or parks.

Children's playgrounds – The over-all space allowance considered reasonable in the past has been 0·3 to 0·4 ha per 1,000 population. (¾ to 1 acre). The National Playing Fields Association however are recommending 0·6 ha per 1,000 (1½ acres) which may be desirable in large towns where common land or other roaming space is not available. The different types of playground needed are:

Under 5's. These must be sited very close to the child's home. Small, frequent provision is more useful than larger areas at a distance. These can be incorporated within the pedestrian system.

Nursery schools need attached playgrounds for the same age group.

Primary school age. One playground for this age should be sited within 400 m (approx. ¼ mile) safe walk from all homes. They may usefully be grouped with primary schools, having interchangeable access from the school and from outside.

Over 11's. These require junior playing pitches and opportunities for adventure.

Adventure play can be provided as constructional playgrounds, scramble courses, canoeing, camping, nature trails, etc. Most of these activities will involve a play leader or other supervision. They will serve all age groups (over 5) but particularly the over 10's. They can often be threaded through the open space system on both a local and regional basis.

The provision and design of play facilities requires special study.

2.6 Cost

Multiple use. This may mean that two or more functions are served by one feature, e.g. timber production and wind shelter, or it may mean that two or more functions are interwoven, e.g. when pedestrian ways are given their setting by passing beside sports fields. Both these forms of multiple use are desirable, and whatever may be the primary function of a site, its possible subsidiary functions should be considered in the site plan. Both capital and maintenance costs are factors in design and their limitations must be considered throughout the development of the plan.

2.6.1. Overall rates per hectare
At the time of first consultations with the client it is useful to be able to give a rough idea of the cost of different types of development. This will be based on an overall per hectare rate.

2.6.2. Unit rates
In some cases it may be possible to estimate rates per unit of development, for example estimates for urban development may be based on a cost per dwelling. Current rates for this must be ascertained bearing in mind the different factors involved. The figure is governed not only by the amount of open space but in particular by the amount of hard surface required and whether all the hard surface will be included in landscape costs or will be partly covered by architectural and engineering costs. The cost of landscape for high density housing may well cost more than for low density because a higher proportion of hard surface will be required. As densities increase, however, the high cost per hectare will be shared among a larger number of dwellings and the cost per dwelling unit ceases to be such a reliable estimating guide.

2.6.3. Estimate of costs by elements
At an early stage in the development of the plan a rough cost check should be made to discover whether the figure originally mentioned is likely to remain accurate. In this check a rough break down of costs should be made listing such elements as:

Excavations.	Hard surfacing.
Grass.	Planting.
Special features, such as pools, walls and buildings.	

A sum should be added for contract preliminaries and contingencies and to cover special site difficulties, such as inaccessibility, lack of topsoil or heavy excavation.

If the result of this check reveals that the final cost is at all likely to exceed the client's expectations, and cannot be reduced without jeopardising the plan, the client should be consulted before the plan is crystallised. More detailed costing will be applied when the plan is completed.

2.7 Maintenance

2.7.1 Standard of provision
The provision which will be available for maintenance is sometimes a difficult factor to ascertain, but unless it is foreseen and planned for, the plan is never likely to reach maturity in the form envisaged. Both the numbers and skill of the staff which is likely to be available must be discussed with the client. Possibilities of maintenance by contract must also be considered. The plan must be adapted to the degree of maintenance which can be foreseen. Instruction on maintenance should accompany site plans. (See also Chapter 11 – Maintenance and Conservation.)

2.7.2 Means of maintenance
The means of maintenance must also be foreseen, e.g. grass areas must either be mown or grazed. If mown they must be accessible and able to be cut; if grazed, protection of adjoining planting must be assured. The use of machinery must be allowed for on all but the smallest sites. Provision must always be made for access for maintenance. The requirements for this depend on the size and type of development and the type of machinery which is likely to be used. The following are typical examples of what may be necessary:

Access for gang mowers to large grass areas and sports fields.
Lorry and machine access to allotments or any large areas of cultivated ground.
Wheelbarrow access to small areas.
Access for lawn mowers to all grass areas however small.
Access for maintenance to patios, roof gardens and window boxes.

Water points must be provided for all areas needing irrigation. Tool sheds, maintenance yards and glass-houses must be planned for convenience of access and working.

2.8 Timing

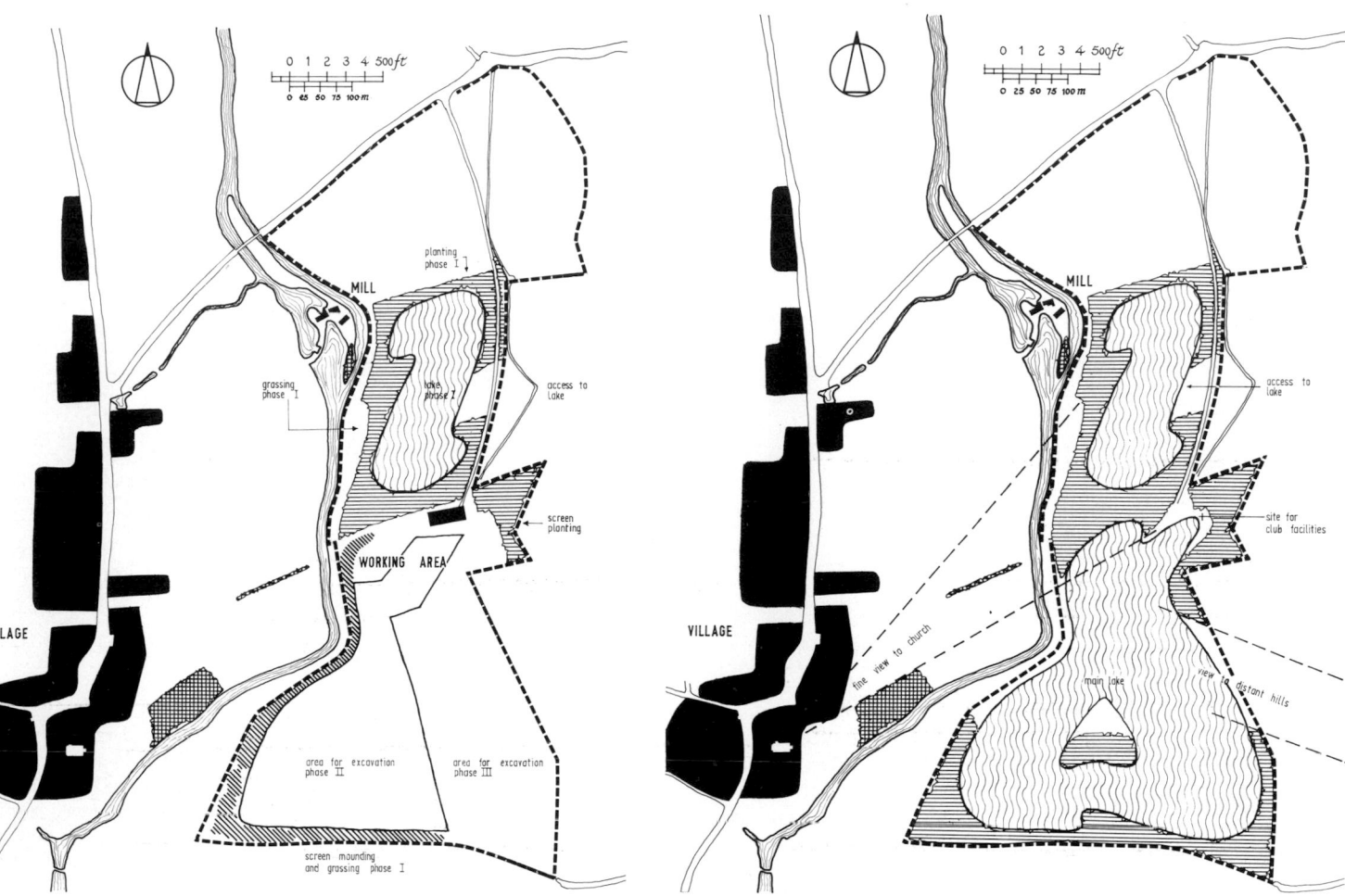

Fig. 2.6. Plan for a gravel working showing immediate screening for working plant and phases of further working.

Fig. 2.7. Gravel working, progressive restoration completed to give final development of lake, related to the adjacent landscape.
Landscape Architect: Sylvia Crowe.

2.8.1 Phasing

The landscape must often be developed in stages for the following reasons:

(a) Future extension of buildings may be planned. In this case temporary landscape may be carried out over the land reserved for future extension.

(b) Finance may only allow the plan to be developed gradually.

In both (a) and (b) the plan must ensure a good appearance in the early stages, and a minimum of wasted cost.

(c) The project may change radically over the course of years. This is the case in mineral workings, where the site plan may comprise at least three stages:

Immediate action to screen or improve the appearance of plant and early workings.
A working programme of progressive reinstatement which will ensure the best appearance compatible with working requirements.
A final plan showing eventual reinstatement of

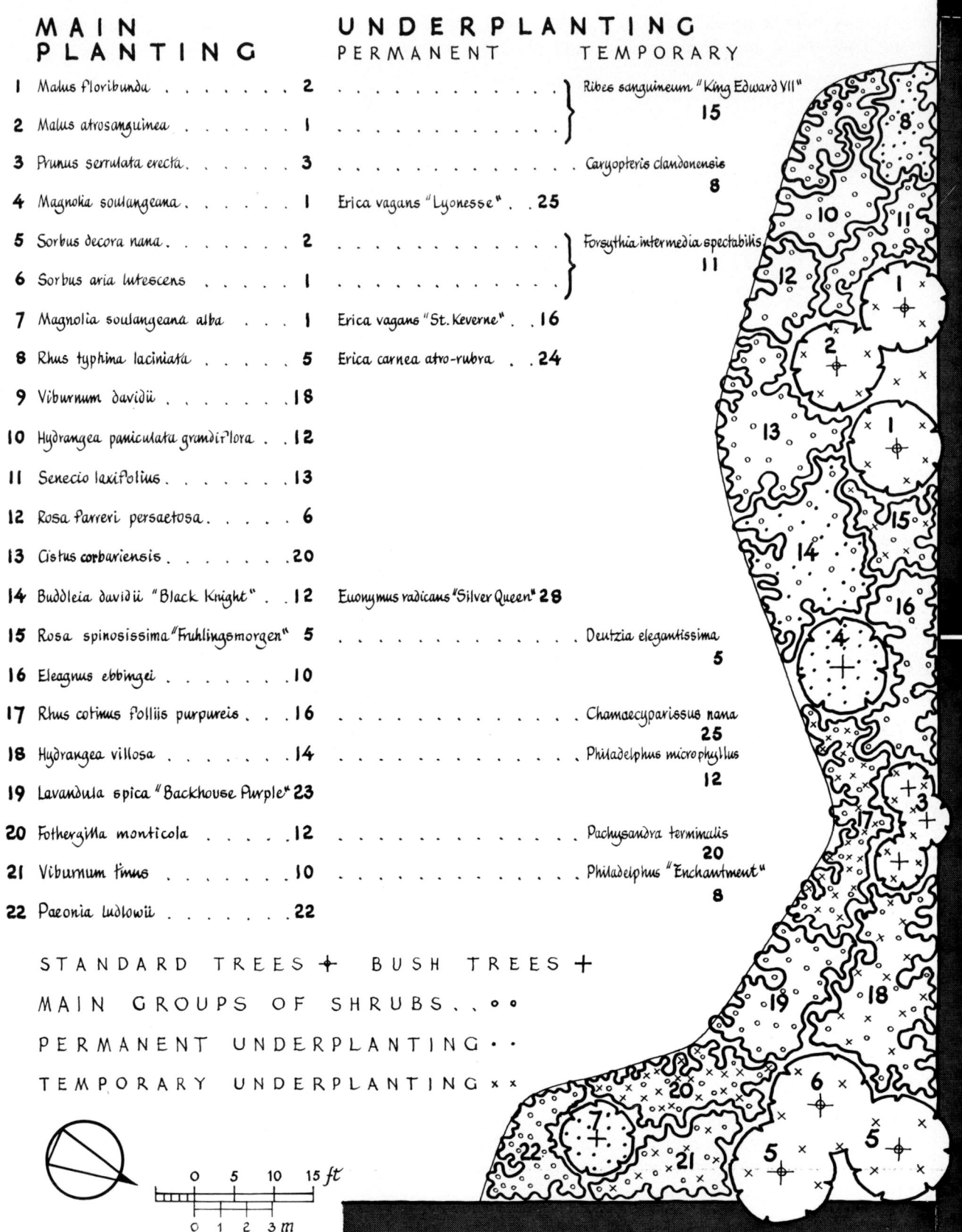

MAIN PLANTING

1	Malus floribunda	. . . .	2
2	Malus atrosanguinea	. . . . . .	1
3	Prunus serrulata erecta	. . . . .	3
4	Magnolia soulangeana	. . . . . .	1
5	Sorbus decora nana	. . . .	2
6	Sorbus aria lutescens	. . . . . .	1
7	Magnolia soulangeana alba	. . .	1
8	Rhus typhina laciniata	. . . . .	5
9	Viburnum davidii	. . . .	18
10	Hydrangea paniculata grandiflora	.	12
11	Senecio laxifolius	. . . .	13
12	Rosa farreri persaetosa	. . . . .	6
13	Cistus corbariensis	. . . . . .	20
14	Buddleia davidii "Black Knight"	.	12
15	Rosa spinosissima "Fruhlingsmorgen"	5
16	Eleagnus ebbingei	. . . .	10
17	Rhus cotinus folliis purpureis	. . .	16
18	Hydrangea villosa	. . . .	14
19	Lavandula spica "Backhouse Purple"	23
20	Fothergilla monticola	. . . . .	12
21	Viburnum tinus	. . . .	10
22	Paeonia ludlowii	. . . .	22

UNDERPLANTING

PERMANENT · · TEMPORARY

PERMANENT		TEMPORARY	
		Ribes sanguineum "King Edward VII"	15
		Caryopteris clandonensis	8
Erica vagans "Lyonesse"	25		
		Forsythia intermedia spectabilis	11
Erica vagans "St. Keverne"	16		
Erica carnea atro-rubra	24		
Euonymus radicans "Silver Queen"	28		
		Deutzia elegantissima	5
		Chamaecyparissus nana	25
		Philadelphus microphyllus	12
		Pachysandra terminalis	20
		Philadelphus "Enchantment"	8

STANDARD TREES ✛ BUSH TREES ✛

MAIN GROUPS OF SHRUBS . . ○ ○

PERMANENT UNDERPLANTING · ·

TEMPORARY UNDERPLANTING × ×

0 5 10 15 ft

0 1 2 3 m

Fig. 2.8. Plan showing slow growing subjects with permanent underplanting and interplanting of rapidly growing shrubs which will be removed as the permanent planting matures.

the workings to form a pleasant and viable landscape (Figs. 2.6 and 2.7).

The same type of problem applies to power stations where ash will gradually accumulate over the years.

2.8.2. Duration of project

Some projects have a foreseeably short life. The landscape plan for these should give the quickest effect possible, but it may still be worth planting trees for the future in the hope that they will be compatible with the succeeding land use.

2.8.3. Short- and long-term plans

It is often desirable to combine planting for quick effect and for long term. The plan should show clearly which trees are to be retained and which removed (Figs. 2.8 and 2.9).

2.9 Elements of the plan

2.9.1 Structures in the landscape

Landscape architects may either site structures in consultation with architects and engineers or if they have dual qualifications they may be wholly responsible. In either case the relationship of structures to the landscape is a vital factor of site planning which must be considered from the outset. This relationship falls into certain categories each requiring its appropriate treatment.

Structures may be so closely related to the land that they appear to grow from it. Typical examples are the mud villages of parts of Africa and the local stone walls and bridges of Britain. Modern structures in this category have been designed in Denmark and elsewhere with turf-covered roofs to let the unbroken green of the landscape flow over them. Small utility buildings such as those housing equipment at the foot of dams can be sunk back into the land formation with only their front elevation showing. This type of treatment is useful wherever an unbroken landscape is required, with complete subordination of minor structures. It may also apply to major structures such as earth and rock-fill dams, or oil storage installations. In all cases any visible part of the structure must be sympathetic to the landscape in texture and colour.

Buildings may form a distinct feature, related to and held within the landscape. This is typified by farms and old villages and depends upon good design, siting and grouping of the building complemented by sympathetic land formation and planting.

Structures may be in complete contrast to their surroundings and yet contribute to the landscape. This applies particularly to engineering structures. A typical example is a bridge of steel or pre-stressed concrete springing across a chasm. Success depends on the siting and design quality of the structure and on a clean transition between natural landscape and man-made structure.

A building which dominates the landscape is typified by the Parthenon. Ideally this demands majesty and perfection of design. Historically these dominant buildings were represented by churches, castles, lighthouses and windmills. Modern types are silos, communication towers and power stations. Landscape around these dominant structures needs to be quiet and simple, avoiding incongruity of scale. Extensive landform may often be helpful in relating the structure to its surroundings and also in concealing small-scale elements such as ancillary buildings and car parks, which would otherwise disrupt the scale relationship.

Since structures form part of the landscape composition they must be designed both in the right relationship to each other and to topography and other landscape elements. Relation to topography can be achieved by informal grouping as in an Italian hill village, or formally as in the Bath terraces. With informal architectural grouping the trees and land formation will also be informal. But in formal layouts the planting may either be axial as in the avenues of Paris, or informal, typified by the planting in Regent's Park, which makes a foil to the Nash Terraces. In close-built urban complexes the trees may be a minor, though important element, complementing the built environment. But such high density areas will also need the contrast of predominantly green areas in the form of parks and town woodlands. In areas of low density the trees may be the dominant and integrating element. Much ugly and formless development occurs where basic function demands a large number of similar units, as in low-cost housing. Here, in particular, a strong concept of the final landscape pattern to be evolved is vital from the beginning. Much can be achieved by extensive tree planting to give cohesion to a landscape which would otherwise be fragmented or monotonous, and the siting of these trees must be part of the basic plan.

In determining the siting and treatment of buildings distinction should be made between those mainly occupied by people, such as schools, hospitals and dwellings, and buildings which are primarily cladding for machines, such as factories and power stations. In the former, views outwards and inwards are of equal importance, in the latter appearance from outside is paramount, combined with working efficiency and consideration for the staff.

All buildings, roads and car parks should be sited to leave the maximum space available for other uses, e.g. a dwelling should be sited to give the maximum space for the enjoyment of the sunniest and most sheltered part of the site. A south-west slope, sheltered from wind and free of frost pockets, is the most favourable for a garden

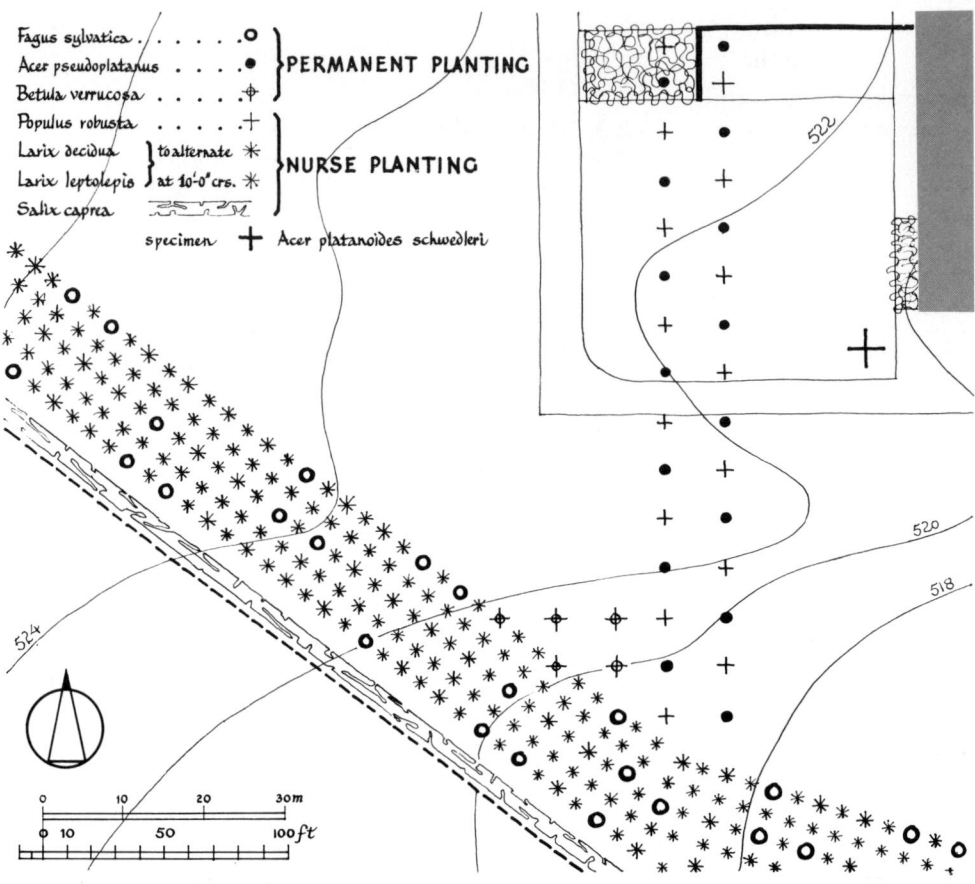

Fagus sylvatica . . . . . .o ⎫
Acer pseudoplatanus . . . .• ⎬ PERMANENT PLANTING
Betula verrucosa . . . . .⌀ ⎭
Populus robusta . . . . .✛ ⎫
Larix decidua ⎱ to alternate ✳ ⎬ NURSE PLANTING
Larix leptolepis ⎰ at 10'-0" crs. ✳ ⎭
Salix caprea ～～～ ⎭

specimen ✛ Acer platanoides schwedleri

Fig. 2.9. Slow growing tree planting with rapidly growing nurse planting to be removed as the permanent planting matures.

and the building. The access road should be contrived so that it does not cut through or overlook the most favourable area (Fig. 2.11).

The same principle applies to hospitals, and to any building whose inmates may wish to enjoy the grounds. The siting of buildings, e.g. schools, requiring extensive games facilities, will be governed by the availability of sufficient level ground for playing fields.

In machine buildings any space not required for working purposes and traffic is likely to have a mainly visual function, and should be allocated where it will most help the surrounding views. For instance an adjustment of a few feet in siting the building in relation to a boundary may enable a screen or some large trees to be planted in a vital position.

Except in the case of a structure which it is intended to conceal, buildings should not be at the lowest point of the site for reasons of drainage. Only very rarely should they be at the highest. Even where it is intended that a building shall be in a commanding position, the brow of the hill is preferable to the actual summit (Fig. 2.12). Where it is desired to screen or partially screen the building and yet give it a good outlook, a position well below the brow is preferable (Fig. 2.13). In the case of a tableland, siting well back from the brow may give con-

cealment from surrounding lower land (Fig. 2.14). Such a position is however likely to be exposed to wind.

Given good architecture, siting on steep ground is favourable to good landscape but both architecture and landscape will be more costly.

2.9.2 Siting the main plant masses

Tree planting.　　　This may be required:

As protection against wind (see Fig. 2.17), noise or fumes.
To screen undesirable views into or out from the site.
To give privacy.
As a visual or ecological link with the surrounding landscape.
To frame views or form focal points.
To give shade.
To form space divisions (Figs. 2.17 and 2.18)

The general positions to serve these needs will make the skeleton of the planting – which may or may not be augmented in developing the plan.

The effects of leaf fall must be taken into account in the case of sewage works and roads. On the latter large leaves may cause skidding. Selection of correct species may often overcome the dangers. In siting trees the effect of their shadows on buildings, etc., must be recognised and the effect of their roots on structures (see Chapter 4.).

Off-site planting. In dealing with large concerns such as power stations or oil installations, which will affect the surrounding countryside, the possibility of off-site planting should be considered. It is sometimes possible to arrange this with the local planning authority or with neighbouring land-owners.

Main hedge and shrub planting. These serve much the same purposes as tree planting but at a lower level. Where complete screening or shelter is required they should be combined with the tree planting. Visually hedges give space division. To register as more than a ground pattern they must be higher than eye level. Shrub planting gives the contrast of solid against the void of unplanted spaces (Plates 2.8 and 2.9). Shrub planting may also be required for ecological reasons, e.g. encouragement of wild life, the formation of game coverts and the amelioration of wet soil conditions. Any flower and colour effects should be considered within the context of the functional planting.

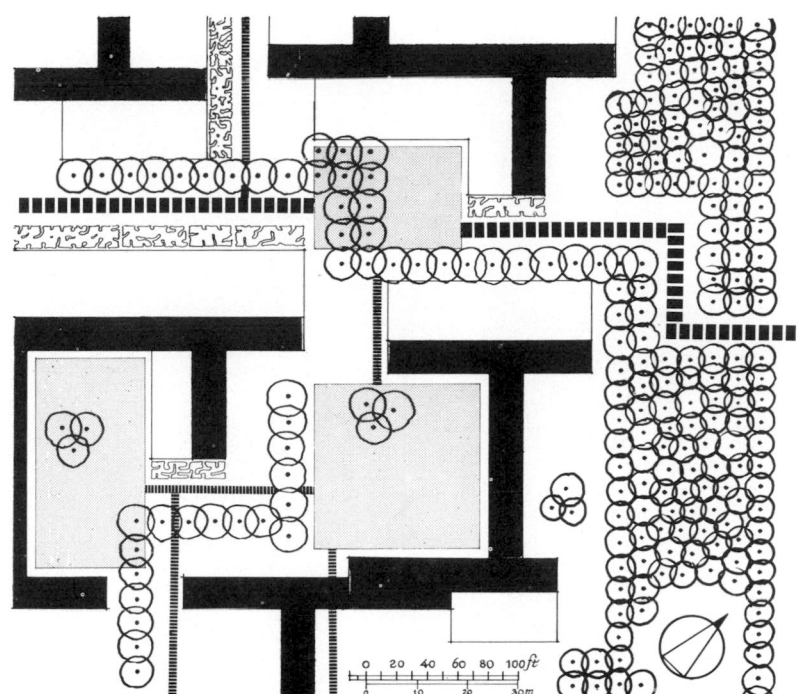

Fig. 2.10. Preliminary diagram for the open space of high density housing, showing the lines of movement and the static spaces.

2.9.3 Contours

Much of the design potential of a site lies in its contours. They affect the siting of all construction. They can be used and manipulated to relate the site to its surroundings or to relate one element to another, e.g. a change of level can provide an access barrier without a visual barrier. If the change of level is sufficient, it can also provide a visual and sound barrier. This device can be used for such purposes as traffic separation, containing noise within a playground in residential areas, forming a noise baffle between heavy traffic roads and residential areas, and separating noisy activities from quiet areas in parks.

Changes of level are one of the most subtle means of creating the desired proportions between one space and another and of creating the element of surprise. Distances appear greater looking downhill, shorter looking up-hill. A very slight cross fall will be obvious seen against a building, while a slight fall away from the building will be imperceptible.

Most constructions produce surplus spoil from underground works. This must be planned for creatively in the site plan. It may be used either to unite the new construction with the existing landscape, or to contribute some new form to the landscape. Banks left at their angle of repose are rarely satisfactory unless used deliberately for a geometric effect. They are difficult to maintain. Any banks formed by the cut and fill of a levelled area must be dealt with in a positive way on the site plan and treated

Fig. 2.11. House well sited for arrangement of a sheltered private garden and for pleasant views from principal rooms.

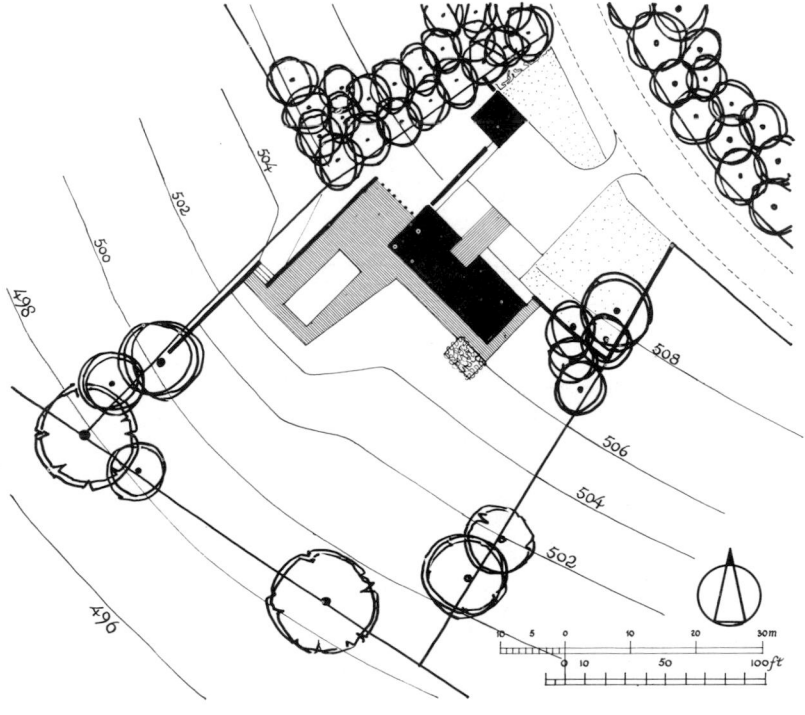

33

Plate 2.8. Hedges above eye level help to create space division. Rous Lench, Worcs.

Plate 2.9. Hedges below eye level form a ground pattern.

as part of the complete design. For details of ground modelling and related problems of drainage, etc. see Chapter 3 – Earthworks.

2.9.4 Site boundaries (see also Chapter 5)

The site plan should always include enough of the surroundings to show their relationship to the site. In the case of a project having a wide field of influence a small-scale location plan is also needed. In this sense the site boundary must not form a mental barrier.

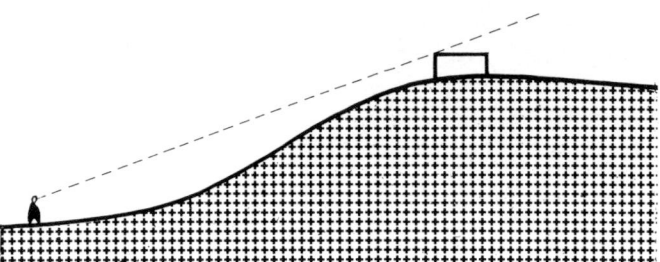

Fig. 2.12. A building in an exposed position, sited on the brow of a hill.

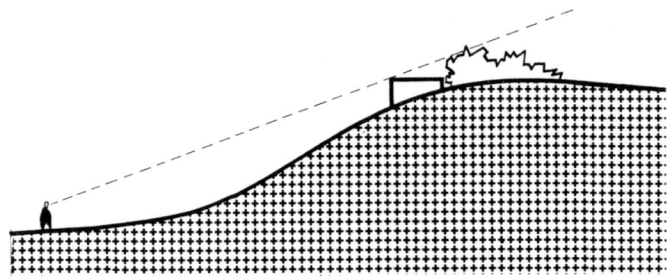

Fig. 2.13. A position below the brow allows both screening and a good outlook.

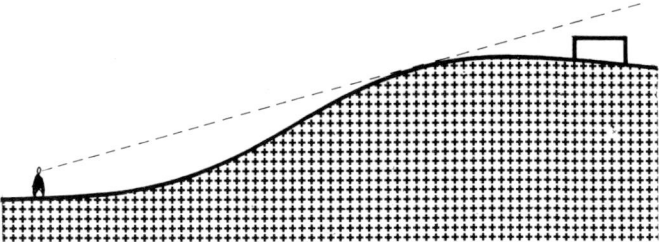

Fig. 2.14. Building on a table-land may be screened by the brow of the hill.

A physical barrier may be required for the following reasons:

Legal definition.
Prevention of trespass, safety barrier, stock and rabbit protection.
Shelter.
Delineation of land use.
Visual sense of enclosure.
A combination of these (Figs. 2.19, 2.20, 2.21, 2.22).

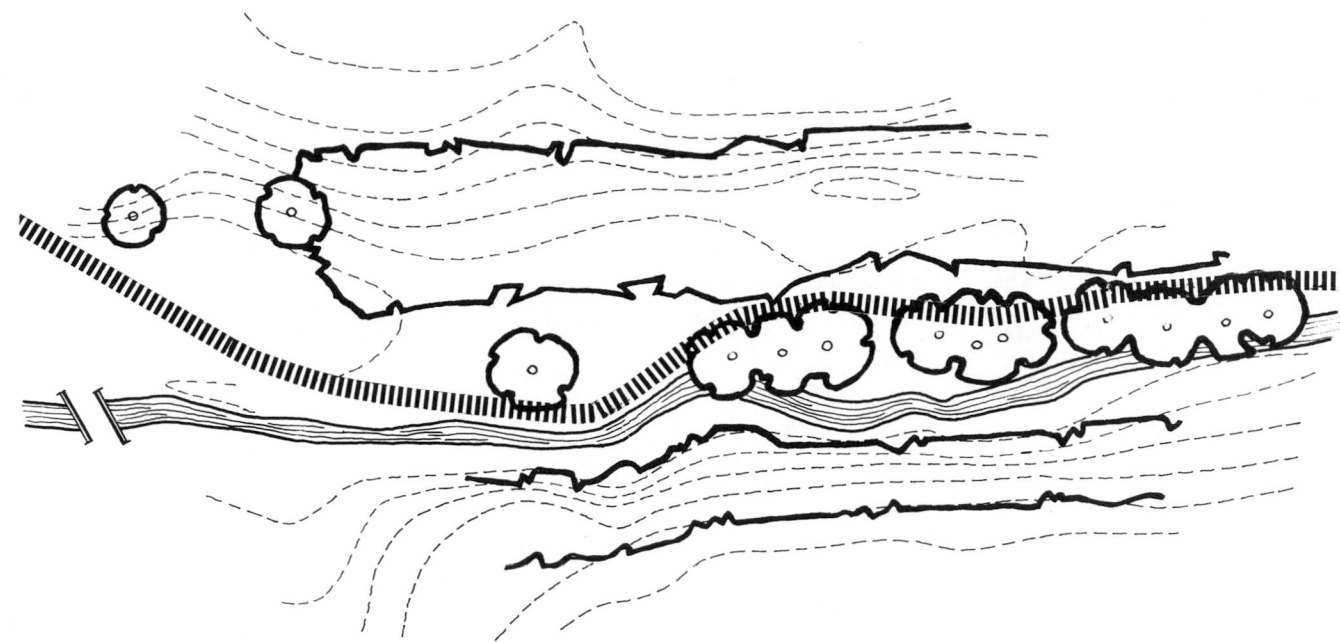

Fig. 2.15. PLAN showing valley siting of secluded footpath.

Types of boundary suitable for each purpose are considered in Chapter 5. The site plan should make clear the reason for and desirable characteristics of each boundary. A client requiring security fencing for certain parts of a site will usually assume that this security fence should follow the site boundary. But this is seldom either necessary or desirable. It will usually be found that a less drastic type of barrier can be used along at least part of the boundary, with the security fence sited back within the site, to protect whatever is vulnerable. This is particularly important where the boundary marches with a public road or footpath. The landscape architect should ascertain the genuine needs of the case.

2.9.5 Water (see also Chapter 7 – Water)
If natural water is to be used, e.g. by the damming of a stream, the siting possibilities will be strictly limited,

and therefore have priority of placing in building up the site plan. The possibility of using water should always be considered because of its unique value in a landscape. Where the possibility exists flooding will often be the best land-use for old workings or low-lying ground, owing to its value for fishing, wild life and recreation and the importance of water conservation for the landscape as a whole.

2.9.6 Street furniture (see also Chapter 6 – Outdoor furniture)
While the detailing of this will not appear in a site plan the positioning of the more important elements may do, and some reference to the type to be used should appear in the report. Items to be accommodated include shelters of various kinds, seats, litter bins, telephone kiosks and other Post Office fixtures, direction posts and notices. It

Fig. 2.16. SECTION showing footpath seclusion achieved by planting.

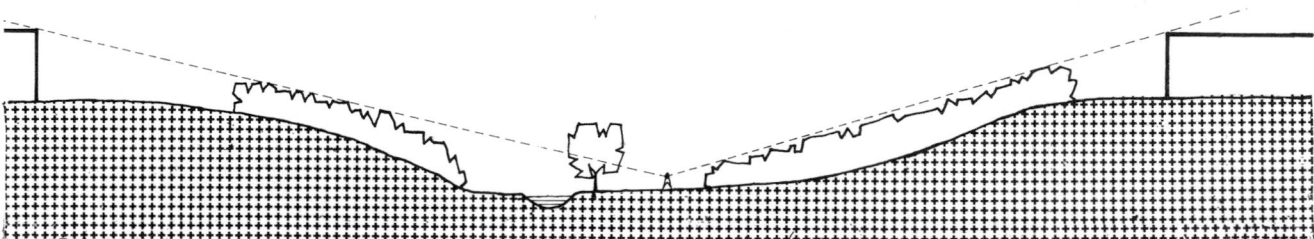

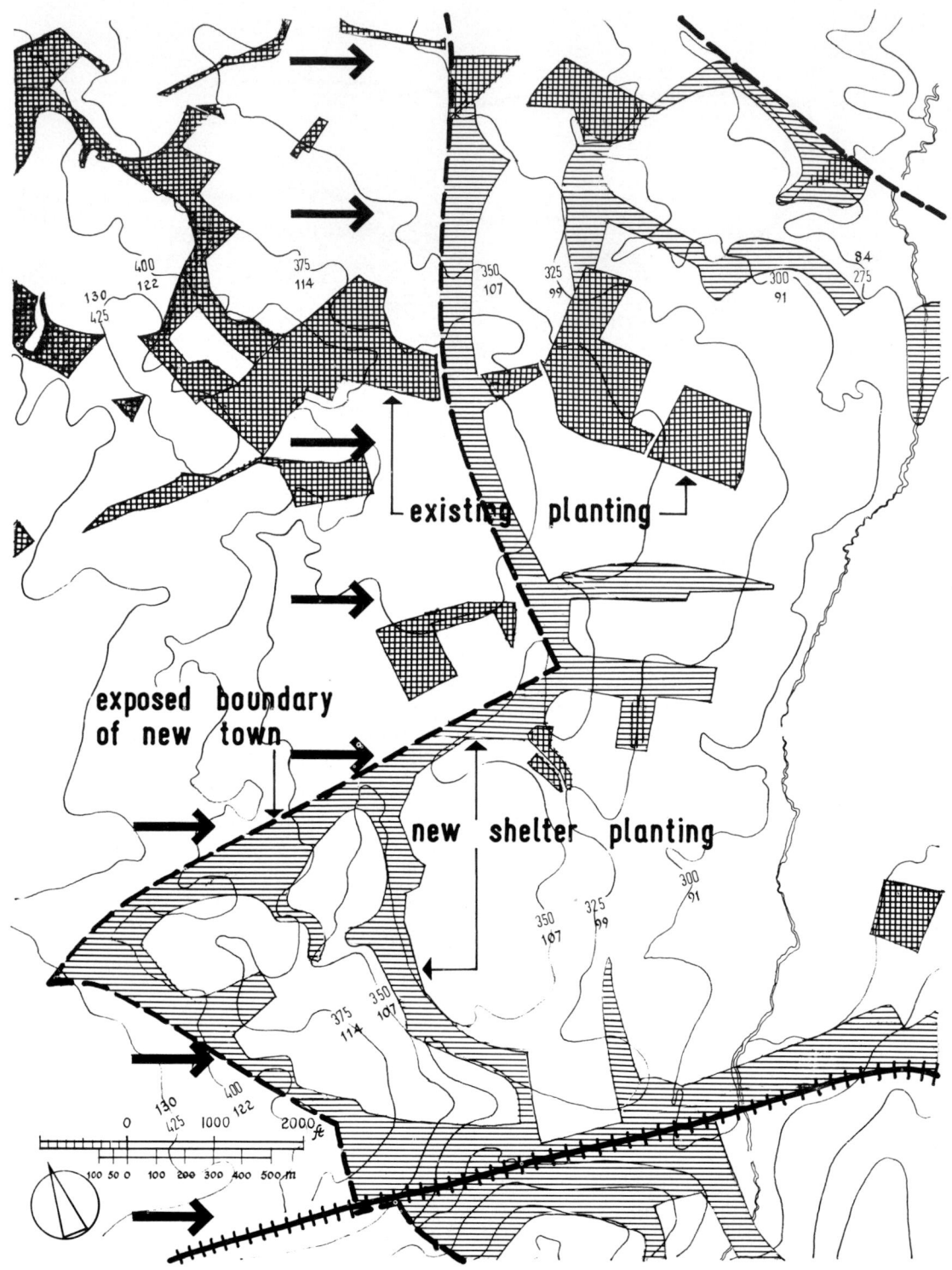

Fig. 2.17. Tree belts sheltering a New Town from prevailing winds and linking into the town's open space system.

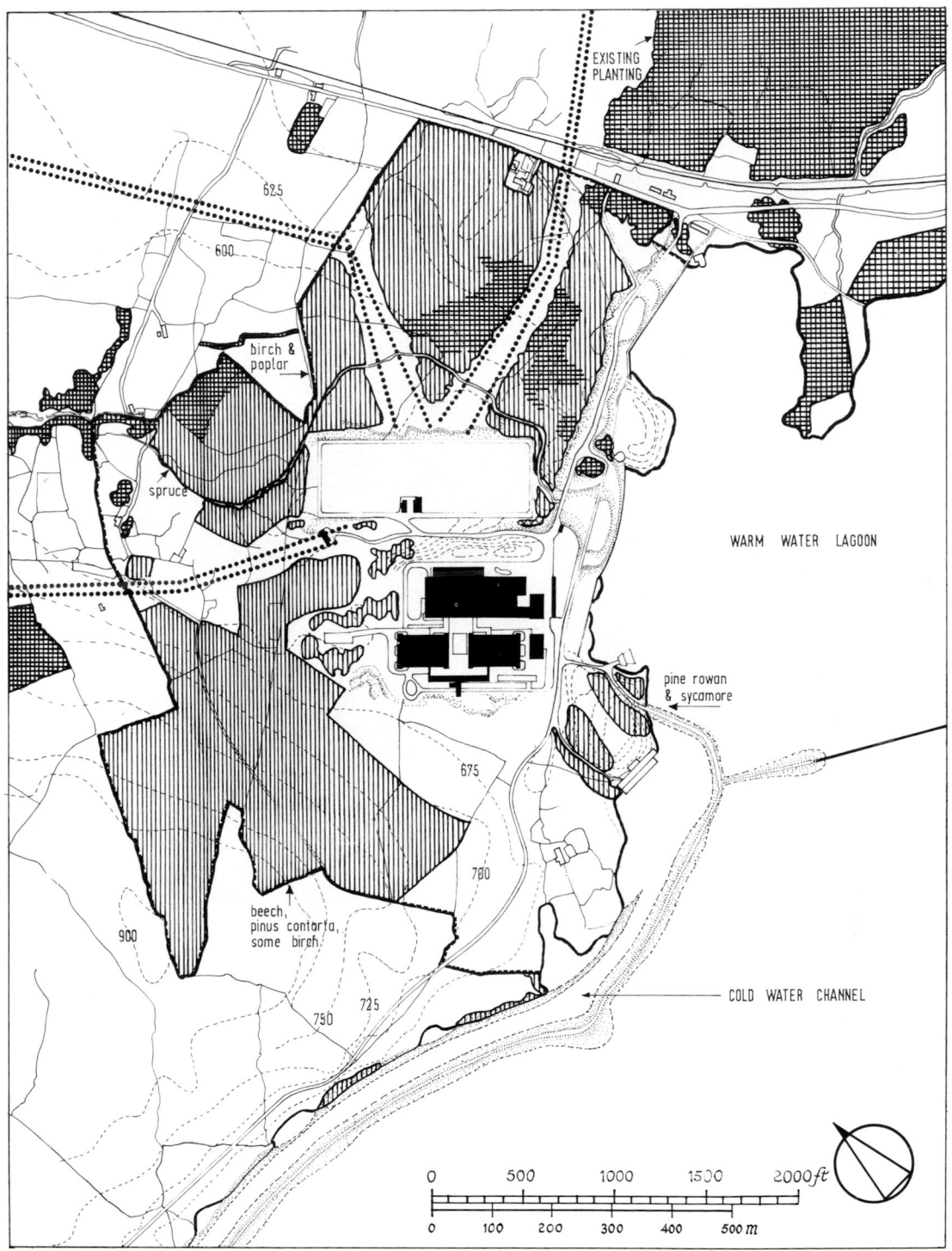

Fig. 2.18. New tree planting forms a link with existing scattered woodland and helps to unite a nuclear power station to its setting in the Welsh mountains.

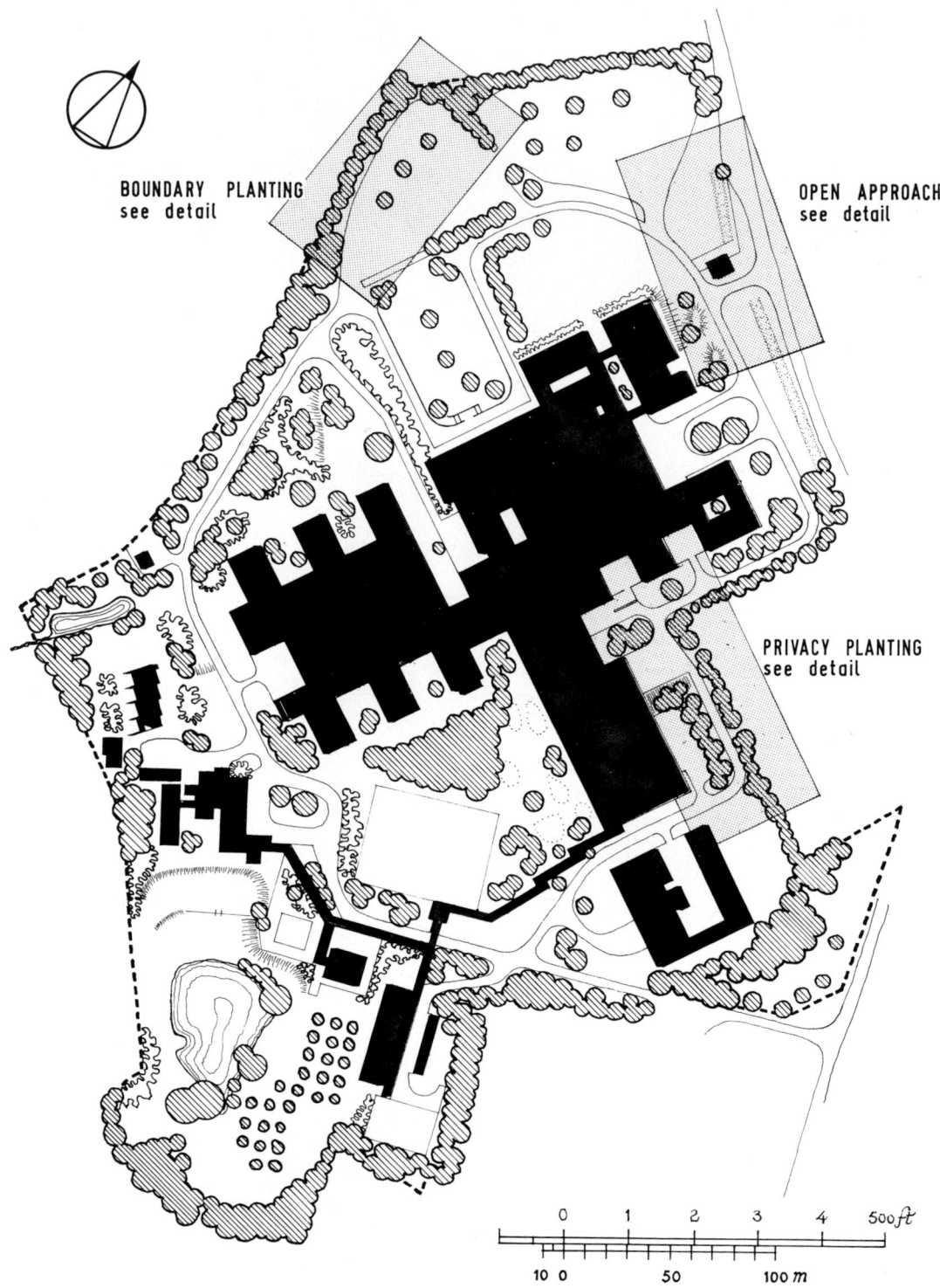

BOUNDARY PLANTING
see detail

OPEN APPROACH
see detail

PRIVACY PLANTING
see detail

Fig. 2.19. A large hospital site where boundaries must be differently designed according to need of security and privacy.

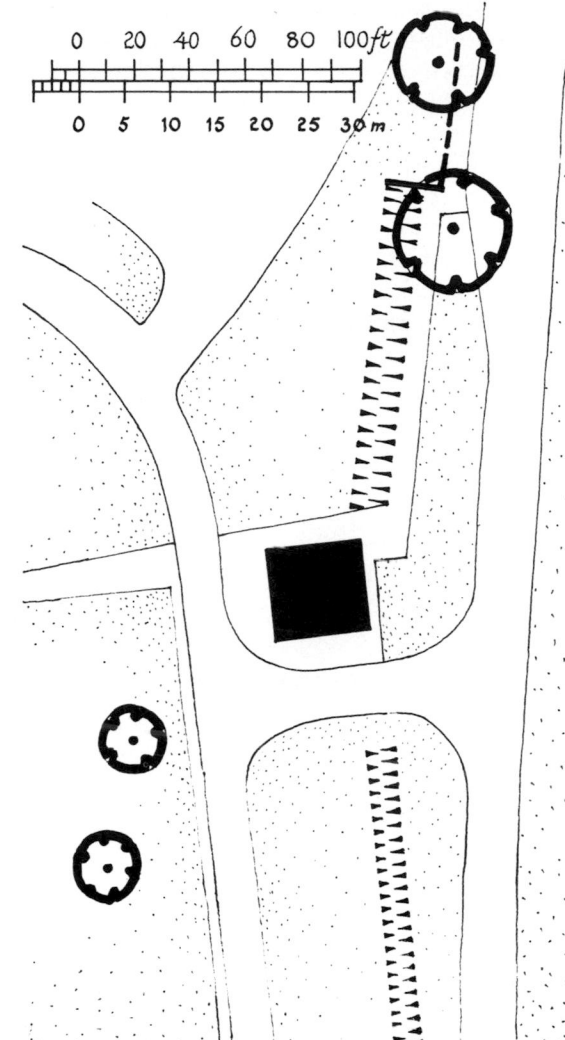

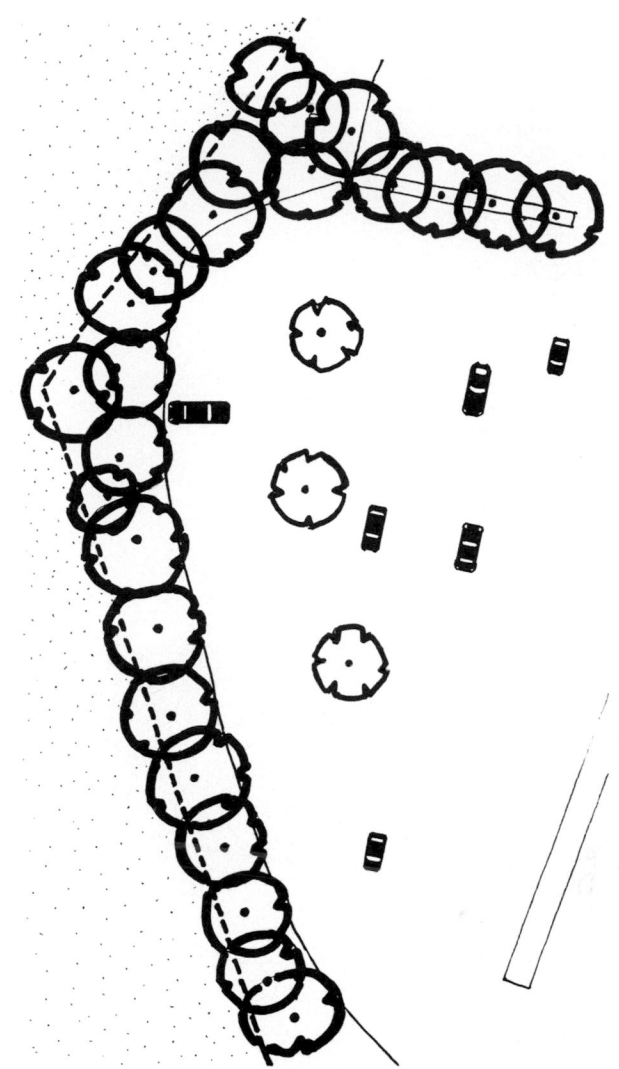

Fig. 2.20. Open approach detail. Ha-ha on boundary to preserve open views.

Fig. 2.21. Park railing defines boundary. Stock-proof but permits open view beneath tall trees.

may be impossible to site those items which are the responsibility of an authority other than the client, e.g. the Post Office fixtures. Constant review of site plans as development proceeds and consultation at the earliest opportunity, is the only method of dealing with these. Most public utility and other authorities in fact prove helpful if personal contact can be made with their representatives on the site and initiative is taken in offering alternative siting which meets their technical requirements.

2.9.7 Lighting (see also Chapter 6)
The general type of illumination, although not the details

of lighting fitments should be included in a site plan. The alternatives are (a) column lighting. There are standard heights for different degrees of illumination. It is also possible to substitute a few very high columns for the regulation number of standard columns, (b) low level lighting, from bollards, hand rails, etc., (c) pavement lighting, (d) lighting fixtures incorporated in the buildings, (e) floodlighting. In plans for projects which are to be kept subordinate to the surrounding landscape, the least conspicuous lighting fixtures are appropriate. But in public gardens the lighting may be displayed as part of the design. Early consultation with the lighting engineers is essential in all cases.

2.9.8 Drainage and underground services

The general configuration of the ground will govern the drainage plan. Undrainable areas on the site should be avoided if possible, but if they do occur must be foreseen and dealt with either by planting moisture-absorbing plants or some other means, such as the creation of a lake as at the University of York.

Drains and other services are often laid across the only spaces on a site which are large enough to accommodate trees without damage to buildings. They should instead be laid compactly, preferably beside a path or fence line (Fig. 2.23). Early consultations on services are essential if the best use is to be made of the available space. Depth, vulnerability to root action and probable needs for access should be ascertained. The position and level of manholes should be agreed and incorporated into the plan.

Plate 2.10. Almondsbury, where the M4 and M5 motorways meet and cross in a three-level interchange.

Fig. 2.22. Solid planting on the boundary to give complete screening for privacy.

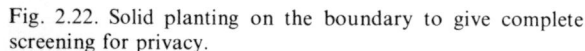

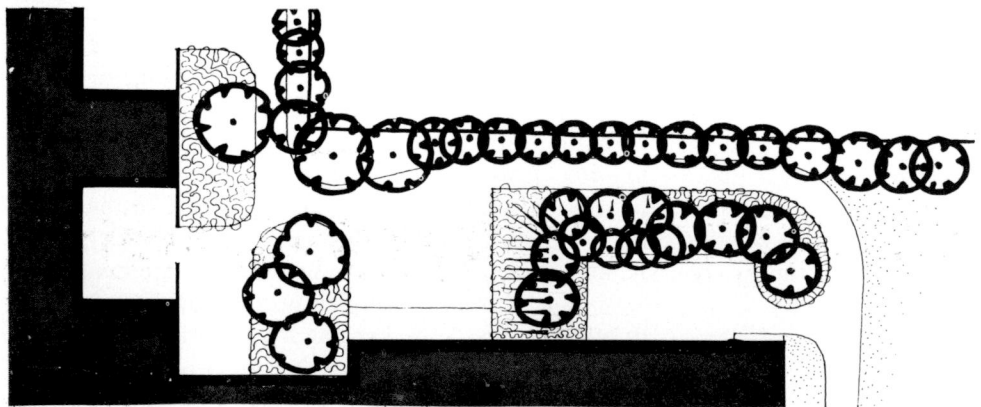

Plate 2.11. Study model used to assist in design of ground shaping for Almondsbury interchange. Contouring is used to give logic and sense of direction to connecting slip roads.

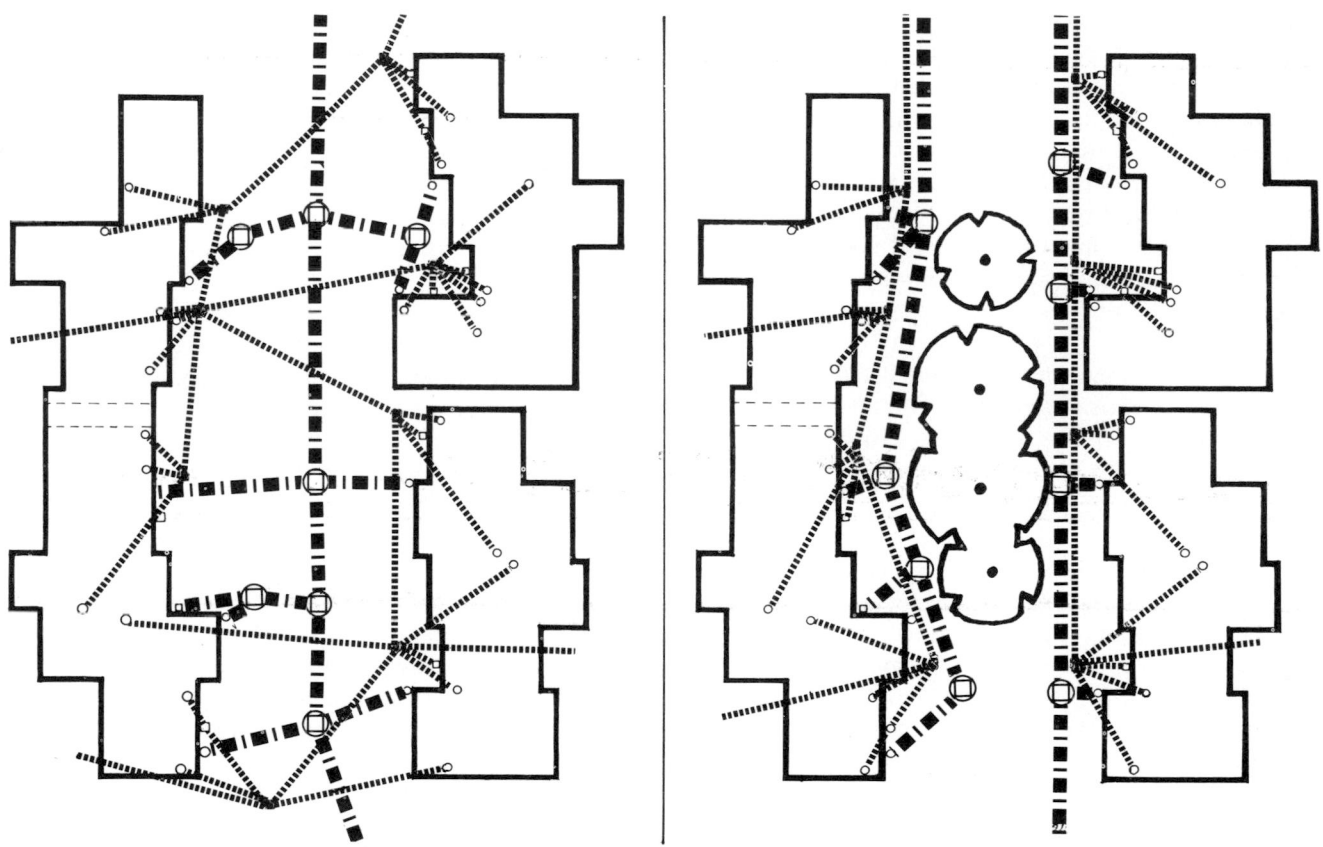

Fig. 2.23. Underground services cutting across a green may preclude tree planting. Rerouting may be possible.

41

2.10 Translation of basic information into landscape plan

The plan must be considered simultaneously as a contribution to the landscape as a whole and as a solution for the use requirements of the site. The first requirement is met by ensuring that the site will accord with, and contribute to, any pleasant character in its surroundings and will ameliorate any unpleasant character. Meeting the second requirement depends on the success with which the functions of the site are translated into an acceptable design form.

The site plan must not only present a solution which will work smoothly and efficiently, but must appear to do so – the most satisfying plans are those which look inevitable. A solution which appears forced or obviously clever is rarely the right one. The guiding principles of the plan will emerge from a study of the two sets of factors, site and use, which have been already considered (see p. 16) but while they may often carry equal weight, and ideally may be synthesised into a new landscape, there are some cases where the site factors, and others where the use factors will dominate. For instance, when siting a camp in a National Park the site factors would have precedence, while in the design of an industrial site in an urban area, the use factors would predominate.

One of the first decisions should be how far the existing character of the site is to be preserved and how far modified. But whatever the decision, it must be realised that to some extent some adjustment is always necessary, since any change of land use or any introduced structure will make its mark on the site ecology and will need to be counteracted, while on the other hand, some of the original site conditions, such as climate and elevation will still be determining factors in the new landscape.

Certain elements of the plan will be seen to have priority in siting, e.g. function may decide the position of the access road or of structures. Site factors may make the siting of shelter-belts in certain positions essential, or the conservation of some particular feature, such as a skyline, a wood, or a view may be of paramount importance. These basic site factors must be grasped at the outset and a mental picture of the essential character of the site should be formed and adhered to, however much the details and arrangements of different elements may change during the evolution of the plan. The plan will evolve by manipulating all major elements into their optimum positions having regard to the site factors and then combining with them the smaller and more flexible elements.

It will usually be found that the functional elements tend to divide themselves into static spaces or rooms, and lines of movement or passages. The distinction and proper relationship between these elements is basic to the plan, and both by siting and treatment they should express repose and movement respectively. This principle applies even when the use of the static space is in itself active, as in a playing field, for it will still require to be offset from the lines of through movement. Equally, a path for strolling may be secluded and tranquil, but it still forms part of the pattern of movement (Fig. 2.10).

The most direct routes of access and communication between the various elements will form the basis of the movement pattern. But these direct routes may be modified in the interests of other aspects of the plan, such as the need for traffic separation, the need to keep certain static areas separated from movement and the general appearance and pleasantness of the site. A devious route may also be used for the sheer pleasure of wandering, but in this case its deviousness should never be apparent from any one point. In adjusting the various traffic flows, there will be priorities for destinations and types of traffic requiring direct routes, and tolerance for routes which can deviate without inconvenience.

The whole plan must be kept fluid until the essential elements have all been satisfactorily settled. Rigidity and premature detailing can cause mental barriers which prevent the emergence of the best solution.

Not only has every element of the plan a minimum size, but most have an optimum size, and it is equally important to allow ample space for those elements requiring it, and to scale down the space for elements requiring a sense of enclosure and intimacy. For instance playing fields not only require a definite playing area (Fig. 2.5) but should also have space for trees, spectators and in many cases parking and car parks, while tree belts need sufficient space not only for the trees themselves but to give the necessary clearance for roots and shade. On the other hand, children's playgrounds and rest gardens need to be scaled down to give a feeling of seclusion and intimacy. These optimum sizes contribute to the variation in scale which is necessary to a successful plan.

At all stages of the plan up to the final dimensioned working drawings, some tolerance of spacing should be allowed to cover possible discrepancies in surveys, or in site constructions.

To summarise, the site plan should be coherent and well balanced, showing clearly its pattern of circulation, its areas for different uses and its structure of land-form and major planting. It should show its relationship to its surroundings and express the character of the site. It should enable the function of the site to operate efficiently remembering that pleasant living conditions and good appearances are part of that efficiency.

Bibliography

Landscape Architecture, John Ormsbee Simonds, Iliffe.

Site Planning, Kevin Lynch, M.I.T. Press, Cambridge, Massachusetts.

Playing Fields and Hard Surface Areas, Department of Education and Science, Building Bulletin 28, H.M.S.O., London.

Design for Play, Lady Allen of Hurtwood, Thames and Hudson, London.

Land and Landscape, Brenda Colvin, John Murray, London.

3 Earthworks and Ground Modelling
BRIAN HACKETT

3.1 Survey (see also Chapter 1 – Survey and Analysis)

3.1.1 Clearing

Earthworks and ground modelling operations will involve on many sites the clearance of vegetation, and this may constitute an element in the total cost. If the site is well covered with trees, a record should be made of the number per acre, whether they have any value for timber purposes, or whether the tree debris must be disposed of by burning. Also a record should be made of the ground level around trees to be retained. Information should also be obtained on the extent of the operations necessary to remove the root system of the trees.

General clearance of tree-covered areas with negligible timber value can be achieved by two tractors moving in parallel and dragging a heavy chain between them. There are also special fitments which can be mounted on tractors for this purpose. These methods may also uproot the root system, but where this does not happen or the stumps of felled trees remain, there are other attachments which are usually effective.

3.1.2 Surveying and levelling

The provision of an accurate record of the dimensions and position of the different surface elements of the site is essential, and the degree of detail to which this should be carried out will be dependent on the scale and nature of the proposed earthworks and ground modelling operations. The objective of levelling operations should be the preparation of a contour plan of the site related to a reliable datum, preferably an O.S. bench mark. The contour intervals will again depend upon the proposals and on the existing topography of the site, but 0·5 m or 1 ft intervals are necessary to the designing of playing field and other 'level' surfaces for surface drainage considerations, and 2 m or 5 ft intervals are the maximum for large scale operations requiring a reasonable degree of accuracy.

It is very important that the survey should carry over the site boundaries in order that earthwork proposals may tie in to the surrounding land form.

3.1.3 Water bodies, etc.

The levels of the water in pools and streams during drought, normal and high rainfall periods are desirable, also the contouring of the pool or stream bed if filling is envisaged. In any event, the maximum depth of water should be recorded. It is also very desirable that the water table levels under different conditions should be noted, and this may require the excavation of several trial pits; in fact, the more information that can be obtained on underground water and springs, the better.

3.1.4 Soil and subsoil

The depths and nature of the topsoil and the subsoil should be noted, and this information should be related to the latest information available from the Geological Survey. Where rock is suspected, it is important that a geological investigation is made.

3.1.5 Access

Information on the accessibility of the site to earth-moving machines and on the room available for manoeuvring is necessary at the design stage.

3.2 Soil and subsoil characteristics

Earthworks and ground modelling operations are concerned with the physical nature of the material moved, rather than its ability to support vegetation. But the design of new land forms must relate to matters like aspect, run-off, drainage and water table, all of which are significant in the development of vegetation. Also, the need to conserve the topsoil should be borne in mind and especially in relation to the new land form design when considering positions for the temporary mounds of topsoil while the earthwork and ground modelling operations are proceeding.

3.2.1 Soil types

The major soil types which are likely to be encountered are gravels and gravel soils (e.g. with sand mixtures, clay mixtures, or both), sands and sandy soils (e.g. with gravel mixtures, clay mixtures or both), fine grained soils (e.g. silts and clays of various kinds), fibrous soils (e.g. peat).

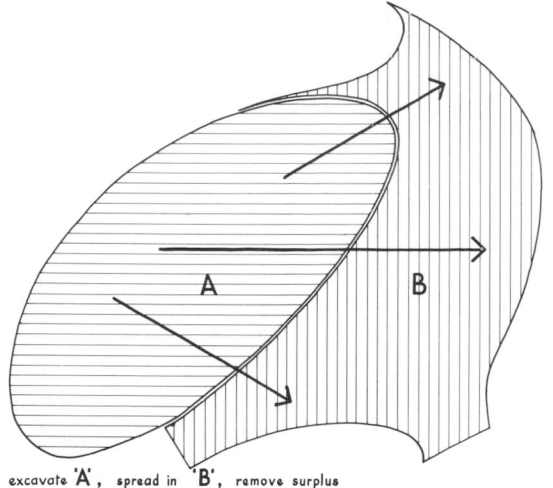

excavate 'A', spread in 'B', remove surplus

Fig. 3.1. DRAFTING METHODS OF SHOWING EARTHWORKS.
A. Movement of material from areas of excavation to areas of fill. Supplemented by site directions.

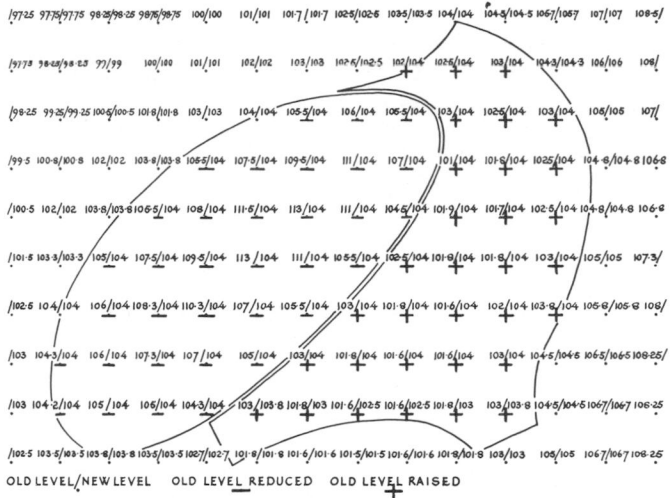

OLD LEVEL/NEW LEVEL   OLD LEVEL REDUCED   OLD LEVEL RAISED

Fig. 3.2. DRAFTING METHODS OF SHOWING EARTHWORKS.
B. Areas of excavation shown by old spot levels reduced to new: areas of fill shown by old spot levels raised to new.

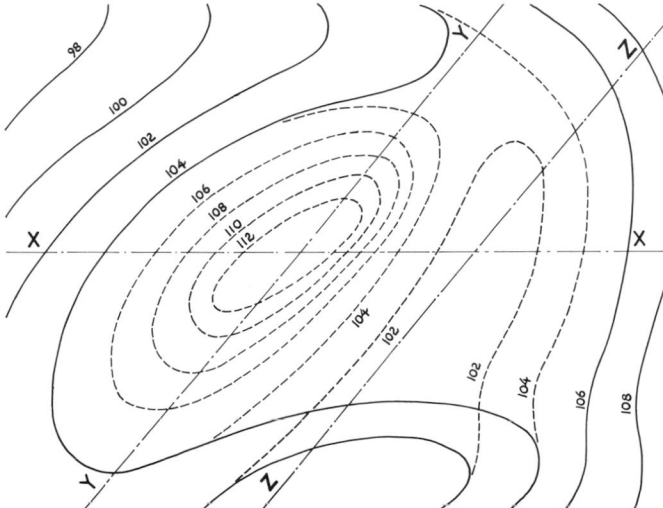

Fig. 3.3. DRAFTING METHODS OF SHOWING EARTHWORKS.
C. Areas of excavation and fill shown by contour lines indicating existing and proposed grades.

The characteristics of soils in so far as movement by mechanical equipment is concerned are as follows:

Sandy gravels, shales, hardpan shale and ripped rock (decomposed or weathered granite, gneiss, etc.) – these present loading problems and cause considerable wear and tear on equipment.
Sands are 'dead' and hard to load and transport, unless carried over a maintained road. Spreading and compacting depends on fill maintenance to prevent wind and other types of erosion as the work progresses.
Clays, silts, loams and variations such as sandy clays, silty clays, etc. – easy to load, spread and compact (excepting excessive moisture in mud).
Fibrous soils – of little use for earthwork formation.

3.2.2 Angle of repose

While the surface covering of vegetation or paving can help to stabilise slopes in soils, each soil has its own particular angle of repose or stability, which may vary with the amount of moisture in the soil. For earthworks which consist of mounds of transported material raised above the original level, the angles of repose will be around the following:

Very wet clay and silt	1:3
Wet clay and silt	1:2
Dry sand and gravel	1:1¾
Dry clay	1:1½
Moist sand	1:1¼

These should not be regarded as finished slopes, which will normally be somewhat flatter. Precise gradients will depend on many factors, including bearing capacity of substrata, loading above the slope, surface treatment, as well as the precise nature of particular clays, sands, etc.

3.2.3 Bearing capacity

Whilst the bearing capacity of soils is likely to require investigation for building and engineering works rather than for landscape development, different soils and other materials are likely to give bearing capacities approximating to the following:

Sandy, sandy-clay and firm clay soils – 11 to 44 tonnes per sq m (approx. 1 to 4 tons per sq ft).
Consolidated clay – 55 tonnes per sq m (approx. 5 tons per sq ft).
Gravel and sandy gravel – 66 tonnes per sq m (approx. 6 tons per sq ft).

45

Compact sandy gravel and soft rock – 88 to 110 tonnes per sq m (approx. 8 to 10 tons per sq ft).
Rocks – 440 to 660 tonnes per sq m (approx. 40 to 60 tons per sq ft).

But, owing to the variation in surface and sub-surface material, proper loading tests should be carried out where weights above the customary use of landscape may be experienced.

Moisture content is closely allied to the bearing capacity of soils and subsoils, and at its optimum (usually given as a percentage of the dry weight) the particular soil is at its maximum compaction state. The maintenance of the moisture content at the level to achieve maximum compaction is sometimes a difficult process under the varying weather conditions and the juxtaposition of excavated or fill material with the undisturbed material behind and under the cut.

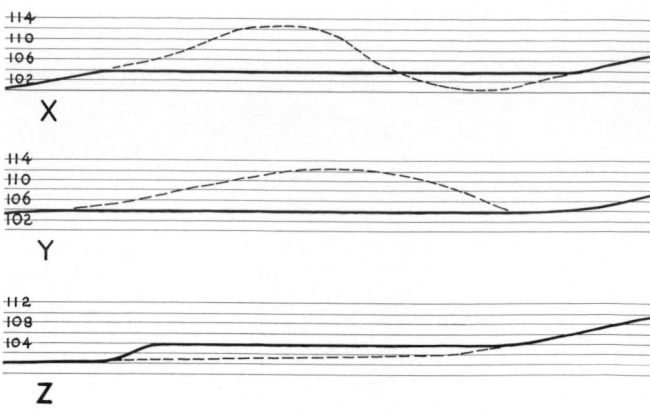

Fig. 3.4. DRAFTING METHODS OF SHOWING EARTHWORKS. D. The use of cross-sections to show the new formation, and the cut and fill.

3.3 Ground shapes

The principles which lie behind the design of a particular land form can be grouped under a number of headings.

3.3.1 Limitations imposed by material and machines

Some of these matters have been referred to under the notes on the angles of slopes at which stability is likely to be achieved. Perhaps the first principle in this group is the difference in volume between soils and subsoils in their original state and during and after removal to a new situation. The design may have to make allowance for 15% and sometimes 25% more cut than fill, but if compaction takes place, the design may have to make allowance for 5% to 10% less fill than cut. The new land forms must also relate to the matter of drainage; for example, cuts or excavations may lead to situations below the surrounding water table or to pits in which the drainage may be trapped, and they should, therefore, be designed so that the flow of surface and underground water can be maintained. Also the direction of slopes of the new landforms may lead to a disproportionate discharge of water in particular areas – either the design should be modified or adequate drainage arrangements made.

In designing the curves in plan of new land forms, it is wise to relate these to the minimum turning circles of the machines to be used. Also, the areas within new land forms (i.e. small valleys and concave forms) should be adequate to allow the machines to manoeuvre. The turning circles vary with the type and make of machine, but the table on p. 47 gives an approximate indication of the minimum curve radii.

The angle of slope of the land forms is more likely to be controlled by the machine's lubrication requirements than by the centre of gravity of the machine, but some machines, like the power shovel, the dragline and the backhoe, can handle slopes well beyond the angle of repose of the excavated material. Limiting slope angles in relation to different machines are given in the table opposite.

3.3.2 Factors influencing costs

The major factors which influence the cost of earthworks operations are:

(a) The location of the site.
(b) Access into the site and manoeuvring room within it.
(c) Availability of the most suitable equipment.
(d) The nature of the material excavated and moved.
(e) Water table and other site conditions.
(f) Separation or otherwise of the topsoil from the subsoil.
(g) Weather conditions.
(h) Time set for completion.
(i) Skill of the machine operator.
(j) Length of haul from cut to fill positions, and the ease with which the cut can be moved to the fill positions. At one time 450 m (approx. 500 yd.) was regarded as the economical haul maximum for large machines, but this factor has decreased in importance.

It has also been shown that there are real cost differences arising from the *type* of design, even when all of the above ten factors are the same as between one design and another. For example, the following design variations do affect cost, provided contractors when estimating take them into account:

46

Machine	Rating	Capacity (m³)	Digging Radius (m)	Max Machine Slope Angle
Power shovels 305	78 b.h.p	0·66	9·00	28°
ditto 406	100 ditto	0·95	9·8	28°
ditto 1405	288 ditto	3·25	12·8	33°
Dragline 305	78 ditto	0·95	*	28°
ditto C34B Pennine	78 ditto	0·95	*	28°
ditto 605 2B	133 ditto	1·9	*	33°
ditto 1405	288 ditto	3·0	*	33°
Wheel type tractor dozer	170 f.w.h.p.	—	5·99	45°
	300 ditto	—	6·68	45°
	400 ditto	—	7·21	45°
Track type tractor dozer	75 ditto	—	*	45°
	105 ditto	—	*	45°
	140 ditto	—	*	45°
	180 ditto	—	*	45°
	270 ditto	—	*	45°
	385 ditto	—	*	45°
Track type tractor scraper	270 ditto	13·00	7·62	45°
	270/385 ditto	20·00	8·84	45°
Wheel type tractor scraper	300	15·30	10·00	35°
	415	23·00	11·45	35°
	550	29/41	12·80/14·02	35°

* Subject to so many variables that difficult to cite a figure

(a) Designs of a 'hill and valley' or 'undulating' type are less expensive to grade than designs of a 'terracing' type. They arc also as visually effective with smaller volumes of earth moved.

(b) On sites up to 0·1 ha (approx. one quarter of an acre) in area, the cost differences between one design and another are insignificant. At 2 ha (approx. 5 acres), the nature of the design is a significant cost factor, but with one exception when the design is such that it can be graded by operations taking place independently within each of say twenty '0·1 hectares' (approx. 1 quarter acres) areas within the major area. Thus, somewhere between an area of 0·1 and 2 ha (approx. $\frac{1}{4}$–5 acres) lies an area at which the designer should carefully review his design in relation to economy.

(c) Designs which allow circumferential and parallel movement lines of the machines as they load and unload material, and within reasonable distances of 450 m (approx. 500 yards) or less, are likely to lead to savings.

(d) Designs which restrict cut and fill operations within separate areas, as opposed to a balance over the whole site, are economical.

(e) Although possibly monotonous, the subdivision of a land form design into roughly equal elements, e.g. the volume of each mound being more or less similar is likely to be a cost reducing factor.

(f) In comparing (1) flat terraces, (2) sloping terraces, (3) undulating topography and (4) hills and valleys formed in a concave basin, the last proves to be the most economical.

3.3.3 Functional aspect of land use

The functional aspect is obviously important in its influence upon the design of earthworks, and has a long historical background ranging from the rice terraces of the Far East and the mound type fortified villages of the Ancient Britons, through the star-like fortifications around cities of the artillery age and the hidden barrier of the 'ha ha' between the cattle and the eighteenth century parkland of England, to the cutting of platforms for contemporary houses on steep sites and the grading around major road flyover junctions.

The situation at the present time errs on the side of the customary arrangement of land uses dominating the land form design, for example, sites are completely

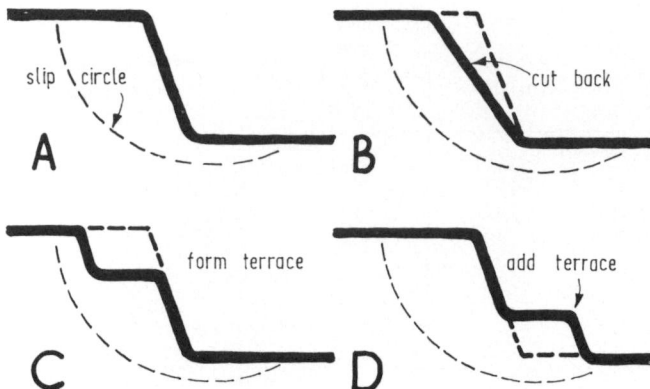

Fig. 3.5. FORMATION OF SLOPES IN CUT.
A. If the slope is too steep there is risk of slip.
B. Risk of slip can be reduced by cutting back slope.
C. Risk may also be reduced by cutting out a terrace or berm.
D. An added terrace will give a counter-balance to check slip.

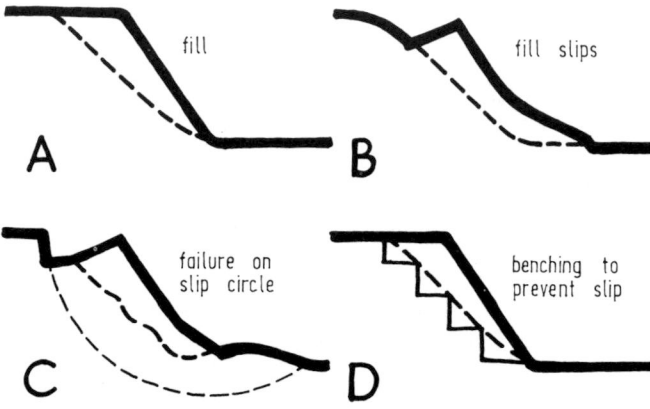

Fig. 3.6. FORMATION OF SLOPES WITH FILL.
A. Incorrect formation of slope. Weight of fill material, probably increased by absorption of heavy rain, may cause slip.
B. Slip of fill material along original formation.
C. Movement, along slip surface of the original formation.
D. Correct procedure, benching cut into original slope to prevent failure shown in B.

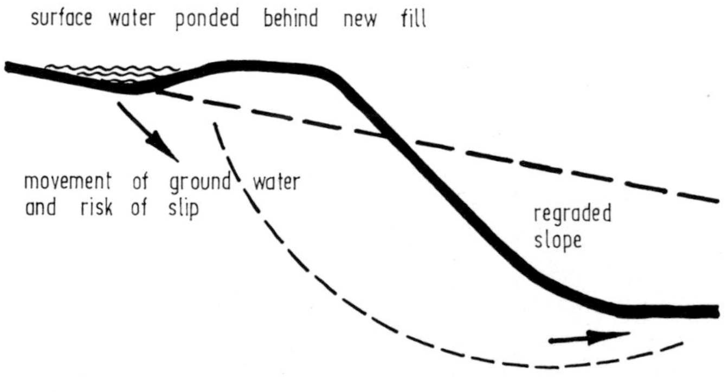

surface water ponded behind new fill

movement of ground water and risk of slip

regraded slope

Fig. 3.7. Undrained areas behind new fill may lead to movement of ground water, excessive loading on regraded slopes and consequent slip.
    If this kind of fill is necessary, provision should be made for drainage at the top and bottom of slope.

48

levelled by a cut and fill operation in order to allow the floor levels of the different factory processes to remain the same. Often, the different processes can equally well take place at different levels, resulting in a more interesting land form design.

Certain land uses present basically uninteresting land forms, especially playing fields with their extensive nearly level areas, though in flat countryside this is acceptable visually. But in sloping or undulating situations, terracing and spectator embankments can be designed to create interest; artificial mounds and hollows may be required, however, to marry up the extensive level areas with the existing topography in a satisfactory manner.

3.3.4 Site physiology

In addition to the function of the land use, the physiology of the landscape (which can be explained by the interrelationship of the land, the water and the atmosphere, and the flora and fauna arising therefrom) constitutes a functional influence upon land form design, because a changed land form can evolve new ratios in the inter-relationship, even to the extent of creating a situation which can never be a stable one. Some of the matters which will need investigation in this respect are:

The water table. Excavation below the water table can lead to flooding or to seepage at the level of the water table and below, necessitating the provision of drainage arrangements.

Angle of slopes. The angle of slopes should relate to the ability of the soil, with or without vegetation cover as the case may be, to withstand the erosive effect of the run-off of surface water. This is not directly connected with the slope angles limited by the angle of repose of the material. It is virtually impossible to lay down an accurate picture of erosion resistant slope angles for different soils, because of the great variation in weather conditions. A low, but concentrated, rainfall in an area with a loose soil cover will do more damage than a heavy rainfall spread over the whole year. In the former cases when the vegetation cover has been well nigh lost, slopes as low as 1 in 50 can be eroded by surface run-off of storm water. In this matter of surface water run-off, the arrangement of the land forms should be such that the run-off is well distributed and is not concentrated in one valley, unless special provision is made for this. The analogy of the streams leading to the tributaries and then to the river is a helpful one in this respect.

3.3.5 Maintenance of vegetation

For future maintenance of the vegetation cover on the slope there are no precise rules but the following constitute a guide to the designer:

Close mown grass surfaces – angle controlled by the powered mowing machine, maximum 1 in 3. Hand mower can operate on this slope for small areas. For steeper slopes, hand scything of high quality is possible, but few gardeners are now equipped in this technique although the Flymo mower is a substitute.

Power scythed grass surfaces – sometimes called 'rough grass' surfaces. Some manufacturers of powered scythes claim 1 in 1 as a maximum slope, but 1 in 2½ is a more realistic angle.

Groundcover plants – plants like ivy (Hedera) can survive and assist in stabilising very steep slopes. The maximum angle is likely to be determined by a combination of the possibility of preventing slip and erosion while the plants are established, and the problem of access for weeding

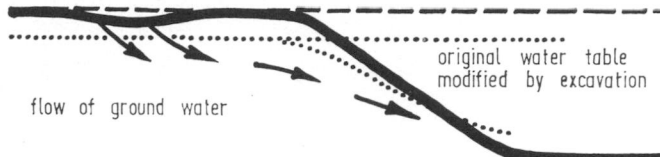

Fig. 3.8. Subsidence resulting from fine material being (indicated by arrows) carried away by the flow of ground water due to modified water table resulting from excavation.
Interceptor drains needed at top and foot of slope.

and firming-in during establishment. Anything much steeper than 1 in 1 will be difficult.

Wild type shrub and tree cover – if pockets or small areas of terracing can be arranged, very steep slopes are possible provided slip and erosion can be controlled initially.

3.4 Grading principles and methods

After the decision has been made to alter the formation of the ground surface of a site, there are certain principles involved in the grading operations which need to be observed. These are listed below.

3.4.1 Stripping topsoil
The stripping of the topsoil after site clearance operations and removing it from the site for use elsewhere as a contribution to the 'national soil bank', or alternatively stacking it in temporary heaps for respreading after grading and building operations, where one or both apply.

3.4.2 Siting topsoil storage
The siting of temporary topsoil and subsoil heaps from the points of view of the site works, building operations and the planning of the grading operations. Also in relation to impeding or facilitating the flow of surface water drainage during the site operations.

3.4.3 Planning grading operations
Planning the grading operations in harmony with the building operations, and also to avoid excessive surface compaction by machines concentrating on one area or route, also the mingling of topsoil and subsoil due to the rutting of the wheels and tracks.

3.4.4 Filling
A decision whether the filled areas must hold true to level or whether on a large project having artificial mounds or hills, some settlement can be accepted. In the former case, depositing fill in horizontal layers, with separate compaction operations for each layer may be necessary. In the latter case, a distinction should be made between (1) 'dumped fill' in which the excavated material is dumped without selection as it comes from the excavation, (2) 'end dumping' in which the excavated material is pushed over the edge of a valley and (3) 'selected fill' in which the excavated material is segregated for different levels and tasks in the filling operations.

3.4.5 Weather conditions
Planning the grading operations in relation to the likely weather conditions prevailing in the different seasons of the year. Long, comparatively dry spells, are likely to simplify the operations and thus reduce costs.

Plate 3.1. Caterpillar 657 Wheel Tractor–Scraper, twin engine all-wheel drive.

Plate 3.2. Caterpillar 631 Wheel Tractor–Scraper. Push-load operation assisted by a D8 Tractor.

Plate 3.3. Motor grader carrying out precision bladework grading.

3.4.6 Water table

The effect of the grading operations on the existing water table. For example, where an excavation cuts across the water table, attention should be given to an adequate method of drainage at this point. Where mounds are formed above the normal land surface, the likely effect of these upon the water table should be considered in relation to the supply of water to any vegetation proposed on the mound; in this respect, the creation of an artificially elevated water table by means of flat saucers formed in an impervious topping to the basic grading (underlying the topsoil) is a solution.

3.4.7 Phasing topsoil replacements

The phasing of topsoil replacement operations to avoid leaving the topsoil longer than necessary in the temporary heaps, and also to prevent it from suffering compaction of the respread topsoil by contractors' equipment which may be still operating on the site.

3.4.8 Preparation before topsoiling

Ploughing or otherwise breaking up the surface of areas which have been excavated into heavy or impervious subsoils before respreading the topsoil in order to improve the soil drainage in those areas.

3.5 Earthmoving methods

The types of machine used for earthmoving are basically divided into fixed and moving machines.

3.5.1 Machines fixed in position when operating

The dragline. This is normally used for large cuts or channels excavated below the level on which the machine is located. It can be used for shaping existing mounds, excavating valleys, and forming embankments and slopes. Whilst standing at a point of operation, the size of the excavation depends on the length of the boom from the end of which an excavating bucket is dragged through the material to be excavated. Machines vary in size with boom lengths normally in the 8–25 m (approx. 25–85 ft) range for machines moving on tracks, and up to 90 m (approx. 300 ft) for walking draglines. The excavated material is usually dumped behind or at one side or other of the machine.

The power shovel. The power shovel also has a boom or jib, but very much shorter than that of the dragline and usually within the range 4 to 30 m (approx. 13–100 ft) long. The bucket operates along the boom instead

Plate 3.4. The ability of modern earth-moving equipment to undertake large alterations to land form is shown in this illustration of a track-type tractor-dozer at work.

Plate 3.5. Progress in the design of earth-moving equipment includes a range of multipurpose machines of the kind illustrated here. The machine combines some of the functions of the bull-dozer with an ability to lift and load excavated material.

51

Plate 3.6. A 'sheepsfoot' roller. A Caterpillar 815 compactor with tamping feet and spreading dozer blade

Plate 3.7. FACESHOVEL. A small faceshovel working against a rock face with a 0·5 m³ bucket.

of along a cable as with the dragline, and it is thus more suitable for working in hard rock which has been broken up first by blasting. The power shovel is very suitable for loading into dumpers and lorries, but only those machines with long booms are likely to be of much use in building up mounds from excavation. Variants of the power shovel are the trencher with an extension arm for deeper excavation, and the skimmer for surface stripping.

3.5.2 Machines mobile when operating

The tractor. This is a basic unit for pushing or pulling earthmoving equipment, and models are available with tracks for slow speeds under bad site conditions, or with wheels for faster speeds and better site conditions.

Tractor attachments. Several types of equipment can be attached to the tractor and these fall into two groups. First, the 'allied equipment' actually mounted on the tractor; for example, bulldozers, angledozers, winches, pipe laying booms, excavator attachments, earth augers. Second, 'towed equipment'; for example,

scrapers, rippers, graders, sheepsfoot tamping rollers, scarifiers and rippers (sometimes also mounted). A wide range of horsepower in the power units is available, usually within the 35–235 hp range.

The cubic metres of earth movable in an 8 hour day vary from approximately 300 for a small unit on a 5 m journey from point of excavation to point of deposition and back again, to 1,100 for a large unit of 130 hp.

Bulldozers are particularly suitable for forming plateaux and embankments. Scrapers can make shallow cuts, and have the advantage of being able to transport large loads over considerable distances. They operate most efficiently in soils lying between the extremes of dry sand and wet clay.

Other machines. There are also several machines which do not precisely fall into either of these two categories. The motor scraper in the smaller horsepower range is particularly suitable for small projects. The loading shovel is useful for moving earth from heaps into lorries. The motor grader is useful for grading roads, forming drainage channels and for trimming work. Several types of transporting equipment are available as lorries, dumper wagons, etc.

52

Plate 3.8. FACESHOVEL. A medium-size N.C.K. Rapier faceshovel loading rock with a 0·95 m³ heavy duty bucket.

Plate 3.9. FACESHOVEL. A large faceshovel. N.C.K. Rapier 1405 with a 3·25 m³ bucket.

3.6 Compaction

3.6.1 Degree of compaction required

The consolidation of the material moved in earthworks and ground modelling is a matter of achieving a balance between a sufficient compaction to give a settlement-free surface, and the avoidance of excessive compaction which may prevent good local drainage within the soil. The most satisfactory solution is likely to be achieved when the fill material is deposited in layers about 150 mm (approx. 6 in thick), each layer being compacted in moderation. Such a solution is not, however, realistic when large depths are to be filled, but good results can often be attained by mass compaction of the lower part, and adopting the layering technique coupled with land drainage in the upper part.

The moisture content of the fill is an important factor in compaction, and the ideal situation occurs when there is sufficient moisture to enable the grains to slide into stable positions without completely filling the voids between the grains. This ideal situation is known as the optimum moisture content and is expressed as a percentage of the dry weight of the fill. The method for ascertaining this is known as the Proctor test.

3.6.2 Achieving compaction

The various ways in which compaction is achieved can be related to types of equipment (see below).

The smooth-wheeled roller. This is available in many different weights with ballast from approximately 1·5 to 18 tonnes (approx. 1½ tons to 18 tons). Compaction is normally achieved up to thickness of 200 mm (approx. 8 in) per layer, and is unlikely to become greater after about eight runs over any one area. This type of equipment is best suited to materials like hard-core and crushed stone, and soils with gravel, sand and clay mixtures.

Pneumatic-tyre rollers. These with ballast are available from about 9 to 50 tonnes (approx. 9 tons to 50 tons). Compaction can be achieved up to 450 mm (approx. 18 in layers), and almost any type of soil will respond, though sands and other granular soils are most responsive.

The sheepsfoot roller. This has projecting feet or spikes mounted on it, consequently it overcomes the problem of crust formation in the top layer of cohesive clays and silts, but it is not very suitable for sandy soils. Compaction can be achieved up to 200 mm (approx. 8 in)

53

Plate 3.10. DRAGLINE. The N.C.K. 305 illustrated is a smaller size dragline machine operating with buckets up to 0·95 m³ and booms up to 15 m length.

thickness, and up to twenty runs over any one area may be required. Various sizes are available from about 2 to 20 tonnes (approx. 2 to 20 tons).

The vibrating roller.   This is similar to the tandem type smooth-wheeled roller, but with a device for vibrating the roller. Its greatest value is with granular soils, such as sandy ones, which achieve their greatest consolidation through the particles being shaken into stable positions relative to one another.

Hand and the pneumatic tampers.   These are used for very small areas, such as for filling in narrow trenches.

3.6.3 Avoiding compaction
In addition to the technique for achieving compaction in a satisfactory manner, the problem of improper compaction frequently arises in contracts. This often occurs when the landscape architect is commissioned at a late stage of a contract or when his authority to control site operations is limited.

Plate 3.11. DRAGLINE. An N.C.K. Rapier 605–2B.

A frequent situation is that of unnecessary surface compaction by building contractors' equipment of a ground level, which is to remain unaltered. A wise procedure is to specify that, where topsoil is to be removed and replaced at a later date, the subsoil should be ploughed up and roughly chain harrowed before the topsoil is replaced. This procedure will improve surface drainage and add to the effectiveness of a land drainage system if installed.

It is also advantageous to limit the areas of operation for the building and/or civil engineering contractor by a clearly worded and enforceable clause in the specification, including also the provision of temporary fencing to protect certain areas.

The specification or bill of quantities can also with advantage allow for a degree of flexibility in the final situation. This is especially important where small slopes, curves and mounds are included, and an assessment of the visual result on the site may suggest slight modifications.

3.7 Filling materials

3.7.1 Waste materials
Many earthwork and ground-modelling projects require working in waste material of one kind or another, and special problems frequently arise. For example, in the reshaping of a coal mine waste heap material may be met which is still in a state of combustion, or has burnt to a congealed mass which cannot be handled as a normal earthmoving operation. Waste material from electricity power stations can create dust problems which become more than usually serious when earthwork operations disturb the material.

Each of these problems is likely to require a special technique, varying from the conventional methods. Material which has an offensive smell, is likely to break down under weathering into fine dust, or may react chemically in the weathering process, is best handled in the same way that certain local authorities dispose of their refuse – by tipping over a moving slope at the edge of a fill, and then covering the fill after each tipping operation with non-active material, such as excavated subsoil, and finally adding a layer of topsoil.

3.7.2 Water-borne soil transportation
In certain circumstances, large-scale earthworks can be carried out by water transportation. This includes the operations of dredging from a river, lake or sea bed, and transporting the material by ship for discharge elsewhere under water or for offloading on to vehicles. The trans- portation of soils by washing through pipelines is, however, an operation closer to the customary earthwork operations likely to be met in landscape design.

The use of pipes for soil transportation can take place over both land and water, steel-drum pontoons being used in the latter case for supporting the pipes. The material excavated is removed by a cutterhead dredge and suction is used to draw back soil and water in the ratio of about 1 to 5 by volume. Several discharge points can be arranged by introducing junctions into the pipelines. The extent of this operation is indicated by the statement that, for a static position of a discharge point, an accumulated fill 1·5 m (approx. 5 ft) deep will slope down at a gradient of about 1:15 for a radius of about 23 m (approx. 75 ft). Skilful control of the operation can lead to successful layering of the fill as part of compaction procedure.

3.7.3 Mechanical handling
Reference is also made to other special techniques, usually associated with the deposit of waste material, like the conveyor belt, the overhead cable and buckets, and the tramline for small trucks depositing at the top of an incline. If the landscape designer is faced with a situation where these special techniques are to be used, economies will result from the design being attuned to the technique, its limitations and possibilities.

3.8 Calculation of cut and fill

3.8.1 Mensuration
The methods of calculating volumes of earth moved are those used in the normal processes of mensuration, such as the areas on triangulation of irregular shapes on plan multiplied by the average height of a series of spot levels giving the difference between the old and new levels at regular intervals on a grid, and the division of volume of cut into a number of sections whose volume can be found. A longer process is involved when it is necessary to achieve an exact balance between material cut and material filled. One method is to design the earthworks in a sand tray model, and by resisting the temptation to increase or decrease the amount of sand as the designer carries out his adjustment to the sand tray model in its original form as a miniature of the site, the result must be an exact cut and fill, and the new levels can be plotted on a drawing which can then be subjected to a more accurate check. Finally, adjustment must be made for the change in volume, which is to be allowed as between cut and filled material, if compaction leaves the fill material in its deposited position at a different density than in its original position from which the cut was made.

Plate 3.12. WALKING DRAGLINE. On large minerals sites very large draglines can be used. The N.C.K. Rapier W.1400 illustrated carries a 15 m³ bucket on a boom 85 m (approx. 280 ft) long.

3.8.2 Visual approximation

The design of a cut and fill balanced operation over and within a site can also be achieved by a two stage method in which the new grades are adjusted by a visual approximation on several cross sections through the site. Then, the existing spot levels are totalled and divided by the number of positions to give an average level; this existing average is compared with the new average. In this method, it is unlikely that the two averages will equal one another at the first attempt, but it is usually possible to achieve comparability within a reasonable degree of accuracy after two or three further adjustments to the figures. The use of an adding machine will save much time and effort in making refinements to a design for the purpose of achieving a balanced cut and fill result. Also, techniques have been evolved which make use of a computer, for example, through a series of calculations along section lines, running parallel across the area over which the land form design is being developed. (For further information on computer methods see Chapter 5 by M. F. Downing of *Landscape Reclamation*, Vol. 1, I.P.C. Science and Technology Press Ltd, Guildford, England, 1971.)

3.8.3 Mass diagram

A method for calculating cut and fill operations which is used for long and narrow earthworks, like roads and railways, is the mass diagram. This is useful for determin-ing the haul distances from points of cut to points of fill, the position and volume of excavations, the situation when it may be more practical to borrow material from a borrow pit, and the type of equipment.

The mass diagram (see Fig. 3.9) consists of a long section through the narrow site of the earthworks. This section is divided into a number of equal stations which are assumed to be the centre of gravity of the volume of earth extending 15 m (approx. 50 ft) in both directions along the section. At each station, the cut is designated as a plus ($+$) volume, and the fill as a minus ($-$) volume. In the computation, the ordinates are cumulative algebraic sums from the first station. These ordinates are plotted on the mass diagram below the profile, and the high and low points of the resulting curve represent the places of no cut and no fill. Also, any horizontal line drawn across the resulting curve represents the length within which a balanced cut and fill operation can take place for the length of haul represented by the line.

3.8.4 Allowance for bulking and compaction

Measurement of earth excavated and deposited is made on the assumption that the earth is 'in the bank', that is in its original state. After excavation the volume can increase up to 45% during handling, but can also decrease to less than its 'in the bank' volume on compaction. Obviously, an earthworks design which relies on an exact balance of cut and fill must specify that the compaction

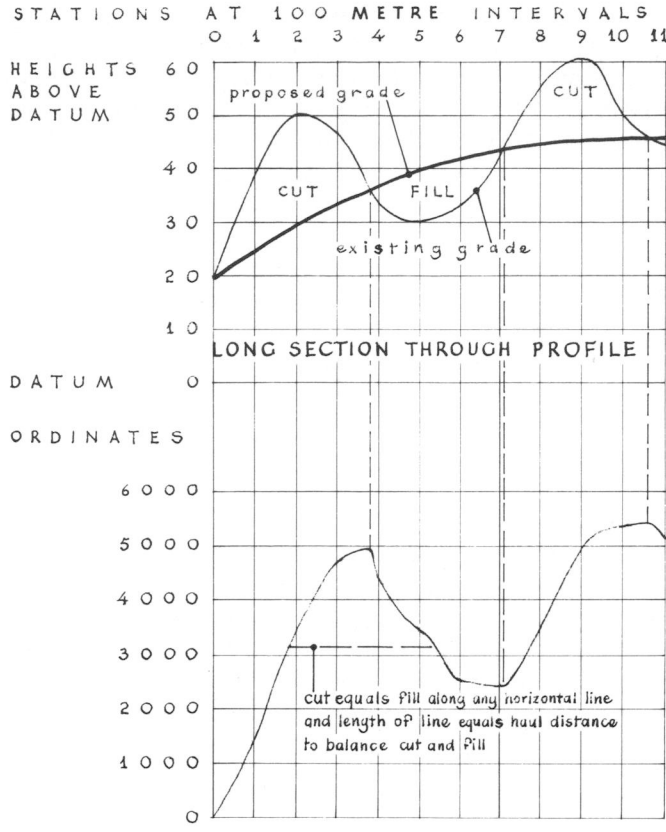

STATIONS AT 100 METRE INTERVALS
0 1 2 3 4 5 6 7 8 9 10 11

HEIGHTS 60
ABOVE
DATUM 50

proposed grade   CUT

40

30   CUT   FILL

20   existing grade

10

LONG SECTION THROUGH PROFILE

DATUM 0

ORDINATES

6000

5000

4000

3000

2000   cut equals fill along any horizontal line
and length of line equals haul distance
1000   to balance cut and fill

0

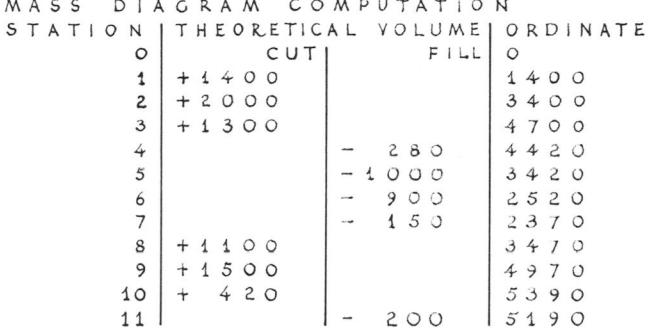

MASS DIAGRAM COMPUTATION

STATION	THEORETICAL VOLUME		ORDINATE
	CUT	FILL	
0			0
1	+ 1400		1400
2	+ 2000		3400
3	+ 1300		4700
4		− 280	4420
5		− 1000	3420
6		− 900	2520
7		− 150	2370
8	+ 1100		3470
9	+ 1500		4970
10	+ 420		5390
11		− 200	5190

Fig. 3.9. THE MASS DIAGRAM for computing cut and fill operations on long and narrow earthworks. Allowances can be made if necessary to the ordinates for shrinkage of the fill material.

process brings the soil which is moved back to its original density. It is, however, wise to include a margin of at least 5% for soil to be brought in to the site, and this allowance can also cover the reverse situation in which it may be found necessary to remove soil from the site.

3.8.5 Quantities

In the calculations of soil moved and in bill of quantities descriptions a distinction between 'major' grading by large machines and in bulk, and 'minor' grading by hand or very small machines is helpful to an estimator and to the efficient administration of a contract. Reference should also be made to the recommendations covering the procedure for measuring and recording excavation in the Standard Methods of Measurement of the Royal Institution of Chartered Surveyors and of the Institution of Civil Engineers.

3.8.6 Roadworks

Earthworks in connection with road embankments and cuttings require not only attention to the balance of cut and fill within reasonable lengths from the points of view of economy and fitting the road to the landscape, but also special attention to the points of change from one curve to another in plan and section. Embankments and cuttings are improved in appearance when the top and the toe are rounded or easily graded into the existing land form. Also, the steepness of the slope should be varied to grade it into the changing topography along the line of the road.

The combination of a long curve in plan with a short vertical curve in the profile of a road grading design between two major slopes can lead to an abrupt modulation in the new topography created by the road grading. If the length of road over which the vertical curve occurs can be lengthened to coincide with the length over which the long curve in plan occurs, the result seen in three dimensions is greatly improved.

3.9 Contracting procedure

3.9.1 Datum and reference points

Wherever possible, new and existing levels of the surface of the ground should be related to an Ordnance Datum bench mark. But where such a bench mark is not present within easy range of the site, a well-established and firm point should be used, for example, the top of a wall or the step of a doorway. If the existing or future land form is so shaped that clear unobstructed visibility between the datum and important positions on the site is impossible, it is advisable to establish additional datum points around the site which are related to the original datum.

3.9.2 Achievement of the new grades

Each firm of contractors will doubtless have their own methods for achieving the correct levels in grading operations. It is, however, helpful to produce a copy of the earthworks drawing on which cut areas are coloured red, and fill areas are coloured blue. The contractor can then arrange how he will move the red areas over the blue areas. He can also cut and fill to the lowest and highest points along a line from the datum or the additional datum points. Having established these key level points, grading can take place around them as the slopes defined

Plate 3.13. WALKING DRAGLINE The N.C.K. Rapier W.1800 dragline illustrated carries a 30 m³ bucket on a boom 75 m long.

by the contours suggest. The positions of these key level points would be set out by the usual methods of measurement from reference points on the boundaries. In practice, most of the machine operators are so skilled that they can achieve new contours by sight judgement. New levels are, of course, checked by normal surveying equipment. A specification should always allow for some refinement of the grading by site direction from the designer. It is also sometimes appropriate to refer to major and minor grading operations in a specification to indicate that some flexibility is necessary to achieve the smooth curves and junctions of curves which do not always appear on a contour plan.

3.9.3 Plans and drawings
Figures 3.1, 3.2, 3.3 and 3.4 show examples of various methods of producing plans to show the contractor the degree and kind of change to the land form which is proposed. Cross sections taken along many lines are a valuable aid to a machine operator. Sometimes it is helpful on particular sites for 'false' contours to be drawn when the real contours would cross a straight mound, which was built up on a sloping piece of ground, instead of running parallel to the mound.

3.10 Drainage

Drainage is concerned with the removal of surplus water from agricultural and urban land. All such water derives initially from precipitation. This may have been directly on the area considered or on an adjacent area from which it has then moved by surface flow or subsurface percolation.

3.10.1 The soil and drainage
The structure of the soil and its mineral composition are intimately concerned with the behaviour of ground water. The soil may have been produced *in situ* or deposited after glacial transport. However, as all soil is derived from the chemical and physical breakdown of rock material the soil characteristics are related to the parent rock minerals. In transported soils mixing of different rock types has taken place and this has produced a wider variety of soils than parent rock material. Soils are not normally homogeneous. Soils may generally be classified according to the sizes of the particles of which they are made according to an internationally agreed scale.

A soil profile normally shows well-defined regions of topsoil and subsoil and, in some cases, of parent rock material in varying degrees of breakdown.

The soil itself consists of solid particles and a fluid medium composed of gaseous air and liquid water. The soil porosity is a measure of the total soil volume not occupied by solid particles, and is usually expressed as a percentage pore space, i.e. the ratio of the volume of fluid to the total volume $\times 100$. The value of soil porosity gives an indication of its water holding capacity. Generally the coarser the particles in a soil and the greater the mixture of different sizes the lower the porosity.

Type of Soil	Average Percentage Pore Space
Coarse sand	28
Sandy loam	37
Silt loam	45
Clay	55

More important than the pore space are the sizes of the interconnecting channels between the pores which will determine the rate of water movement. Water will flow through the soil in response to an applied force. This may be gravity, causing a downward percolation, or a hydraulic potential, causing a flow in the direction of decreasing hydraulic gradient. Those soils with the smaller channels will exhibit the lower rates of flow. Coarse sands have a low value of porosity but drain rapidly while clays have a greater pore space, but drain very slowly.

The water table in a soil is the upper limit of the pores which are completely filled with water. It thus separates the saturated region below from the unsaturated region above. In a waterlogged soil the water table is at or very near the soil surface. Water will drain from such a soil until that soil reaches field capacity. Further water can only be removed from the soil by evapo-transpiration. Most agricultural crops grow best in soils that have a water content slightly less than that at field capacity.

The rate of water movement through soil is measured by its permeability in units of mm/hr. Some typical values are:

Soil Type	Permeability (mm/hr)	(in/hr)
Coarse sandy	475·0	18·7
Sandy loam	3·05	0·12
Silt loam	1·09	0·043
Clay	0·152	0·006

Actual soil profiles show varying permeability with depth. Three general cases exist:

(a) Increasing permeability with depth, e.g. loam soil overlying chalk – no drainage problem.

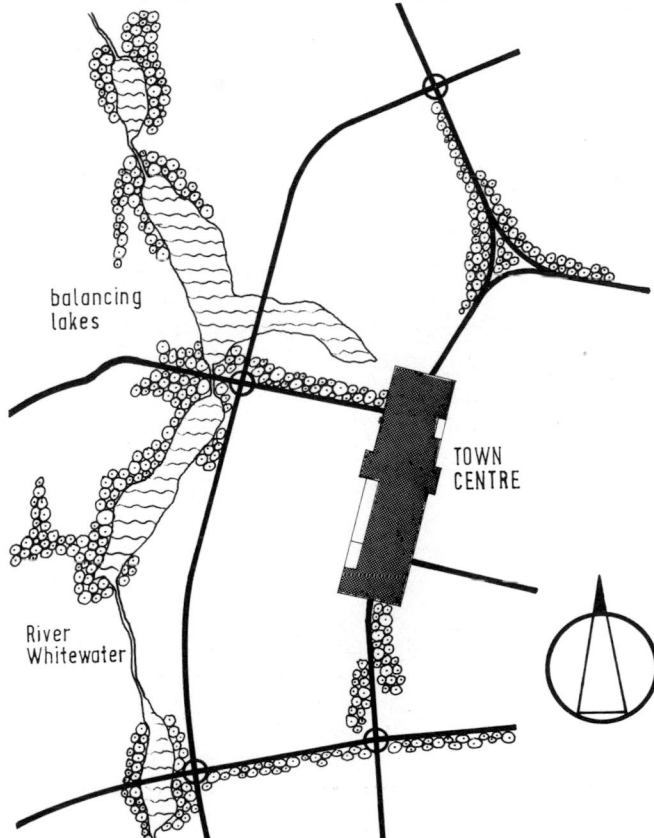

balancing lakes

TOWN CENTRE

River Whitewater

Fig. 3.10. THE HOOK PROJECT – balancing lakes used along the River Whitewater.

(b) Decreasing permeability with depth, e.g. a worked clay loam overlying a clay subsoil.
(c) Variable permeability with depth, e.g. boulder clays with perched beds of sand and gravel.

The maximum flow rate through a soil is fixed by the layer with the lowest permeability through which the water has to pass.

Rainfall rates in excess of the minimum permeability will cause water to accumulate in the soil or on the surface giving flood conditions on level ground and surface run-off on sloping ground. If the speed of surface run-off is excessive soil structure is destroyed and soil particles are transported giving rise to soil erosion.

Drainage is concerned with the removal of water in order to restore a soil to field capacity or to remove surface water which would accumulate on sites of low permeability.

3.10.2 Run-off and soil erosion
Rational formula. A rational calculation of the rate of flow (Q) of run-off water from a site may be made in imperial units by multiplying the average intensity of rainfall over one hour (i) by the site area (A). Multiplications by a dimensionless run-off coefficient C reduced the calculated peak run-off rate to account for water absorbed on the site.

Thus $Q = CiA$

The rational formula is equally applicable in S.I. units but an additional constant is now required if the coefficient C is to remain dimensionless.

Thus $$Q = \frac{CiA}{350}$$

where Q = Peak run-off rate m³/sec
C = Dimensionless run-off coefficient
i = Rainfall intensity mm/hr
A = Site area hectares.

The formula is used by selecting appropriate values of C, i and A. While A can be measured and i estimated from rainfall data, an estimate of the value of C is more difficult to obtain. The British Code of Practice 303:1952 suggests values of C as follows:

Roofed buildings and concreted areas	0·95–0·99
Roads	0·75–0·90
Pathways	0·50–0·75
Gardens, lawns and wooded areas	0·10–0·15

Design formulae for predicting peak run-off rates. The design of structures to deal with surface run-off is now generally based on information obtained from use of Bilhams formula for accepted recurrence intervals and duration of rainfall.

3.10.3 Ground modelling to control run-off

Reducing the peak intensity of run-off. The maximum peak rate of run-off from a site is directly proportional to the maximum intensity of rainfall expected for the time of concentration and within the recurrence interval selected.

An increase in the time of concentration enables a lower value of rainfall intensity to be selected in predicting the peak run-off rate. This can be achieved by delaying the discharge of surface water from an area being developed by constructing impounding or diversion dams or ponds. These smooth out the main fluctuating discharge from the watershed to a low safe rate of water release to the main channel.

Decreasing size of watershed. A decrease in the size of the collecting area will also reduce the peak intensity of run-off but will also lead to a greater number of structures to deal with the total run-off from an area although the dimensions of each structure may be reduced.

Grass lined waterways. The time of concentration may also be increased by impeding the surface flow of water as for instance by a grass sward in established waterways. This is an important method in controlling run-off from agricultural land because, in addition to the peak intensity, it also produces a more stable soil surface capable of withstanding higher water velocities. Vegetative cover is a vitally important factor in controlling soil erosion because it safely absorbs the kinetic energy of the raindrops.

3.10.4 Piped run-off of surface water

This may be achieved by structures offering less resistance to surface flow than that occurring naturally. In such cases open channels or, in extreme cases, underground pipes, of suitable dimensions to deal with the predicted run-off are used. Attention should be paid to the final discharge point. Such pipes rarely flow full and may be considered as special cases of open channels.

3.10.5 Piped drainage of underground water

Conditions requiring piped under drainage. In soils with a low inherent permeability or with small slopes or low lying land, natural drainage is a slow process because of the small size of pore interconnecting channels. Porous pipes laid with a grade in such a soil will receive water from the surrounding soil by virtue of the hydraulic gradient existing between the pipe (which is in connection with the atmosphere at its outlet) and the soil water adjacent to it. Such water can then be discharged from the pipe to an adjoining ditch easily and speedily.

The usual type of such underground drains is the 'clay tile drain' made in unglazed baked clay in 300 mm (12 in) lengths and various diameters between 40 mm and 200 mm (1½ in and 8 in). The more usual diameters employed are 75 mm (3 in) for laterals and 100 mm (4 in) or 150 mm (6 in) for main lines. These tiles are laid end to end in a hand or machine dug trench with a specially formed base to locate the tile accurately and ensure accurate butting. Water enters these drains mainly through the small gaps between each 300 mm (12 in) length. Concrete land drainage pipes are also used but are more costly, partly by reason of their shortened life compared with clay tiles in soils having marked acidity or alkalinity and partly because of their material cost. Attempts have been made to lay such pipes automatically by injecting liquid or semi-liquid concrete behind a tine working to the required depth and then forming the concrete drain *in situ*. This requires a more expensive machine but economises in the cost of trenching.

New materials. Many new materials are now becoming available for land under-drainage in the form of plastic pipes produced from special grades of polyethylene. Water enters the pipe from the soil through specially cut slots 30 mm (1¼ in) long at 50 mm (2 in) intervals and the pipe is currently available in 6 m (20 ft) lengths and 120 m (400 ft) coils.

Slightly more expensive in initial cost, savings can be made in transport and laying cost because of its light weight and applicability to machine laying. A porous backfill is normally used with the pipe to increase the hydraulic gradient in the soil surrounding the pipe and to equalise vertical and horizontal pressures on the pipe during soil settlement after laying.

Some specialist machines are also available which form a circular cross-section drain pipe on a former pulled through the soil from a continuous sheet of plastic foil material. The flat sheet is passed down the leg of the implement, is turned through a right angle, formed into a tube and the slotted edges latched together. These drains do not require trenches to be cut.

Mole drains. In pure clay soils a drainage channel can be formed *in situ* by drawing a cylindrical plug through the soil. If done under moist conditions a water carrying channel is produced with an average life of about 3–5 years. The gradient of the mole drains should be between 1 in 300 and 1 in 100 in most cases, these extremes being dictated by the need to avoid silting up on the one hand and washing on the other. Decreases of grade should also be avoided.

3.10.6 Patterns of laying drainage pipes

(a) In 'thorough' drainage a herringbone or straight pattern of laterals is laid which lead into main drains which in turn discharge into ditches or watercourses. A 75 mm (3 in) lateral size is standard with a 100 or 150 mm (4 in or 6 in) main line.

(b) In 'natural' drainage a single line of drains is laid along the natural lines of water discharge. This is specially applicable to the drainage of isolated wet areas in an otherwise dry location.

(c) 'Interceptor' drainage is practised to control the lateral movement of subsurface water. Interceptor drains laid on a suitable grade to obtain effective discharge are laid across the land slope and just above the seepage line. In this way the water is trapped and discharged before reaching the surface at the spring line.

Soil type	Spacing m(yd)	Depth m(ft)
Clay	3·6–6 (4–7)	0·6–0·75 (2–2½)
Loam	7–11 (8–12)	0·75–0·9 (2½–3)
Sand	11–20 (12–22)	0·9–1·2 (3–4)

Depth and spacing of the drains. Empirical methods are at present used to establish the spacing and depth of drain tiles.

The greater the clay content of the soil the shallower and closer should be the drain tiles. Water will not reach deep drain tiles in an impermeable soil which, after heavy rain, may be observed to have a waterlogged surface without any discharge from the drain ends.

Laying of tile drains. The trench should only be excavated to the required depth. The depth and grade may be obtained by using boning rods and two sight rails previously levelled to the required grade. The base of the trench should be rounded to fit the tile surface. In a soil with a high silt fraction the surface sod and topsoil should be placed in the drain before the rest of the backfill. In certain parts of the country a porous backfill is used. The gradient of the laterals should be greater than 1 in 250 and the gradient of the mains will suit the level of the discharge point and the designed carrying capacity. Junctions between mains and sub-mains and between sub-mains and laterals should be carefully made. Any junction at which a change in rate of flow is expected should have a silt trap with a removable inspection cover.

Protection of end of main. The point of discharge of the main line into a watercourse or ditch should be protected against the ingress of vermin and should be in glazed pipe to resist frost action. A hard surface to receive the discharge water is essential to prevent wash and the ditch side should be stone or brick faced around the discharging main. A main line should not pass within 2 m (6 ft) of a hedgerow unless made of glazed pipe laid with sealed joints to prevent blockage by plant roots.

3.10.7 Ditches and French drains

Ditches. Important in controlling the level of the water table in the adjacent soil profile and in removing large volumes of water collected by tile drainage systems. They suffer from the disadvantage of restricting the movement of surface vehicles. The size and shape of a ditch will largely be governed by conditions at the site but as a general rule in a well-proportioned ditch the top width will be equal to the bottom width plus depth with the sides sloped at 45°. This may be varied according to the soil conditions. The gradient of a ditch will largely depend on the discharge level required, variations for different rates of discharge being taken into account in the cross-sectional dimensions of the ditch.

French drains. A ditch not full of water will control the water table in the adjacent soil. To improve the accessibility of areas interlaced by such channels, to ease maintenance and prevent land slip into the ditch a steeper sided trench may be used which is then filled with coarse stone or gravel to provide a French drain. These are always used in preference to open ditches on the sides of roads and railway cuttings to control the seepage which would otherwise occur on such slopes.

3.10.8 Machines for land drainage

Trenching machinery. A wide selection of machines for digging straight sided trenches is currently available. These fall into three main categories (a) the continuous rotary or endless-bucket trenchers, (b) the single-bucket diggers and (c) endless chain diggers. Group (a) tend to be more expensive, but achieve a higher rate of work in rock-free soils while group (b) are cheaper and with a slower rate of work can deal with soil with rock obstructions. They may also be fitted with special buckets for digging trenches of different widths and to a uniform depth. All are used for trenching operations in conjunction with laying underground drains but group (b) may also be used for ditch construction although specialist side-arm dragline machines are preferred for this purpose.

Machinery for the automatic laying of drainage pipes.
The rotary bucket trenching machines are particularly adaptable to the automatic laying of drainage pipes because of their steady continuous operation. For clay tiles a platform for storing tiles is required in addition to a chute on to which the pipes are placed end to end to travel down into the trench behind the machine. For plastic pipe a carrying rack for the 6 m (20 ft) lengths is necessary and again a chute into which the pipe lengths are introduced by an operator on the machine. 120 m coils of plastic pipe are carried on drums and fed down a chute to the sole of the trench cut by a rotary wheel or chain trencher. New machines are continually being developed for trenchless pipelaying, using plastic pipe, and for placing permeable backfill in the trench prior to the normal backfill being placed. One of the most successful new machines for trenching uses an endless chain with coal-cutting type blades attached to every 4th or 6th link so that when raked at 45° and moved forward a slot is cut in the soil.

Special devices are required to maintain the true and correct grade so important is this work.

3.10.9 Disposal of run-off
Artificial drainage increases the volume of water which the rivers have to carry unless special provision is made to delay the flow of water to the rivers in times of heavy rainfall. An example of this is the provision of balancing ponds and lakes along the watercourse as in the L.C.C. New Town Project at Hook (Fig. 3.10). Without such provision artificial drainage tends to increase the risk of flooding from the overflow of rivers and streams.

River and Water Authorities. The catchment areas of the principal rivers of England and Wales were controlled by twenty-six river authorities, with general responsibility for land drainage within their catchment area and for the control of discharges into rivers. From April 1974 the twenty-six authorities were replaced by ten water authorities.

Legislation. There is a considerable volume of legislation relating to the problems of the disposal of run-off. The annual reports of the Water Resources Board, which was set up under the 1963 Water Resources Act, provide information and data on developments in this subject area. Some of the relevant statutory publications of H.M.S.O. are:

The Land Drainage Act, 1930
The Water Act, 1948
The Rivers (Prevention of Pollution) Act, 1951
The Land Drainage Act, 1961
The Rivers (Prevention of Pollution) Act, 1961
The Water Resources Act, 1963
The Water Act, 1973.

Bibliography

'Basic design in land form', Brian Hackett, *I.L.A. Journal*, February 1960.
Data Book for Civil Engineers, vols. 1, 2 and 3, E.E. Seelye, John Wiley.
Drainage of Agricultural Land, U.S.D.A. Water Information Center, New York.
Field Drainage, M.C. Livesley, E. and F.N. Spon.
General Excavation Methods, A. Brinton Carson, F.W. Dodge Corporation, New York.
'Ground modelling', David Thirkettle, *I.L.A. Journal*, February 1961.
'Land form design and cost factors', Brian Hackett, *Landscape Architecture, U.S.A.*, July 1964.
Land Modelling, Brian Hackett, Public Works and Municipal Services Congress 1964: Final Report.
Soil and Water Conservation Engineering, R.K. Frevert, G.O. Schwab, T.H. Edminster and K.K. Barnes, John Wiley, New York.
Soil Mechanics, Foundations and Earth Structures, G.P. Tschebotarioff, McGraw-Hill, New York.
Soil Physics, L.D. Baver, Chapman and Hall.

4 Hard Surfaces

TIMOTHY COCHRANE

4.1 Introduction

Hard surfaces are important elements in landscape design, especially in our increasingly urbanised civilisation. This chapter gives a general coverage of the major points to be considered in paving schemes, with references as necessary for more detailed information. The emphasis is on *paving for pedestrians* in courtyards, precincts and squares rather than on footpaths. Vehicular and sports surfaces are only briefly mentioned as they are well covered by many publications. *It is important to realise that what is said in this chapter must be related to differing local conditions.*

4.1.1 Function of pavings

The first function of any paved surface is to provide a hard, dry, non-slip surface which will carry the required load for pedestrian or vehicular traffic. It may also have other functions; it may indicate:

Direction – This can be suggested by the use of smoother flags on which people naturally walk to lead them across a grassed or gravelled courtyard; or by the use of cobbles to deter people from wandering off route (Plate 4.1).

Traffic hierarchy – It should indicate – by its texture or otherwise – pedestrian/vehicular priorities.

Hazard – Where vehicles meet pedestrians changes in the paving material will indicate change of function. Changes in paving materials can also draw attention to changes of level negotiable by steps or ramps.

Plate 4.1. WOODSTOCK, OXFORD – A classic example of paving for function and delight where each bend and kink of the path has a purpose. Stone setts channel the rainwater to and past the trees on the left.

Repose – Paving patterns can indicate subtly focal points where people pause in a paved area.

Ownership – Change of level and/or material can indicate differing ownerships (e.g. spaces beside public pavements outside hotels, shops, etc.).

4.1.2 Choice of pavings

With function decided upon it is possible to consider the available materials and to assess them on grounds of cost, appearance, etc. The following list should assist in selecting an appropriate paving:

Cost and availability – Is the material one with a high first cost matched by low maintenance costs, or *vice versa*? Has it durability, freedom from cracking and other failures, matched to the life expectation of the project, and is it readily available in the area?

Appearance, weathering, cleaning – Textural range, colour suitability for plain or patterned work should be considered, not only when first laid, but also when weathered. In this respect, natural materials tend to weather unevenly, but in doing so usually become more attractive. It may however be necessary to select materials which can be cleaned down by washing and hosing; or if by mechanical vacuuming or sweeping, design should be of a structural strength to carry at least light machines. In some locations a dark and heavily patterned material such as setts may be used to conceal oil stains which cannot be readily cleaned off any surface.

Safety, noise, light reflectivity – Is the area one affected by liability of local authorities, or otherwise affecting public safety, and do conditions suggest selection of non-slip materials? Softer and coarser paving textures may cause less impact noise at source and provide absorption for other sounds. In some cases, light reflection, causing glare around buildings may be a consideration.

Subsoil, drainage, services – Do subsoil conditions suggest the use of an impervious surface, with full drainage, or can the paving be chosen to absorb rainfall? Must underground services be accommodated and what are their access needs, by means of manholes, etc., or by occasional excavation? *In situ* materials should not be used where they may be dug-up frequently. Manhole covers should be integrated into paved schemes.

Comparative cost of surfacing materials – Costs are very much affected by local conditions, soil structure, labour and transport costs, availability of materials (including wastes) and on the size of the contract. The local council engineer or surveyor could help here with local knowledge, but it must be remembered that his experience may be related more to roads than pedestrian surfaces. Table 4.1 gives a rough and ready comparative guide to some of the most common materials in use.

4.1.3 Patterns

After years of neglect paving design has now come into its own in this country. As Elisabeth Beazley comments, 'Good paving is nearly always the background of a scheme and should reinforce the character of the design as a whole; it might be deemed equally unsuccessful if attention is drawn to it either by its monotony (i.e. being out of scale with its surroundings), ingenuity or colour. Rare exceptions, e.g. mosaic pavings are not considered here. If a pattern is wanted, and it may be necessary to reduce scale, it is best introduced by a material already in use in other parts of the scheme (e.g. in the buildings or screen walls) or by varying the shade but not the actual colour of the material. Otherwise acceptable schemes (e.g. of precast concrete slabs) are often made garish by the use of two colours. Drainage channels can be most useful in giving scale.'

Technical aspects – See sections 4.4.1 and 4.4.2 for notes on trim, setts, bricks, etc. Additionally concrete offers an infinite range of finishes and patterns due to the many ways in which its jointing can be designed. For flexible materials, only use as dividers those materials which will withstand rolling (e.g. setts, not concrete or stone). Costs can go up steeply when paving materials are mixed, and to avoid extra screeding costs it is as well to consider using materials of similar depth together (e.g. 50 mm (approx. 2 in) paviors with 50 mm (approx. 2 in) flags; or cobbles with 50 mm (approx. 2 in) flags in 75 mm (approx. 3 in) concrete; while 25 mm (approx. 1 in) hot asphalt on concrete fill can be used as infills to 50 mm (approx. 2 in) flags). Jointing patterns can be varied widely but note that herringbone patterns need elaborate setting out and constant checking as against straightforward coursing.

4.1.4 Paving for vehicles

Common surfacing materials are concrete, bitumen macadam, tarmacadam, cold and hot asphalts, sealed and unsealed gravel. Increasing the thickness of the sub-base and base or the addition of 100–150 mm (approx. 4–6 in) concrete will render many of the materials in this chapter usable for light vehicular traffic. This can be especially important for pedestrian precincts with their service traffic, vehicle crossings, or hard-standings. Pavement corners and other vulnerable locations can also be reinforced in this way.

For detailed consideration of vehicular pavement design, consult the publications of the following organisations:

D.O.E. Transport and Road Research Laboratory, Crowthorne, Berks.

TABLE 4.1: COST COMPARISON OF PAVED SURFACES

Up-to-date costs of all landscape materials are given in the current edition of Spons Landscape Price Book.
This table will therefore give only a very approximate comparison of costs as between different surfaces. Geographical availability of materials and paving area obviously have a profound influence on choice and cost, while mixing materials can add 25–50% to cost.

Surface, including thickness* of depth of finish only (mm)		Capital† cost guide (1–100)	Level of maintenance required Low/medium/high	Coverage/weight guide Weight in tonnes/100m²
FLEXIBLE				
Gravel	50	5	High	9·0
Gravel (with bitumen sealer)	50	6	Low/medium	9·5
Hoggin	100	5	medium	17·5
Cobbles (loose)	50–75	25	medium	—
Chippings (loose)	25	9	medium	—
Tarmacadam (tarpaving)	50	9	Low/medium	10·5
Tarmacadam (tarpaving)	75	11	Low/medium	15·5
Fine cold asphalt	20	7	Low/medium	4·0
Rolled asphalt	40	9	Low/medium	8·0
RIGID				
Concrete (plain finish)	100	14	Low	22·5
Concrete (exposed aggregate)	100	18	Low	22·5
UNIT				
Flags p.c. smooth	50	12	Low	11·5
Flags p.c. exp. aggregate	50	20	Low	11·5
Flags yorkstone new	50	63	Low	11·0
Flags yorkstone second hand	50	42	Low	11·0
Flags slate	20	100	Low	9·0
Bricks – stretcher bond stocks	75	19	Low	18·0
Bricks engineering	75	26	Low	26·0
Setts, new	100	44	Low	26·5
Setts, second hand	100	40	Low	26·5
Cobbles in concrete	75	47	Low/medium	—

* Only includes the thickness and weight of the finish.
† Includes for sufficient basework for pedestrian and light vehicular traffic only (where appropriate).

Their *Road Notes* cover all aspects of road design. *Road Note No. 29* (1970) is the key one on construction covering design of flexible and rigid pavings together with M.O.T. *Specification for Road and Bridge Works* (1969) (all obtainable from H.M.S.O.). Their Reports (obtainable from T.R.R.L.) features articles and items of research.

Cement & Concrete Association, Wexham Springs, Slough, SL3 6PL.

Asphalt and Coated Macadam Association, 25 Lower Belgrave Street, London, SW1W 0LS.

These produce various publications on materials for estate and minor roads.

4.1.5 Pavings for recreation

These include pavings for athletics: running tracks, field events, jump approaches, throwing circles and steeplechase tracks; and all ball-games. (Rugby football is the only one which cannot be played on a hard surface.)

There are two basic types of paving for recreation:

1. Hard porous (waterbound) surfaces. Composed of crushed hard limestone, whinstone, burnt red shale or ash, they depend on hygroscopic action for stability. The surface can therefore often be affected by frost and frost heave, while good drainage is essential to get water away quickly. These surfaces are common ('Redgra', 'Dripla', etc.), relatively cheap, but require regular brushing, watering and rolling.

Colours are in the black/buff/grey/red range and they have the lateral 'give' required for hockey and football.

2. Allweather surfaces. (*a*) Concrete, asphalt or coated macadam are old-established examples of non-resilient impervious surfaces unaffected by weather conditions, but which have no 'give'.

(*b*) A new family of surfaces have come in during recent years – based on bitumen/woodfibre and the newer synthetics using acrylics, elasto/polymers and even using nylon bladed 'grass'. Many of these newer materials combine the genuine all-weather characteristics of 2(a) with the resilience of 1. They are expensive but are becoming increasingly economic in obtaining continuous use in high-priced urban land situations.

It is important to consider each sport separately due to different requirements. Up-to-date references are essential and the following organisations should be consulted as to the latest literature available.

National Playing Fields Association, 25 Ovington Square, London, SW3 1LQ or the Sports Council (Technical Unit for Sport), 70 Brompton Road, London, SW3 1EX.

Playgrounds. Much of the foregoing information is applicable also to playgrounds. Generally, softer materials are used throughout, with concrete or paving slabs and other hard materials at access points and other areas of heavy pressure. Rolled asphalt (hot laid) gives a good finish, being more durable than cold asphalt, and smoother than macadam finishes which are too rough to fall down on.

Bitumen sealers with various admixtures have been used with mixed success. Cork chippings are good but need annual replacement.

Many new synthetic materials are now available for vulnerable areas under slides and climbing frames. Mainly composed of varying mixtures of rubber and/or synthetic polymers they come in red, green, grey and tan colours. Still relatively expensive – manufacturers are still experimenting to reduce costs, and the N.P.F.A. have available updated lists of manufacturers and surfaces with prices.

4.1.6 Roofs

Roofed or decked areas are now being increasingly used in urban areas. They require special consideration and various treatments are possible. These include light decking, more heavily modelled sculptural shapes in reinforced concrete, or a treatment which gives an illusion of normal ground by superimposing a naturalistic garden design.

Waterproofing is necessary – 'Waterproof Concrete' and 3-ply felt have not been successful. Tanking with 25–35 mm asphalt appears to be the only foolproof way. There must be adequate provision for rainwater disposal.

Lightweight screeds (for example vermiculite) can be used with cobbles, etc., set directly into them. Patent surfaces for roofs include asbestos–cement tiles, cement–grano paving laid *in situ*; both being laid on bituminous sheet membranes. Use can also be made of lightweight timber deckings laid duckboard style on rot-proof battens over the membrane. Care is needed with soil for planting on roofs, while water supply and drainage are

necessary. See *Handbook of Urban Landscape*, Ed. C. Tandy, Architectural Press: Landscape Information Sheet 42, Roof Gardens.

4.1.7 Foundations

The function of the pavement is to distribute point loads over the soil itself. Macadam pointed out that 'it is the native soil which really supports the weight of traffic, and that while that soil is in a dry state, it will carry any weight without sinking' (see Fig. 4.1 for terms used in paved surfaces).

In other words good drainage is of paramount importance.

Subsoil – Gault clay, heavy clay and peat give rise to difficulties and are especially susceptible to uneven movement.

Lighter clays, silts and gravels may be taken as more normal, but some, such as sand, are only stable when contained. Rock and compacted gravels give good foundations. Excess water in the subgrade reduces bearing capacity and can also give rise to frost heave. This can be controlled by waterproof surfacing and adequate falls which restrict rain penetration. Ditches and land drains can be used to control ground water.

Preparation – Organic topsoil must be removed and any fill should be a suitable base material well compacted in 300–600 mm (approx. 1–2 ft) layers. The formation should be rolled and compacted to required falls and cambers. On difficult soils likely to be affected by rain penetration during construction it is possible to apply a sprayed bituminous binder at the rate of 1·1–1·8 litres/m² according to traffic. For gravel and other flexible pavements, the formation should be treated with a weedkiller applied in accordance with the manufacturer's instructions. Sodium chlorate is effective at the rate of 10 kg/80 litres of water applied to each 500 m². This is however toxic to tree roots and where these are present use may be made of simazine (Geigy) at the rate of 1 kg/1,000 litres of water applied to each 1,000 m², or of one of the other monoglycomates which fix in the surface and do not travel down.

Base – In flexible pavements the base is the main load distributing layer. It may be any material with an 80% CBR* when compacted, and which remains stable in water and is resistant to frost.

Well-graded gravel, sands, hard core, hard clinker or slag will generally be suitable, but ashes are likely to be unstable when wet. With rigid pavements the loading is transmitted by the slab and the base would only be necessary to protect a poor subgrade from frost or to provide a suitable working surface.

* *California bearing ratio* – A measure of the bearing capacity of soils, commonly used for vehicle roads – see *Road Note 29*, H.M.S.O., for design guides.

4.2 Types of hard surface

4.2.1 Flexible surfacings

These are layers of compacted materials with no tensile strength and which spread the load directly over the soil and can be surfaced to keep water and frost from the sub-soil. The material may be laid loose or incorporate a binder.

Unbound surfaces – If laid loose consists of a base and sub-base as needed laid directly on formation level without binding materials. The base is usually 100 mm (approx. 4 in) clinker or hardcore.

Unsealed gravel – Has a precinctual and informal character and is, of course, useful around trees as it allows their roots to breathe, and avoids rigid paving lines round the trunks. It is cheap and suitable for occasional car parking. Treatment with weedkiller is necessary in spring (see section 4.1.7). Granite dust and pea shingle may also be used though the latter tends to be slippery.

Some self-binding gravels are available which lightly cement together after watering and compaction. They must be laid to falls. Colours vary according to the locality of source. Some include dust from lead and copper mines which has the additional merit of inhibiting weed growth. One type is hoggin, a gravel/sand/clay mix. This above all materials depends on good craftsmanship, which is now difficult to find.

Construction – Heavy rolling at all stages is essential (8–10 tonnes for vehicular areas, but a 500–750 kg hand roller may suffice for paths). Specifications vary greatly with subsoils and loads, but the following is fairly general (all are finished thicknesses): Sub-base as necessary, 100 mm (approx. 4 in) base of hardcore, clinker, etc., 50 mm (approx. 2 in) gravel (50 mm mesh), 25 mm (approx. 1 in) fine gravel with some hoggin as binder, and finished with 20 mm (approx. $\frac{3}{4}$ in) fine gravel, fine grit, shell or stone chippings (20 mm mesh) spread and rolled.

Plate 4.2. Interlocking pavings in a public garden over a multi-storey car park. Baden, Switzerland.

Ashes or cinders as a surfacing are suitable only for rough paths and running tracks. More than any other material construction varies with local conditions. Graded mixes (3 : 1 household/hard fine ash) can be compacted and rolled to total thickness of 125 mm on 125 mm (approx. 5 in on 5 in) base.

Cobbles and ballast. *Laid loose* – When laid directly on hoggin or hardcore loose cobbles or stones provide an excellent hazard and are good by trees especially where the ground level by trees has to be raised. They can be used also as recessed trim between dissimilar materials, but give rise to cleaning difficulties. Sizes approximately 30–100 mm (approx. $1\frac{1}{4}$ to 4 in) diameter. For reasonable economy it is essential to investigate local sources of supply. Indiscriminate digging from beaches and rivers is not permitted but some firms have rights over defined areas. Ballast/gravel rejects are split rather than waterworn.

Cobbles are available from beaches (grey/fawns) waterworn, potteries (wash mill flints) and quarries (flint cobbles – dark–blues). Granite chippings and other coarse aggregates can be used similarly.

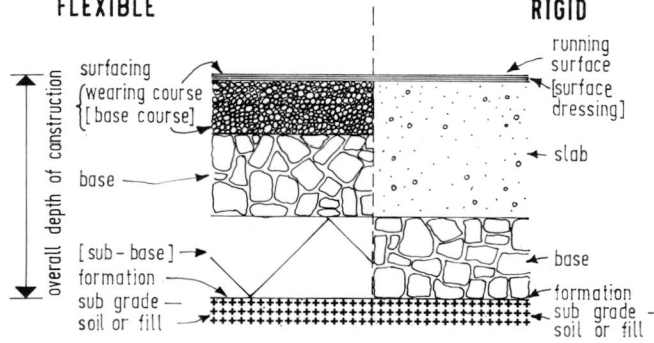

Fig. 4.1. PAVED SURFACES – DEFINITIONS – This covers the standard terminology of most types of paving. Items in brackets are those not always used, while 'formation' denotes the top of the sub-grade.

Bound surfaces (with waterproofing binders and/or surfacings). Surface dressings for both old and new pavements utilise hot tar or bitumen (also available in emulsion form). Wearing courses are provided for waterproof and non-skid surfaces, while the base course protects the base from traffic load (see Fig. 4.1).

Surfacing varies from open-textured coated macadams to the smooth and more expensive black toppings of the hot and cold asphalts. The Asphalt and Coated Macadam Association's technical advisory service will advise on the best combination of materials for differing conditions. Coated macadams – consist of graded aggregates that have been coated with tar and/or bitumen (B.S. 4987). Textures are variable – open looks much better, but they are more vulnerable to weathering and thus less durable.

Cold asphalt (B.S. 4987) – originally laid cold – hence its name – it is still used for patching but now often laid warm for footways, roads or tracks.

Rolled asphalt (hot process) (B.S. 594) – a dense surfacing used on most city streets for very heavy traffic. It is the cheapest and most common of the hot asphalts.

Mastic asphalt (B.S. 1446 and 1447) – smoother cleaner finish – a heavy-duty finish for bridges etc.

Non-slip qualities and appearance depend largely on the aggregate chosen and black tops can in fact be lightened by their use.

Construction of flexible toppings. Thickness 35–100 mm (approx. 1½ to 4 in) depending on the traffic and the texture required. A.C.M.A. recommends 50 mm (approx. 2 in) for foot traffic, although 35 mm (approx. 1½ in) has been used. The minimum for vehicles is 60 mm (approx. 2½ in) laid in one or two courses. *Road Note No. 29* gives design charts.

Compaction is achieved by 1 to 3 tonnes (approx. 1 to 3 tons) roller for playgrounds, up to 6 to 9 tonnes (approx. 6 to 9 tons) for roads, but with use of a 500 kg (approx. 10 cwt) hand roller round manholes and awkward spots.

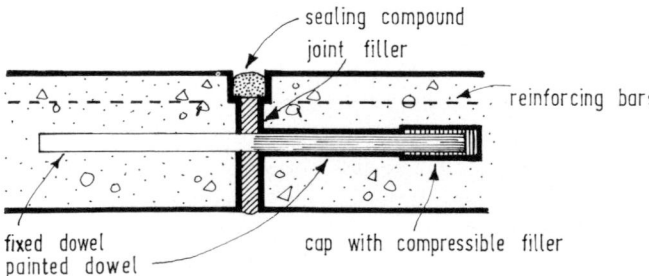

Fig. 4.2. CONCRETE SLABS – EXPANSION JOINTS – Reinforcement is stopped as shown and joint filler and sealing compound fills the gap. Where heavy traffic is expected dowels are used to transmit load.

Plate 4.3. GARDEN, HAMBURG – This composition of exposed aggregate and smooth concrete slabs with its water channels shows an imaginative treatment of the material.

Stabilised soil base. This is best described as a weak flexible but cheap concrete of cement mixed with earth,* which needs surfacing. It can be used for roads, car parks, cycle tracks, playgrounds, etc. It is only applicable where the ground is suitable (gravels, coarse sands, but not organic soils, while clay needs special processing), and where the contract is big enough to justify soil tests, expert advice, and careful supervision.

4.2.2 Rigid pavings

Rigid paving structures are those which utilise the tensile strength of the construction to transmit loads to the soil, as in the case of concrete slabs for roads or pavements. The most common is *in situ* concrete which is cheap, easy to use and popular, but it is important that the surface should be finished correctly and carefully with imaginative use of jointing and textured finishes. Even with the extra cost of these finishes and joints it is still far cheaper than many other materials. It is at its best combined with other surfaces or trim, and good detailing and workmanship are vital. Concrete is chosen for its finish, use on bad soil (if local materials available), or its combination with other materials as it obviates rolling.

Minimum thicknesses are 75 mm (approx. 3 in) unreinforced for pedestrian traffic, 150 mm (approx. 6 in) unreinforced for vehicular traffic, or 100 mm (approx. 4 in) reinforced, with the addition of 50 mm (approx. 2 in) to each for vehicles over 1·5 tonnes (approx. 30 cwt).

Normal mix is 1:2:4. For pedestrian surfaces reinforcement would normally only be used for crack con-

* Cement stabilised materials for road and air field pavements, A. A. Lilley, C.C.A. Tech. Report, Nov. 1971; 'Soil-cement roads', Fixed equipment of the farm, Leaflet 19, M.A.F.F.; Road Note No. 15, Specification for the construction of housing estate roads using soil cement, T.R.R.L.

trol (square mesh about 50 mm (approx. 2 in) from top) increasing the spacing of joints needed from every 4·5 m (approx. 15 ft) if unreinforced to 12 m (approx. 40 ft) with mesh reinforcement approximately 2 kg/m² (approx. 4½ lb/sq yd). Bad subgrades, embankments over 1·2 m (approx. 4 ft) high, or paving over high water tables may also require reinforcement. Expansion joints need special construction detailing (Fig. 4.2). (See *Road Note No. 29* for design chart.)

Textured surfaces offer an excellent range of finishes. They rely on exposure of the aggregate by brushing while still damp, spraying or using retarders or by mechanical means (crimping rollers, board patterns or even by bush-hammering and grit-blasting). A wide range of aggregates is available, in whites, pinks, greys, blues, greens, browns and blacks while colour of cement should be carefully chosen either to harmonise with, or to set off the chosen aggregates* (Plate 4.3).

Untextured concrete which relies solely on coloured cements for effect can look crude and artificial. *Jointing patterns* and mixture with other materials can be very effective.

4.2.3 Unit pavings

Bases for pedestrian traffic: use 75 mm (approx. 3 in) well-consolidated good hardcore or sand-blinded clinker (well-burnt) rolled to paving falls. For occasional vehicular traffic add 100 mm (approx. 4 in) weak mix concrete, 38 mm (approx. 1½ in) aggregate, laid directly on formation or 75 mm (approx. 3 in) base.

Large units (flags). These may be laid in several ways:†

Set on 50 mm (approx. 2 in) sand bed. Traditional. Satisfactory where sand cannot be washed out at edges or through open joints.

Bedded and jointed with mortar. The mix (usually 1:3 cement or lime/sand) should be suited to the slab. Essential for wheeled traffic but not over services due to lifting difficulties.

Laid on five mortar dots at corners and at centre (1:5 mix) – easy to lift to access to services, and to level the slabs. Good if pavior is skilled, but not recommended for heavy pedestrian traffic.

Joints – Butt joints are best for normal pavings and formal effects, as they keep water from the base and discourage weeds. Grout joints or brush in dry mix (5:1).

* Sources of aggregate (D.S.I.R.), H.M.S.O.
† Laying precast concrete paving flags. H.S. Mildenhall, C.C.A. 1974.

Where plants are needed – spread sand on foundation, lay slabs with 25 mm (approx. 1 in) joints, fill with fine soil and top up for the first few weeks.

Stepping stones – Flags laid at 750 mm (approx. 2 ft 6 in) centres and 38 mm (approx. 1½ in) below grass level. Can also be laid *in situ* in grass but this is not easy. Cut out turf and lay 75 mm (approx. 3 in) concrete (1:2:4) on sanded clinker with a minimum of 300 mm (approx. 1 ft) between *in situ* concrete to protect grass.

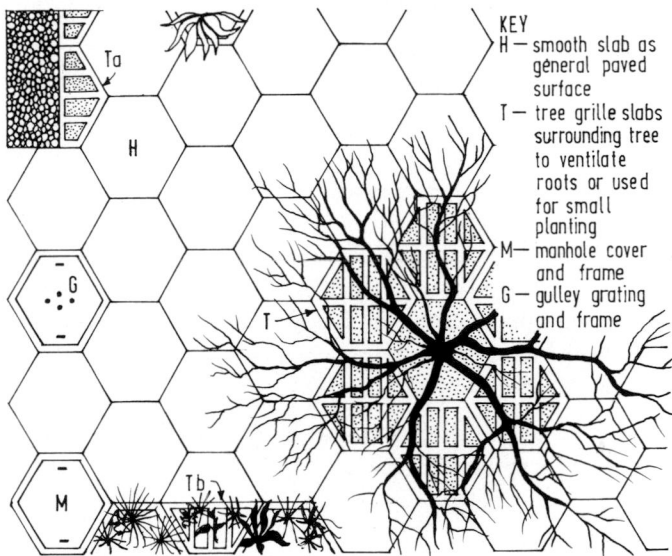

Fig. 4.3. HEXAGONAL PAVING – Note the varied details possible; tree grids (*Ta* + *Tb*) and gully grating covers *G* while manhole covers *M* are also integrated into the pattern. (Acknowledgement: Wettern Bros.)

Materials – Precast concrete is the most common material, to sizes as follows: Flag dimensions (B.S. 368) A 600 × 450 mm (approx. 2 ft × 1 ft 6 in), B 600 × 600 mm (approx. 2 ft × 2 ft), C 600 × 750 mm (approx. 2 ft × 2 ft 6 in), D 600 × 900 mm (approx. 2 ft × 3 ft) (thicknesses 50 and 63 mm (approx. 2 and 2½ in)). For pedestrian traffic 50 mm is normal (approx. 2 in) but 63 mm slabs (approx. 2½ in) are often used for occasional light vehicle traffic as at garage crossings, precincts, and at pavements subject to mounting by service vehicles. Slabs 450 × 450 × 100 mm (approx. 1 ft 6 in × 1 ft 6 in × 4 in) are now being used in vehicular areas particularly shopping precincts – as these smaller units combine better resistance to wheel stresses and a more human scale. These units are also more adaptable for lifting for services. Most slabs are mass-produced and made to a dense, high quality, by hydraulic pressing in steel moulds. They normally have a smooth creamy finish, but can be coloured or have the aggregate exposed by acid washing or bush hammering. Open mould casting is also done. At a much higher cost this opens up a further variety of finishes including exposed coarse aggregates, textures impressed by rubber mats, and non-slip inserts of rubber or carborundum. Slabs which are not hydraulically pressed lack very high density and strength, but vibration can be used to produce a sound and durable concrete.

Aggregate exposure or texture finishes, or colours (grey, greens, buffs, reds) can be used to improve the somewhat dull appearance of concrete slab pavings, but discretion is needed. Shapes are also available, including hexagons, but they need very careful detailing to avoid awkward junctions (Fig. 4.3).

Precast stone – This is dearer than precast concrete, yet much cheaper than stone slabs. Almost any stone can be 'reconstructed'.

Natural stone and slate – These are relatively costly, quarried in small quantities, but still most durable and pleasant materials. Slight irregularities and more organic weathering provides a welcome relief from that of manufactured materials. If locally obtained, secondhand stones are much cheaper. Being already weathered they can look better, but cost more to lay. (Usually Yorkstone from broken-up pavements.)

> *Laying* – consult quarries as to sizes and adjust design to suit seams being cut.

Granite – Very hard and durable but expensive and rarely found in large slabs.

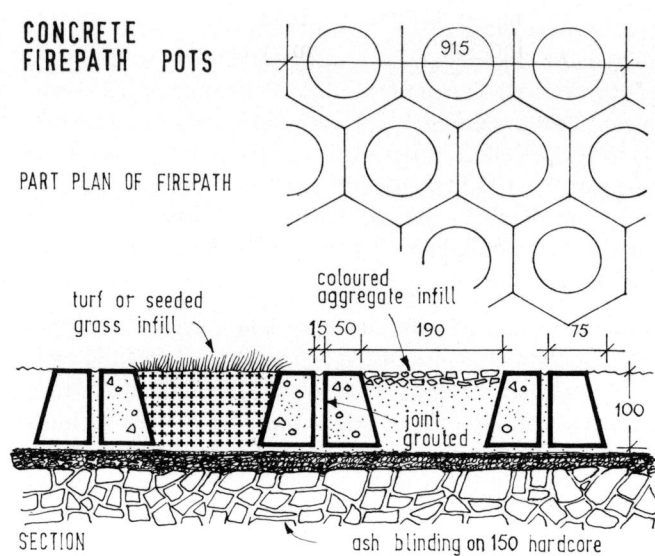

Fig. 4.4. CONCRETE FIREPOTS – Useful where a fire appliance access must be routed through a grassed area. (Acknowledgement: Wettern Bros.)

Yorkshire – Best known is sandstone, buff-brown, also bluish. Riven faced, rubbed finish is more expensive. Similar stones from Lancashire and the Forest of Dean. Slabs 38–63 mm (approx. $1\frac{1}{2}$ to $2\frac{1}{2}$ in).

Portland Stone from Purbeck and Portland are soft grey/whites. Slabs 50–63 mm (approx. 2–$2\frac{1}{2}$ in). Other stones are generally not robust enough for external pavings.

Slate – is good but expensive. Lancashire, Westmorland and Cornwall – green, browns and Welsh slates – purplish, grey-black, are usually split to natural riven face. Sanded and rubbed finishes are available at greater expense. Usual thickness 20 to 40 mm (approx. $\frac{3}{4}$ to $1\frac{1}{2}$ in).

Small units. These are particularly useful for small-scale patterns (as in domestic work), where a change of scale is needed inside a larger area or for ease of lifting over services. Many of them are relatively expensive but the small precast concrete unit, often used so successfully in Europe, is now generally available here.*

Bricks† – Many hard, well-burnt, non-dusting bricks can be suitable for use, but they must be chosen with care to resist frost and sulphate attack. If anything they should be slightly over-burnt. Usually they are attractively well-textured and therefore non-slip. Colours – dark blues, plums, browns and reds. Some bricks are available with

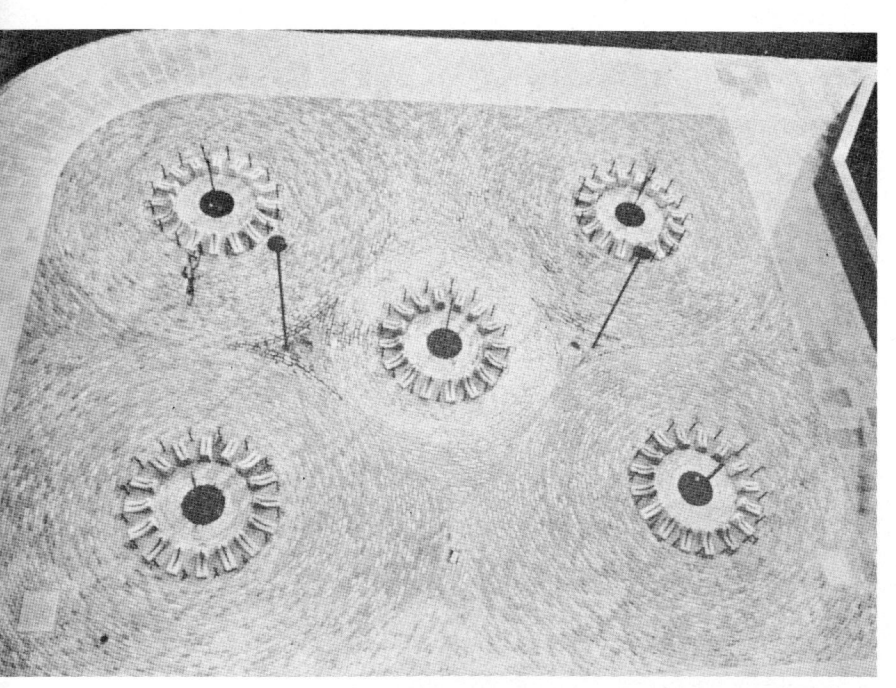

Plate 4.4. CYCLE PARKING AREA, CAMBRIDGE – The swirling circles of setts combine to present an interesting pattern. Drainage is to gullies by the lamp posts while gravel and setts laid in sand around trunks provide water and air to the trees.

---

* *Laying concrete block paving.* A. A. Lilley and J. R. Collins, C.C.A.
† *Brick floors and brick paving*, K. Thomas and L. Bevis, Brick Development Association, Technical Note.

slots for drainage and aeration of tree roots, while engineering seconds make excellent paving bricks.

Paviors – Wirecuts and pressed. Surface sizes are usually as for other bricks, but 25 to 50 mm (approx. 1–2 in) thick. They are tough, with hard smooth or textured surfaces, and also have non-slip patterned faces. Colours – red (south) and blue/brown (north).

Laying – Many permutations are possible: on edge or face, herringbone, stretcher or basketweave bonds, etc.

An adequate camber or cross-fall is essential to facilitate drainage and avoid slipperiness. Laid on sand or sandlime (1:4) bed, or on a mortar bed. Colour and type of jointing is an important factor in the overall appearance. Ordinary bricks have grouted 10–20 mm joints while engineering bricks are butt jointed.

Tiles and mosaics – These are usually limited to small areas of special emphasis. A large variety of sizes, shapes and colours is available; clay quarries – browns, reds; semi- and fully vitrified tiles or mosaics – wide colour range. Pattern-making tiles (as quarries but in interlocking shapes) are available in great variety from U.K. and continental sources. Only a few clay tiles are frostproof.

Laying – Tiles 16–32 mm (approx. $\frac{5}{8}$–$1\frac{1}{4}$ in) thick, laid on 100 mm (approx. 4 in) concrete (1:2:4) with 20 mm (approx. $\frac{3}{4}$ in) cement/sand screed (1:3) and 5 mm (approx. $\frac{3}{16}$ in) joints of cement/sand (1:2). Mosaics 3–5 mm (approx. $\frac{1}{8}$–$\frac{3}{16}$ in) thick. Various proprietary methods of laying, utilising latex cements.

Setts – Granite and whinstone (B.S. 435) the hardest wearing surfaces of all, are the most common, but limestone (B.S. 760) and sandstone (B.S. 706) setts are also made. From 100 mm cube up to larger and rectangular blocks, they can be obtained new (very expensively) or secondhand. They are laid either with a fairly flush surface, or a rough surface to discourage access; used to create bold patterns (Plate 4.4), or as scaling-down trim (Plate 4.2). Its ability to stand rolling makes it suitable as a permanent shuttering to other materials, such as tarmac.

Laying – On 25 mm (approx. 1 in) sand bed, rammed 10 mm (approx. $\frac{3}{8}$ in) joints grouted after racking with chippings. Alternatively butted tight and laid on

Plate 4.5. GRANITE SETTS AND TIMBER DECKING – The jutting mound contrasts pleasantly with the smooth sophistication of the open timber decking.

25 mm (approx. 1 in) cement/sand (1:3) with joints brushed in with dry cement/sand (1:6).

Cobbles – see section 4.2.1. There are many ways in which cobbles can be used; random, roughly coursed, or laid in patterns; either flush or proud of the surface to give differing degrees of pedestrian control.

Laying – On 50 mm compacted sand lay 50 mm concrete (1:2:4) (approx. 2 in on 2 in) and place cobbles as required in this base. Other methods: lay dry and water with watering can. (Use concrete base for vehicles.)

Timber – Formerly this was used as tarred road setts, and it is still possible to exploit the qualities of timber as a paving material on terraces and patios, and especially on roofed areas where its resilience, lightness and smooth surface drainage can be utilised. Durable hardwoods or treated softwoods can be laid with 12–25 mm (approx. $\frac{1}{2}$–1 in) gaps. A well-trafficked area with coarse-textured timber, adequate falls and good ventilation and drainage should be reasonably non-slip, and would offer a welcome change from many of the other heavier paving materials used (Plate 4.5).

Precast concrete firepaths – Several types are available, 'waffle grids', hexagonal pots, both of which can be bedded and jointed on ash over a porous hardcore base, while the hollows are filled with grass or soft paving materials to give the appearance of a lawn (Fig. 4.4). Small interlocking paving units are also made for this purpose, but without interstices for planting.

4.3 Drainage and services

4.3.1 Surface water drainage

The aim of drainage is to get the water off the impermeable surface quickly by means of cambers or falls through gutters, channels or gullies to the disposal system. It can either be handled unobtrusively or designed as an attractive element of the paving pattern. Cross falls and cambers have generally replaced older methods of 'dishing' to separate gullies. In handling falls it is necessary to be bold. Quite steep falls (within limits as shown) have been used in traditional work and can be very effective, but it may be necessary to counteract any visual 'sliding' by using central channels in narrow places.

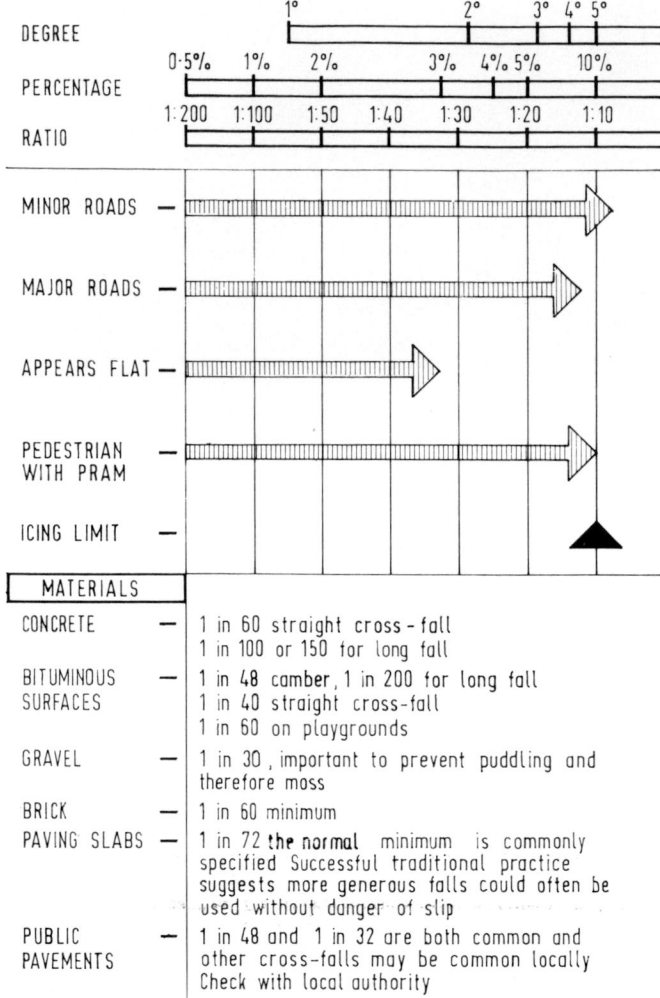

DEGREE			1°		2°		3° 4° 5°
PERCENTAGE	0·5%	1%	2%		3%	4% 5%	10%
RATIO	1:200	1:100	1:50	1:40	1:30	1:20	1:10

| MINOR ROADS — |
| MAJOR ROADS — |
| APPEARS FLAT — |
| PEDESTRIAN WITH PRAM — |
| ICING LIMIT — |

MATERIALS	
CONCRETE —	1 in 60 straight cross-fall 1 in 100 or 150 for long fall
BITUMINOUS SURFACES —	1 in 48 camber, 1 in 200 for long fall 1 in 40 straight cross-fall 1 in 60 on playgrounds
GRAVEL —	1 in 30, important to prevent puddling and therefore moss
BRICK —	1 in 60 minimum
PAVING SLABS —	1 in 72 the normal minimum is commonly specified Successful traditional practice suggests more generous falls could often be used without danger of slip
PUBLIC PAVEMENTS —	1 in 48 and 1 in 32 are both common and other cross-falls may be common locally Check with local authority

Fig. 4.5. FALLS TABLE–A comparative table showing falls in varying conditions. Note that minimum falls increase with surface roughness.

Three-dimensional checks are essential in consideration of the effects of the ensuing warped planes against any strongly horizontal surfaces. Suggested falls are shown in Fig. 4.5, but it is always as well to check on local practice. Around buildings the paving should fall away at 1:50 minimum for about 3 m (approx. 10 ft) to avoid 'splashback' from rain.

4.3.2 Surface water disposal
Calculation of water run-off is usually by means of a modified version of the 'rational' (Lloyd–Davies) formula. The T.R.R.L. hydrograph method is only used in really large schemes, anything requiring a 600 mm (approx. 24 in) sewer or bigger (see Chapter 3 – section on Drainage, for formulae).

For paved areas and roads generally the permissible fall in channels or pavings (see section 4.3.1) governs spacing of gullies. Former *ad hoc* methods of gully design on 'flat' roads gave a spacing of 45 m (approx. 150 ft) for gullies – governed by the minimum longitudinal fall of 1:250. B.S. standard 508 × 451 mm (20 × 18 in) gullies would drain 150–250 m² according to conditions. When sizing gullies allow for 0·2 m² of grating area to 1 m³ min. flow (plus factor of safety for obstruction by leaves, overrun, etc.).

Disposal may be to combined surface and foul water or to separate surface water systems (check with local authority). Soakaways (at least 3 m (approx. 10 ft) from buildings) must be used if there is no sewer. Several small ones are better than one large one. Storage chambers should hold 15 mm (say ½ in) rainfall over area × impermeability coefficient, and should penetrate at least 500 mm (about 2 ft) into permeable strata.

4.3.3 Surface items
Collection points for drainage, and points of access to underground services, appear on the surface in ways which must be carefully considered and if possible co-ordinated in their overall design. Drainage and service lines can be routed or re-routed within reasonably defined limits. Gullies and covers can be selected from standard ranges or be specially designed. Finally paving types can be selected bearing in mind particular needs to accommodate known drainage and service requirements. Efforts to hide or camouflage are seldom successful, but tidily ordered elements become relatively unobtrusive. In this respect rectangular covers should fit squarely into the paving pattern. If this is not possible circular gratings and covers present an acceptable alternative – especially in monolithic surfaces.

Manhole covers (see Table 4.2). There are many good traditional patterns available in cast iron in circular, rectangular, square, double triangular and single triangular shapes. Non-rocking covers should be specified. Steel is also used; it is stronger and more expensive but rusts more quickly. Recessed covers, medium and light

Plate 4.6. Dished and perforated stone gully set in brick paving.

TABLE 4.2
Gradings of manhole covers and road gully gratings according to B.S. 497 (1967) – (cast iron and steel).

Manhole Covers and Frames: Grades

A	Double triangular Single triangular	Heavy duty – for carriageways (to take wheel loads up to 11·43 tonnes)
B	Circular Rectangular	Medium duty – domestic access etc. (note – for oil tanker – use grade A)
C	Rectangular Square	Light duty – in areas inaccessible to wheeled vehicles

Road Gully Gratings, Covers and Frames

D	Double triangular	Heavy duty – for carriageways (to take wheel loads up to 11·43 tonnes)
E	(1) Straight bar (for gradients under 1:50) Stormbar (for gradients over 1:50) (2) Kerb type	Medium duty for normal commercial vehicles (14·22 tonnes max gross weight)

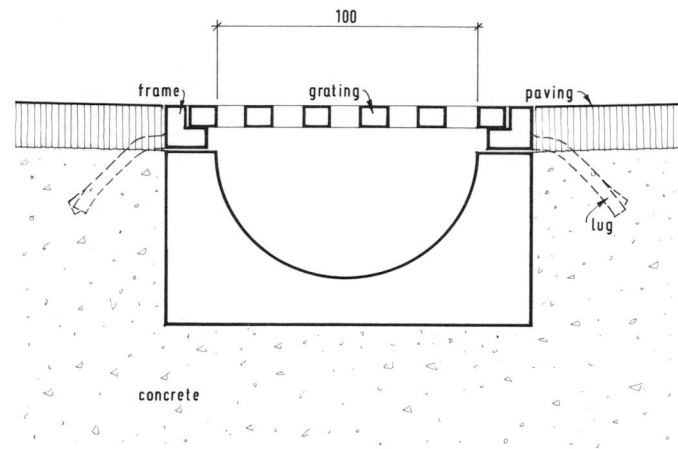

Fig. 4.6a. CHANNEL – Shows half-round channel with grating cover. Medium duty for foot and very light vehicular traffic.

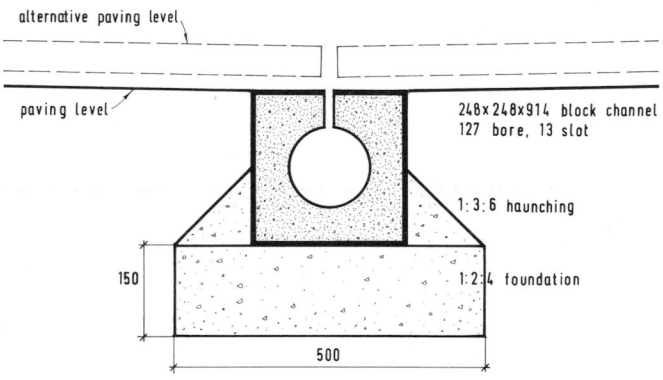

Fig. 4.6b. CHANNEL – Concrete channel with drainage slots.

grades only, can be filled with paving material to match that of the surroundings. They are not always a perfect solution but are more successful with small paving units.

Setting of manhole covers is all-important and these points should be covered in the specification. Covers should always be parallel to the overall pattern and set either well within the paving or away from the edge into planting to obviate the untidy sight of manhole walls projecting and manholes astride two materials. Also keep the covers parallel to sloping surfaces. Round covers fit better into *in situ* pavings.

Concealed covers; this is sometimes done with service manholes. The G.P.O. use a small triangular marker plate usually at the corner of a paving slab to indicate the presence of a concealed junction cover. Simply, the

Plate 4.7. A straightforward grille detail draining an area of exposed aggregate paving.

manhole is terminated with a cover below paving level and the paving (slabs on dots) or gravel, loose cobbles, etc., is continued over it. Other covers include those for all the major services, including hydrants, air valves, meter boxes, sluice valves and stopcocks. All are available in 100 × 100 to 600 × 900 mm (approx. 4 in × 4 in to 2 ft × 3 ft).

Gullies and gratings (see Table 4.2).   Back inlet gullies provide the neatest system for rainwater downpipes. Other gullies which are open to receive direct discharge from rainwater pipes or to collect water from channels have grating covers to check entry of leaves and litter. They are removable to give access for cleaning. For gratings cast iron is almost universal. Steel is sometimes used for its high strength to weight ratio. These notes refer to cast iron but also apply to steel.

Many sizes and patterns are available including those with hinges and which can be locked in position.

73

Plate 4.8. STREET PAVING, BASILDON – Cobbled cycle areas and tree grids combine to form an excellent articulation to this pavement separated from the shopping parade by a neat channel grille.

direction of flow: gradients of 1 in 50 and over

1 straight bar double triangular grating: lift out pattern	2 plain grating: hinged	3 storm gulley grating: hinged
Grade D	Grade E	Grade E
508×457	200×200	406×355
	300×275	508×355
	300×300	

Fig. 4.7. GULLY GRATINGS – Three typical heavy-duty types.

Channels. These are used where hard surfaces meet kerbs and where two falls intersect. As well as channelling water run-off they also act as trim, especially useful on rolled surfaces where the roller cannot get up to the edge.

Materials may be *in situ* concrete, precast concrete (B.S. 340) or granite and whinstone, in various dressings to B.S. 435.

Sandstone (B.S. 706) is seldom used but traditional setts are useful for texture change. Cobbles also give texture change but their rough surface slows the flow of water. Hot asphalt can be ruled as a smooth margin to otherwise textured asphalt paving. Cast iron, in half round sections may suit special cases. Surrounding surfaces should be dished to channels; alternatively the channels themselves can be dished at higher cost. Some can be covered with iron gratings or grilles to 150–375 mm (approx. 6–15 in) width (Plate 4.7 and Fig. 4.6a).

Monsoon drains – concrete channels with continuous slots to drain below afford a neat and simple trim/drainage detail (Fig. 4.6b).

Plate 4.9. Care is needed when using bold patterns on warped planes. Hay Hill, Norwich.

4.3.4 Public utilities

The traditional method of laying mains for the public utilities still remains messy, wasteful and disruptive – due to the difficulties and dangers, imaginary or otherwise, of co-ordinating the various utilities constructional programmes. The report of the Joint Committee on the Location of Underground Services (1963) gives suggested spacing and depths for the other services below 1·8 m (approx. 6 ft) or preferably 3·15 m (approx. 10 ft 6 in)

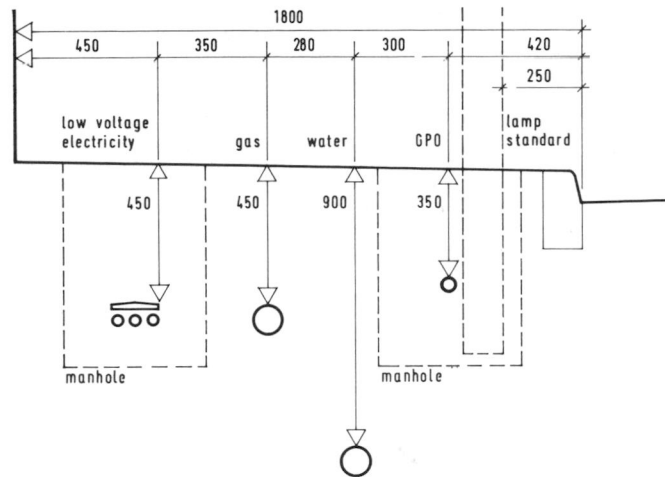

Fig. 4.8a. Suggested arrangement of services under a 1·8 m (approx. 6 ft) wide footway based on recommendations by the Joint Committee on the Location of Underground Services. Sewers are not shown as they are separately laid to independent falls.

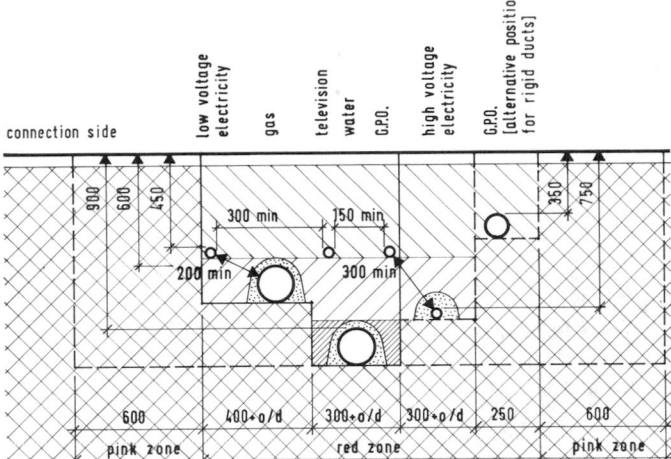

Fig. 4.8b. COMMON TRENCH – Suggested layout which permits relative ease of access for maintenance.

Plate 4.10. Rain water taken to a central slit drain concealed under paving. London Street, Norwich.

footpath. From this it is possible to develop a reasonable system for fitting services into paved areas. In complicated cases, three-dimensional checks are useful especially for crossings and for sewer connections (Fig. 4.8a).

Drains and sewers have to be laid separately as they require regular falls and cannot therefore be combined easily with other services.

The D.O.E. are encouraging the idea of the common trench for all public utilities. This leads to a much more logical and tidy site, while individual services can be located easily for maintenance. The suggested layout (Fig. 4.8b) overcomes many traditional objections to common trenches. Water mains are laid at the bottom to obviate freezing; gas gets maximum separation from electricity and water, to obviate risks of explosions and short circuits. Normally services are laid below footpaths, verges and paved areas to minimise disturbance

to traffic. When below paving, services should be laid below small-scale paving units rather than below *in situ* paving, to obviate patchy making good after repairs or additional connections. Access boxes and markers are also easier to fit in. Table 4.3 covers some basic information on the various services. Hydraulic mains, district heating lines and land drains are also met with. Fire hydrants and sluice valves are usually 275–300 m (approx. 300 yd) apart and if possible kept at least 7·5 m (approx. 25 ft) from buildings so that they will be usable in an emergency.

4.3.5 Trenches and ducts

The biggest source of paving failure is faulty compaction of trenches. They should be filled in 225 mm (approx. 9 in) layers with approved granular material. If of inferior quality, add 5% cement. Flooding during backfilling should not be permitted. The soil should be spread and compacted at its natural or optimum moisture content. Compaction is best done by power-driven rammers. Trenches for service pipes often become water traps. If so, surrounding saturated ground should be excavated and replaced with well-consolidated good subsoil or a suitable base material. Trenches should be routed as far away as possible from trees with at least 1·5 m (approx. 5 ft) clearance. If necessary pipes can be tunnelled under

TABLE 4.3

Services	Materials and access needs	Minimum cover
WATER mains WATER branches	Mainly 100 mm ϕ C.I., steel or asbestos 75–300 m ϕ, common; largest is 3·9 m ϕ 12·5–50 mm ϕ. Manholes for stop valves and branches also access for bursts and new connections. Polythene useful, unaffected by soils or frost. Some grades not always allowed for drinking water due to risk of gas absorption.	900 mm depth (up to 300 mm ϕ) 1,100 mm depth (up to 600 mm ϕ) 750 mm depth
GAS mains GAS service GAS branches	100 mm ϕ min, C.I. or steel 25 mm ϕ min, W.I. steel 12·5 mm ϕ min. Fall to main (for condensation). Access rarely required. Valves, pumps and vents needed for condensation.	600–750 mm 400–600 mm less than 450 mm
ELECTRICITY mains (H.V.) ELECTRICITY (L.V.) to lights, kiosks, etc.	Low voltage is wasteful on long runs, so street lights run off spurs from main below. Laid direct in ground or drawn through 100 mm earthenware ducts in busy areas. Underground link disconnecting boxes 750 × 600 mm m.h.'s at street intersections 120 m length usual maximum. Armoured cable with tile covers.	450 mm or by agreement with highway authority Just below paving
G.P.O. telephone	Polythene cables in ground or in ducts. 50–85 mm asbestos and pvc ducts encased in concrete. 155 m max between surface junction boxes.	225 mm (protected cable) 350 mm (steel or self-aligning duct) 450 mm (90 mm earthenware ducts with 1, 2, 4, 6 and 9 ways)
DRAINAGE	75 mm ϕ (100 mm for soil). Clayware/ci/concrete/asbestos cement/pitchfibre. M.h's at all changes of direction/gradient and in any case at 90 m apart max. Covers 0·75 × 0·7 min to 0·9 × 0·6 or 0·55 ϕ for deeper m.h.'s.	Variable according to local public health regulations

large roots while small cut roots should be trimmed square and tarred. Drying movements in heavy shrinkable clays can cause damage down to 1·5 m (approx. 5 ft) deep to pipes and drains. Where fast growing thirsty and suckering trees such as the poplar, elm or willow are used, damage can extend down to 3 m (approx. 10 ft) below the surface. The only solution is to avoid these trees on such soils.

Ducts are used where ready and frequent access is needed, or to carry services through a concrete road, bridge or foundation. They vary from multiway earthenware tubes as used by the G.P.O., tubes in concrete formed by inflatable rubber/plastic tubing, through the usual 225 m (9 in) or so ducts, to large crawlways with services hooked on to built-in lugs at the sides. Due to expense, progress towards integrated ducting of public utility services has been slow in developments except where enforced as a condition by the controlling authority.

4.3.6 Heating of paved areas
This is installed mainly to prevent ice formation and also to thaw snow. Radiant heating in slabs is now used for elevated roads, shopping precincts and subway ramps. It can also be used to provide greater comfort conditions in spring and summer evenings and is particularly effective in sheltered areas with 'ceilings' of trees or awnings overhead. It is not so effective in windswept locations. The T.R.R.L. have monitored pioneer schemes on roads in this country and note that costs are still high – many times the cost of chemical treatment for ice and snow. The usual method is to have embedded electrical coils. These may be at mains voltage with insulation cable, or at low voltage with uninsulated steel mesh conductors through transformers. Power required is 100/130 watts m² for sheltered areas to 150/200 watts m² in exposed areas. Embedded pipes with heated fluid have been used in the U.S.A. for roads but are really only suitable for pedestrian areas.

4.4 Trim and changes of level

Nothing can enhance or destroy the character of a paved area so much as its 'trim' or edge detailing. Trim should therefore be carefully chosen to accord with the character of pavings and their surroundings, urban, suburban or rural. Far too many inappropriate details appear especially in the use of heavy 'town' kerbs in village roads.

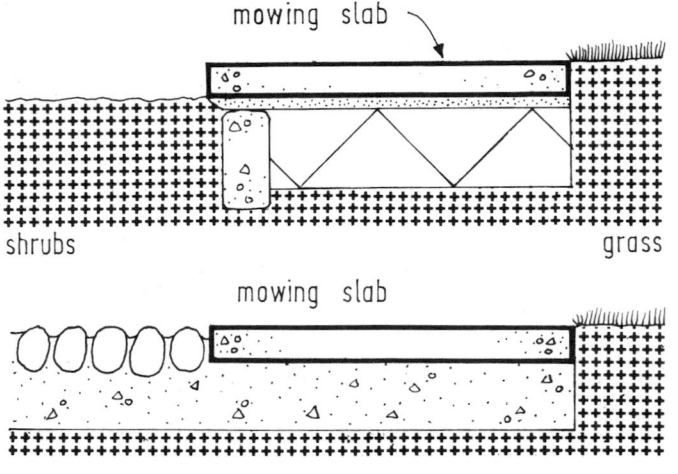

Fig. 4.9. MOWING STRIPS – Necessary at edges of paved areas and desirable against walls. Slabs can be of stone or concrete.

4.4.1 Functions of trim

Kerbs and edgings are needed to prevent lateral spread of flexible paving. They denote changes of level and can provide hazards, physical and psychological – especially to indicate segregation of pedestrians and vehicles. Boundary definition may be required. It need not be continuous, but act as a reminder especially under water or snow. Surface water drainage is often taken to margins and these are clearly visible either as raised kerbs or depressed channels. Mowing margins 25 mm (approx. 1 in) below grass level are provided as an aid to easy maintenance (Fig. 4.9). Junctions of materials generally are

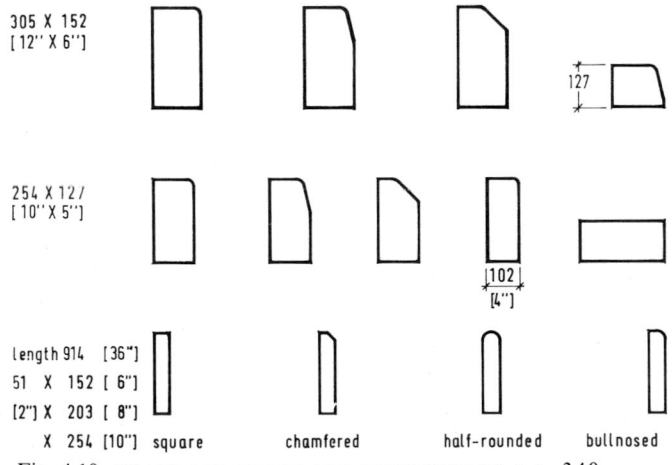

Fig. 4.10. STANDARD KERBS AND CHANNELS TO B.S. 340.

best detailed by inclusion of a joining or insulating strip or 'trim'.

4.4.2 Types of trim

The many types of trim include those proud of surface, flush or depressed and may be continuous or intermittent. Materials must be durable for all purposes: granite, sandstone, precast concrete (heavy or thin), brick. For kerbs only: timber edging, metal trim, stone slabs on edge, stones and boulders for intermittent spacing. For flush and depressed trim only; various stones, slabs, setts, cobbles, asphalt, concrete and loose materials including gravel cobbles, ballast. Other forms of trim include: low walls, fences or rails (see Chapter 5 – Enclosure).

Kerbs and channels conform to B.S. 340 (precast concrete), B.S. 435 (granite and whinstone), and B.S. 706 (sandstone). These B.S.'s are old and all are still in imperial dimensions (with exact metric equivalents only)

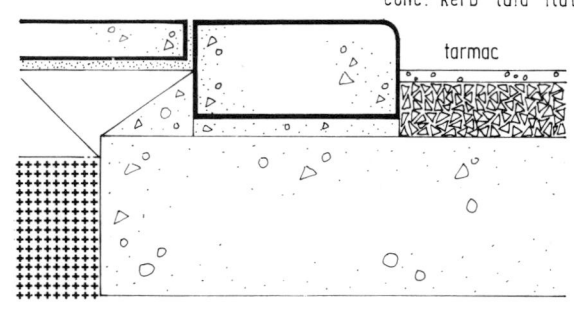

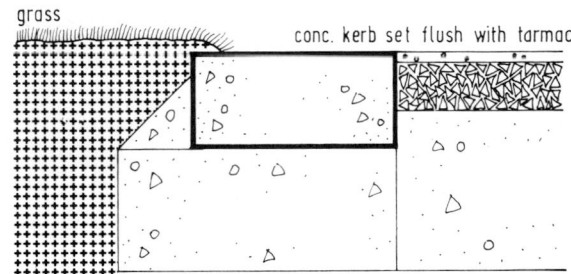

Fig. 4.11. FLUSH KERB – Contains the flexible surfacing while the grass provides an informal edging.

and are consequently difficult to work in with metricated paving slabs.

Raised kerbs are used mainly for roads, but elsewhere as character dictates. *Granite and whinstone* are good and really tough, but can cost three times as much as precast concrete, so are now used only in special circumstances. Finishes range from fine to rough, in rectangular sections of minimum length 500 mm (say 1 ft 9 in), 100–300 mm

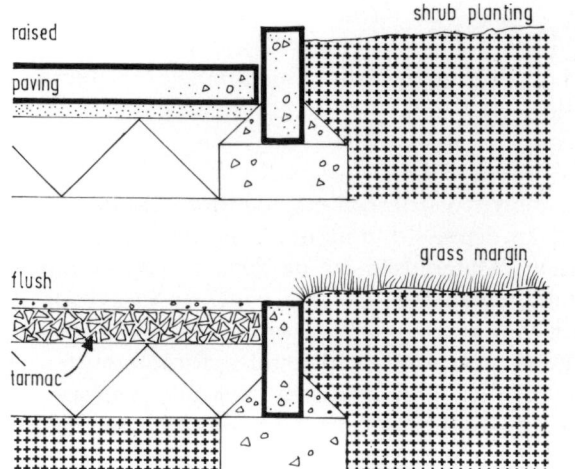

Fig. 4.12. TRIM – Standard 50 × 150 mm edging. The details show an upstand kerb to retain planting and a flush kerb recessed below grass border.

(4–12 in) wide × 150–300 (6–12 in) depth. *Sandstone* sizes are generally as granite, but longer sections are more readily available. *Precast concrete* is popular and relatively cheap. It has a natural finish, smooth and creamy, which can be improved and still be much cheaper than granite. Square and splayed sections in 610–914 mm (2–3 ft) lengths to sizes shown in Fig. 4.10. Reconstructed granite kerb made of granite aggregate and tooled to resemble the natural material is available at half the price of granite. Flush kerbs (Fig. 4.11) to roads and driveways give a much better appearance, and are available in the above materials and lengths but splayed kerbs if laid flat will need *in situ* concrete kerbs at curves to match. Mean-looking but cheap 51 mm (approx. 2 in) wide precast concrete edgings are available as trim to contain gravel and tarmac paths and their bases (Fig. 4.12). Setts or other flat-laid trim give much better appearance but at higher cost.

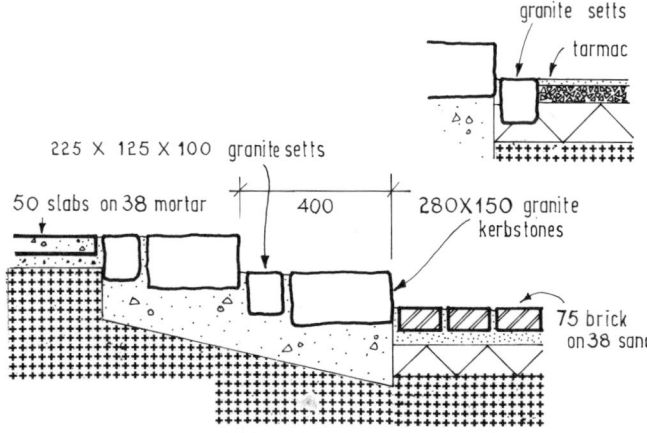

Fig. 4.13. STEPS – Secondhand materials, including those found on site, can often be incorporated in constructional detailing. The example shows steps formed from granite setts and road kerbs.

4.4.3 Changes of level

The potentialities of exploiting changes of level are limitless; retaining walls, paved banks, steeply sloping steps, wide sweeping flights of steps with spacious landings, gently curving ramps or perrons. (See Chapter 5 for retaining walls and banks.) Due to the greatly increased sense of scale outdoors, widths and goings of stairs and ramps must be as large as possible in the context of the adjoining landscape, especially so where overhanging or encroaching planting is envisaged.

Steps. These can be solid, sculptural, floating or cantilevered; or be in the form of a plinth. Domestic scales for the angle of descent are generally inappropriate although a really steep flight can have a character of its own. Favourite formulae are $R \times \text{Tread} = 1.9$ m (75 in), and $2R + \text{Tread} = 685$ mm (27 in) and a 110 mm ($4\frac{1}{2}$ in) riser are suggested for a leisurely ascent, while a 300 mm

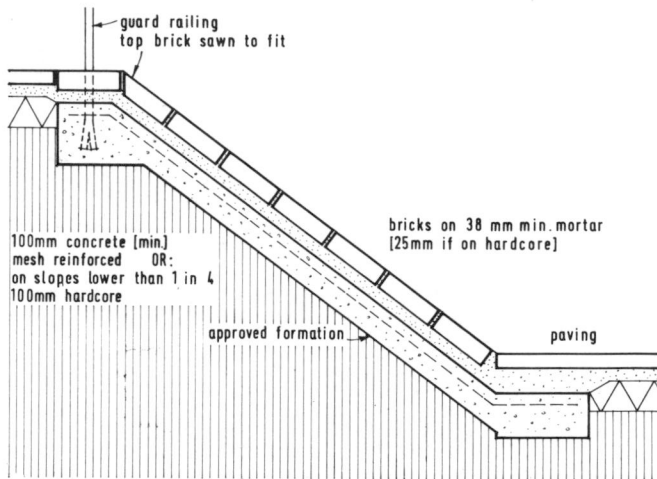

Fig. 4.14. BRICK BANK – Section illustrating brick paving on a bank.

(12 in) tread is a normal minimum for external use. It is generally accepted that three steps are the minimum for a flight but innumerable examples of safe single steps exist in obvious places at changes in paving functions as at road kerbs. Long flights of steps should be broken up into flights of say 10–14 steps, with generous landings.

Construction can be of reinforced or mass concrete (stiff broom or hand tamped finish for slip resistance), concrete slabs on brick or concrete risers, or of macadam, gravel, etc., surfaces with timber risers. Treads can also be of concrete, concrete paving slabs, setts, stone, brick, slate or even timber. Materials should be chosen with care as steps are a hard test for any material. Of stones, yorkstone is probably the best for the purpose. Non-slip inserts of carborundum can improve the slip resistance of concrete steps. Projections and depths of nosings or overhangs should be generous.

Ramped steps or perrons. These can be useful on a long slope as they enable a steady ascent. Allow for three paces to each tread while risers and nosing should be clearly marked. Maximum incline should not exceed 1:12 and risers should not exceed 100 mm (4 in) if people with prams are to use it.

Ramps. An angle of 1:10 is the usual maximum up which prams or wheelchairs can be pushed, although 1:12 is preferable. It is also the critical limit for reasonable safety in icy conditions although electric heating (see 4.3.6) may be used in important locations and a gradient of 1:7 is negotiable for very short stretches. Many methods are available for non-slip surfaces; ruled, gridded or other patterns in concrete, crimping roller for concrete and tarmac, and special non-slip pavings. Drainage is vital and any pattern should shed water sideways gently to recessed gutters for collection in channel gratings or gullies. Ramps may also be placed alongside short easy flights of steps particularly for the use of disabled persons and prams (preferred maximum 1:12 slope and 1·2 m (4 ft) minimum width). (Cf. Access for disabled required by *Chronically Sick and Disabled Persons Act 1970*.)

4.5 Planting in paved areas

4.5.1 Selection of planting positions
The check list in Table 4.4 covers some general points to note in selecting and designing planting positions in paved areas. Some solutions to overcome local difficulties are suggested.

4.5.2 Trees
Existing trees. Many established trees in paved areas can exist without irrigation as they still continue to collect nourishment from underground water from other catchment areas percolating through the subsoil. Where paving is lower than the tree allow ample room for roots, with good irrigation; where paving is raised make up level with washed gravel or with vertical drains round it to original level.

New trees. For these, adequate watering, staking and tree guards are essential, while tree trunks should be wrapped with water-miscible plastic to prevent excess transpiration due to reflected heat from paving.

Choice of trees for paved areas. Names are listed in reputable catalogues and other books under headings for 'Town and smoky localities', 'Street trees', 'Plants for shady places'. Note that these lists are only a guide to be interpreted with great care and discretion taking full account of local conditions. Lists commonly err towards normal town conditions and seldom deal with adverse conditions found in some heavily polluted urban areas, or heavily trafficked areas exposed to petrol and diesel fumes. The best guide is to examine any available site evidence which shows what is already growing there, and note whether it is thriving, growing or just struggling. Do not select those trees with excessive leaf fall, branch shedding characteristics, such as elms and, in clay soils, those with voracious rooting and suckering systems such as poplars and willows. Soils have a marked influence on selection. They vary from shrinkable clays, where planting should be kept clear of buildings and pavings where drainage pockets can be troublesome, to the other extreme of light sandy soils where trees can be placed close to pavings and services but will need extra irrigation to counteract rapid drainage.

4.5.3 Shrubs and ground cover planting
Artificial soil conditions are easily provided for smaller planting at paving level, in raised beds, in plant boxes or containers with a minimum height of 150–225 mm (approx. 6–9 in). Care is needed in positioning, and in particular to avoid north-east winds. Flush planting is easily introduced into path edges, crevices in steps, etc., but raised beds with kerbs are much less vulnerable to damage and litter. With ground cover or alpine plants, the kerb height should be sufficient to allow for plant overhang. For dwarf shrubs and conifers, excavate plant holes to a depth of 450–600 mm (1 ft 6 in–2 ft) and backfill with good soil, giving each plant a 600 mm (2 ft) square station, then lay paving with 225–300 mm (approx. 9–12 in) aperture at the plant positions. This allows room for plant feeding below the paving.

4.5.4 Drainage and irrigation
A correct water balance is vital for plants. In paving, planting is unnaturally constricted and artificial methods are necessary to ensure sound growth. Ideally water should stay long enough in the root area to nourish the roots before percolating slowly into the subsoil. Where conditions do not allow this, drainage is necessary to prevent 'ponding' of stagnant water. In impervious clay subsoil further excavation and filling with washed ballast may be necessary. Always crown bottoms to fall to land drains laid around the circumference with vertical drains or outlets to catchment areas; there must be adequate safeguards against poisonous substances (see section 4.5.1).

Natural water supply. Extra run-off from paving can be channelled to planting areas, while unsealed gravel, cobbles or gravel rejects form an excellent paving

TABLE 4.4

Problem	Solution
Frost pockets occur in low areas without air drainage.	Leave gaps in enclosing walls.
Draught funnels – All too common amongst tall buildings.	Use wind hardy plants and avoid north east draughts. Use permanent or temporary screens for establishment.
Waterlogged areas – Often in clay or peaty areas.	Provide drainage or use raised beds.
Vandalism – Normally experienced in towns and can be acute in housing areas.	Use grouped planting away from access points, tough, spiny plants, and heavy standard trees rather than saplings. Good staking and tree guards will help.
Excessive drying out – Urban areas are usually warmer than country. Intensified by heat storage and reflective qualities of paving, isolated trees dry out quicker; growth is advanced and more exposed to damage by spring winds or frost.	Use darker colour and less reflective pavings. Seek or provide shelter. Protective wrappings for delicate plants and young tree trunks. Transpiration retarders, spraying and irrigation are needed during the establishment period.
Overshadowing by buildings. *Atmospheric pollution* – Direct by solids and sulphur, also diesel and petrol fumes; and indirect by light restriction.	Use shade bearing plants. Use plants which are known for their resistance to urban conditions.* Avoid conifers.
Run-off pollution from paved areas – Salt, petrol, oil, tar, soapy water, etc.	Use kerbs, and provide proper traps or interceptors if the water is used for irrigation.
Drip from overhead cables – Copper wires.	Avoid these positions.
Gas main leaks – Even a small one caused by traffic vibrations can be harmful.	Oxygenation necessary – pump in compressed air. Repair pipe and replant as necessary.
Animals – Urination, scratching and digging.	Design for relative inaccessibility.
Root restriction and amputation – Due to hard pavings and excavations for trenches, services and buildings.	Careful planning of pipes and planting. Leave ventilation spaces in paving.

* 'Plants and Air Pollution', P. J. W. Saunders and C. M. Wood, *Landscape Design*, February 1974, pp. 28–30.

around trees. Treated with non-penetrative weedkiller it is neat and simple and allows air and water to penetrate. Trees, in fact, offer a difficult problem as their catchment area extends around the perimeter of their spreads. Open joints can be left in paving or filled with weak mortar or sand, although slight frost heave may result with minor undulations appearing. In impervious pavings, use cast iron or precast concrete tree grids or slotted bricks laid flush with the surrounding paving. These can be linked by open or storm drains to even out water intake. Paving slabs or bricks with holes or grilles are useful around tree perimeters where the roots get their nourishment.

Artificial water supply. This is often necessary especially due to excessive evaporation and overheating of tree roots through shallow pavings. Comprehensive irrigation schemes for planting would include time-controlled sprinklers for small planting and outlets for shrubs and trees. At the other end of the scale a tree grid can be lifted out, a shallow saucer scooped out in the soil and 100–200 litres of water run slowly in. For smaller plants, adequate water is necessary for the first year after planting but after establishment in suitable conditions, most alpines and conifers will thrive quite happily with only occasional watering.

Bibliography

'The Delight of a City', George Perkin, *Concrete Quarterly*, No. 99, Oct.–Dec. 1973.

Design and Detail of Space Between Buildings, Elisabeth Beazley, Architectural Press.

Specification, Sections on Roads, Landscape and Floors, ed. D. Harrison, Architectural Press.

Spons' Landscape Price Book, Derek Lovejoy and Partners, E. & F. N. Spon.

Handbook of Urban Landscape, ed. Clifford Tandy, Architectural Press.

Hard Landscaping in Concrete, M. Gage, Architectural Press.

5 Enclosure
FREDERICK GIBBERD

5.1 Need for enclosure

5.1.1 Function and materials

Enclosure means to shut in and the technical need for it is to give security, privacy or shelter. These functions are provided by a physical barrier, a visual barrier, or both. It is important to recognise that there can be a fundamental difference between visual and physical barriers. With the former the object is to conceal the view; it is a process of space-defining and therefore a raw material of the art of landscape design. With the latter, the problem is the relatively simple one of providing a physical obstruction. Shelter from the elements is a by-product of visual barriers but it also exists in its own right, as in tree planting for a wind break.

There are two broad groups of materials, plants and man-made structures. Plants, being organic, provide enclosure which is constantly changing in form, colour and texture; with artifacts there is no modification of form and the only changes that may take place are surface ones of texture and colour, through processes of weathering or the application of colour. Plants cannot be left unattended and if their form has been shaped, as in a hedge, there must be periodic attention by clipping, pruning or training but man-made structures can require very little maintenance – granite bollards, a brick wall. Plants are most often chosen for their aesthetic effect, or for man's innate love of growing things but a whole range of man-made structures, like fences, are used solely for functional reasons – which is not to say that they must not be beautiful objects in themselves. As barriers formed by natural materials may take some time to establish, the two groups are sometimes combined, as when a hedge is planted against a chain link fence. The design choice for either of these two groups is determined, in the first place, by considering the functional requirements – what is required of the barrier and what its life should be – the amount of money available for the job and the maintenance necessary which has, of course, to be balanced against the initial cost. Since man is conscious of the appearance of things, the functional solution needs also to be considered in terms of appearance, both of the object itself and the object in relationship to the environment as a whole. This aesthetic choice is largely based on intuition and experience but unfortunately trained designers are seldom involved. In the past, with its limited range of materials and craft techniques, this did not matter, but today the complexities of materials and construction make it imperative that the trained designer should be involved in choosing or designing the method of enclosure; that he is seldom so involved largely accounts for the chaotic appearance of the visual scene.

5.1.2 Physical enclosure

The design basis for a physical barrier is its function and the objective must be to perform it with the least possible material. It is necessary, therefore, to be quite clear what kind, or kinds of access it is being erected to prevent – if, for example, a barrier is to be erected to prevent a car running off a carriageway, must it also exclude dogs? The answers to these questions can produce such widely different solutions as a bollard or tubular steel rails filled with chain-link. Whilst the function of barriers is to prevent access, they are also used to delineate property ownership and, as such, are debased structures. The Englishman's over-developed sense of privacy and sense of personal property has given him a passion for enclosure and the scene suffers from a superfluity of barriers. In addition, design is often over-emphatic or over-elaborate, thereby causing unnecessary disturbance to the view. It is not always appreciated that physical barriers are possible as minor incidents such as bollards, or with no disturbance at all, such as the ha-ha.

5.1.3 Visual enclosure

Visual barriers have the simple functional use of concealing the view of an object, either to give privacy or to hide the object from the scene but they have a much wider and more fundamental use which is that of space defining. Visual barriers can enclose spaces for particular functions and make of them particular places in a far greater degree than can a physical barrier – thus, a fence round a bowling green will keep people off it but a hedge, by visual enclosure, makes it an environment, a room, with its own identity. In their wider use as space-defining objects, visual barriers are one of the raw materials of

81

landscape design. As such, they have an unlimited range of application from large-scale landscape design, where trees can be combined with land forms to make broad spatial compositions; through urban design, where visual barriers can be an extension of architecture to create the different space zones of a town; to the formation of small-scale intimate local spaces, as in garden design.

5.2 Plants for enclosure

5.2.1 Types and qualities

Plants are primarily used for visual enclosure and for shelter; as physical barriers they are limited to hedges, used as an alternative to fences or walls. Their choice over artifacts is because of their association with other organic material (field hedges), because of the desire to obtain contrast between the works of man and nature (a tree screen behind architecture), or simply because of man's love of natural things. Being organic, plants present the problems of growth and time; the time interval before they are either effective visual or physical barriers and the limited length of life before they need to be replanted. They may, in some instances, involve considerable maintenance costs, as their form is only constant when clipped, pruned or trained. Of the two broad groups, evergreen and deciduous, the choice, planting conditions being similar, is primarily aesthetic. Evergreen plants give the most complete visual enclosure, except in broad-scale or dense planting, such as wood or copse. Deciduous plants provide complete changes of form, colour and texture over the seasons; they are often abhorred by those responsible for the upkeep of the urban scene because falling leaves have to be disposed of; but this is no reason for depriving the townsman of his right to enjoy one of nature's most remarkable gifts. Evergreen and deciduous plants used for enclosure can be placed in three broad groups; trees, shrubs and hedges; and there is a vast range of material to choose from. The first selective processes are ecological ones, as set out in Chapter 8 – Planting Techniques, section 8.3.2. Beyond this, limiting the species to those that are indigenous to the district will preserve the character of the environment. If new species are required, the selection will be based on those that give the most effective enclosure; functional expression is the objective. Beyond this it is largely a matter of the composition of the landscape; should the hedge unobtrusively follow the contours of the landscape? – may a tree screen break the silhouette? – and so on. Each design poses its own particular set of problems and only by asking the most searching questions will the pitfalls of decoration be avoided.

Plate 5.1. A hedge clipped to take on the architectural character of a wall.

5.2.2 Trees

The use of trees for enclosure falls into three broad groups: space defining, screening against view and screening against wind. Space-defining is the art of landscape enclosure, and trees combined with land form, are its raw materials. The subject is dealt with elsewhere in this book (Chapter 2 – Site Planning, and Chapter 10 – Tree Planting) and mention must be made of an admirable book, *Trees for Town and Country* (Lund Humphries). Tree screening to hide ugly structures of disfigured landscape, like planting for visual enclosure, is primarily an aesthetic problem and little need be said here, except to mention that there are many alternatives to the common technique of masking the object with a row of fast-growing trees, like Lombardy poplars, close against the boundary. Thus trees may be used to distract attention from the unpleasant view; they may be planted close to the view point, to cut out the prospect – the nearer the trees are to the view point, the greater will be the effect – and the species can be selected to have a formal relationship to the object to be obscured. Shelter belts or wind breaks are formed by belts of trees singly or in systems or by small blocks of trees of various shapes. The effect of the wind break is to reduce the surface wind velocity to the leeward of the belt and partly to the windward. The barrier deflects the on-coming air stream upwards and accelerates it somewhat but eventually the original pattern of wind velocity is re-established at ground level, at a distance of about thirty times the height of the barrier. If the barrier is solid, air currents from the main flow may be drawn downwards to cause vigorous eddies within 3 to 4·5 m (approx. 10 to 15 ft) of the barrier; on the other hand, if some wind can penetrate the shelter belt, it will reduce the turbulence and the airstream deflected over the top will re-establish itself more gradually. The degree of permeability which achieves optimum shelter has been established at about 40%. With agricultural land the shelter falls into three broad categories: arable areas, upland pastures and exposed grazing. Each type has its own problems and reference should be made to *Shelter Belts for Farmland* (Leaflet 15, Ministry of Agriculture, Fisheries and Food) which deals most thoroughly with the subject.

5.2.3 Hedges

Hedges are the alternative to fences for physical enclosure and to walls for both physical and visual enclosure. As wind breaks they are more effective than solid walls because they are permeable. Hedges are the complement of trees and land shaping in the art of landscape enclosure; they largely provide the English agricultural field pattern resulting from the Enclosure Acts of the seventeenth and eighteenth centuries; in town design

they define space for different functional uses – such as playing fields and in gardens they provide the partitions and dividing screens which give the design structure. As with trees, the choice is a very wide one indeed and is based on the considerations outlined elsewhere (see Chapter 8 – Planting Techniques). Hedges that are to provide a physical barrier are generally strong-growing plants with thorns, those that are to form a visual screen tend to be evergreens; and those that are to be windbreaks are sturdy and dense in growth. It is of importance to consider the appearance of the hedge as a whole rather than as a series of individual plants – a beech hedge is a very different thing from a beech tree and, as with the grouping of different species of trees in a clump, hedging plants may be combined to give variety in colour and texture throughout the year – tapestry hedges. Thus beech, combined with holly and yew, will have contrast between the three different species and the contrast will differ in the winter from the summer, when the beech leaves turn brown. J. L. Beddall has made a useful study of hedging, *Hedges for Farm and Garden* (Faber and Faber). The following are the more common types.

5.2.4 Evergreen hedges

Yew (*Taxus baccata*), 'the aristocrat of hedging plants'. Strong, compact growth and dense texture make possible shaping into precise forms that may, on the one hand, take on the architectural character of walls or, on the other, the exuberance of topiary work (Plate 5.1). Its sombre dark colour makes a beautiful contrast with ground covers such as grass and pavings and a fine background for flowers. The disadvantages are cost and slow growth, 1 m (approx. 3 ft) in five years. The latter may be overcome by double planting with a cheap, quick-growing hedge such as *Lonicera nitida*, which is subsequently grubbed up. Holly (*Ilex aquifolium*) has characteristics

Plate 5.2. A random rubble retaining wall.

Plate 5.3. A coursed stone retaining wall surmounted by a hedge.

other types, *Cupressus macrocarpa* and *Escallonia macrantha* may be mentioned for their resistance to wind on the south coast but are not hardy in the north.

5.2.5 Deciduous hedges

Quickthorn (*Crataegus oxycantha*), said to be introduced by the Romans, provides a tough, impenetrable fence for field enclosure and is an integral part of the English agricultural scene. Large scale, mechanised farming and the high cost of maintenance is resulting in many miles being grubbed up with loss of shelter for crops, animals and wild life. Two deciduous species of particular value as visual screens, because they retain their leaves in winter, are beech (*Fagus sylvatica*) and hornbeam (*Carpinus betulus*). Both are slow starters but make a fine hedge up to 6 m (approx. 20 ft). Of similar appearance, the winter leaves of beech give a warmer brown colour. Beech does well on light and chalky soils and hornbeam will often succeed where the former is unsatisfactory, as on heavy clay.

5.2.6 Decorative hedges

A very wide choice of plants for decorative hedges can be found under the broad headings: coloured stems for winter effect; leaf colour; autumn foliage; berries and fruiting; and flower colour. J. L. Beddall again gives a wealth of advice in *Colour in Hedges* (Faber and Faber). Most of the plants are more closely associated with garden rather than landscape design. Typical evergreen decorative hedges are laurustinus (*Viburnum tinus*), with attractive winter flowers; barberry (*Berberis stenophylla*) for a dense informal hedge up to 3 m (approx. 10 ft) with yellow flowers in spring; *Cotoneaster salicifolia* for a good tall hedge with red berries in autumn. Of the deciduous types, *Cotoneaster simonsii* can be trimmed to narrow width, has tinted foliage and vermilion berries in autumn; *Philadelphus* has single or double white flowers, for informal hedges; and a whole range of roses, the more robust of which, such as *Hugonis*, *Canina*, musks and rugosas will withstand children and dogs.

of yew of close texture, slow compact growth and high cost and it forms an excellent alternative. It is not so dense and has the particular qualities of a shiny, light-reflecting leaf and, due to the leaf spikes, greater resistance to animals. Box (*Buxus sempervirens*) may be bracketed with yew and holly for its excellence but it has neither the sombre, light-absorbing qualities of yew, nor the shine of holly. Compact but slow growth makes it an expensive but excellent visual barrier. Privet (*Ligustrum ovalifolium*) makes a good barrier up to 3 m (approx. 10 ft) in exposed places but it is often considered to be less attractive than the previous examples, possibly because of its suburban associations: growth is moderate and it is a gross feeder; cost is reasonable. *Lonicera nitida* is characterised by its small-scale form, tiny leaves and rapid growth, 1·5 m (approx. 5 ft) in five years; it tends to straggle and become top-heavy, limiting its use to comparatively low hedges and, being both cheap in cost and fast in growth, it is useful for rapid effects. Of the many

5.3 Walls for enclosure

5.3.1 Types and functions

Walls for enclosure have the characteristic that they can form complete physical and visual barriers of very long life. They are an essential part of urban and village design but in open landscape they are only used as an alternative to fences and hedges in those districts where stone is found in abundance. The most impressive historic use for walls is for defence; not only is the fortified wall a splendid thing in itself but it draws a sharp distinction between town and countryside which subsequent generations have so far failed to achieve by mere legal definition. Walls for enclosure may be divided roughly into four

main types: (1) Walls higher than eye level, used to form a complete physical and visual barrier: they are often associated with architecture such as screen walls linking dwellings together and giving continuity of facade. (2) Walls for partial enclosure, below eye level in height but still providing visual obstruction, generally used as an alternative to hedges or fences, such as the eighteenth and nineteenth century rear garden wall. (3) Dwarf walls, where a strong physical barrier of architectural qualities is required as an alternative to trip fences or low hedging; they are often associated in design with pavings or combined with other barriers – a metal fence over a dwarf wall. (4) Retaining walls, used to form changes in level, either for formal reasons, as an alternative to land shaping, or for functional purposes, such as a cutting. The subject is a large one and those not familiar with building construction might consult Davies and Petty or W. B. McKay, for general information (see bibliography at end of chapter).

5.3.2 Rubble walling

Rubble walls, used as boundary fences, are a characteristic of those areas of the countryside where timber is scarce and stone readily available. There is a shortage of masons and stone walling is expensive but those who do use local stone have the satisfaction of making a construction that looks inevitable and one that will outlast by many years all other alternatives. It is encouraging that some authorities, like the Central Electricity Generating Board, advise their consultants that the question of cost should not preclude stone being considered where it is the obvious answer. Stone walling should never be imported for decorative purposes in an environment foreign to it – Cotswold stone for raised traffic islands or flower beds is a nauseating sentimentality. As the kinds of stone vary enormously (gritstones and shales of the north and Wales, the limestones of the Peaks and the Cotswolds, sandstones of the Midlands, granites of Cornwall) there are many different local building techniques. The general principles that apply to almost all of them are: that the walls are always built with a batter, or inward slope, of about 35 mm in each 300 mm ($1\frac{1}{2}$ in in each 12 in) of height; the foundations and courses are horizontal but a wall built on the slope is finished at the top to follow the contour of the land and care is taken to break the vertical joints. The core of the wall is gener-

ally packed with small stones, stone chippings and sometimes earth and long stones are used as ties across the wall. The bond is either random rubble, or random coursed, with some stones selected or roughly dressed into shape to allow coursing. The traditional dry wall is being largely replaced by mortar-jointed walling, as less skill and less stone are required. Rubble walling is built of stones, either irregular in shape or squared but not dressed to the same degree as ashlar and having comparatively thick joints. The subject is well described and illustrated in a British Standard Code of Practice (C.P. 121:201 (1951) Masonry Walls ashlared with natural or cast stone). (Fig. 5.1.)

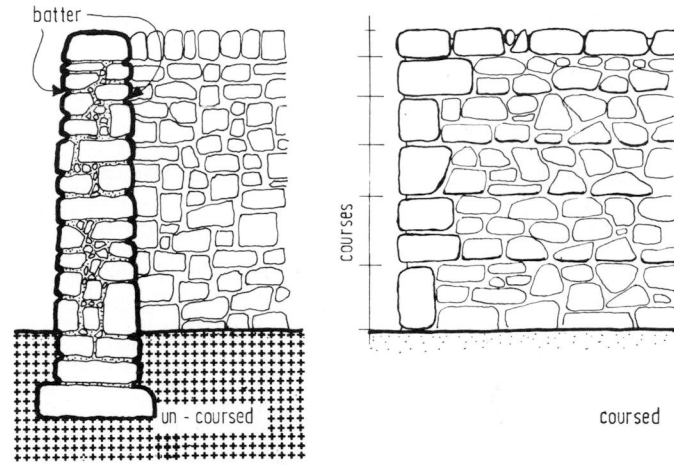

Fig. 5.1. RUBBLE WALL – Random and random coursed, showing batter and capping detail.

FREE-STANDING BRICK WALLS: CONSTRUCTIONAL DETAILS

	Thick-ness (mm)	Max. Height (m)	Piers		Expansion Joints		Mass Concrete Founds		Notes
			Size (mm)	Spacing (m)	Preferred Spacing (m)	Max. Spacing (m)	Min. Width (mm)	Min. Depth (mm)	
1	112	1·2	225 × 112	4·5	9	9	337	150	Expansion joint at every second pier position; 12 mm joint between 2 No. 225 × 112 mm piers
2	112	1·8	337 × 225	4	8	9	337	150	Expansion joint at every second pier position; 12 mm joint between 2 No. 225 × 225 mm piers
3	112	2·4	337 × 225	2·6	7·9	9	337	150	Expansion joint at every third pier position; 12 mm joint between 2 No. 225 × 225 mm piers
4	225	1·8	—	—	6	9	675	225	
5	337	2·75	—	—	6	9	1,012	337	

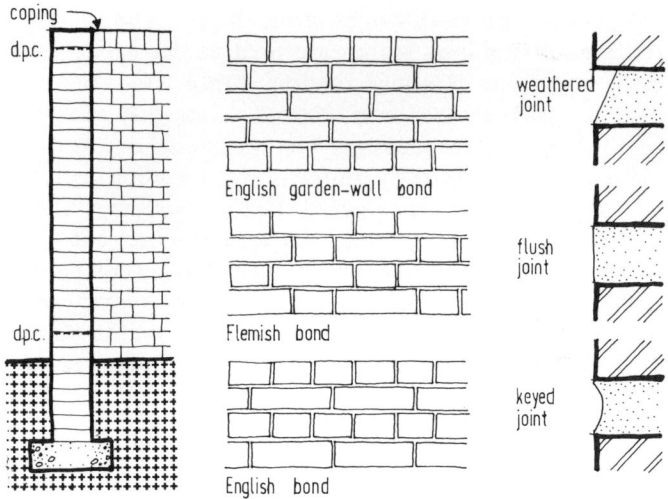

Fig. 5.2. BRICK WALL – Various bonds and jointing details are shown, together with capping, foundation and d.p.c. details.

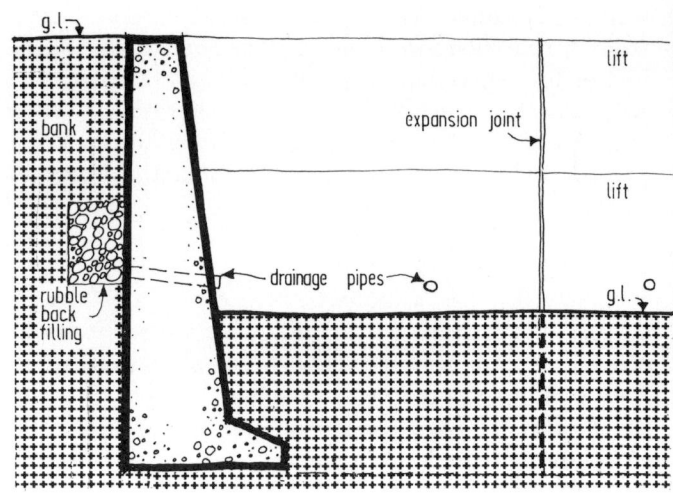

Fig. 5.3. MASS CONCRETE RETAINING WALL – Note the rubble backfill and provision of drainage pipes.

5.3.3 Brick walls

Brick walls are covered by a Code of Practice (C.P. 121:101 (1951) Brickwork). Being composed of small prefabricated units laid in horizontal courses, they are less flexible in form than stone. In particular, they cannot take up changes in level without stepping the top of the wall which means they cannot 'flow' with the land form, as can stone walls or hedges and so, apart from their association with farm buildings, they are an urban building form. The appearance of a brick wall is dependent on the colour and texture of the brick itself, the type of mortar joint and the bond. The days when it was impossible to use an ugly brick are over and very great care is needed in the choice of modern machine-made varieties, as eccentric textures, unpleasant arrises and fierce colours are common. If costs are so tight that a reasonable brick cannot be specified, it is better to turn to some other material. The aim in design should be to get a direct and simple expression. Joints should preferably be in lime-cement mortar as there is a wider colour range and less shrinkage and cracking than with cement alone; the finish can be with a bucket handle or wiped over with a rag; pointing, or special architectural effects, such as raking out the horizontal joints for emphasis, will seldom tell in a landscape scene. Similarly, with bonding, complicated patterns are seldom worth the trouble and expense. Flemish bond, with headers and stretchers alternating in each course, is generally less monotonous in appearance than the alternating courses of headers and stretchers of English bond; an alternative is English garden wall bond, where a course of headers alternates with two to five courses of stretchers. The table opposite sets out construction detail for free-standing brick walls under normal conditions. The expansion joint referred to is a continuous vertical joint filled with a material like bitu-

menised canefibre to allow compression and decompression without permanent deformation. A damp-proof course (B.S. 743:1970) must be provided at a minimum of 150 mm (approx. 6 in) above ground level and one is advisable immediately beneath the coping (Fig. 5.2).

5.3.4 Concrete walls

Concrete walls can be divided into two broad groups: *in situ* and block. *In situ* walls seldom occur in landscape design except as retaining walls, owing to the comparatively high cost of shuttering. Block walls are of three main varieties: (1) plain blocks (B.S. 2028, 1,364:1968), which have a comparatively smooth grey concrete surface, suitable for use in open countryside (say, farm buildings); (2) profiled blocks, in which the block is cast in a mould to give it an irregular surface, either to a geometric pattern or one reminiscent of natural materials, 'rock-face' – their advantage over plain blocks is that marking from atmospheric pollution is not so visible; (3) exposed aggregate blocks composed of aggregates chosen for their colour and texture which are exposed by removing the cement skin – their advantage over the two previous types is that as the greater part of the surface is of a natural material, the block weathers well, the blocks are normally only faced on one side, their chief use being in cavity wall construction or as permanent shuttering to *in situ* concrete walls. Plain concrete blocks are normally 450 mm × 225 mm × 100 mm, 150 mm or 200 mm (approx. 18 in × 9 in × 4 in, 6 in or 8 in) thick but profiled and exposed aggregate blocks vary in size with different manufacturers.

5.3.5 Retaining walls

Retaining walls set the following problems: the construction of the wall itself to withstand the earth pressure,

Plate 5.4. HARLOW CIVIC CENTRE – London stock 9 in brick walls with heavy concrete coping, between water garden and town hall forecourt. The same detail is repeated in the dwarf walls in the foreground. Architect: Sir Frederick Gibberd.

the expansion of the wall along its length, and the drainage of moisture from the retained earth. Most forms of block construction are suitable for retaining walls but where there is considerable earth pressure (as in a cutting), concrete either *in situ* or reinforced is tending to supersede traditional materials like blue brick or granite blocks, because of the cost. In all but the simplest structures, the advice of a consulting engineer should be sought on design. As a rough guide for a simple retaining wall, say 2 m (approx. 6 ft) high, the wall in reinforced concrete will not be less than 150 mm (approx. 6 in) thick and in mass concrete 300 mm (approx. 12 in) thick. Walls of any length will require expansion joints whatever the material, e.g. a 300 mm (approx. 12 in) thick reinforced concrete wall 2 m (approx. 6 ft) high will require expansion joints at approximately 4·5 m (approx. 15 ft) centres. Drainage at the foot of the wall is normally achieved by back-filling with hardcore and providing weep holes through the wall – 75 mm or 150 mm (approx. 3 in or 6 in)

pots are a usual device (Fig. 5.3). Of considerable importance is the texture, uniformity and finish of the exposed wall. In a tall wall the design should recognise that there are horizontal junctions between lifts, otherwise there will be unsatisfactory making good and rubbing down. A textured surface will help to take up inconsistencies in construction and in weathering and so the use of rough board formwork shuttering, such as flat sawn Douglas fir, might be considered. The illustration (Plate 5.6) shows a retaining wall in engineering bricks with its expansion joint and clay drainage pot and a hard surface at the foot, to keep the design precise.

5.3.6 The ha-ha
The ha-ha, that unexpected ditch by which the eighteenth-century landscape architect was enabled to tear down the enclosing wall or hedge to let the garden extend into the countryside, is virtually a retaining wall sunk into the

87

Plate 5.5. Ha-ha wall being constructed of standard concrete blocks with alternating headers and stretchers laid to a slight batter.

exclude water from penetrating to the walling below. There are marked differences between copings used for the free-standing walls of enclosure and those used in buildings; the latter are designed to throw the water clear of the wall surface and are backed up by a waterproof membrane as no water can be allowed to penetrate the wall into the rooms of the building but neither of these factors is of great importance in, for instance, a garden wall.

Furthermore, as a wall is a simple and bold structure compared with a building, its coping needs to be simple and bold. If the coping as a design component can be omitted altogether, then so much the better; thus, random rubble stone walls look far more convincing when finished with the traditional methods of a top course of stones on edge, or stones roughly shaped to a batter. Similarly, brick walls can be finished with a course of brick on edge or the standard saddle-back or bull-nose brick, all of which will preserve the brick-like quality of the wall. Thin concrete copings generally look out of scale on most walls, unless they are in architectural context. Concrete copings can be satisfactory on low walls but if they project beyond the wall face they can easily be displaced and when thin tend to look mean; 75 mm (approx. 3 in) is probably the minimum thickness but there are many instances where a really robust section with a bold weathering will be far more in scale with the scene. The picture (Plate 5.7) shows a bold triangular-section pre-cast concrete coping to a dwarf wall enclosing a car park.

ground. It is not, as is generally supposed, an English invention but was devised by the French as a means of obtaining a *claire voie* of open countryside at the end of formal alleys.

The ditch is about 1·2 m (approx. 4 ft) deep with the wall on the garden side sloping down to its foot. The ground slope should not be more than 1 in 3 for ease of maintenance and the wall is to normal retaining wall construction described in the previous section. The illustration (Plate 5.5) shows a 1·2 m (approx. 4 ft) deep ha-ha construction from standard concrete blocks with alternating headers and stretchers laid to a slight batter, with the interstices filled with soil.

The ha-ha has been little used during the last century but the revival of large-scale landscape design, coupled with the modern inventions of muck-shifting machinery and ready-mixed concrete, make it a practical method of enclosure without visual obstruction.

5.3.7 Copings
The purpose of a coping is to finish the top of a wall and

Plate 5.6. Retaining wall in engineering brick, with expansion joint, drainage and hard surface at the foot of the wall.

5.4 Fences and railings

5.4.1 Types and choice

Fences and railings are used for so many different functions, they have defied classification. Their prime use is as a barrier, either an actual physical one or a deterrent to access; only a few types of fence, such as close-boarding, provide visual screening. There are three main groups, as follows: (1) unclimbable fences, generally vertical bar types, 1·2 m to 1·8 m (approx. 4 ft to 6 ft) high, which are difficult to get over; (2) boundary fences, the most common being post and wire and post and rail fences, seldom more than 1·2 m (approx. 4 ft) high, which form a barrier to animals and generally discourage

Plate 5.7. A bold triangular-section pre-cast concrete coping to a dwarf wall enclosing a car park.

access, mainly a rural type; (3) trip fences or rails which can be stepped over but which discourage access simply because they are there. Types of fences with special functions are traffic barriers, temporary fences, security fences and screens. The first question to be asked in considering the type of fence and rail to be used is whether it is necessary at all. There is a great deal of quite unnecessary fencing for the following reasons: the responsibilities that rest on local officials for public safety; the desire of lawyers and owners to have properties emphatically defined; and the dislike of the divided responsibility for the maintenance of fences that are jointly owned. These, together with the Englishman's passion for fencing for its own sake, are responsible for the kind of visual disorder that is illustrated in Plate 5.10 – this, it is to be noted, is in a new town where a positive attempt was made to prevent multiplication. Fences are largely standardised articles, prefabricated in sections or lengths and they are all the better for that; personal expression with secondary elements seldom helps the scene. The choice of fence is considered in the first place in terms of function, cost and maintenance. Particular aesthetic questions that need asking are – is it well-proportioned, is it simple and unfussy, will it fit happily into the ground shape, will its direction look inevitable, will its forms confuse the prospect and is it in character with the *genius loci*?

5.4.2 Strained wire or strained line wire

Strained wire fences (B.S. 1722: Part 3), are most commonly used in agriculture as a barrier against farm animals; as an urban form, they are limited to temporary fencing, generally associated with a hedge – as between rear gardens. The structural principle is to stretch wire between posts of wood, metal or concrete. There are innumerable ways of doing this, from wires fixed to rough and ready wood posts, to prefabricated proprietary systems where the materials are reduced to the minimum; but in all cases they depend for their efficiency on the tautness of the wire. With all post and wire fences the critical visual element is the post, for the wire is hardly seen and so, by comparison, throws the former into prominence. Heavy posts, or light-coloured posts, such as concrete, can cause great disturbance to a rural scene and thin timber or black-painted metal sections are preferable. The object in design is to reduce the structural members to the absolute minimum section compatible with keeping the wires taut; the lighter they are, the cheaper the cost and the better the appearance. Thus, instead of a fence with posts of equal thickness, there can be two sizes: main posts or straining posts, between which the wire is stretched and which are braced; and intermediate posts which keep the wires the right distance apart. A typical timber line wire farm fence (Fig. 5.4) will be 1·2 m high and have 150 × 150 mm straining post braced by 100 × 100 mm with 75 mm intermediate posts at 2·75 m centres. The wire is fixed by adjustable hook or eye bolts to the straining posts and by staples to the intermediate ones. Full constructional details of this and other types of farm fence are contained in the Ministry of Agriculture's admirable leaflets, *Permanent Farm Fences*, Ministry of Agriculture, Fisheries and Food, Leaflet No. 5. A further saving of material and labour can be effected by substituting droppers for some of the intermediate posts: these are light bars which are suspended between the wires to keep them apart without giving physical support. The droppers are light timber or metal sections and most proprietary line wire fencing systems adopt them. A development of the use of droppers is the 'spring dropper fence' (Fig. 5.5). Here the posts are placed as widely apart as possible (50 m (approx. 55 yd) is generally taken as the maximum) and the droppers are placed between them at 3·33 m (approx. 11 ft) centres. Such a fence is elastic and it is an ideal form for farm use as animals dislike anything which springs back when pushed or lifted and it has the

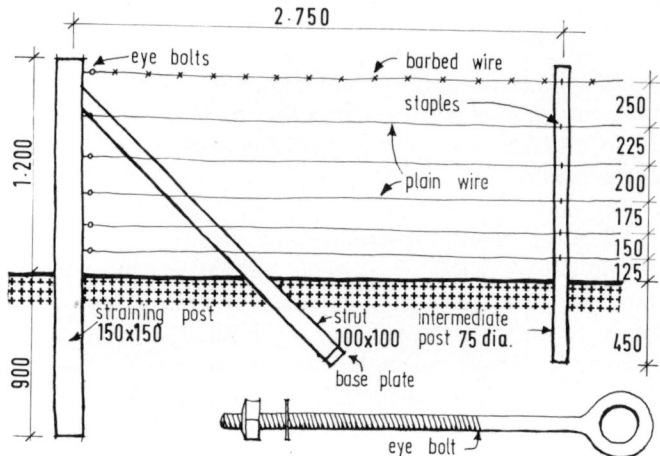

Fig. 5.4. STRAINED WIRE FENCE – Braced timber straining and intermediate posts; plain wire topped by barbed wire.

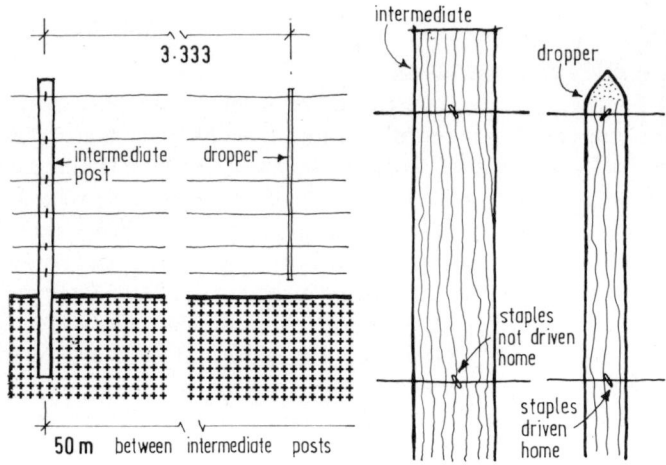

Fig. 5.5. SPRING DROPPER FENCE – This construction of wire fencing permits wide spacing between intermediate posts.

additional advantage that the farm worker can pass under it anywhere on its length – squeezing through line wires makes them sag in time.

5.4.3 Woven wire fences

Woven wire is a rectangular wire mesh in which the vertical wires act as droppers: in other words, it is a prefabricated strained wire fence (Fig. 5.6). The posts are the same as for line wire fences. So that the horizontal wires are all equally tight and the verticals perpendicular, they are attached to a metal stretcher bar, which is itself bolted to the straining post. The wires are so widely spaced that the fence looks light and open and has none of the mesh-like quality of chicken wire. It is not to be confused with the heavy diamond mesh of the chain link fence, to which it should be used in preference for all normal agricultural purposes. The fence is covered by B.S. 1722, Part 2.

5.4.4 Chain link fences

Woven chain link diamond mesh wire is the strongest and heaviest post and wire fence and the most objectionable in appearance. The height is from 1·2 m to 1·8 m (approx. 4 ft to 6 ft) and it is essentially a barrier fence because it is so difficult to scale. The structural system (B.S. 1722: Part 1) is similar to woven wire fences excepting that line wires are required to support the mesh. Posts are in metal or reinforced concrete, the latter being most clumsy, particularly the straining post. Chain link is seldom necessary for agricultural use but it has become a familiar part of the suburban or urban scene, as a cheap substitute for metal or wood barrier fences. It is one of the ugliest of modern inventions and, if it must be used, then it may be planted up with a hedge which will, in time, obscure the rusty mesh. There is a case for chain link as a security fence, because other alternatives are so costly. When used as such, the posts may be rolled mild steel angles or T's which, when painted black, make a lighter and more

homogeneous fence than concrete posts and rust stains will not be so visible. As an alternative, rectangular-section hollow tubes, with welded top caps, make a neat and tidy job. The mesh is normally galvanised mild steel which has a limited life (corrosion sets in, under most conditions, between 5 and 7 years), and for a more permanent job aluminium alloy, stainless steel or plastic-coated mild steel may be considered.

5.4.5 Wood post and rail

Posts and rails, 900 mm to 1·4 m (approx. 3 ft to 4 ft 6 in) high, of wood or metal, make a more permanent fence than posts and wire. They are a physical barrier against animals but the rails provide a convenient foothold for trespassers. Both wood and metal are used extensively in rural areas as boundary fencing and look an inevitable part of the scene (Plates 5.8 and 5.9), but neither is normally associated with urban building. The fences have a strong horizontal direction and it is important that the

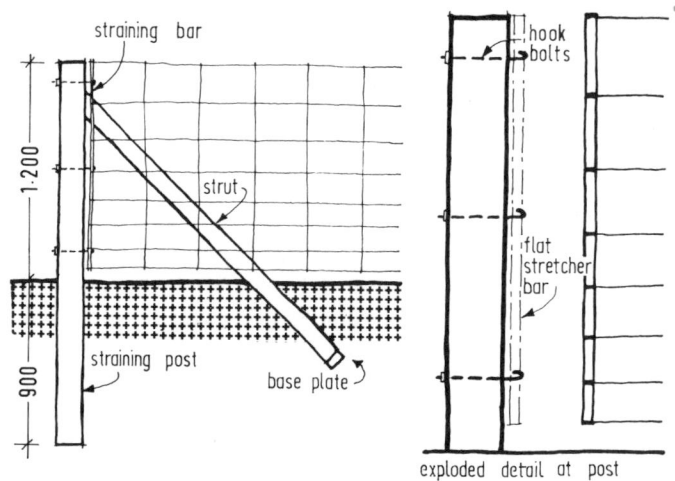

Fig. 5.6. WOVEN WIRE FENCE – A rectangular wire mesh fence.

Plate 5.8. Continuous metal bar estate fencing in a rural setting.

rails should follow the contours of the land. The traditional wood types have two or three horizontal rails supported by vertical posts sunk in the ground and projecting above the top rail (Fig. 5.7). The Ministry of Agriculture Leaflet No. 5 again gives valuable data and the construction is covered by a B.S. 1722: Part 7. Timbers which can be left in their natural state for posts in the ground are oak, larch and Spanish chestnut. Softwoods, such as Douglas fir and spruce, require preservatives. There is a variety of fixing methods, the simplest being nailing and, perhaps the most durable and best-looking, mortising; a compromise between the two is widely-spaced mortised posts with one or two lighter section nailed posts, 'prick posts', between them (Fig. 5.8). Metal straps, brackets or bolts for fixing tend to make the joint look over-elaborate and clumsy.

5.4.6 Metal continuous bar

Metal post and rail, or continuous bar fencing (B.S. 1722: Part 8) is an alternative to wood for boundary fencing in rural or open areas. It provides a much lighter and less obtrusive fence than wood with predominantly horizontal lines which reflect the shape of the land. The traditional type is of mild steel or wrought iron with round bars threaded through flat section standards. The commonest type today is prefabricated in 4·5 m (approx. 15 ft) lengths with joiner standards at each end and intermediate standards at 900 mm (approx. 3 ft) centres, the

top rail is round or square section and the lower rails flat, making a much stiffer structure than with round rails. Where greater strength is required the flat standards are replaced by T or H sections (Fig. 5.9).

5.4.7 Vertical bar railing

Vertical bar railings are panels of closely-spaced vertical mild steel bars held at the top and bottom by a flat rail; the panels are supported by standards at a maximum of 2·75 m (approx. 9 ft) centres. Heights are from 1·2 m to 2·1 m (approx. 4 ft to 7 ft) and the absence of horizontals

Fig. 5.7. WOOD POST AND RAIL FENCE.

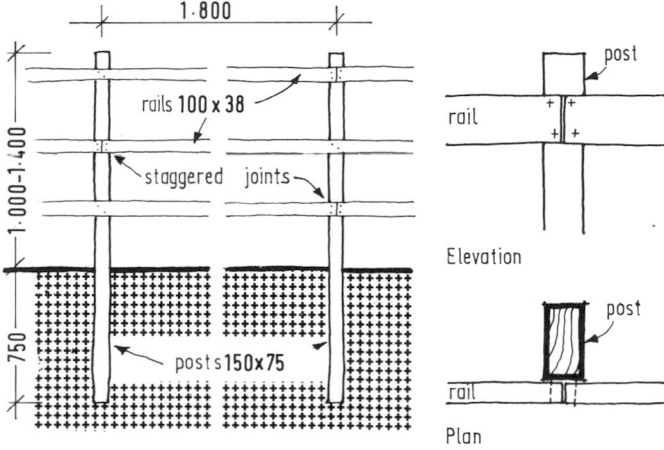

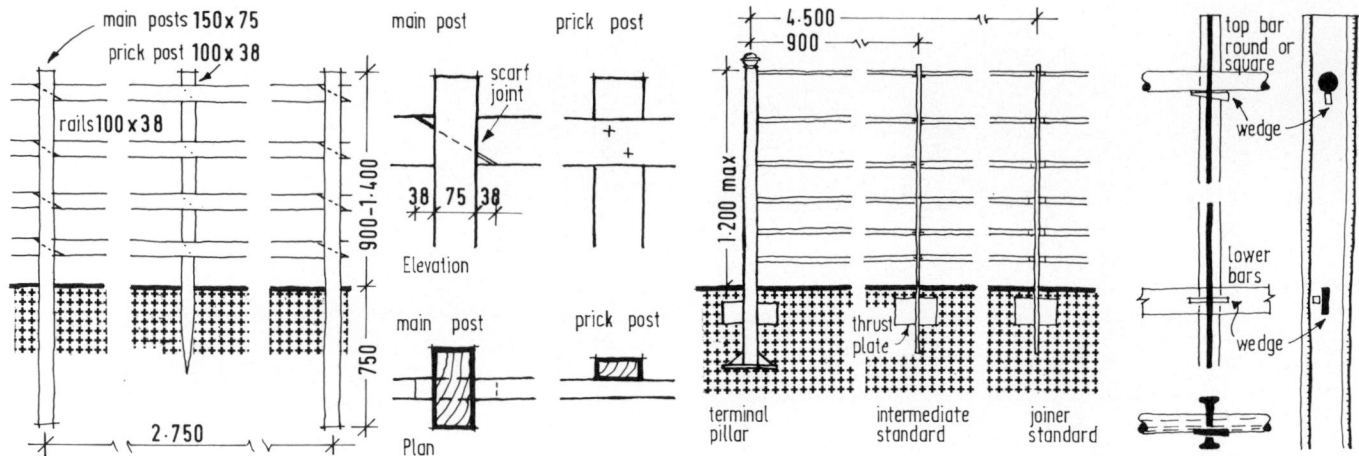

Fig. 5.8. WOOD POSTS WITH MORTISED RAILS.

Fig. 5.9. METAL CONTINUOUS BAR FENCE – A light horizontal bar fence.

for a foothold puts the fence into the category of unclimbable. The fences are covered by B.S. 1722: Part 9, with the laborious title of *Mild Steel or Wrought Iron Unclimbable Fences with Round or Square Verticals and Flat Standards and Horizontals*. The normal vertical bar fence is self-adjusting; that is, the bars are slotted through the horizontals, enabling the fence to follow the angle of the ground to a maximum gradient of 1:6. The fence is primarily urban in character and has its antecedents in the wrought iron railings of large town and country houses – public gardens or playing fields are typical modern usages. In the countryside it is seldom functionally necessary and when it is used it tends to look foreign because

of its strong verticality. There is a wide variety of design but the bars are generally at 125 mm (approx. 5 in) centres, of square or round sections. Decorative effects are obtained by treatment of the top of the bar; this is normally passed through the top rail and finished with a spike but blunt top bars are common (Fig. 5.10); a less effective but more friendly type has the bars bent over in semi-circular form, like a hairpin. Vertical bar fences are also made as rigid fences with the bars welded or riveted to the rails. They have to be manufactured to specified levels and are a less flexible and more 'architectural' fence – a common usage is over dwarf walls.

Plate 5.9. Timber post and rail fence.

Plate 5.10. A multiplication of fencing leading to visual disorder.

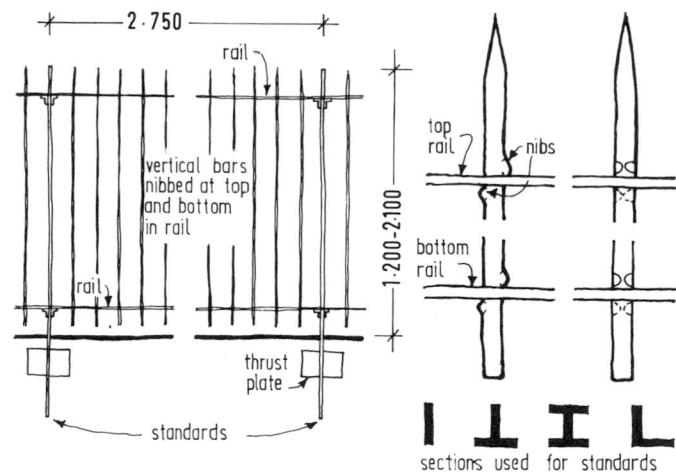

Fig. 5.10. VERTICAL BAR RAILING – Closely spaced vertical bars held at top and bottom by a flat rail.

5.4.8 Palisade fences

The traditional palisade fence is of wood and consists of closely spaced flat vertical sections spiked to top and bottom rails, supported by posts at about 2 m (approx. 6 ft 6 in) centres. It is a greater barrier than timber post and rail because there is little foothold and the projecting tops of the pales make it difficult to scale. Although coming into the category of an unclimbable fence, it is not as efficient as iron post and bar, as it is less strong and the spikes are not so formidable. The palisades vary from 100 mm × 25 mm to 75 mm × 25 mm (approx. 4 in × 1 in to 3 in × 1 in) and are generally spaced with the gaps slightly wider than the pales. The ease with which the tops can be shaped has resulted in all kinds of designs from rounded to spiked forms and this, together with the bold and rhythmical silhouette, gives the fence its decorative qualities. The fence is covered by B.S. 1722: Part 6 and, as it is difficult to produce a bad design, there are many satisfactory proprietary makes. The fence is essentially one of country associations and one of the many charms of the English village is the white-painted palisade fence made by local craftsmen (see Plates 5.14, 5.17, 5.18); whilst permissible in a suburban environment, it usually looks out of place in the town. The most satisfactory finish is white paint; green merges with the background and the rhythm and precision are lost; black looks heavy in large areas; and other colours tend to look 'arty'. Where a stronger palisade and one with less maintenance is required, proprietary concrete palisade fences are sometimes substituted – happily less frequently than in France, where some quite astounding patterns have been produced. It generally looks out of place in the countryside and in urban areas is a heavy substitute for iron vertical bar railings.

5.4.9 Trip fences and guard rails

The normal purpose of trip fences and guard rails is to protect grass or planted areas from being trodden on. As they are not more than about 600 mm (approx. 2 ft) high, they are a visual rather than physical deterrent. Whenever possible they should be used in preference to boundary fencing, as they are so much more inconspicuous. When the fences are set in the edge of pavings the

Plate 5.11. Metal rod fence and gate.

93

Plate 5.12. Vertical bar railing and gate.

standard boundary fencing. Mild steel posts and rails are superseding hoops because they are less conspicuous, will take curves more easily and are cheaper. The rail is generally 300 mm (approx. 1 ft) above ground and the standards or posts are between 900 mm and 1·5 m (approx. 3 ft and 4 ft 6 in) centres, depending on the strength of the rail and the rigidity required. The posts are split at the foot and set in concrete and finishes are either galvanising or painting, which must have a corrosion-inhibiting primer. Traditional and standard designs are usually based on 22 mm (approx. $\frac{7}{8}$ in) diameter rails passing through standards but rails can be square and standards I section. As an alternative, round or square section tubes can look equally simple and efficient, providing the joints are the sleeve variety, but they cannot so easily take up curvatures. Concrete is sometimes used for the posts instead of metal but they look clumsy as the posts appear out of scale with the rails. When a strong rail is required, such as a barrier to motor cars, timber posts and rails are a possible alternative to dwarf walls or bollards. The rail should be a heavy section (150 mm × 50 mm, 175 mm × 38 mm), with half-lapped joints over stout posts (say, 100 mm × 75 mm) chamfered on top. Such a rail is not to be confused with traffic barriers, used to prevent vehicles running off a carriageway, where corrugated or trough section metal is bolted to heavy wood posts for greater strength and ease of replacement.

standards need relating to the joints and, when in grass, they should be set in a concrete mowing strip, to avoid trimming by hand. Trip fences are usually of mild steel and there is a variety of proprietary designs based on hoops and pales, most of which are cut-down versions of

Plate 5.13. Formal 'architectural' fencing surmounting a brick wall.

Plate 5.14. Example of timber palisade fencing.

Plate 5.15. Example of timber palisade fencing.

Plate 5.16. Example of timber palisade fencing.

5.5 Bollards

5.5.1 Types and functions

Bollards are vertical barriers which, being free-standing objects, are one of the most unobtrusive ways of preventing access; they have no great height and no horizontal line is drawn across the scene. Their common use is to prevent motor cars encroaching on pedestrian areas by narrowing a space. Other uses are the sub-division of paved areas to direct the flow of traffic, the marking of property boundaries and the protection of property – such as the corners of buildings from casual traffic. There are a variety of bollards for special purposes, such as illuminated types for traffic direction, removable tubular steel bollards for cases where very occasional access is required and hinged tubular steel bollards for reserving individual parking spaces. Traditional bollards are of natural stone, such as granite and cast iron and some very beautiful designs are still to be seen. Both types are rapidly being superseded by reinforced concrete owing to cost but a revived interest in cast iron might encourage manufacturers not to destroy all their old moulds. Although reinforced concrete is used for all kinds of conditions, wood (not less than 100 mm × 100 mm) is satisfactory for pedestrian control and mild steel tubes are sometimes substituted. Neither of the latter materials has the strong and robust appearance of the traditional bollard and they have closer affinities to post and rail fences.

5.5.2 Concrete bollards

With the increasing practice of pedestrian/vehicular segregation, concrete bollards are becoming a familiar part of the urban scene. They are favoured because they provide a strong, reasonably cheap barrier with its own decisive character which causes few of the disturbances to the floorscape that occur with kerb, wall or rail. The materials used are Portland cement, concrete aggregate from natural sources and rolled steel bars. The form

should be robust and simple; thin or over-elaborate shapes do not express strength. There is a variety of pleasant proprietary designs on the market, obtainable in different finishes, such as white concrete, bush-hammered granite, lightly exposed, crushed gravel and reconstructed stone: over-complicated textures detract from the character of robustness. As a barrier to vehicles, the bollards are placed with 1·5 m (approx. 5 ft) clear between them. Their total height varies from 900 mm

Plate 5.17. A row of stone bollards marking off the edge of the carriageway.

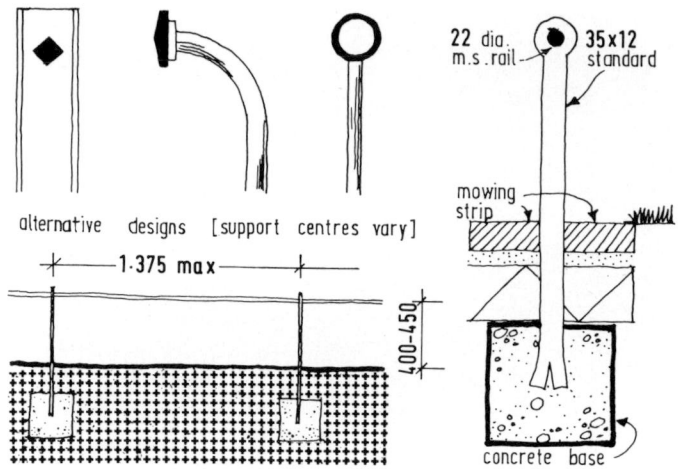

Fig. 5.11. TRIP FENCE – A low fence to protect grass or planted areas.

Plate 5.18. A metal bollard protecting the corner of a pavement.

to 1·5 m (approx. 3 ft to 5 ft) and they are set 300 mm to 450 mm (approx. 12 in to 18 in) in the ground, on a 100 mm (approx. 4 in) concrete base. When set in pavings, the bollards may be surrounded by cobbles, shingle or some similar material to avoid cutting the slabs.

Bibliography

Brick Information Sheets, Nos. 7, 8, and 12, National Federation of Brick Industries.

Building Construction, vol. 1, W. B. McKay, Longmans Green.

Building Elements, Davies and Petty, Architectural Press.

Colour in Hedges, J. L. Bedall, Faber and Faber.

Hedges for Farm and Garden, J. L. Bedall, Faber and Faber.

Permanent Farm Fences, Leaflet No. 5, Ministry of Agriculture, Fisheries and Food, H.M.S.O.

Shelter Belts for Farmland, Leaflet No. 15, Ministry of Agriculture, Fisheries and Food, H.M.S.O.

Shelter Belts and Windbreaks, J. M. Caborn, Faber and Faber.

The Small Garden, C. E. Lucas Phillips, Heinemann and Pan.

Trees for Town and Country, Brenda Colvin and S. R. Badmin, Lund Humphries.

6 Outdoor Fittings and Furniture

IAN PURDY

6.1 Seats and sitting areas

6.1.1 Description, principles and uses

Simplicity of form and detail, ease of maintenance, cost, durability, finish and resistance to vandalism are all important factors guiding selection of seats.

In considering the basic requirements of a comfortable seat it should be borne in mind that the seat height should be low enough for the body's weight to be borne by the feet so that there is no pressure on the thighs. If the seat is higher than the length of the sitter's lower leg some thigh pressure is unavoidable. Also the depth of seat should not be so long that the edge of the seat causes pressure behind the knees. Work carried out for the design of seats for offices suggests certain essential dimensions which are shown in Fig. 6.2.

The type of seat to be used in any particular area is dependent on its siting. In metropolitan areas the seats should be monumental in character, the design forming part of the urban landscape; in the country they should be rough and workmanlike, the key quality being simplicity, often emphasised by using the local material such as stone, slate or timber, but care must be taken to avoid false rusticity. Scale is important and materials should be in character with the surroundings. In small spaces the simplicity of bench or chair is essential and the attempt to attract attention by an overdressed design or intricacy of finish merely looks silly. Visually it is better to have seats designed as benches without backs, a form which is least obtrusive in the landscape, but seating in public places must take into account requirements of old people and other users who will require seats with arms and backs. Seats as an element of design need a background, whether this consists of planting, walls or trees and they should be related to other objects in the landscape and should be co-ordinated wherever possible with other street furniture (Fig. 6.1).

Urban seating may be back to back, continuous, pedestal or wall mounted. In some cases *in situ* seats cantilevered from walls can be used or retaining walls can be wide enough to act as a bench; circular or multi-sided seats may be useful around trees or other features. If seats or benches are to be used as a permanent fixture it is preferable for them to be open underneath, particularly

Plate 6.1. Bench seats and plant-holders, Bath Technical College, Architects Frederick Gibberd and Partners.

PRINCIPLES
BENCHES and SEATS should be simple in design.

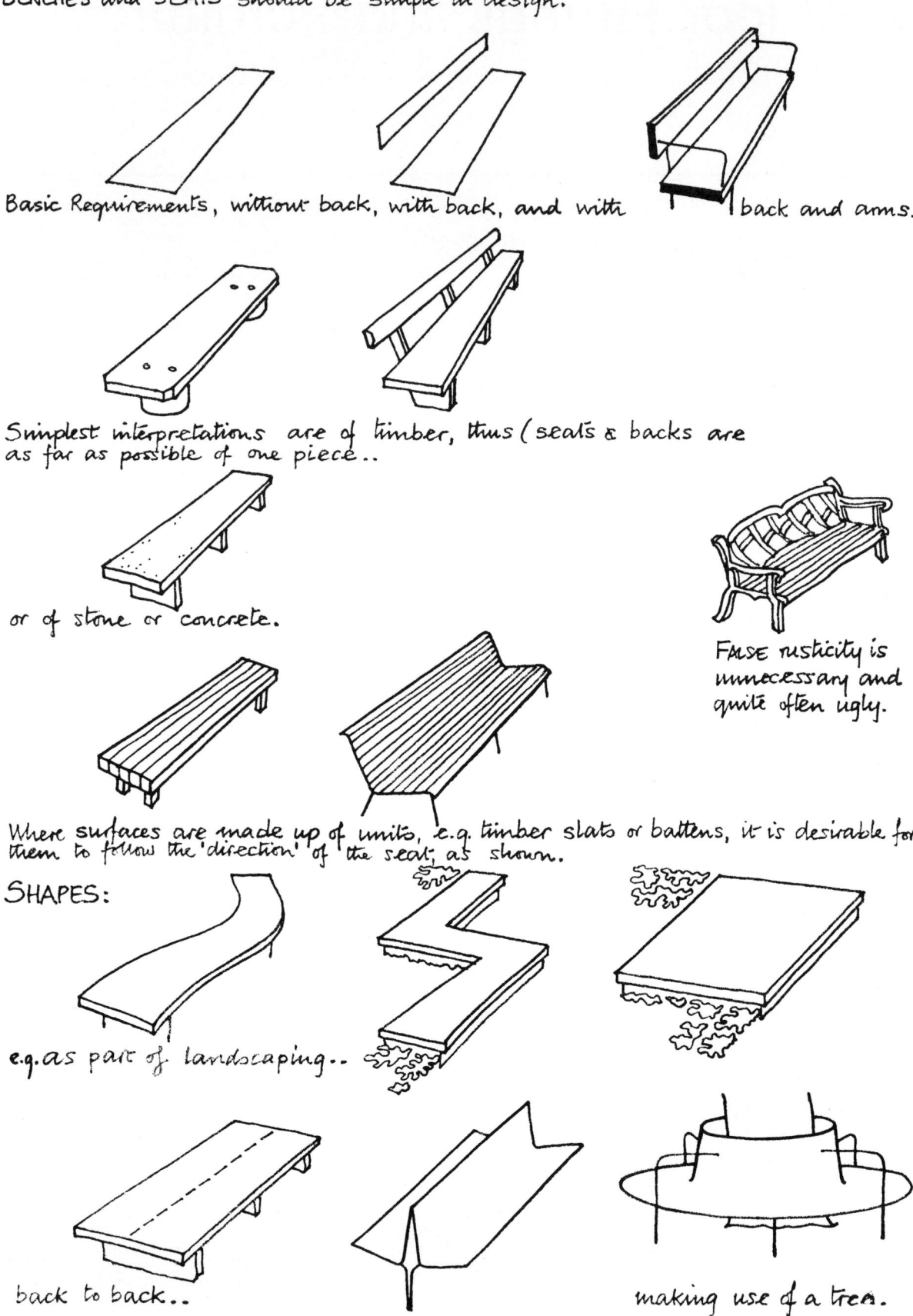

Basic Requirements, without back, with back, and with back and arms.

Simplest interpretations are of timber, thus (seats & backs are as far as possible of one piece..

or of stone or concrete.

FALSE rusticity is unnecessary and quite often ugly.

Where surfaces are made up of units, e.g. timber slats or battens, it is desirable for them to follow the 'direction' of the seat, as shown.

SHAPES:

e.g. as part of landscaping..

back to back..

making use of a tree.

Fig. 6.1. Design principles for seats.

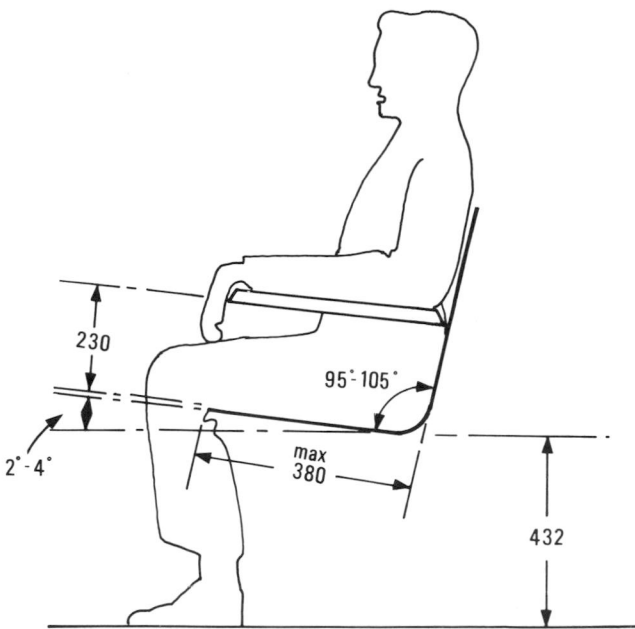

Fig. 6.2. Guide to seat dimensions.

where a feeling of lightness is desired or where a line of vision should not be stopped. This is especially important where paving or grass continues beyond the seat.

Stacking or removable chairs are suitable for private gardens, open spaces and public parks which are adequately controlled or policed. In areas which are not policed, seats should be fixed either to the ground, walls or other suitable points. Supports and fixing must be of a form which will resist easy removal. Seat bolts should be countersunk and nuts riveted to discourage removal. Where supports are carried below ground level to form a foundation the depth should not be less than 600 mm (approx. 2 ft).

6.1.2 Sitting areas

The location of seats and sitting areas must take into account climatic conditions; some should be in the shade, some in the sun, but all should be sheltered from wind or draughts. It is important to ensure that people sitting in seats close to footpaths do not impede pedestrian movement along them. Generally seating should be situated a minimum of 2 m (approx. 6 ft 6 in) back from pathways, and it is preferable that seats are placed to give a view of the landscape rather than sited to look at areas of pedestrian movement.

Seats should be well away from children's play spaces, but in playgrounds seats are an important factor in ensuring the maximum use of the playground. Mothers do not wish to stand up when supervising their children and ample seating accommodation, sheltered from the wind but sited to catch sunshine, should be provided. Seats are

also an essential part of any playing field equipment and adequate numbers should be provided particularly near facilities such as tennis courts, bowling greens, etc.

The ground surface around sitting areas receiving intensive use needs careful consideration. Where the surface is grass the turf very quickly becomes worn and patchy and is always damp in wet weather. In designing and laying out sitting areas durability and hard wearing surfaces with adequate drainage are required. The materials used around the seat should also be related to, and in keeping with, the surrounding ground surfaces.

6.1.3 Costs

Some types of seat available and comparative costs are summarised in Table 6.1 below.

TABLE 6.1: COMPARATIVE COSTS FOR SEATS

Materials	Cost* £	Notes
Teak or other suitable hardwoods	40–120	Curved seats are available from some manufacturers
Concrete frames or supports, hardwood slats	35–80	Depending on aggregates and finishes required
Tubular or square steel frames, hardwood slats	32–75	Iroko frequently used for slats. Metal frames available – nylon coated or stove enamelled

*Prices are for comparative purposes only, based on single seats at 1978 prices. Reductions are available for quantities. Detailed information and costs should be obtained from manufacturers.

6.1.4 Materials

Points to be remembered when considering the various materials available include:

Timber – Probably most durable when constructed in Burma teak (*Tectona grandis*) but other suitable woods include afrormosia, oak, iroko, keruing, agba, afzelia, African mahogany, African walnut, utile.

Concrete – This is mainly used in the form of a composite construction in conjunction with timber seats or backs, but simple benches consisting of slabs and supports can be pre-cast. Usually the slabs are of a steel-trowelled finish with supports having a smooth or textured exposed aggregate finish. Other alternatives include reconstructed stone – finishes available include Hams Hill (warm buff), Doulty (cream) and Portland stone (greyish white). Where exposed aggregate finishes are used heavily textured surfaces should be avoided and the careful choice of the grading of aggregate with the right degree of exposure is important. Aggregate faced finishes include shingle, Cornish granite, grey or black granite and pink limestone.

Plate 6.2. Bench seats. Players factory, Nottingham. Architects Arup Association.

Metal – Bench or park seats are made with stove enamelled or plastic coated (frequently nylon coat in white, grey or black), rectangular hollow steel frames. Painted cast iron and aluminium alloy frames are also available.

Where aluminium is used care must be taken with the fixing to avoid corrosion through galvanic action. Also when salt is present in the atmosphere moisture corrosion is accelerated, and for this reason the direct contact of aluminium and other metals in marine atmospheres should be avoided. Where steel bolts are used for fixing they should be galvanised. Certain timbers, such as oak and chestnut amongst the hardwoods, liberate organic acids in damp environments and when the timber is unseasoned. This may cause severe corrosion of aluminium and it is wise to treat any timber, which comes into contact with it, with a suitable wood preservative, followed by the use of an aluminium or bituminous paint.

Plate 6.3. Double seat in Burma teak, Loughborough. Architects: Richard Shepphard, Robson and Partners.

Plate 6.4. Reinforced concrete frame exposed aggregate finished afrormosia seat design by L. Berger A.R.I.B.A. Made by Neptune Concrete Limited.

100

6.2 Plant containers

6.2.1 Function

Containers can be used to provide vegetation in urban areas or used architecturally to emphasise spaces, pedestrian ways or as an element of building design. They may act as a barrier separating or articulating the spaces between buildings, defining areas available for pedestrians and vehicles, identifying and indicating changes in ground level and they can give 'scale' to the street scene, particularly as their proportions can be related to the human figure. Plant containers should not be used where it is possible to grow plants naturally in the ground. Normally containers should be grouped, the number being dependent on the design requirements. Single plant holders, other than those used as window boxes, should be avoided.

6.2.2 Siting

The first consideration for deciding the siting of any sort of plant container must be the welfare and success of the plants themselves.

In congested urban areas light is the most vital factor and this must be considered in a photographic sense, the requirement is not sunshine but adequate light. All flowering plants and most foliage plants need uninterrupted top light and care must be taken in siting them to avoid overhanging balconies, canopies, etc. Other conditions to avoid include traffic fumes, smoke, winds and draughts. Particular care must be taken to avoid unnecessary draught conditions in passage ways, doorways and entrances.

6.2.3 Principles of design

Plant holders should contain sufficient body of soil for the plants' nutrition, have adequate water retaining capacity, be provided with adequate drainage and be capable of easy maintenance; portability may also be a requirement (Fig. 6.3).

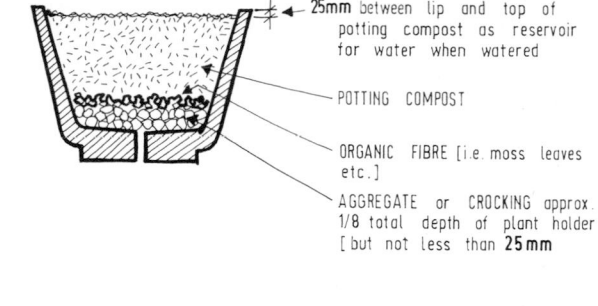

25mm between lip and top of potting compost as reservoir for water when watered

POTTING COMPOST

ORGANIC FIBRE [i.e. moss leaves etc.]

AGGREGATE or CROCKING approx. 1/8 total depth of plant holder [but not less than **25mm**

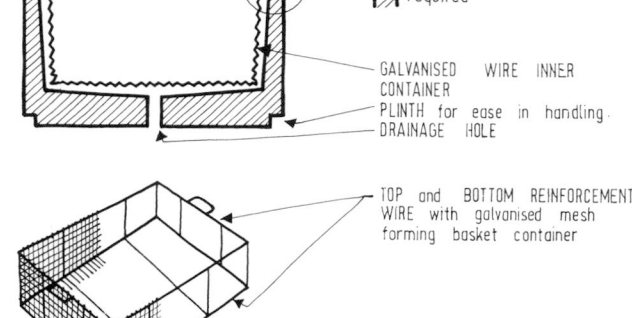

LIP if plant holders are required

GALVANISED WIRE INNER CONTAINER

PLINTH for ease in handling

DRAINAGE HOLE

TOP and BOTTOM REINFORCEMENT WIRE with galvanised mesh forming basket container

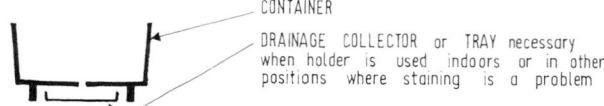

CONTAINER

DRAINAGE COLLECTOR or TRAY necessary when holder is used indoors or in other positions where staining is a problem

Fig. 6.3. Design principles for plant holders.

Plate 6.5. Plant craters constructed in granite setts with a brick lining at the Owen's Park Student Village, University of Manchester. Architects: Sir George Grenfell Baines of Building Design Partnership.

Plate 6.6. Precast concrete plant holders, Stevenage Town Centre. Architect: L.G. Vincent C.B.E., F.R.I.B.A., consultant Architect and Planner to the Stevenage Development Corporation.

6.2.4 Sizes

Generally the maximum volume of soil which two men can handle without mechanical assistance is approximately 600 mm × 600 mm × 300 mm (approx. 2 ft × 2 ft × 1 ft). Sizes of plant holders will, however, be dependent on the design and type of use. Their depth, however, should never be less than 300 mm (approx. 12 in) to ensure an adequate amount of growing medium. If trees are intended to be used in containers the minimum depth should be increased to 600 mm (approx. 2 ft).

6.2.5 Drainage

Holders should contain sufficient broken material of a large aggregate at the bottom to allow water to pass through. Drainage itself can be provided by a simple hole in the bottom, but care must be taken to avoid external staining from the drainage holes.

6.2.6 Growing media

Growing media can be soil or inorganic materials, e.g. vermiculite or water. Vermiculite has the advantages of lightness and cleanness and is very suitable for use on roofs or indoors; but as a growing medium it does not retain, unlike soil, the plants' nutritional requirements. Care must be taken therefore to ensure that adequate nutrient is provided. Composite mixes normally used in plant holders consist of 3:2:1 loam, peat and sand or 6:4:1 loam, peat and sand, the growing medium normally being dependent on the plants to be used. The use of organic fertilisers may be required as a reinforcement to the growing medium dependent on particular conditions.

6.2.7 Maintenance

Plants will be put in containers either on a permanent or temporary basis. Where they are temporary they can be lifted either individually or collectively, but it is preferable if the plant container has an inner wire basket which may be lifted out and the plants removed. The wire basket should be of galvanised wire and the sides packed with polythene or sphagnum moss.

6.2.8 Materials and types available

Plant holders can be square, circular, rectangular or triangular in plan with parallel or tapering sides, traditional or special shapes also being available. Materials used are stone, concrete, clay, terracotta, metal, timber, glass fibre and asbestos cement.

Stone – Stone containers are usually traditional in form, heavy in weight and most appropriate for permanent planting. Types of stone used include York, Portland stone, various granites and marbles.

Designs should provide for adequate drainage since, owing to the thickness of the material, the amount of porosity is very limited through the sides of the container.

Concrete – Normally light reinforcement is used in the concrete but the extent of this depends on design of the plant holder. Exposed aggregate finishes can give a wide variety of colour and texture but care is necessary to ensure that the simplicity of form is not destroyed by exaggerated exposure of the aggregate. Surface finishes include brushing, bush hammering, and rubbing; and the use of textured or corrugated formwork should be considered. Glass smooth surfaces can be obtained by casting concrete against formwork lined with plastic sheet.

Shapes available include conical, tubular, hexagonal, rectangular and curved. These are usually manufactured in white or grey concrete. The walls of the containers vary between 38 mm and 50 mm (approx. 1½ in and 2 in) thick and some types are available without bases for deep-rooted plants. Hexagonal and timber plant kerbs are also produced which can be built up into tiers of any required height. Reconstructed stone holders are made in the form of square tubs, vase and bowl shapes.

Plate 6.7. Teak plant holders, Nuclear Physics Laboratory, Oxford. Designers Arup Associates.

Clay or terracotta – Porosity of the surfaces is important. There is a tendency for these materials to harbour disease in the pores of the walls. Care must be taken to wash the pots, especially when new, but also when any replanting takes place. Terracotta is used for the production of various traditional forms of holder – mainly conical in shape but also as pots or large vases.

Timber – Where timber is used a waterproof lining should always be provided. In some cases it may have advantages because of the insulation it gives to the roots against sudden temperature changes. Where timber is painted, care must be taken to ensure that non-toxic paints, stains or preservatives are used. Round and square tubs, rectangular boxes and barrel tubs are available from a number of manufacturers. Timbers used include Burma teak, iroko and oak.

Glass Fibre – Until the last few years it has been principally used to manufacture various forms of reproduction antique urns or tubs but now glass fibre reinforced polyester units are available in many shapes including hexagonal, square, rectangular and cylindrical forms. A wide range of colours is possible and units integrated with bench or various forms of seating are produced.

Asbestos cement – Conical, rectangular and curved moulded units are manufactured in natural grey asbestos or various coloured finishes. Interlocking rectangular trays which can be built up to various heights are available.

Metal – When any form of metal is used care must be taken lest it comes into contact with the planting media. Metal should always be protected or coated, generally with a bitumastic paint to avoid the toxic effects of metallic salts on the plants. In hot weather there is a tendency for the temperature rise in the holder to cause rapid drying out of the planting material and consideration should be given to the use of a suitable insulating barrier between the outside container and the growing medium. Possible insulating materials include polystyrene or Asbestolux.

Metal in the form of lead, painted galvanised iron, zinc or aluminium is principally confined to special designs and most often used for window boxes.

6.3 Lamps and lighting

6.3.1 Lighting requirements
The optical requirements of outdoor lighting resolve into three principal types:

(*a*) Lighting for carriageways.
(*b*) Pedestrian or amenity lighting.
(*c*) Lighting of a decorative nature suitable for gardens, illumination of plants, statuary or buildings.

Street lighting is of a complex technical nature and normally the landscape architect's responsibilities would be confined to lighting which is of a decorative nature or only suitable for pedestrian ways.

The B.S.I. Code of Practice 1004 recommends both the appropriate intensity of light and normal mounting heights, 9–12 m (approx. 30–40 ft) for A roads and 6 or 8 m (approx. 19½ or 26 ft) for B roads. Mounting heights have been increasing steadily in recent years and high mast lighting is now seen at large-scale intersections. Higher mounting and light sources may mean a reduction in the number of columns necessary but the colour and daylight appearance of column and lantern is extremely important in making a choice for a particular setting. Consideration should be given to the scale of the installation (including consideration of wall mounted fittings), colour and character of design. Details of well-designed modern columns and lanterns can be found in the Design Council approved list.

103

TABLE 6.2

	Tungsten	Mercury/ Fluorescent	Sodium	Fluorescent	Tungsten Halogen
Colour	Yellow/white	Green/white	Yellow (monochromatic)	White	White
Colour rendering	Very good	Good	Poor	Very good	Very good
Lamp wattage range	40–1,500	50–1,000	45–140	40–125	300–2,000†
Normal life (hr)	1,000	5,000	5,000	5,000	2,000
Lamp dimensions	Normal domestic size 165–335 mm long	Similar to tungsten	Approx. 500 mm long	Sizes vary from 300 mm to 2·5 m, circular and bulk-head fitting available	Between approx. 50–250 mm in length, diameter of only approx. 12–20 mm
Lantern types	All types	Similar to tungsten, choke and capacitator usually housed in column base	Medium size lantern	Large lantern	Small flood lighting lantern
Cost of typical 5 m column and lantern‡	£44	£42–52 (control gear extra)	£55	£45 (control gear extra)	£43–53 —

† Lower wattages for special applications.

‡ Cost of electric service will be dependent on site conditions and availability of existing supply.

The figures given in this table only outline the principal characteristics of various lighting sources; detailed information is available from manufacturers. Costs based on 1978 prices.

Important points to remember in the choice of fittings are the relationship between lamp post and lantern, the structural requirements of the column, the provision to be made for terminating the main supply, control gear, fuses, time switches and ancillary equipment required by the lantern (Fig. 6.4).

6.3.2 Light source
The design of the lantern itself relates to the type of lighting source and Table 6.2 sets out in outline the characteristics of light sources generally used for street or amenity lighting.

Generally gas discharge and tungsten lamps are compact in size and light source, but require accurate optical control to distribute the light properly and avoid glare. Fluorescent lamps are popular with some authorities because of the advantages of the natural colouring, the low intensity at the light source and the long lamp life. A disadvantage is the size of lantern required which, when related to the lamp posts, often results in a clumsy design and unfortunate daylight appearance.

A new type of light source based on sodium but giving good colour rendering has now been produced by the lamp manufacturers. This light source which is known as the High Pressure Sodium Vapour Lamp has a very high luminous output and in a well-designed lantern

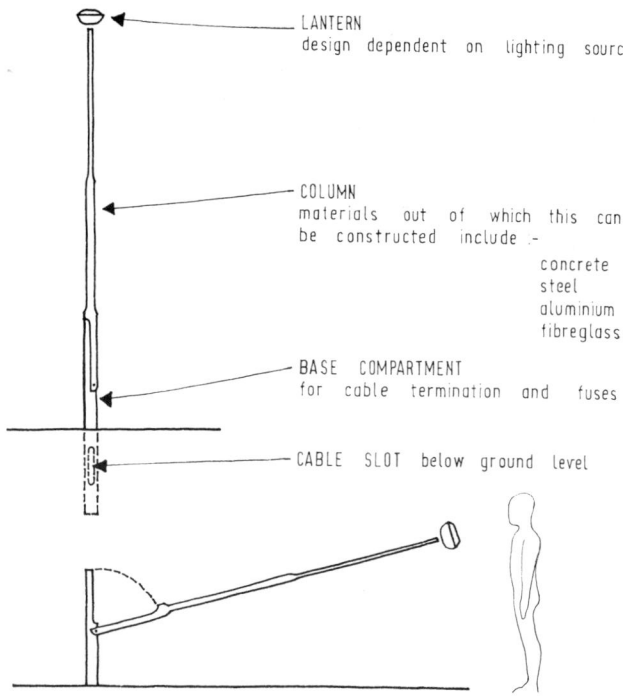

LANTERN
design dependent on lighting source

COLUMN
materials out of which this can be constructed include :-
concrete
steel
aluminium
fibreglass

BASE COMPARTMENT
for cable termination and fuses

CABLE SLOT below ground level

Fig. 6.4. Lighting columns: components. A patented lighting column designed for lowering to a convenient height for maintenance by means of a hinge at the base (up to 10 m, approx. 33 ft, mounting height). Locking mechanism at the hinge is released by special lever supplied with column. A spring or hydraulic counter balance unit can be attached to the base of the column during lowering if required.

Plate 6.8. Illuminated bollard for low level pedestrian area, lighting manufactured by Abacus Municipal Limited.

could enable columns to be spaced at distances much greater than at present.

6.3.3 Amenity lighting

This can be defined as lighting suitable for the illumination of areas such as pedestrian walks, squares, parks or the forecourts of buildings where vehicular traffic is not normally found. Its function is also connected with the adequate policing and security of areas and 'morality' lighting. As the requirements for amenity lighting are less stringent, more use can be made of the decorative effects of both fittings and illumination.

Bulkhead fittings can illuminate steps, wall fittings, pathways and passages; floodlights playgrounds or large pedestrian spaces.

In siting lighting fittings consideration must be given not only to the functional requirements but also to the relationships with other street furniture, buildings, trees or planting and must take into account such points as the annoyance caused by lighting falling on bedroom windows of houses, etc. Fittings used should be robust in construction and of a type suitable for their particular siting. Vandalism can be a considerable problem and

must be borne in mind when deciding on the design of lantern to be used, the biggest danger being the destruction of the lantern glass. Acrylic or polycarbonate bowls are generally used in situations where vandalism is prevalent.

Plate 6.9. 4·5 m (approx. 15 ft) steel column and lantern with provision for litter bin fixing. Designed by R. Steven, P. Rodd and J. Barnes. Made by Atlas Lighting Limited.

105

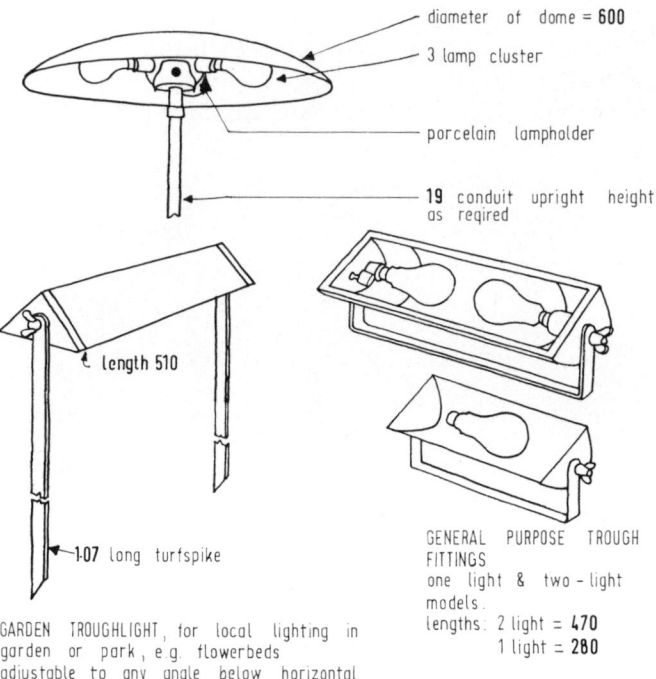

diameter of dome = **600**

3 lamp cluster

porcelain lampholder

19 conduit upright height as reqired

length 510

1·07 long turfspike

GARDEN TROUGHLIGHT, for local lighting in garden or park, e.g. flowerbeds adjustable to any angle below horizontal

GENERAL PURPOSE TROUGH FITTINGS one light & two-light models. lengths: 2 light = **470** 1 light = **280**

Fig. 6.5. Typical garden lighting fittings.

6.3.4 Decorative lighting

Decorative or garden lighting can be used in three principal forms:

(a) To illuminate paths, walks, steps, living areas for use at night.
(b) To illuminate and dramatise plant material.
(c) As another decorative element in the garden – in fact, gardening with light.

Lighting can either be direct light where the illumination is from the source directly to the tree, flowers, plants, pools, etc. and where in all cases the source of light should be hidden or, alternatively, indirect light where a reflecting surface directs the illumination to the area or object to be lighted (Fig. 6.5).

The use of glow light as a major element of the landscape design should also be considered. In this case the light itself becomes the object to be seen and is not intended to have any great illumination value. This is illustrated by the classical Japanese use of stone and paper lanterns which were often placed where paths cross or in the middle of a shrubbery or on the banks of a lake. Trees or a bush were planted close by the lantern so that the leaves partially concealed the lighting but gave the light a shimmering appearance (Fig. 6.6).

The final arrangement of night lighting is best done by trial on the site, but it is important in all cases (except where glow light is used) to avoid excessively harsh lighting effects and generally it is preferable to baffle the source of light.

106

Plate 6.10. Pedestrian precinct lighting, Bretton Centre, Peterborough Development Corporation.

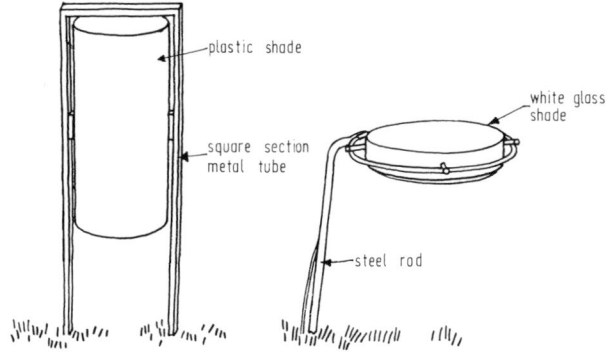

plastic shade

square section metal tube

white glass shade

steel rod

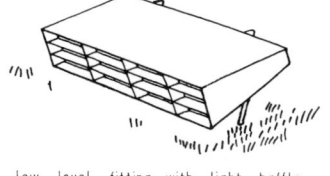

low level fitting with light baffle

Fig. 6.6. Continental examples of low level lighting fittings.

The hue of light can be chosen either to give a reasonably favourable rendering of the colours (incandescent lamps or tungsten halogen lamps) or alternatively to intensify or change the colour of the foliage. The blue light from mercury vapour lamps intensifies the colour foliage of conifers, cedars, thuyas. Sodium vapour lighting can be used for leaves yellowed by the Autumn, red light can emphasise the colour of copper beeches.

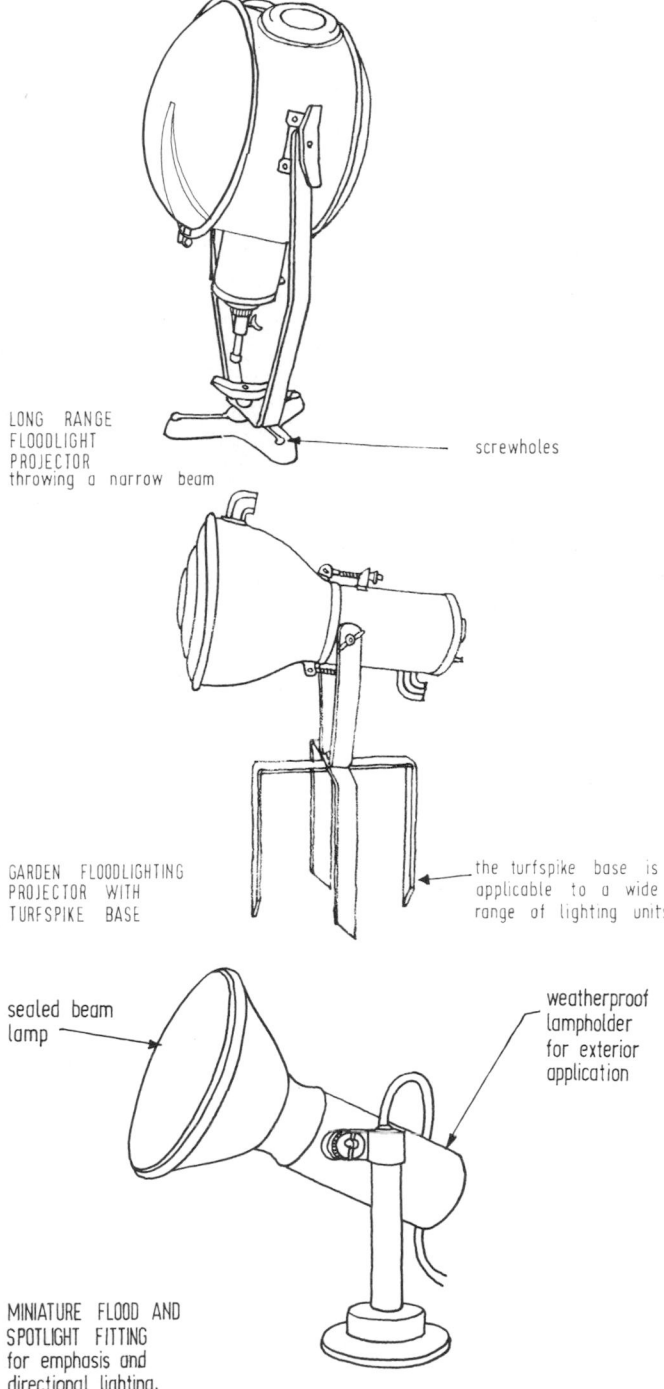

LONG RANGE FLOODLIGHT PROJECTOR
throwing a narrow beam

screwholes

GARDEN FLOODLIGHTING PROJECTOR WITH TURFSPIKE BASE

the turfspike base is applicable to a wide range of lighting units

sealed beam lamp

weatherproof lampholder for exterior application

MINIATURE FLOOD AND SPOTLIGHT FITTING
for emphasis and directional lighting.

Fig. 6.7. Typical floodlight projectors.

Plate 6.11. Lighting, pedestrian route, Church End, Cambridge. Architect: I. M. Purdy, City Architect. Manufactured by Thorn Lighting Limited.

The use of fluorescent tubes for the lighting of trees and shrubbery has become very popular in this country primarily because the fluorescent tube is considerably more efficient than incandescent lamps with colour filters and because the electrical load is very much reduced.

Coloured tubes are manufactured in pink, blue, green or gold and in lengths from 600 mm to 1·5 m (approx. 2 ft to 5 ft).

The green colour tube can be used for the lighting of dense shrubbery and, particularly, evergreens. Gold or pink tubes have been used for the lighting of tree trunks and branches and pink, in particular, for the lighting of copper beeches. The initial cost is much less than that of sodium or mercury vapour lamps and with weatherproof control gear installation it becomes relatively simple. Automatic colour change dimmers are available for hire or direct purchase if required.

107

Plate 6.12. Lighting column with fluorescent fittings. Stevenage Town Centre. Architect: L. G. Vincent, C.B.E., F.R.I.B.A., Consultant Architect and Planner to the Stevenage Development Corporation. Landscape Architect: Gordon Patterson.

6.3.5 Lighting equipment

Permanent outdoor lighting must be weatherproof. The need is for small, easily adjustable units which can be either spiked direct into the ground or provided with suitable base plates. Types available include, downward lighting fittings for illumination of flower beds or other planting, either in the form of dome lights (Fig. 6.5) about 600 mm (approx. 2 ft) in diameter for use with incandescent lamps (the outside of the dome available in various colours) or, alternatively, trough lights with incandescent or fluorescent lamps, fitted with turf spikes adjustable to different angles and suitable for general illumination (Fig. 6.7). General purpose trough fittings for highlighting features, fitted with glass panel front covers, are also available and these are often suitable for ground lighting where a wide beam of light is required. For isolated trees, thickets and statuary some form of directional floodlighting may be necessary. Small and large projec-

tors are produced with narrow or broad angle lighting beams. Small low wattage sealed beam reflector lamps are also available which can be used with simple weatherproof housings, illuminating objects 5–6 m (approx. 16–

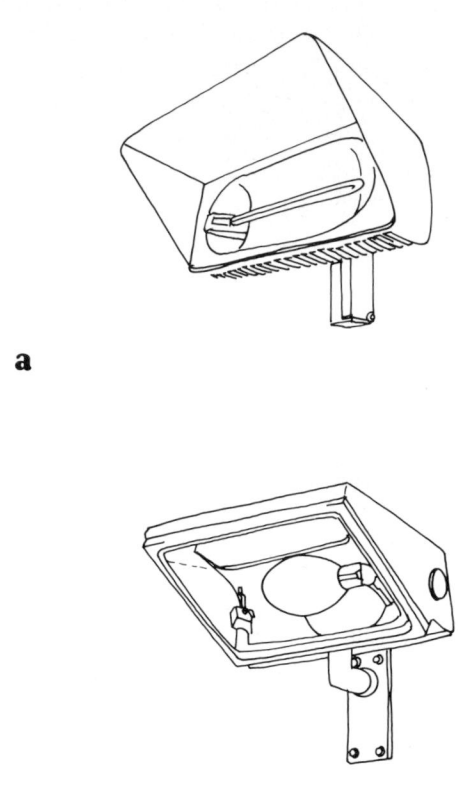

a

b

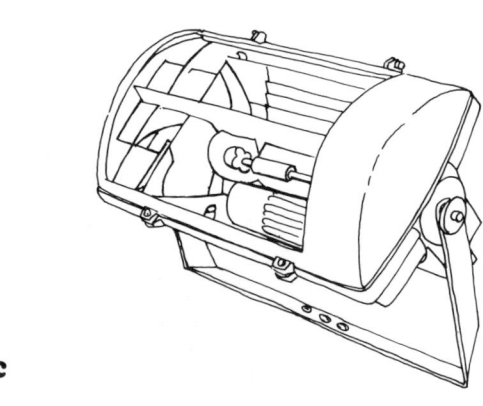

c

Fig. 6.8. Typical floodlight projectors. (*a*) Tungsten halogen floodlighting fitting: available with post or wall mounting. Wire guards available for lamp protection. (*b*) Area floodlight: available for post top stirrup or wall bracket mounting. (*c*) Floodlight available for narrow or medium beam. Various light sources.

108

20 ft) away. Projection floodlights are available from a number of manufacturers with turf spike mounting bases as an alternative to normal bases.

6.3.6 Cables and wiring

Cables and wiring for street lighting would not normally come within the scope of the landscape architect's responsibilities, but he will be concerned with requirements for decorative lighting.

Where decorative lighting is used it may be an advantage to return to store during the winter the lighting fittings, conduit and other equipment. There is, therefore, an advantage in making and using temporary installations or, alternatively, incorporating a permanent 'ring main' system through which temporary installations and surface cables can be connected. The cables likely to be used for temporary or permanent decorative lighting or floodlighting are:

Mineral insulated copper-covered cable – This form of cable can be laid directly in the ground, but to ensure protection from any corrosive elements in the soil it should be sheathed in P.V.C. It is considered good prac-

tice to lay a tile on top of the cable wherever required for protection.

P.V.C. cable with an earth continuity conductor – This cable will require laying in a conduit and must be properly protected wherever it is used.

P.V.C. sheathed armoured cable – Armoured cable must always be used and specified when running connections directly on the ground and for all temporary installations where mechanical damage may occur to cables at ground level.

In all cases cables must be terminated in weatherproof outlet boxes. All lighting fittings and switches must be weatherproof and it is essential that all lamp fittings should be efficiently earthed and care must be taken to meet the requirements of the Health and Safety at Work Act. Where cables are permanently installed trenches should be dug and the cables buried at least 450 mm (18 in) below ground level. If it is necessary to place cables at shallower depths they must be protected and protection must always be provided where they enter or leave the ground.

6.4 Litter bins

6.4.1 Principles and uses

Litter bins should be simple in character, robust and easy to maintain, easy to empty and handle. There are advantages in having separate wire or metal baskets inside the main container because there is then less danger of damage when being emptied. A good bin should not only hold litter but should, as far as possible, conceal the litter it holds. Containers should be as indestructible as possible and preferably fireproof (Fig. 6.9).

In urban settings there is a need for co-ordination with other street furniture. It is preferable for containers to form part of other elements in the street. They should related to such items as lighting columns, shelters, seats or walls. In a more diverse landscape such as parks, public gardens, rural areas, etc., containers should be sited adjacent to the main circulation areas or routes and should be immediately available for use and be easily seen and identified.

Although litter bins should be related to other street furniture and are often required close to seats in public parks, gardens or other open spaces, the problem of unpleasant odours must be remembered. In some areas, such as holiday resorts, bins quickly become full, particularly at the height of the season and in hot weather they can become so offensive that would-be sitters are discouraged. In cases where this may happen litter bins with lids, possibly worked by foot pedals, may be advantageous.

When they are placed adjacent to roads or lay-bys

where infrequent servicing is likely, containers must be large enough to hold considerable quantities of waste and be designed to be weatherproof with some form of cover to prevent litter blowing about and to discourage foraging by animals or birds. Special types are available for temporary use and for outdoor functions such as race meetings, fairs, etc., but care must be taken to see that the design of the container used does not itself form an element of litter in the landscape.

The act of emptying a bin will vary from tipping a small container into a handcart to shovelling quantities of a wide variety of rubbish by hand into a lorry. The cleans-

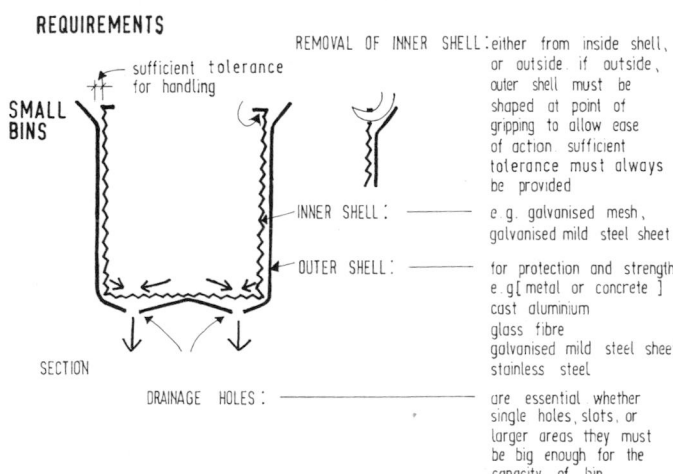

Fig. 6.9. LITTER BINS. Diagram showing main requirements.

109

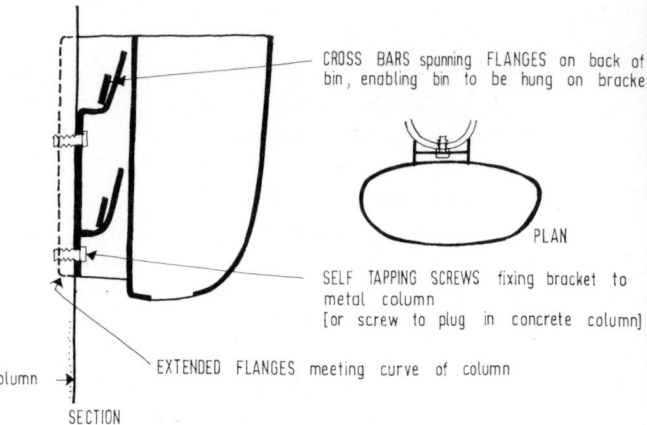

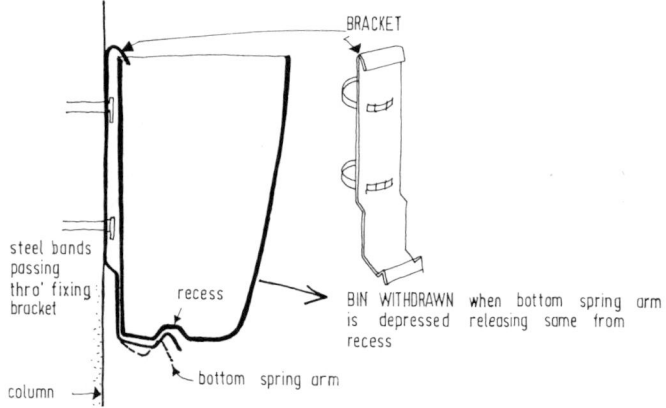

Plate 6.13. Wall- or column-mounted litter bin in sheet metal. Designed by John and Sylvia Reid A/A.R.I.B.A.

Fig. 6.10. LITTER BINS: Fixing to columns.

ing of containers varies from practically nothing to laborious burning and scrubbing out. It must be borne in mind that the term 'litter' embraces a strange assortment of objects and substances particularly in over-crowded areas. Similarly vandalism varies from being almost non-existent through various stages of occasional bonfires and minor damage, to that of almost complete demolition. It is not unknown for a concrete bin to be completely shattered by children, and insecurely fixed containers may be thrown about or stolen. Factors other than human ones have to be contended with and squirrels and birds may be a problem in one place, and deer or ponies may pose an entirely different one elsewhere. Where consideration is given to hooded or protected bins care must be taken that the mechanical function does not lead to excessive wear and tear, accidental damage or dif-ficulties in emptying. Generally the public are reluctant to push a dirty or sticky flap to dispose of their rubbish and the advocates of an open-mouthed container that 'invites' litter may well be correct in their arguments. Hygiene is important and must be coupled with good design.

6.4.2 Types of litter bin
There are five principal types of container. These are:

(a) Containers for mounting on lighting columns or poles (Fig. 6.10).
(b) Wall-mounted types or types for fixing to vertical surfaces (Fig. 6.11).
(c) Free-standing litter bins (Fig. 6.12).
(d) Large capacity bins or containers for public spaces or sites adjoining roads.
(e) Movable containers for temporary use.

The list of approved designs for street furniture is avail-able from the Design Council Catalogue.

6.4.3 Materials
The choice of litter bin to be used will be dependent on its siting, its relationship to other street furniture, its capacity and its method of emptying. Materials available include:

Sheet Metals – Galvanised sheet metal with a galvanised wire removable inner container forms the traditional type

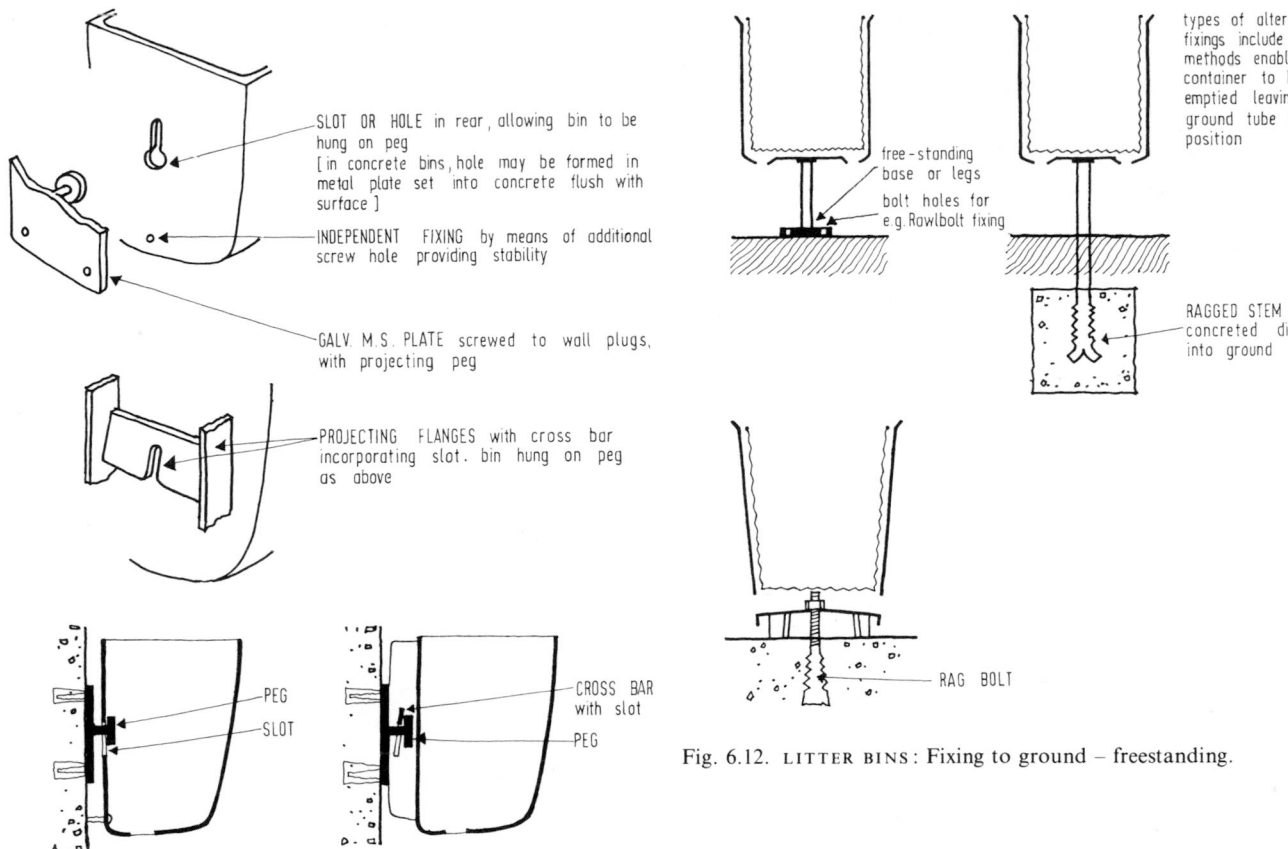

SLOT OR HOLE in rear, allowing bin to be hung on peg
[in concrete bins, hole may be formed in metal plate set into concrete flush with surface]

INDEPENDENT FIXING by means of additional screw hole providing stability

GALV. M.S. PLATE screwed to wall plugs, with projecting peg

PROJECTING FLANGES with cross bar incorporating slot. bin hung on peg as above

PEG
SLOT

CROSS BAR with slot
PEG

SECTIONS

EXAMPLES taken from a typical manufacturers product

Fig. 6.11. LITTER BINS: Fixing to walls.

types of alternative fixings include methods enabling container to be emptied leaving ground tube in position

free-standing base or legs
bolt holes for e.g. Rawlbolt fixing

RAGGED STEM concreted direct into ground

RAG BOLT

Fig. 6.12. LITTER BINS: Fixing to ground – freestanding.

of litter bin. The metal is normally galvanised or lead coated steel sheet and is usually available in any British Standard colour either stove-enamelled or spray painted. Perforated metal sheet is also available and plastic coated steel is offered by some manufacturers.

Aluminium – Cast aluminium is used for some litter bins generally cast in one piece with flanges, slots and drain holes; primed ready for painting as required on site. Removable wire baskets are provided either in galvanised mild steel wire or coated in plastic to any required colour. Care must be taken when using aluminium that fixings or any other adjacent metals are protected to ensure that no galvanic action takes place with the aluminium.

Timber – Various designs of litter bins are produced in oak or oiled teakwood slats mounted on galvanised steel strip. Inner baskets are either galvanised or of stove-enamelled sheet steel, or of a heavy gauge wire mesh.

Glass Fibre – Resin impregnated reinforced glass fibre or press-moulded containers are increasingly being used by local authorities. The glass fibre is self-coloured with smooth wall finishes on both surfaces and often fitted with a removable galvanised sheet metal inner container or alternatively a wire mesh basket.

Concrete – A number of containers are available constructed with a cast concrete outer shell; these are usually cast in one piece with fixing plates and holes. Generally the thickness of the shell varies from 30 to 60 mm (approx. $1\frac{1}{4}$ to $2\frac{3}{8}$ in) and normally the finish is smooth grey, using granite based aggregates, but alternative aggregates can be provided if an alternative finish is required. Removable internal wire baskets are provided in galvanised mild steel wire.

6.4.4 Costs
Table 6.3 sets out some comparative costs and materials available for pole-mounted, wall-mounted and free-standing litter bins.

6.4.5 Large capacity bins
These may often be designed as specific pieces of street furniture for urban or rural use. Where this type of con-

111

Plate 6.14. Reinforced precast concrete bin. Removable wire basket. Manufactured by Mono Concrete Limited.

These consist of free-standing containers with metal supports holding paper bags. The holders are galvanised or plastic coated and have either open tops or rubber or plastic lids. The sack of a high wet strength paper, or black–grey or dark-green polythene, is clipped to the top of the holder and is designed to be easily dismantled. Wire protectors for the sacks are now available against vermin attack. Stands can be in concrete or metal with wheels or legs and in some cases can be provided with pedal-operated lids. Wall-mounted types are also produced and further refinements in the design of the sacks include the introduction of polythene which is available in black or dark green.

tainer is used the design must take into account the infrequent servicing. Covers or lids are preferable; adequate self-drainage is needed and there are advantages with very large containers if arrangements can be made to burn the refuse whilst still in the container. Fig. 6.13 illustrates certain of the principles of this type of design. Standard designs are available in concrete, perforated metal, heavy duty polyethylene, and glass fibre, though the very large containers are usually specifically designed for their particular site.

6.4.6 Movable containers
The problems of litter disposal for functions of a temporary nature such as fairs, race meetings, processions, etc., have been considerably eased with the development of movable containers using disposable paper sacks.

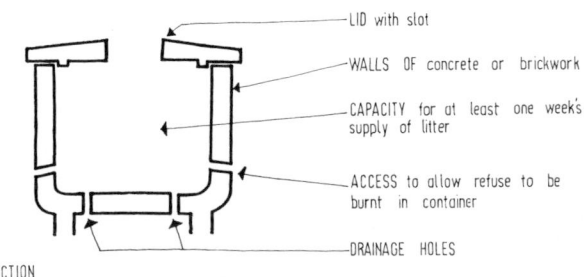

LID with slot

WALLS OF concrete or brickwork

CAPACITY for at least one week's supply of litter

ACCESS to allow refuse to be burnt in container

DRAINAGE HOLES

SECTION

Fig. 6.13. Large capacity bins.

Plate 6.15. Free standing litter bin made of steel and stove enamel. Designed by Design Research Unit.

TABLE 6.3: COMPARATIVE COST OF LITTER BINS

Materials	Cost* £	Notes
FREE-STANDING BINS Timber slatted	16–50	Slats in teak or other suitable hardwood
Galvanised steel sheet	12–33	Depending on finish or design
Concrete	30–57	Higher price range for large capacity bins
Galvanised mild steel refuse sack holders	9–30	With paper or polythene sacks. Lids in rubber or P.V.C.
Galvanised wire	8–13	Higher price range for large capacity bins
POLE- AND WALL-MOUNTED BINS Timber slatted	10–30	Interior containers usually stove enamelled or galvanised steel or wire
Steel sheet, galvanised, stove enamelled or plastic coated; aluminium Galvanised wire	6·50–60 11–13	Depending on size and design

* Prices shown are for comparative purposes only, detailed information should be obtained from manufacturers.

Plate 6.16. Double-sided litter bin forming part of co-ordinated system of street furniture, Birmingham. Designed by David Pearson. Manufactured by Urban Enviroscape Limited.

6.5 Signs and signboards

6.5.1 Design principles

Signs should be designed to ensure instant recognition by the clarity of the message. Uniformity of appearance, consistent application of symbols in preference to text, standard support structures, colour and type face, and uniform positioning of signs are essential aids to legibility. The more detailed the information the weaker is the impact of the message or its 'retention value'. Signs should be as few in number as possible and not add to the visual clutter; frequently too many signs only impede and confuse the public seeking information. This is particularly important for car drivers. Multiplicity of diverse signs defeats its own object and only produces visual chaos.

Where possible, therefore, signs should be mounted together and should be as small as compatible with their function and effectiveness. Motorway signs are very large; they are designed to be read from a great distance to give the driver travelling at speed adequate information in time; correspondingly sign areas can be reduced and become quite small where they are intended for pedestrians, provided they are not dwarfed by adjacent advertising or other messages.

Care should be taken that signs are not sited so as to be obscured by structures or growing trees or hedges.

They should easily be seen both by day and night, and the design must take into account the problems of illumination or the use of reflective materials.

In order to reduce the number of obstructions on the footpath, signs should be fixed to walls and other suitable structures where at all possible, but careful consideration should be given to their mounting height. The eye level of a driver in a car is substantially below that of a pedestrian; signs for vehicular traffic should not be more than 0·9–1·2 m (approx. 3–4 ft) measured from the ground to the bottom edge of the sign. Consistency of mounting height is most important since it will avoid unnecessary searching for vital information.

6.5.2 Types of signs

Signs fall into three types:
- (a) Signs giving definite instructions
  - (1) Mandatory.
  - (2) Prohibitory.
- (b) Warning signs.
- (c) Information signs.

There is no universally acknowledged classification for pictorial symbols, but those most frequently recognised, and identified, are road signs, and particularly those proposed at the 1949 Geneva Conference, which have since

Plate 6.17. Cast concrete town boundary marker, Saint Quentin En Yvelines, France. Designed by Kinneir Calvert Tuhill, London.

been adopted by most countries. The addition of a shape to a pictorial or typographic legend can invest a sign with extra meaning and colour is often a help to differentiate one category of information from another. Certain colours have accepted connotations when associated with danger and emergency, and should not be used for other purposes. As important as the face of the sign is the rear and support structure, which should be as inconspicuous as possible, and, in practice, is usually coloured black or dark grey.

6.5.3 Methods of sign manufacture
These include:

Silk screen reproduction. Modern screen printing is largely based on the use of stencils made from drawn or painted originals. A very wide range of materials can be printed, wood, metal, glass, fabrics, etc. The process is economic for small numbers.

Transfer lettering. This consists of printing on a thin film with either water or spirit soluble gum so that the layer of paint or ink forming the lettering or symbol can be slid off the face of the temporary carrier and stuck on to the permanent surface. It is possible to transfer complete notices in one operation.

Scotchlite and Scotchcal reproduction. A patented process, using a heat-vacuum application which causes a printed adhesive coating of Scotchcal or films of Scotchlite reflective sheetings to bond permanently on to a suitable backing, and enables superimposed lettering and emblems in these materials to become integrated with the backing material. The resulting sign should have a very much longer life than ordinary painted notices.

Photographic reproduction. Photographic prints of type setting are often used for temporary applications such as exhibitions, but can also be incorporated in a

114

laminated plastic which provides weather resistance. Because of cost, signs are largely confined to black and white. In spite of the laminated protective coating it is likely that colour photographs would fade under ultra-violet light (sunlight).

Three-dimensional signs. Formed by incised or raised lettering of many types. Materials used in the manufacture of solid letters and signs vary widely, e.g. they can be cut out of sheet plastic, sheet metal, cast in aluminium, engraved on plastics or metals or fabricated from wood. The choice depends on a number of factors and consultation with an expert sign-maker is advisable.

Painted signs. In spite of the methods for fabricated signs set out above painted signs are invaluable where only a few are required and renovation presents no problem. The success of a painted sign depends invariably on the skill of the craftsman signwriter. Control of painted signs is difficult since invariably a signwriter will have his own method and 'preferred alphabet'. A full size

template is invaluable in ensuring that the design is faithfully executed by the craftsman.

Carved or sculptured signs. In small park settings carved and painted timber signs are frequently quite appropriate and can enhance the character of the setting. Other suitable materials include stone, slate or concrete.

6.5.4 Materials for construction of signs

The choice of materials for sign panels or letters is generally determined by cost, appearance, durability and maintenance factors. Signs can be made from non-ferrous materials such as aluminium or aluminium alloy which are reasonable in cost, resist corrosion, are light in weight and can be embossed when in sheet form.

Vitreous enamel on a steel base is often used and has the advantage of colour fastness and long life (e.g. signs on railway stations and Underground stations), but it is liable to 'starring' from flying stones, etc., which can then destroy the finish. Enamelling can also suffer if any distortion occurs to the steel base and care must be taken

Plate 6.18. Neighbourhood boundary marker, Saint Quentin En Yvelines, France. Designed by Kinneir Calvert Tuhill, London.

Bold	Classical
VERTICAL	VERTICAL
New Haas Grotesque	New Clarendon
ITALIC	ITALIC
Doric Italic	*Ultra Bodoni*
CONDENSED	CONDENSED
Playbill	Roman Compressed
EXPANDED	EXPANDED
Egyptian Expanded	**Wide Latin**

Fig. 6.14. The examples illustrate some of the wide range of type faces available for signs and signboards.

in the fixing of the sign to its supports. Plastic signs usually of acrylic sheet are used either solid or transparent and illuminated from behind (e.g. petrol stations). If the number is large enough master moulds (which are expensive) will justify a three-dimensional treatment. Acrylic signs are particularly suitable in corrosive atmospheres and situations where the minimum of maintenance is required. Here again expert advice from the sign maker is essential at an early stage.

Other materials include plastic sheet, plywood or block board, aluminium, stainless steel, glass, laminates and perspex, all of which can be treated to aid cleaning, and for protection against weather and industrial fumes, etc. Weaknesses can, however, occur at the edges and in most cases protective film or lippings should be considered to keep the weather out.

6.5.5 Lettering

Lettering should be bold and simple. Sans serif lettering in upper and lower case is now used on traffic signs and the spacing of the letters has been rationalised as the result of the Traffic Signs (Worboys) Committee Report. This can well serve as a guide for many types of signs on which a landscape architect may be asked to advise. Where it is proposed to use type faces which are designed for printed text care should be taken not to misunderstand the nature of the type design. Type faces are designed flat compared with signs or lettering which are

two- or three-dimensional. They are intended to be seen at a certain distance and the subtleties of detail identifying the particular type face are only valid for these distances. They may diminish or become very obtrusive outside a limited range of sizes. The truly functional type face is the one that properly spaced makes its message clear from the distance from which it is intended to be read.

When considering the selection of lettering for signs it should be confined to as few type faces as possible and it must be decided if a classical or bold type is required; also whether an expanded or condensed type face is best suited to the particular layout or sign. Fig. 6.14 indicates some differences between bold and classical letter types.

The degree of clarity and legibility of any lettering is not only determined by the size of the letters themselves

Plate 6.19. Standard entrance sign for the Milan Underground.

116

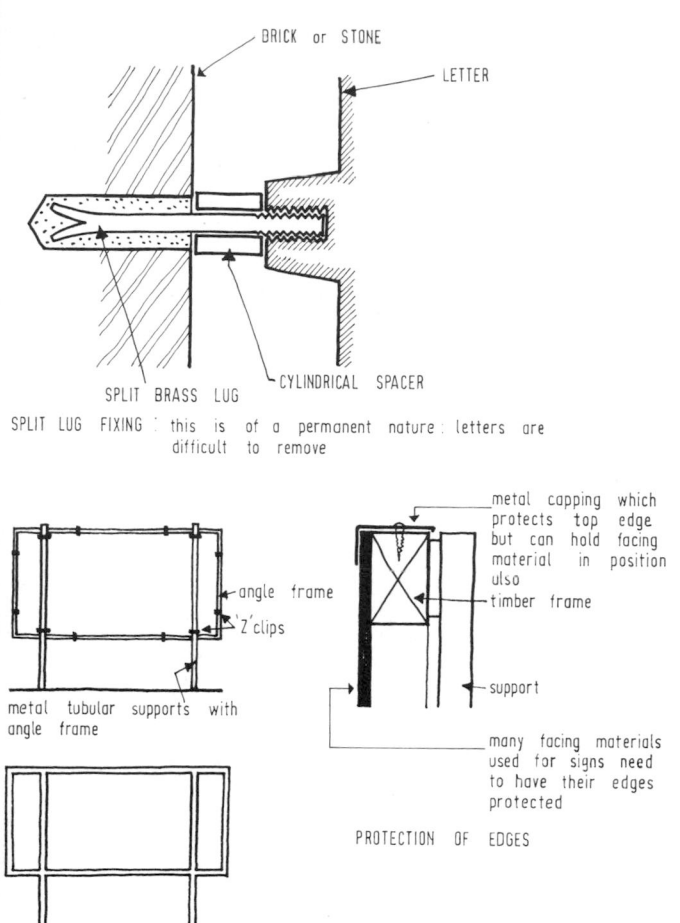

SPLIT LUG FIXING : this is of a permanent nature : letters are difficult to remove

metal tubular supports with angle frame

simple timber frame

SIGN SUPPORTS

PROTECTION OF EDGES

Fig. 6.15. Fixing methods for signs.

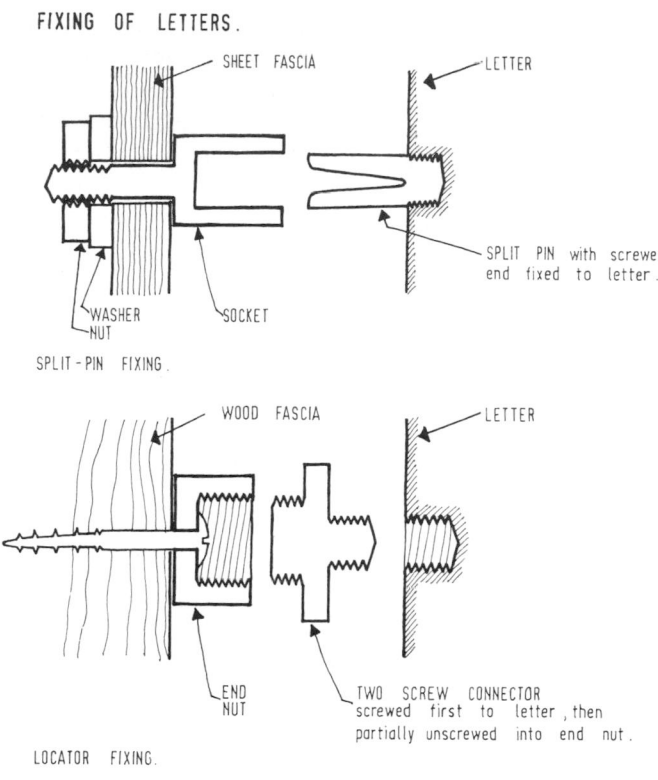

FIXING OF LETTERS.

SPLIT-PIN FIXING.

LOCATOR FIXING.

Fig. 6.16. Fixing of letters.

but should be borne in mind that the pleasing appearance of lettering depends as much on the spacing between the letters as upon their shape. A type face should be selected that offers freedom of space and if special titling of descriptive material is required the use of lower case letters may prove helpful.

Lighting. Lighting is an essential factor in the effective function of a sign and it may be necessary to increase this either with individual spot-lights or by a generally higher level of illumination. Interior back-lit signs have some problems and will only be effective if they are made of the right materials including the appropriate light fitting to enable easy replacement of lighting tubes or lamps.

6.5.6 Fixings
The fixing of signs can be broadly defined into side projecting, top hanging, flat mounted and free-standing. Top hung signs should either be firmly fixed to avoid damage through movement by wind or be allowed to swing freely.

Plate 6.20. Direction sign. Heathrow Airport.

Projecting signs should allow for stress or strain at weight bearing points. Fig. 6.15 illustrates various forms of fixing the different types of signs. Where applied letters are used the most satisfactory type of fixing, in most cases, is a locator, which provides the letter with a stand-off from the facia. This eliminates the risk of weather staining and also allows the letters to be easily removed, or replaced (Fig. 6.16).

Bibliography

Better litter bins, *Design*, December 1960.
Floodlighting of Buildings, Technical Report No. 6, Illuminating Engineering Society.
Flower boxes and architecture, W. R. Watson-Smyth, *Architect and Building News*, 22 May 1952.
Lettering on Buildings, Nicholete Gray, Architectural Press.
Lettering for Architects and Designers, Milner Gray and Ronald Armstrong, Batsford.
'Lighting of parks, statues and water displays', L. Gaymond, *A.P.L.E. Conference Report*, 1963.
Pride of Place (how to improve your surroundings), Civic Trust.
Street Furniture, from Design Index 1979, Design Council.
A Sign Systems Manual, Crosby, Fletcher and Forbes, Studio Vista.
Traffic Signs, Report of Committee on Traffic Signs for All-Purpose Roads, H.M.S.O.
Street Scene, Design Council 1976.

7 Water

D. G. THORNLEY

This chapter incorporates many of the items on water features in landscape design dealt with by G. A. Jellicoe who was the chapter author in the 1967 publication of *Techniques of Landscape Architecture*. The present version has been re-written to deal with water at the large landscape scale, in reservoirs and recreation areas especially, where the landscape architect works in collaboration with planners and engineers. A specialist section has also been provided by O. L. Gilbert to outline biological techniques which can be employed in design and maintenance.

7.1 Introduction

7.1.1 Water as an element in landscape design
Water may appear as an important element in both natural and man-made landscapes and in either it may assume a wide variety of forms of the largest and smallest scale. In the case of natural landscape the landscape architect may be called upon to prepare schemes related

Plate 7.1. Buttermere. Land form and water related at a large scale.

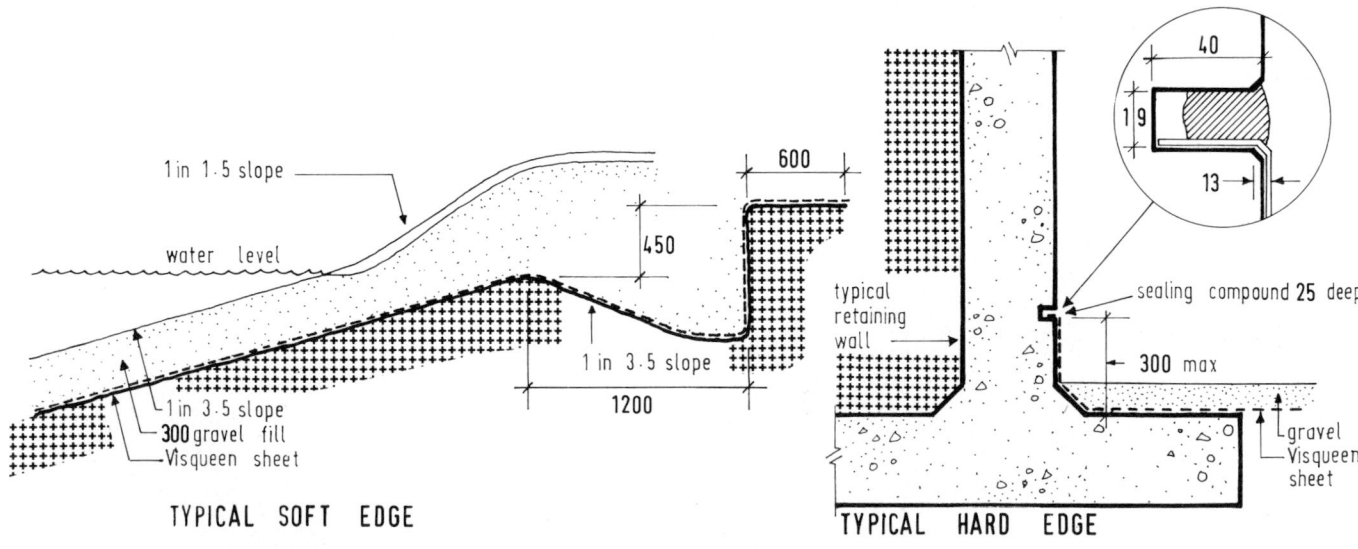

Plate 7.2. Marlow-on-Thames. A highly humanised riverside landscape.

to the sea coast, lakes and river banks as well as stream courses and smaller areas of water. In the man-made landscape the range is equally great, and extends from functional water works such as reservoirs, canals and drainage schemes to purely decorative features such as fountains, cascades and similar elements which for so long have formed part of the normal repertoire of garden design.

Fig. 7.1. Details of soft and hard edges to pools lined with polythene sheeting.

120

Artificial lakes have provided focal elements and a horizontal base around which the scenery may be composed in informal man-made landscapes since the early eighteenth century, while in earlier periods in history the more severe lines of canals and tanks have helped to provide a geometrically ordered framework for the formal garden. More recently the increasing demands for both water and recreational facilities have led to proposals for schemes combining several functions and conceived on the very largest scale in riverside developments, reservoirs and the bay-barrages which are at present under consideration.

Water as a landscape material has its own very special qualities of change, movement and a variation under the play of wind and light which set it apart from all other materials. The fact that it is at times unpredictable in its changes and even somewhat difficult to control only adds to its interests and general appeal.

This section provides an introduction to the design of water elements in landscape schemes.

7.1.2 Water supply

Natural.　　　　Running water from a spring or stream is usually very fertile. It is important to make sure that the supply is not significantly reduced in the dry months of the year with the result that stream courses dry up or ponds are reduced in level. The use of any water from a stream, river or underground source requires the permission of the appropriate section of the Regional Water Authority.

Piped water.　　　　This provides a guaranteed supply and can be obtained from the local Water Authority with a payment according to the requirements. Because of the cost involved and the need to conserve water the supply is usually recirculated and topped up to make good evaporation losses, etc. Piped water has normally been filtered and treated chemically and is, therefore, infertile.

7.1.3 Water retention

In an excavation in the ground water will normally be retained at or near the level of the water table. This may be well below the ground surface and may be changed by modifications to adjoining ground levels or by the extraction of water from the substrata. If there is any doubt the holding capacity of ponds, lakes, etc. may be tested with trial sumps over a period of several weeks.

There are a variety of retaining materials available which are suitable for lining ponds, lakes and water courses. These include puddle clay, reinforced or mass concrete, timber and the more recently introduced plastic materials. The choice of one or other of these materials will be influenced by the nature of the problem being dealt with, appearance and cost (see Fig. 7.1).

7.2　Tranquil water

7.2.1　Natural rivers, lakes and pools

Where it is desirable to create an informal or apparently natural sheet of water, the treatment of the banks is of paramount importance. The problem is to create artificially a system of defence against water that would take a long time to evolve naturally. There are two main methods of dealing with the effects of scour water in motion; that of following the *natural way*, which with an existing hard material such as rock depends upon the nature of the rock itself, and care in choosing a line which will expose the right shape and amount of rock. Careful stripping to cleavage and bedding planes will allow a more ready weathering and help to avoid a long period of rawness if the rock is one which normally weathers reasonably rapidly. With soft soil it may be possible to establish a vegetation margin, which if temporarily protected during early stages, will become sufficiently durable as a 'natural' bank. It is a method that has been studied over a long period in Germany under Professor Seifert, but because of the discouraging time factor there is little experience in this country. The other way is the *artificial way* where the visual effect is informal but not necessarily naturalistic. In certain stone counties such as Oxfordshire it is still economic to use the traditional method of random stones deposited dry against the bank, and generally used at the bend of rivers. If a formal surface such as timber or concrete is used, it must finish as close as reasonable to the water surface, with the soil and plants so disposed as to conceal the edge.

If the water is fertile the natural bottom of pools presents no problems of aesthetics, however difficult may be that of cleaning (see section 7.1).

7.2.2　Artificial canals, lakes and pools

Depth.　　　　Care should be taken to decide the correct depth, which depends upon the purpose. Paddling pools are described below, but non-paddling pools in public places should be not less that 525 mm (approx. 21 in) deep in order to discourage children but not too deep for safety. A water lily pool may vary from 200 to 400 mm (approx 8–16 in) or more, depending upon the variety of plant. A reflecting pool, giving the same effect as a puddle, may be as shallow as is practicable, taking evaporation loss into account. A fish pool can be deeper, and should provide also for privacy. Boating and amusement lakes need to be deep enough for rowing, but for safety and economy should not exceed this depth. Unless the designer has other good reasons, it is an axiom in pool design that the water level be as close to the rim as is consistent with wind disturbance; a pool is most convivial when it is abundantly full and 'winking at the brim'.

Floors. Although reflections are the main pleasure of static water, the eye penetrates the surface especially when looking down from above as from a bridge or an upper window. For this reason it is wise to design the bottom to give added interest remembering that it is to be seen through water and consequently the view is confused by light refraction. The following are a few of the examples that are within range of decorative design:

A surface of rough stones set in concrete: these will collect plants and will soon be transformed into a green bottom of great charm. The following for infertile water only: a pattern of circles or other designs of movement incised in the surface concrete before it has set; painted surfaces of all kinds; large pebbles spread loose upon the surface, chosen and disposed for their colour pattern; if in a public place these should only be used where there is proper supervision. In a public garden a rough surface uncomfortable to the bare feet discourages paddling.

Weirs. In any large scheme it is essential that levels over the whole area be taken exactly, for an opportunity may arise for making weirs and cascades even on apparently level sites. Where there is an abundance of water, there should be a lip so that water falls clear of the vertical. The specification must state that this lip is to be exactly level, and no approval should be given until the first water test has been made. As the water course may need to be drained off, a pipe or similar opening should be provided through the bottom of the weir wall which can be opened when required. If the water flow is small or likely to be so in dry weather, it is advisable to assist the effect of falling water by an illusion such as channelling the water into vertical grooves in the face.

Overflows and drainage. The overflow should be inconspicuous unless developed as a feature such as a cascade: its level should be determined exactly beforehand, and not an approximation. For emptying purposes the floors of all artificial pools, etc. should fall to a drainage outlet (Figs. 7.2 and 7.3). Small pools can be satisfactory without any plumbing. Unnecessary equipment is to be avoided in such cases. Filling can be by hosepipe, and emptying by portable pump or syphon. The overflow may irrigate bog plants; alternatively a soakaway can be arranged under a pebbled area.

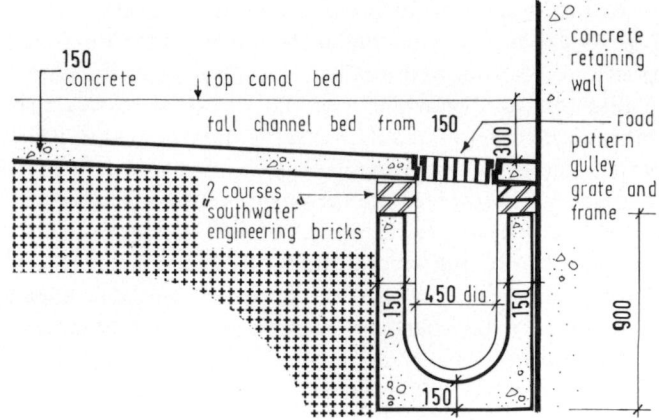

Fig. 7.2. Section through a typical cleaning channel.

7.2.3 The diversion of running water during progress of works

It is imperative that during the preparation of the designs a phasing plan be drawn up to indicate how the contractors can divert a stream or river upon which the landscape architect has set a new design. This problem may sometimes determine the actual design; in any case diversion may be costly. To make the canal dry for the contractors at Hemel Hempstead, the river was let into a new but unused sewer and pumped out to rejoin the old bed downstream.

7.2.4 Construction of a large pool

The services of an engineer are advisable. The following is a description of a typical construction:

The foundation naturally depends on site conditions, but in general a 150 mm (approx. 6 in) minimum thickness of well-consolidated hardcore, with 50 mm (approx. 2 in) of blinding concrete is required, any soft spots being excavated and filled with hardcore. It is desirable to cover

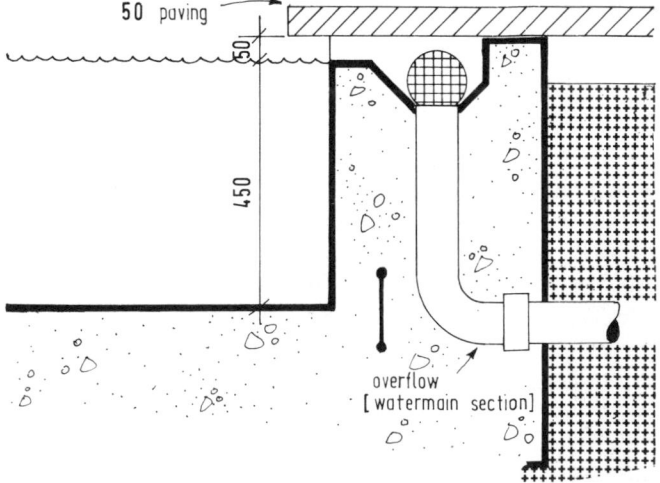

Fig. 7.3. Section through the concealed overflow of a garden pool.

122

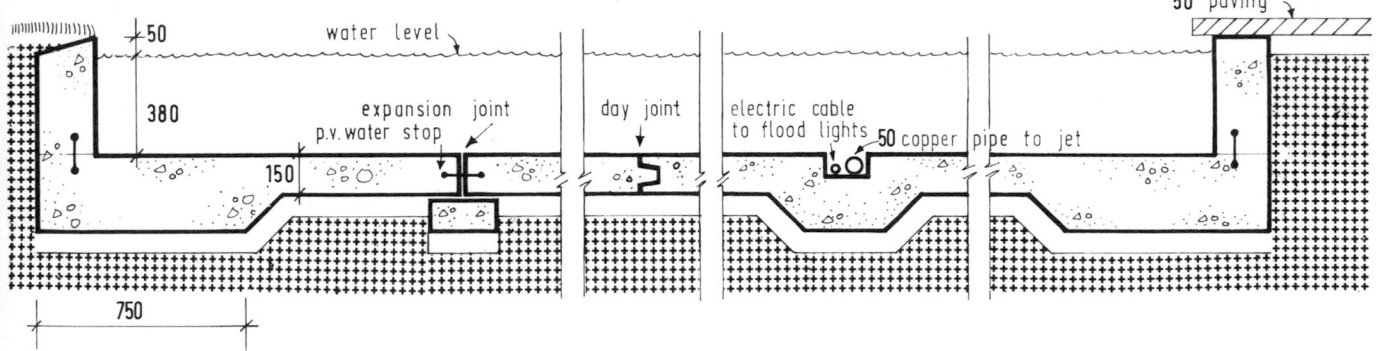

Fig. 7.4. Section showing jointing details and alternative edge designs for a reinforced concrete pool.

the blinding concrete with a layer of waterproof paper or plastic sheeting to enable the structural bed to move freely and so permit any movement to occur at predetermined joints (Fig. 7.4).

The design of the structural bed depends on the depth of the pool and the site conditions. For deep pools constructed on sites with high water table levels, consideration must be given to the pressure of water acting under the pool. This pressure not only affects the strength of the bed, but it can also lift the whole pool should it be emptied for cleaning or other purposes. The slab may have to be increased to provide dead weight, and specially reinforced to resist outside pressure when empty.

In general the minimum thickness of the structural bed should be 150 mm (approx. 6 in) of vibrated reinforced concrete of 1 : 2 : 4 mix with 19 mm (approx. $\frac{3}{4}$ in) maximum sized aggregate. Precautions must be taken to prevent shrinkage cracks which occur when concrete dries out. This can be achieved by dividing the bed into a number of bays not exceeding 20 sq m (approx. 215 sq ft). Individual bays are then cast and isolated from the adjoining bays by 450 mm (approx. 18 in) gaps, the edges of the bays being shuttered to form continuous grooves or rebates. After 2 or 3 days, when each bay has dried out and shrunk, the gaps are carefully filled in. It should be noted that the reinforcement must be continued across the joints.

Expansion joints are also required to allow for movement which may occur in the concrete bed due to temperature changes. The joints should divide the bed into bays not exceeding 9 m (approx. 30 ft) in width or 85 sq m (approx. 915 sq ft) in area and where they terminate at the edge of the pool they must continue up and into the wall. The joint is constructed by casting a water stop into the edges of two slabs which are 25 mm (approx. 1 in) or so apart, the gap being filled with a flexible filling to within 25 mm (approx. 1 in) of the top and later com-

pletely sealed with mastic. The water stop is a strip of P.V.C. or rubber 150–225 mm (approx. 6–9 in) wide and shaped rather like a dumb-bell in section. It should be noted that, unlike the day joint, the reinforcement must not continue over the gap. Because of this the two slab edges should be supported on a continuous concrete strip beam.

The wall of the pool will naturally vary in thickness according to the depth of water retained and the amount of reinforcement employed, but in general 200 mm (approx. 8 in) should be adequate for most pools. The wall should be cast in maximum lengths of 6 m (approx. 20 ft) with joints similar to those used in the bottom slab. Expansion joints as previously mentioned should be a continuation of the joints used in the bed. The wall is usually shuttered on top of the edge of the structural slab and as there will be a horizontal joint at this point, a continuous water stop should be used. Alternatively a continuous groove or rebate can be cast into the top of the slab at this point and after the surface has been thoroughly roughened by hacking, the wall can be shuttered and cast on.

7.2.5 Construction of small pools

Any variation from the rectangle or straight line will affect the material used. Curved shuttering to concrete is expensive and usually beyond the capacity of a small contractor; small units such as bricks are more flexible and familiar. Fibreglass in one piece is now used for very small pools; the designer should acquaint himself with its properties.

7.2.6 Swimming pools

Location. This must be sunny and protected from wind. Pools need a supply of water and electricity, and enough space to contain the chlorinating plant, which is not easily concealed. Siting should be not too

123

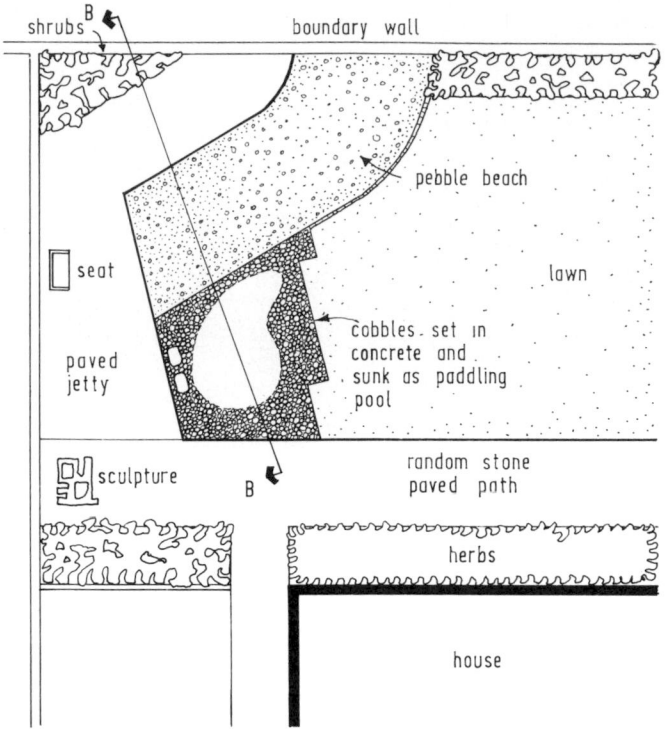

GARDEN PLAY AREA

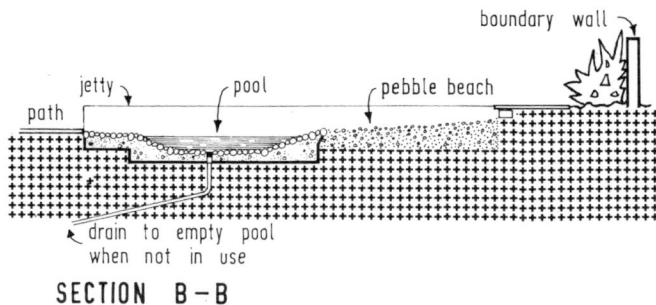

SECTION B—B

Fig. 7.5. Paddling pool, with associated detailing.

close to trees, because of falling leaves. The immediate surroundings must include sufficient hard surface as durable margins and for sunbathing.

Construction and equipment. In principle the construction is similar to that of a large pool, but because of the technical complexities such as that of the chlorinating plant, the heating plant, if there is one, cleanliness generally, and safety precautions, it is advisable to take expert advice from the many firms who now specialise in standard construction and equipment. If the pool is tiled special attention should be given to the expansion joints of the concrete; tiles have been known to buckle in an empty pool twenty years after completion. It is often

desirable to depart from a standard design, but the landscape architect must thoroughly understand the constructional principles which are usually established by long experience. Many of the specialist firms provide a design service and build pools and supply and instal all necessary purification and maintenance equipment.

The effect of chlorinating plant. The water is defertilised and is therefore manifestly artificial. The usual commercial colour of light blue is given by chlorinated rubber enamel, but this can be obtained in alternative tones, such as pure white which tends to emphasise the colour of the water itself. In small private pools the inflow of the circulating water is usually invisible, but in larger pools and lidos this can be a considerable feature as a cascade.

Natural heating. It is now possible to cover small pools with polythene, which collects the sun's heat and raises the temperature. In practice it is troublesome to cover and uncover, and looks disagreeable in the landscape.

7.2.7 Paddling pools
The isolated paddling pool recalls natural conditions and therefore should have a shelving beach of a material, such as smooth pebbles, associated with nature. The floor under the water should be enjoyable to the soles of the feet. It should not be so deep as to cover children's knees. It must be able to be easily cleaned (Fig. 7.5).

Facilities for children paddling are becoming a feature in rivers and lakes in urban areas. Care must be given to the problems of scouring, cleanliness, and the safety of those who adventure into deeper water (Plate 7.3).

Plate 7.3. Paddle pool, Elm Tree Road, London (see Fig. 7.5).

Plate 7.4. Water barrier between factory and public highway, Moreton, Cheshire.

7.2.8 Water barriers

The modern water barrier corresponds to the eighteenth century ha-ha, for its purpose is to provide a fence which, although not itself invisible, nevertheless conceals its true purpose. Like a normal so-called unclimbable fence, its intention is not to keep out the determined attack but rather the casual. It should be more than jumping width and too deep for paddling; its water must be fresh under one of the systems described above; it should be decora-

tive in appearance. Its traditional forbear in England is the cattle moat round a manor house, rather than the impregnable castle moat (Plate 7.4).

7.2.9 Water and industry

Modern industry needs huge volumes of water for cooling. This water may be recirculated together with additional make-up water, or cooled and returned to the river. In either case a considerable structure is called for, and the opportunity of creating a landscape asset should be seized wherever possible. For instance, there is in the central area of St. Helen's, Lancashire, a display of cooling fountains probably unequalled anywhere and yet not recognised for more general application of their spectacular potential.

It must be accepted that there is at present no more efficient way of cooling water than the enclosed vertical cooling tower which creates a forced upward draught. But where circumstances allow, there is opportunity for the cooling lake and fountains. The use of tepid water for fish farming or for stocking with tropical fish has still to be explored.

7.2.10 Drainage and erosion prevention as landscape features

Drainage ditches may appear as very prominent features

Plate 7.5. Noord-Oost Polder, Holland. The scenic structure determined by drainage channels, land sub-division and shelter planting.

Plate 7.6. Eroded gulley, East Lothian. Wicker dams built to reduce mechanical erosion.

Plate 7.7. Eroded gulley, East Lothian. Colonisation of stabilised gulley by coarse plant material.

in the landscape and particularly so in flat country where they may impose a regular rectangular grid on the field and boundary pattern. The most obvious case of this latter kind is the polder land recovered from the sea in Holland. The introduction of balancing pools intended to accommodate an abnormal run-off of large quantities of water where drainage conditions are poor may also provide opportunities for the creation of fairly large bodies of water as elements in the landscape. Where these features are likely to appear the Drainage Authority for the area concerned should be consulted.

Erosion problems may call for special measures in order to prevent rivers changing their course or an unacceptable degree of erosion on river banks and on the shores of lakes which are exposed to wave action. These measures may take the form of pitching on the bank with rock, concrete blocks or a similar hard material, the introduction of sheet piling where conditions are severe, or the introduction of gabions formed of moderately sized pieces of stone held together in a regular mass by galvanised wire mesh. All these features are likely to form very visible elements in the local scenery.

Serious erosion problems may also occur where stream courses run down steep slopes formed of an unstable material such as shale. In these cases very deep gullies may be formed on the lower levels of the slope and may work their way upwards as erosion continues. In pasture land, and particularly in high ground, the erosion may be aggravated and kept active at the head of the gully by sheep or cattle sheltering beneath the overhanging rim. The first measure to be taken in eradicating the very prominent scars which may be formed on the hillside is to fence off the area to keep sheep and cattle out and to prevent plant material which colonises the gullies from being grazed. Forestry type netted fencing which keeps out rabbits and hares as well as cattle is appropriate for this purpose. In order to reduce the physical erosion of the subsoil by the stream course small dams constructed of wicker hurdles or other similar material should be built across the stream course at 5–6 m (approx. 16–20 ft) centres. These may need repairing from time to time until the ground has been recolonised by plant material as the amount of shale and gravel retained can be considerable and may result in the dam being deformed or burst open. In addition, the rapid colonisation of the eroded area can be encouraged by introducing small quantities of fertiliser and seeding the gully with rank and rapidly growing species. Mustard and Rose Bay Willow Herb have been used with success in establishing the first stages of plant cover (Plates 7.6 and 7.7).

7.3 Turbulent water

7.3.1 Fountains in water

Apart from conveying water irrationally and delightfully from one spot to another, fountains can also have functional purposes, for example to cleanse the surface of the water by spraying; to cool it for industry or to discourage paddling.

Originally fountain design was governed by gravity supply of water. Fountains have never been so popular in England as in the hot countries, probably wholly because of climatic conditions; they should therefore be used with discretion since in wet weather they add to the sense of gloom and dampness. Partly for this reason, the study of fountain design in this country has lagged behind that of the continent; we are almost entirely inexperienced in not only what effect we want, but how to get it. The circulating and pressure pump have overcome dif-

126

ficulties of supply and head, and the appropriate power can be calculated by the manufacturer when he knows the total number of jets and their sizes and the height of throw required.

Location. In principle the jets should come at some time between the spectators and the sun, since the jet of water is most spectacular when it appears luminous. Fountains should not be in too enclosed a space, for climatic reasons. The distance from any public path should be at least three times the height of the jet owing to wind gusts; this may be modified if height can be controlled by valves.

Design. Unless the landscape architect is thoroughly experienced in fountain design, he will find it impossible on the drawing board to reach anything other than a first approximation of design. Probably the most technically proficient of all fountains are those at Versailles, where experience was gained continuously over a number of years. The problem in Britain is that the demand for original fountains is small and the expenditure on each is so modest that neither professional nor contractor can afford to spend a great deal of time in experimenting. But it is important that a contingency is included in the estimate for rearranging nozzles on site, adjusting some to new design arrangements, and if necessary changing them. Generally it is possible to fix on paper the placing of nozzles, but it is not possible (without great experience) to foresee the exact arcs and interlacing lines of the jets themselves.

Pipe sizing and power. These requirements vary according to the design, and early advice should be taken from the manufacturers. Precautions must be taken, especially where there are leaves, that the return flow is protected by a wire basket (or something similar) to prevent blockage.

Pipe lines. The simplest method is to run the pipes along a groove or chase in the surface of the bottom of the pool or basin and fill in with a weak mortar. This can easily be removed should repairs be required. Normal materials are copper and iron and where they pass through a concrete wall or bed, a puddle or otherwise waterproofed flange must be fitted and cast in with the concrete wall.

Plastic pipes are also suitable and are sometimes claimed to be invisible, although in practice this is not the case.

Height of nozzles. These should normally be concealed, but when projecting above the surface of the water should do so to the minimum height consistent with efficiency.

Plate 7.8. A modern fountain in Freiburg, West Germany. The jets are programmed to vary their height at intervals in groups.

Mechanical variation of flow. A recent development in fountain design has been the introduction of variations in the direction and rate of flow of water by mechanical means or by controlled variation of the rate of flow of the water supply. This may involve the tipping and emptying of containers when filled, or alternatively a series of jets which rise and fall at intervals in accordance with a prearranged programme. This kind of device can be entertaining in some circumstances such as public squares and noisy urban situations, but care should be taken in introducing such features in situations where quiet and repose are an important factor in the general design (Plate 7.8).

Although piped water is normally sterile, the introduction of water plants into pools and basins can rapidly produce extensive biological activity. This frequently leads to the coating of flooded surfaces with moss and fine green slime. It is worth remarking that while this may be perfectly acceptable and even improve the appearance of conventional stone fountains and cascades the appearance of green biological material on brightly polished

Plate 7.9. Trevi Fountain, Rome. Probably the most masterly work in existence combining sculpture, water and rock form. (Designed after Boromini.)

Plate 7.10. Bubble fountain, West Germany Pavilion, Brussels Exhibition, 1958.

stainless steel surfaces in modern water features may be most unfortunate.

7.3.2 Fountains and sculpture
In design it must be decided whether the water or sculpture motif is to predominate. In practice the sculpture should be wholly wet or wholly dry, unless it has been previously planned otherwise as in many compositions on a grand scale, e.g. Trevi Fountain, Rome (Plate 7.9).

7.3.3 Bubble fountains
These are an interpretation of a natural spring. Their purpose is to keep adjoining material damp; they should be used in conjunction with materials such as the English marbles, which best display their quality when wet. A recent design from Germany was installed in Russell Square where the bubble emerged from the hole in the centre of a stone; clearly care must be taken to ensure evenness of distribution, and an agreeable surrounding overflow such as through pebbles (Plate 7.10).

7.4 Biological aspects

7.4.1 Water and vegetation
Biologists recognise two types of freshwater. Oligotrophic water is unproductive and usually acidic and, due to the low concentration of certain major nutrients, colonisation by plant and animal life is minimal so the water remains clear. Water of this type is becoming increasingly rare in Britain but good examples can still be found in the uplands where Water Authorities delight to get their hands on them. Most lakes, ponds and streams in lowland Britain contain eutrophic water rich in nutrients such as nitrogen and phosphorus and with a pH in the range 7–8. These highly productive waters support abundant rooted vegetation, large fish populations and dense plankton crops which may give rise to waterblooms in summer and autumn. The Shropshire Meres, the Fens, all canals, farm and village ponds and most arti-

ficial shallow water bodies are of this type. Waters intermediate between these two types are designated mesotrophic.

Under natural conditions the pattern of marginal aquatic vegetation is the same for both types although the species involved may differ. Marsh vegetation on the seasonally waterlogged soils of the bank passes into a tall emergent reed swamp dominated by monocotyledons rooted in shallow water. In deeper water beyond the reed beds a belt of plants with floating leaves usually occurs and beyond this again, often only accessible from a boat, is a zone of dense, totally submerged vegetation. Factors such as grazing, exposure, an unfavourably coarse substratum or a fluctuating water level can upset this classic pattern. The hydrosere – invasion of open water by plants – is fast in eutrophic waters but under oligotrophic condi-

128

tions it proceeds infinitely slowly except around the inflow and in sheltered bays.

The water body most commonly created or manipulated by landscape architects is the shallow eutrophic lake. These pose a challenge as if poorly designed they can quickly silt up, become choked with vegetation, vast blankets of floating algae may appear or the water may turn green and start to smell.

At the design stage these problems can be reduced by providing for a good depth (2 m (6 ft 6 in) over two-thirds of the area) and flow of water and if possible arranging for particularly dirty or nutrient rich water, i.e. from roads or playing fields to follow a bypass system. One should be wary of the ambition of civil engineers to direct all storm water into the nearest stream. Large numbers of water fowl should not be allowed on small lakes as they exacerbate eutrophication problems and excessively enriched water is passed on to the next user. If it is policy to keep ducks off a lake as at Bath University, island refuges and plants which provide food for them should be avoided. In most lakes a certain turbidity of the water after rain and algal mats in summer will have to be accepted as natural.

7.4.2 Techniques for design and management
Planting. Water plants are very mobile and for the first years after filling a new lake can be expected to arrive naturally at the rate of 1–2 species per annum.

We have a wide range of native species in this country and water schemes can be successfully stocked using these. It is important to remember that they like a sunny position and not to plant deeper than the depth at which you can see a white saucer on a sunny day. Certain marsh species are very typical of eutrophic waters especially meadowsweet (*Filipendula ulmaria*) and Great Hairy Willow-Herb (*Epilobium hirsutum*) which increase spectacularly if sewage or agricultural fertilisers get into a pond or ditch. Table 7.1 provides a guide to the requirements of some common aquatic species. There is no need to plant large amounts of most water plants as given the correct conditions they spread vigorously. Many grow too well. Over 28 tons of vegetation (mainly the reed-mace *Typha*) are removed annually from the ambitious water scheme at York University and our countryside is full of lakes which in summer are solid with water lily.

Maintenance. Most water schemes require some maintenance if details of the original design are to be retained. When attempting to control aquatic vegetation it should be pulled up and not cut as cutting only stimulates new growth. This can conveniently be done by a man in waders working with a rake. The most suitable method of control in polythene-lined lakes is to restrict the use of the growth medium (topsoil or river silt) during construction. The use of algicides or herbicides is not

Plate 7.11. Broadleaved pondweed (*Potamogeton natans*) and bur-reed (*Sparganium erectum*).

Plate 7.12. Detail of ornamental pond in a Sheffield Park. White water lily (*Nymphaea alba*) is zoned beyond a marginal reed bed composed mainly of the grass *Glyceria maxima* var *variegata*. In seeking to achieve a balance between water and aquatic vegetation it is important to remember one value of open water is that it provides reflections.

129

TABLE 7.1: HABITAT PREFERENCES OF A RANGE OF AQUATIC PLANTS

Species	Oligotrophic	Water type Mesotrophic	Eutrophic	Guide to planting depth		Approx. maximum depth*	
Emergent				mm	(in)	m	(in)
Acorus calamus (Sweet flag)	—	*	*	75–150	(3–6)	0·5	(20)
Alisma plantago-aquatica (Water plantain)	*	*	*	0–150	(0–6)	1·5	(59)
Butomus umbellatus (Flowering rush)	—	*	*	75–150	(3–6)	2·0	(79)
Glyceria maxima (Reed grass)	—	*	*	50–150	(3–6)	0·7	(28)
Iris pseudacorus (Yellow flag)	—	—	*	50–125	(3–5)	0·5	(20)
Mentha aquatica (Water mint)	—	*	*	0– 75	(0–3)	0·5	(20)
Phragmites communis (Reed)	*	*	*	75–200	(3–8)	1·0	(39)
Rumex hydrolapanthum (Great water dock)	—	—	*	0– 75	(0–3)	0·4	(16)
Sagittaria sagittifolia (Arrowhead)	—	*	*	75–150	(3–6)	1·5	(59)
Sparganium erectum (Bur-reed)	—	*	*	75–150	(3–6)	0·5	(20)
Typha latifolia (Great reedmace)	*	*	*	75–150	(3–6)	0·6	(24)
Floating leaved							
Callitriche stagnalis (Water starwort)	—	*	*	50–100	(2–4)	0·5	(20)
Lemna spp. (Duckweed)	—	—	*	A floating plant			
Nuphar lutea (Yellow waterlily)	—	*	*	up to 900	(36)	1·5	(50)
Nymphaea alba (White waterlily)	*	*	*	up to 900	(36)	1·6	(63)
Polygonum amphibium (Water bistort)	*	*	..	0–300	(0–12)	1·0	(39)
Potamogeton natans (Broadleaved pondweed)	*	*	*	150–500	(6–20)	2·0	(79)
Submerged							(ft)
Callitriche intermedia (Water starwort)	—	—	*	† see note		1·0	3
Chara spp. (Stonewort)	—	*	*			2·5	8
Elodea canadensis (Canadian pondweed)	—	*	*			3·0	10
Hippuris vulgaris (Marestail)	—	*	*			4·0	13
Myriophyllum spp. (Water milfoils)	—	*	*			1·5	5
Pontamegaton crispus (Curled pondweed)	—	*	*			6·0	20
Zannichellia palustris (Horned pondweed)	—	—	*			2·0	7

* The optimal depth for establishment is invariably shallower than the maximum depth to which a species will spread by vegetative means. Only very approximate depths can be given as this depends almost entirely on the clarity of the water. The figures are adapted from Spence's *Survey of Scottish Lakes* (1964) and the author's own observations.

† These are often just thrown in. They are unlikely to become rooted at depths below about 4 m.

recommended as they produce only temporary results. It is better to aim for a well-stocked ecosystem and let it achieve its own equilibrium with the prevailing conditions and management schedule. The ecological instability experienced after the construction or dredging of lakes gradually disappears.

Conservation. The number of ponds and ditches in the British countryside has declined sharply in recent years. Landscape architects should give some thought to redressing the balance by creating small waterbodies where appropriate and incorporating existing ones into their schemes. In Cardiff, collaboration between local naturalists and the City Parks Department resulted in the handsome pink-flowered rush (*Butomus umbellatus*) being moved to thirteen sites in the city a fortnight before its last native site in Glamorganshire was destroyed by tipping (Dennis 1972). Rescue operations of this sort are rare.

7.5 Water in storage reservoirs

7.5.1 Water catchment

With the increase in world populations and the increasing demands of industry, water conservation and distribution has become a matter of great importance for the community as a whole. Since April 1974 the responsibility for water supply together with the surveillance of rivers and the disposal of sewage has been vested in the nine Water Authorities which between them cover England and Wales. In Scotland and Northern Ireland the responsibility still lies with local Water Boards and Local Authorities.

Generally the Water Authorities deal with the broad strategy of conservation of water resources including ground water, while distribution is dealt with by local

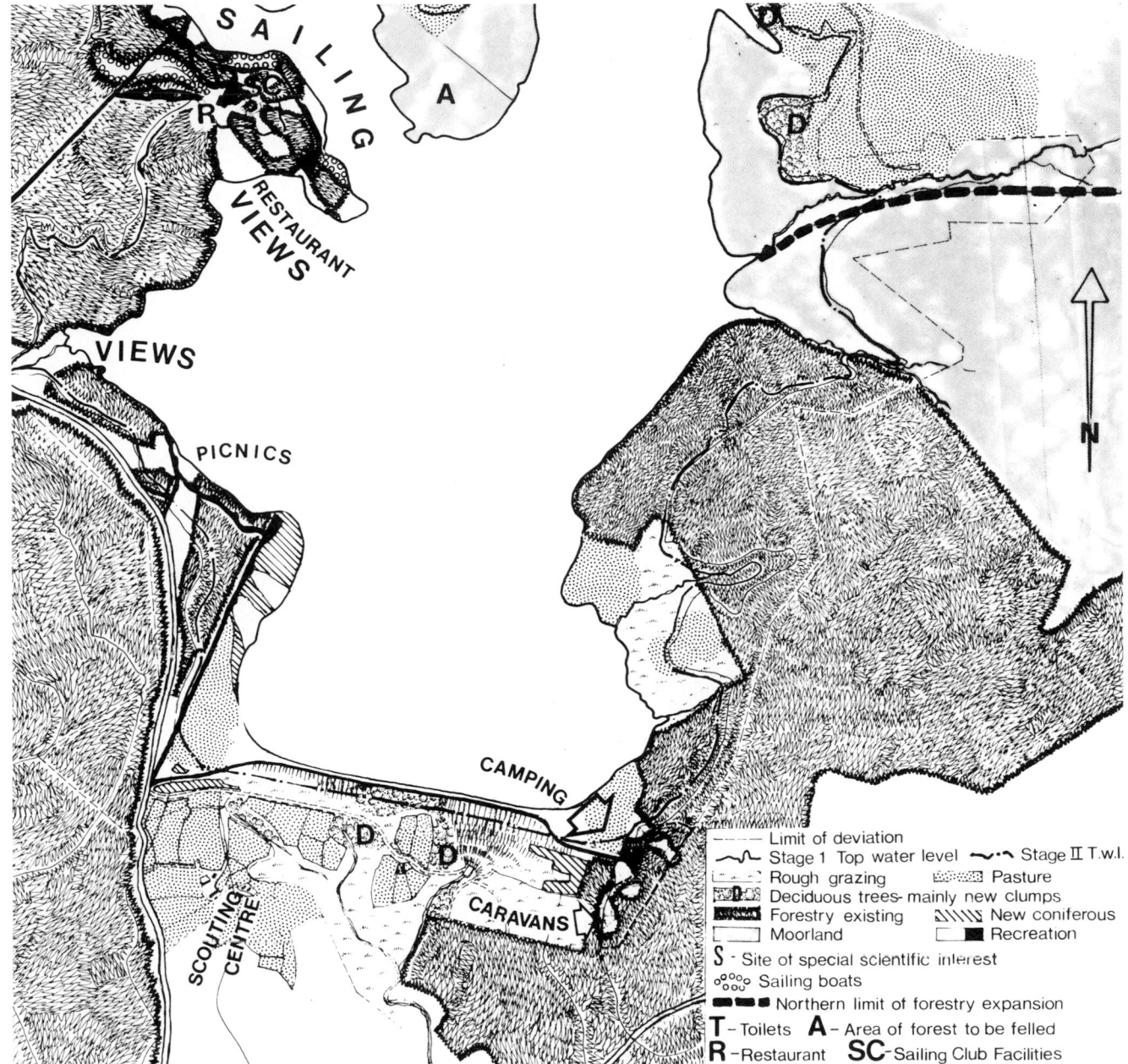

Fig. 7.6. Plan, Brenig Reservoir.

Legend:
- Limit of deviation
- Stage 1 Top water level — Stage II T.w.l.
- Rough grazing — Pasture
- Deciduous trees- mainly new clumps
- Forestry existing — New coniferous
- Moorland — Recreation
- **S** - Site of special scientific interest
- Sailing boats
- Northern limit of forestry expansion
- **T** - Toilets **A** - Area of forest to be felled
- **R** - Restaurant **SC** - Sailing Club Facilities

Water Divisions, Water Boards and some private companies. It may be assumed that any scheme which involves the creation of substantial bodies of water, the modification of stream or river courses or the use of water in quantity including that recovered from underground sources would be of concern to the appropriate Water Authority.

In the past most reservoirs were built in upland country where rainfall was heavier and where there was less danger of pollution from the smaller population. More recently pumped-storage reservoirs and bunded reservoirs in lowland country have become common while very large-scale barrage schemes sited in river estuaries are being subjected to feasibility studies. While the upland reservoirs almost inevitably occupy sites in areas of high scenic amenity lowland sites may occur both in high amenity areas and in areas of relatively flat and featureless landscape close to major centres of population. In all cases the creation of a new reservoir offers great opportunities and makes great demands in terms of landscape design and particularly so in view of the many conflicting interests which emerge during the proceedings related to the promotion of schemes of this kind.

131

Plate 7.13. Derwent Reservoir, Northumberland.

7.5.2 Construction

The most common form of reservoir involves the impounding of water behind an embankment built of rock or similar material or a dam built of concrete or stone, the method of construction depending on local conditions and the availability of materials. Since the water surface follows the adjoining ground form the lake created can assume a very natural appearance particularly where side valleys and smaller indentations in the surrounding slopes lead to the formation of a highly articulated shoreline. A reservoir with a complex plan normally offers more promising opportunities in terms of landscape design than one of a very regular and homogeneous shape.

7.5.3 Method of filling

In the case of most upland reservoirs, water is provided by the direct run-off from adjoining hillsides and the siting of the reservoir and the size at which it may be maintained is determined by the run-off available. Water obtained in this way is normally fairly pure and can be put into supply with a minimum amount of treatment. This condition may impose restrictions on the availability of the reservoir for recreational purposes and the use of adjoining land.

Some reservoirs, and particularly those on lowland sites, are operated on a pumped-storage basis in which water is pumped from adjoining river sources during seasons of heavy rainfall and purified before being put into supply. Since the water is taken from the relatively impure source of a lowland river, the processes of purification used are more elaborate and more expensive, and the restrictions on the use of the reservoir for recreational purposes are likely to be less severe.

7.5.4 Method of use

In the past it was normal practice to pipe water from the collection and storage point in an upland reservoir to the point of supply in urban areas. This procedure involved both the laying and maintenance of expensive pipelines and considerable modification of the existing landscape situation along the route chosen.

In recent years direct supply reservoirs of this kind have been superseded by regulating reservoirs which are now regarded as a more effective form of water management. In the case of the regulating reservoir, water is impounded in upland country at the head of a river system and the water allowed to run into the river to maintain a constant flow at a predetermined level. This applies particularly in the dry season when the river would norm-

132

ally run at a low level. The water required for supply purposes is then extracted and purified at a point sometimes many miles downstream of the reservoir and even, in some cases, immediately above the highest point of tidal flow in the river estuary. Advantages gained by this method of operation include the additional water obtained from the normal run-off along the course of the river, the maintenance of the river itself in a more hygenic condition during the dry season, and the omission of the expensive pipeline system. The principal disadvantage is that the water recovered from the river requires a more elaborate system of purification before it can be put into supply. As in the case of pumped-storage reservoirs, recreational use of the reservoir is less likely to be subject to restriction than is the case with a direct supply reservoir.

7.5.5 Embankments
The most economical form of embankment is normally one built of broken rock on a straight line in plan with a slope of approximately 1:3 on the upstream face and 1:2½ on the down stream face. The upstream face is protected against water erosion by natural stone, precast blocks or concrete slabs while a wave wall is normally built at the head of the slope to prevent waves breaking over the top of the embankment and eroding the downstream face (Fig. 7.7).

Where natural stone is available it is common practice to use this material in the form of random pitching for those sections of the upstream face which normally lie below water level and to use cast blocks or similar material in the upper sections of the embankment face where erosion conditions are likely to be continuous and severe. Although rough stone and large boulders would often be more acceptable in terms of appearance, there have been some cases of the failure of this material under heavy wave action with serious consequences for the stability of the embankment. For this reason the less stable forms of surface material should be treated with reserve.

The down stream face is grassed and may include a series of horizontal platforms 4 to 5 m (approx. 13–16 ft) wide referred to as 'berms'. Embankments of this type are normally rendered water-retaining by the introduction of a puddled clay diaphragm about 4 m (approx. 13 ft) wide running vertically through the centreline of the structure from bedrock to the top edge.

It is often suggested that an embankment curved in plan would be more acceptable than a straight one as an element in the landscape. This is by no means always the case, and a curved embankment can appear artificial and contrived because of its calculated geometry. To curve an embankment in plan even on a large radius of 1,220 m (approx. 4,000 ft) or more will increase the cost of the structure in direct proportion to the increase in its length and, because of the high cost of this feature in proportion to the total investment for the reservoir, the sum may be such as to be unacceptable. It is, however, normally poss-

Plate 7.14. Vertical air view of main embankment. Errwood Reservoir, Derbyshire.

133

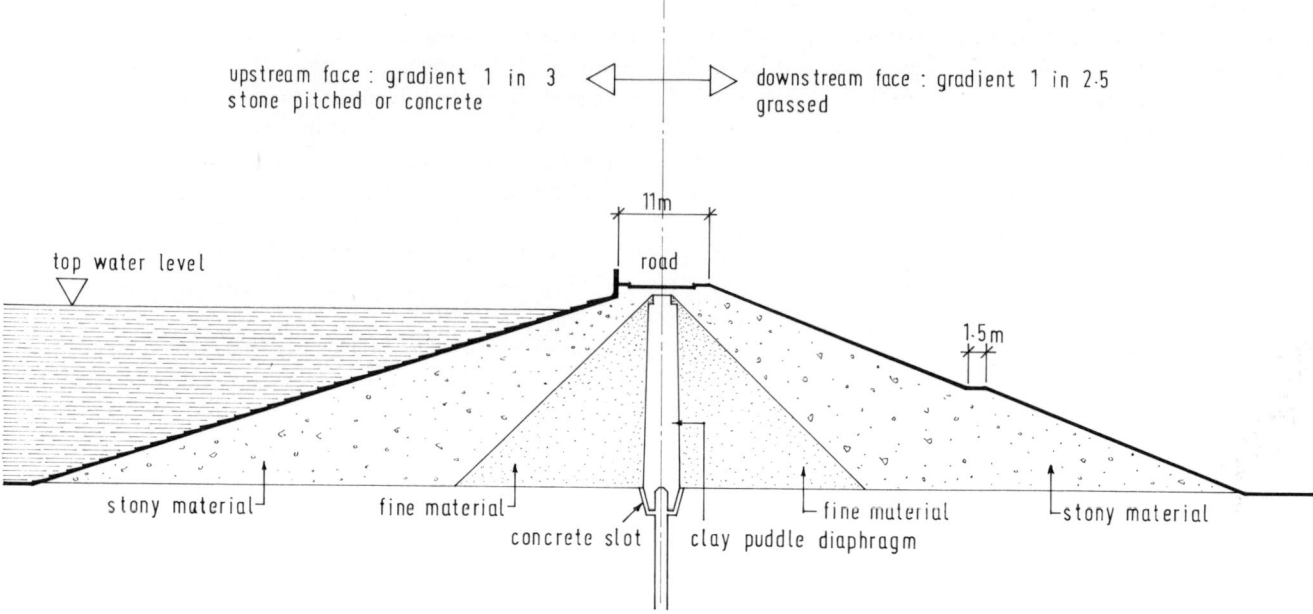

upstream face : gradient 1 in 3
stone pitched or concrete

downstream face : gradient 1 in 2.5
grassed

11m

top water level

road

1.5 m

stony material   fine material   concrete slot   clay puddle diaphragm   fine material   stony material

Fig. 7.7. Section through typical reservoir embankment.

ible to curve the ends of the embankment into the adjoining natural landforms without introducing an abnormal increase in costs. It is this line of junction or mitre between the natural and artificial forms which calls for careful attention if the embankment is not to appear as a somewhat artificial and intrusive element. A surface drain is often introduced on this line of junction and it is a great advantage if means can be found to conceal this feature (Plate 7.18).

In some cases it has been found possible to extend the lower and narrower levels of the down stream face of the embankment to form projecting platforms which relate closely to adjoining landforms without too great an increase in cost. In general it is a considerable advantage if the ends of the embankment can be related to natural headlands or return faces in the valley sides in order to make the structure appear as an inevitable element in the scenic composition with a close formal relationship to the site on which it stands (Plates 7.15 and 7.16).

Normally trees cannot be planted on the basic structure of the embankment except at the lowest levels of the down stream face and if shale or similar materials are used for constructional purposes the restrictions are likely to be even more severe. Shallow rooted shrubs may be acceptable on the upper levels but any danger of root systems extracting moisture from the puddled clay diaphragm must be avoided.

An embankment will include an overflow system which may be in the form of a cascade running down the embankment face in a stone or concrete channel or a bell-mouthed outlet standing in the area of water and leading to a tunnel below the embankment. In either case the overflowing water will be fed into a stilling basin in which turbulence is reduced before the water is fed back into the natural river bed. The buildings related directly to the embankment will normally consist of small control houses and draw-off towers which are not subject to very exacting functional requirements. They, together with the other features already mentioned, are capable of providing telling contrasting elements in the general landscape composition but it is of the greatest importance that the civil engineering, architecture and landscape architecture should be considered together from the outset with one common purpose.

Plate 7.15. Model of Overwood Reservoir embankment illustrating projection of lower levels of downstream face.

7.5.6 Draw-down

Any reservoir will be drawn down to a level below normal top-water level at some period or periods during the year, and the beaches exposed may lead to serious problems

134

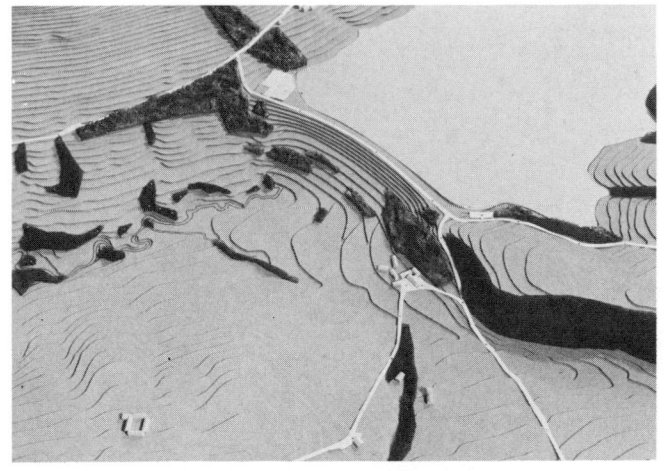

Plate 7.16. Model of Farndale Reservoir embankment designed on a 1,220 m (approx. 4,000 ft) radius with the ends and lower slopes turned into the natural land form.

in terms of visual amenity. The most difficult case to deal with is one in which the natural slopes adjoining the reservoir are the same throughout its perimeter with the result that a regular sloping beach completely surrounding the reservoir is exposed. Where the land form of slopes surrounding the reservoir is more varied the exposed beaches will be less monotonous and with projecting headlands and shallow areas of limited length, the scenic effect can be quite acceptable.

Where the geology of the site leads to the formation of beaches of broken rock, gravel or sand these can readily contribute to the general scenic effect when exposed. It is, however, important that the beaches should be considered as scenic elements and included in the general composition when a landscape scheme for a reservoir is prepared and much can be done in this respect by suitable arrangements of small tree groups and individual trees along the water's edge.

Where the geology leads to the formation of beaches made up largely of mud, the circumstances are less promising, but in these cases the encouragement of colonisation by suitable plant material and the formation of small islands and reed beds can do a great deal to improve the appearance of the exposed areas.

Because of the cost involved it is not normally possible to reconstruct the bed of the reservoir in order to remove the shallow areas which would normally be exposed during periods of draw-down. It is, however, sometimes possible to arrange that material for the main embankment and other engineering structures could be extracted at advantageous points in order to eliminate the less desirable shallow areas. In these cases it is an advantage if computer-based predictions of the occurrence of various levels of draw-down can be used in order to determine the most frequently occurring situations which call for remedial measures. In some cases broken stone has been introduced to cover what would normally be

Plate 7.17. Drawing of the main embankment at Ogston Reservoir.

135

Plate 7.18. Air view. Ogston embankment illustrating the berms on the downstream face and the clear mitre between the embankment and the natural land form.

exposed mud banks, but in the absence of wave action the appearance of this material after a period of time may not justify the expense involved.

Where narrow inlets occur which might dry out completely during periods of draw-down, consideration may be given to the introduction of bunds or small earth embankments which would retain water during the periods when the main reservoir is at a low level. Since these structures would be sometimes below water and sometimes exposed their construction involves some difficulties in terms of both stability and appearance. Moreover, when the structure of this kind would involve the impounding of a volume of water greater than approx. 22,730 cu m (5 million gallons), the structure would become subject to the legal requirements imposed on major embankments with a consequent increase in both

technical difficulties and in the cost involved.

Where draw-down conditions persist for more than a few weeks, colonisation by plant material may take place on the exposed reservoir bed, and attempts have been made to identify species which could be introduced in these circumstances. Strong wave action may, however, preclude this kind of remedy on the more exposed upland sites. There have been cases where deliberate seeding has been carried out and even of circumstances where crops were recovered from the sites, but this could only be done where a fairly long period of draw-down could be accurately predicted.

The exposed beaches can be rendered less attractive visually by the presence of dead tree trunks, rubbish and similar material. In some cases the circumstances have been improved by introducing measures to remove this rubbish regularly whenever the reservoir is drawn-down.

In view of the circumstances created by the drawing-down of the water level, it is a matter of the greatest importance that the original landscape features which will lie below the normal water level, including disused sections of roadway, walls, hedges and the remains of buildings, should be removed or concealed before the reservoir is filled. This measure should be extended to below the level to which the water drops at intervals during normal periods of draw-down.

7.5.7 Borrow pits

Where conditions are suitable the material required for the construction of the main embankment and other similar works will be recovered from the bed of the reservoir. This will include not only rock and the harder fine materials, but also clay for the diaphragm in the embankment. Where no suitable rock is available softer forms of shale may be used for the main embankment structure, but in these cases the slopes must be much shallower and the embankment becomes very much more bulky in appearance.

Since the normal geological processes which lead to the formation of the general structure of the landscape leave the harder materials as hills and headlands some distance above the valley bottom, it often occurs that the building materials can only be obtained from sites well above the final top water level. In these cases the quarried area is almost always left as a new and prominent feature in the landscape and steps must be taken to ensure that its final form is acceptable.

7.5.8 Pipelines

Where extensive pipelines across country form part of the scheme it is normally necessary to complete a careful study along the routes in order to avoid the destruction of important landscape features. The strip cleared for the laying of the pipeline and to create working space during the laying may be 20 m (approx. 65 ft) or more wide and the replanting of trees above the pipeline after laying is not acceptable. Minor re-routings in order to avoid woodland or other important landscape features is normally possible without an undue increase in costs.

7.5.9 Land purchase

When authority is given for a reservoir to be constructed, a legal boundary outside which no working must extend is defined, and this is referred to as the limits of deviation. It will apply to new roads and other similar features as well as the reservoir itself. The limits of deviation may correspond to the limits of land purchased by the authority constructing the reservoir but excess land would normally be resold and returned to farming or other use once the scheme was completed. Since it is important to retain good quality farming land in farming occupation, the area of land available for planting and recreational use in relation to the reservoir may be very restricted and it is important that the requirements for planting and similar purposes should be understood from the outset. The limit of deviation and the limit of purchase may follow existing field boundaries, but this is not inevitably the case and it is sometimes possible to arrange to fence the site on lines related to the field boundaries rather than to the new line of ownership. In any case, it may be necessary to re-site the existing field boundaries where these run into the water in order to avoid unfortunate relationships between the shore line and these features.

It is also an advantage in some situations if farming activity can be continued to the water's edge. Otherwise the fenced-off strip of land can raise very serious maintenance problems and produce an area of scrub and neglected ground quite out of keeping with the areas of well-maintained adjoining farmland. Where the farming involves cattle, fencing on the water's edge may be essential because of insurance requirements.

7.5.10 Nature conservation

Nature conservation has assumed considerable importance in relation to some new reservoirs and this particular land use can normally be reconciled with recreational uses by the introduction of zones which are free from disturbance. Generally the shoreline on the windward side of the reservoir is regarded as more suitable than that on the leeside for the establishment of reserve areas as it is free from wave action and general disturbance which can discourage some natural species including water fowl. Low-maintenance areas on the shoreline of the type referred to in the previous section may provide ideal circumstances for purposes of nature conservancy.

Advice and assistance in relation to both establishment and later maintenance is normally available from the Nature Conservancy and from the county naturalists trusts. The possibility of nature conservancy in relation to local educational requirements and the establishment of nature trails for the general public should also be considered.

7.5.11 Planting

Because of the size of most water storage reservoirs, planting related to them assumes the scale and character of afforestation, and while advanced nursery stock and semi-mature trees may be used at particularly important points where screening or early evidence of planting are essential, forestry techniques and the size of stock normally planted for forestry purposes would be used elsewhere. Most new blocks of planting would be fenced and because many individual blocks are likely to be used, the cost of fencing would be high and could be similar in amount to that of all the other planting activity put together.

The planting of large numbers of deciduous trees, particularly, oak, can lead in the autumn to the water in the reservoir being contaminated by the rotting leaves and assuming an unpleasant taste which is very difficult to eliminate. For this reason some Water Authorities stipulate that no deciduous trees must be planted within twenty-five yards of the water's edge and a similar distance on either side of all main feeder streams. It is important to retain existing areas of woodland where possible and to extend these where necessary by additional planting. Where the land available for large-scale planting is inadequate, it may be possible to arrange for the County Planning Authority to carry out large blocks of planting in the surrounding landscape as part of the general scheme. This may be done under normal planning legislation and is normally a matter of agreement between the County Council and the landowner rather than one of compulsory purchase.

A large reservoir scheme may take up to five or six years to construct and this amount of time may elapse before the reservoir is filled. In order to avoid the large area of land being blighted by the effects of the construction works during this period, every effort should be made to discourage the clear-felling of the site during the early stages of construction. It may be also highly desirable to retain much of the area which is eventually to be flooded by the reservoir in farming use during the construction period. During this period it may also be possible to move existing trees from the site to form new plantations in relation to the ultimate landscape scheme. It is also an advantage if some of the ultimate planting can be completed during the construction period so that the effects of the scheme become evident at the earliest possible date.

7.5.12 Recreation

During recent years it has become common practice to provide recreational facilities of various kinds at water storage reservoirs and these features are incorporated in the initial design of the scheme and submitted as part of the normal planning application. It is also normal that a requirement for the provision of such facilities for the public should be included in any water order issued by the government to permit the construction of a reservoir.

In planning the facilities it is often difficult to reconcile the requirements of the various interests concerned including not least those of the adjoining landowners, and this situation is best dealt with by the formation of a joint consultative committee representing the various interests. Any scheme which is likely to attract even a moderate number of visitors to a reservoir site will need to include appropriate toilet facilities and arrangements for

litter clearance. The provision of these latter features is normally a matter for arrangement with the local authority. One cause of serious concern on the part of adjoining landowners is the danger of visitors wandering over adjoining land and damaging crops. For this reason it is often good policy to concentrate public facilities in a restricted area on the site and to ensure that this is adequately fenced.

Sailing may be established on quite small areas of water although club and competitive sailing is only likely to flourish where adequate space is available. The number of boats accommodated can vary from as few as 1·25 per hectare to as many as 5 per hectare (1 boat to 2 acres–1 to half an acre) in some circumstances. Experience has shown that approximately 50% of the membership boats would be sailing at one time at peak periods and, therefore, the dinghy park should accommodate at least twice as many boats as the area of water. Experience has also shown that 0·67 car parking places would be needed for each boat having permanent membership of the club. Where deep water exists and the reservoir is large in area, moorings and other facilities for keel boats may be needed. In selecting a site for the sailing club it is important to consider possible racing courses on the water and also the fact that the starting line should be so sited that a large fleet of boats may start conveniently to windward, particularly into the prevailing wind.

Casual sailing by visitors is difficult to control and unauthorised power-boating may also present problems if cars and trailers can be brought close to the water's edge at points which are not under supervision. Normally authority over boating of various kinds and responsibility for supervision is vested in one club or in one joint committee.

In the case of fishing the facility may be leased to a club or may be operated on a day-ticket basis by the Water Authority concerned. A small building is required with some car parking, and the accommodation would include a ticket office, lavatories and space for weighing and recording catches. On some waters regulations apply which stipulate that each fisherman must be separated by at least 23 m (approx. 25 yd) from adjoining fishermen on either side. It is also accepted that due to the wind direction which affects casting and the movement of fish only 60% of available shoreline is likely to be eminently suitable for fishing purposes at any one time. Boat fishing may be included but in general this is not as popular as bank fishing and is more likely to cause interference between the fishing and sailing interests.

It is not possible to reconcile game and coarse fishing on the same water, and local demand should determine which type of fishing is provided. The Water Authority have a statutory responsibility to maintain and improve fishing and they would have the final say in this matter.

138

The presence of water plants, including reeds, in areas of shallow water and the planting of trees along the water's edge may seriously interfere with fishing. Normally the fishing interest asks for facilities along the water's edge to permit the clearance of weeds. It may be necessary to provide fish-rearing tanks immediately below the main embankment and these can extend to occupy considerable space and to become a prominent feature in the landscape.

Water-skiing is also possible on reservoirs although power boating is generally discouraged because of the danger of serious contamination by petrol and the interference with the amenities by the noise created.

Swimming is not normally encouraged in reservoirs partly because a non-tidal shoreline requires considerable maintenance if it is to remain in a sanitary condition when used by large numbers of people for swimming.

Underwater swimming is increasing in popularity and there is a considerable demand for suitable water. In this case the ruins of farm buildings which have been flooded and similar features add considerably to the attraction of an area of water for this type of recreation.

7.5.13 Traffic generation

In catering for a large number of visitors attracted to a new reservoir, consideration must be given to the generation of traffic and the need for car park facilities. In practice it has been found that a substantial increase of motor traffic on networks of narrow roads and lanes is unacceptable, and this fact may determine the access routes for facilities and the location of many of the recreational features. In the case of visiting fishermen it is not normally possible to accept casual parking on the road network close to the water's edge and parking areas will need to be provided at intervals. In some cases a minibus service for fishermen has been proposed as an alternative.

7.5.14 Bunded reservoirs

On relatively flat sites reservoirs may be formed by building bunds to enclose areas of up to a mile square or more and filling the enclosures with water to a depth of 15–18 m (approx. 50–60 ft). For reasons of economy in construction reservoirs of this type tend to be near-circular in plan with almost no irregularities in the line of the enclosing bunds. Up to a capacity of about 4·5 million cu m (approx. 1,000 million gallons) the bund may be built with a vertical reinforced concrete retaining wall internally and a grassed sloping embankment similar in form to the down stream face of a normal reservoir embankment externally. Above this capacity it becomes more economical to build the bund of a mass filling material with a slope both internally and externally and a general structure virtually identical with that of the normal embankment already referred to.

If a bunded reservoir is built on a wholly flat site it would not be possible to see over the area of water except from the top of the bund itself and the area of the reservoir would be walled off from the surrounding scenery. Since the top water level would normally be only a short distance below the crest of the bund there would be little space for the parking of boats or the provision of similar recreational facilities. It would, moreover, be very costly indeed to extend the area covered by a section of the bund in order to create areas suitable for the development of picnic sites and similar features.

Where the natural ground level rises to above the intended top water level on part of the perimeter of a bunded reservoir, a normal shoreline is created and this may be used to advantage for the establishment of recreational facilities and picnic sites with views over the water. Most forms of recreation which could be introduced on normal reservoirs would be appropriate but there would only be limited possibilities of nature conservancy owing to the lack of shallow water.

Generally a more satisfactory landscape scheme could be created in relation to a bunded reservoir where this formed one element in a much more extensive area of development planned on a very large scale. On a site in a suburban area where the scale is small and the character domestic, and where little additional land is likely to be available for related planting, the situation is much less promising.

7.5.15 Barrage schemes

The barrage schemes which are at present being considered take the form of one or more very large bunded reservoirs sited at the point where the river begins to widen out into an estuary. The water level would again be considerably above normal high-tide level and the conditions created would in many ways be similar to those described in relation to bunded reservoirs. Most of the schemes so far studied include the river itself, adjoining areas of water which may be tidal outside the bunded areas and extensive highway developments as well as very large-scale recreational facilities. They offer quite magnificent opportunities in terms of combined built-form and landscape studies on the very largest scale.

Recently schemes of this nature have been canvassed widely by the conservation interests as an acceptable alternative to the alienation of farming land and the modification of existing scenery in high amenity areas which would be brought about by the construction of additional reservoirs of a normal type.

7.5.16 Sand and gravel workings

Although workings of this nature differ from water storage reservoirs, both in their purpose and their method of development, the final result is almost invariably flooded and is similar to a reservoir in most respects. In the case of the sand workings the pit is flooded soon after excavation commences and from then on the sand is pumped out suspended in water. Gravel workings may also be flooded and the gravel dredged mechanically, but in some cases the excavations are pumped out and kept dry during the working period.

When the workings are finally flooded the water will lie at the level of the normal water table which may be well below the natural ground level. The banks formed round the area of water during extraction are normally too steep to appear natural or to be convenient for recreational purposes while the creation of a shallower slope would either extend the site occupied unduly or lead to an unacceptable loss of material which would otherwise be extracted. For safety reasons a flat platform is normally introduced in the slopes just above the final water level. This prevents visitors falling down what may be a fairly steep slope into rapidly deepening water and facilitates rescue operations should this happen.

In spite of the somewhat limited possibilities of the smaller sites and the relatively long working period of twelve years or more, some consideration is normally given to after-use at the planning application stage. The areas of water created are in most cases too small for club sailing while the possibilities of development for nature conservancy purposes will be limited unless shallow areas and islands can be created artificially by the use of unwanted spoil.

On some larger sites of gravel workings alongside major rivers it has been possible to exploit local circumstances in order to create very large-scale facilities for rowing and other activities.

Bibliography

Dee Estuary Report, 1971. Also the second similar report prepared by the Dee Estuary Committee for the Department of the Environment.

Everyman's Nature Reserve, 1972, E. Dennis, David and Charles.

I.L.A. Journal, No. 104, November 1973.

Picnic Sites, H.M.S.O.

Recreation at Reservoirs, Countryside Commission and Water Resources Board.

Terrace and Courtyard Gardens (Chapters 19–21), A. D. B. Wood, Collingridge.

The Vegetation of Scotland, 1964 (Chapter 9 by D. H. N. Spence), Ed. J. H. Burnett, David and Charles.

Water Gardening, Francis Perry, Country Life.

Works of Humphrey Repton, and particularly observations on the theory and practice of landscape gardening.

8 Planting Techniques

PATRICIA BOOTH

8.1 Introduction

Plants are the most vulnerable of the materials that a designer can use in the landscape, and the success of any planting scheme will depend largely on whether it can be maintained to develop in accordance with the designer's vision.

Planting design will evolve mainly from site conditions but will be influenced at all stages by the quality of maintenance considered desirable and possible. Until comparatively recently plants were cared for by either the forester or the gardener and planting design followed the traditional patterns which could be maintained by these skills. Now there are many areas which can only be looked after by new methods of landscape maintenance and planting patterns have to be devised to suit a wide range of sites between the woodland and the garden.

The basic landscape design will ensure that planting areas are sited only where growth of appropriate plants is possible and they can develop as functional or decorative elements in the landscape. Circulation and use may be guided by planting but even mature plants will not deter determined trespassers unless reinforced by ground modelling or fencing.

This chapter outlines the factors affecting the detailed design of the planting areas envisaged in the main landscape plan; general planting methods are given for plants other than trees, but special techniques, e.g. hydroseeding or mechanical planting, may be more appropriate on difficult or extensive sites. Successful planting will depend on a number of factors:

(a) Appreciation of the client's requirements and the money available for capital and maintenance costs.
(b) Appreciation of site conditions; choice of material to suit these conditions and selection of good strong plants.
(c) Suitable preparation of the ground.
(d) Careful planting when soil and weather are favourable; regular aftercare to establish the plants.
(e) Maintenance to maturity in accordance with the intentions of the designer.

The most important factor for success in any landscape scheme is to choose the plant which is exactly right for any particular situation. *The Basic Plant List* published by the Landscape Institute gives a limited selection of plants which are likely to be of fairly frequent use; for difficult sites and specialised planting much more detailed lists will be needed.

8.2 Plants and the soil

8.2.1 Plant nutrients

For plants to grow they need light and regular supplies of the essential plant nutrients in a readily available form. Carbon, hydrogen and oxygen are obtained from the carbon dioxide in the air and from water taken up from the soil. The other plant nutrients are taken up from the soil in solution and good soil structure and aeration are essential to ensure a healthy root system and efficient nutrient uptake.

8.2.2 Function of roots

Roots have four main functions – absorption, conduction, storage and anchorage. Absorption and anchorage are intimately associated with the soil and any cultivations are done with the object of improving these functions. Roots need oxygen to live and poor soil structure which prevents free water movement can prevent roots functioning efficiently and create a deficiency in the plant. Many plants are enabled to grow in poor soil conditions by the presence of mycorrhizae which extend the root system and develop particularly in soils low in nitrogen and phosphorus. The addition of suitable mycorrhizae can sometimes be helpful in establishing plants on poor soils.

8.2.3 Soil components

Soil consists of mineral particles (sand, silt, clay), organic matter, living or dead, water containing plant nutrients, and air spaces. The proportions vary from soil to soil and in depth in the same soil. Mineral particles give soil its textural qualities; the texture of a fertile soil provides a continuous stable system of fine and coarse air spaces throughout.

Organic matter provides plant nutrients and influences soil structure tending to produce a good physical condition. Soil micro-organisms help in the decomposition of organic matter and the recycling of nutrients.

Soils may be loosely grouped according to the dominant constituent which affects their characteristics and the type of plants which will grow on them.

Clay soils – These contain a high proportion of very small particles which retain moisture and nutrients but impede water movement. They are very sticky when wet and set very hard when dry, making cultivation difficult. Compaction can be avoided by not working when the soil is wet: rough cultivation is best done in the autumn and the soil left to be broken down by frost action until it can be prepared for planting in the spring. Some drainage may be necessary and organic matter and sand will improve the physical condition; under intensive management their structure can be improved by adding lime or soil conditioners. Clay soils are potentially fertile and will support a wide range of plants.

Sandy soils – These have a high proportion of relatively large particles which cannot retain moisture and are liable to dry out. It is easy to establish plants in sandy soil provided that sufficient water and nutrients are made available; organic manures are preferable since these will retain moisture as well as provide plant foods. Sandy soils should not be left bare for any length of time as they are liable to erosion, nutrients are quickly leached out and weeds soon become established. When acceptable it is better to plant small plants out of pots, or to sow seeds *in situ* since these will become established more quickly.

Loams – These are a mixture of particles of all sizes to form an easily worked fertile soil. This may be described as heavy, light, medium according to the proportions of clay and particles; loams are the ideal soil for most plants and the easiest to cultivate.

Chalk soils – Such soils are those where an excess of calcium carbonate gives a soil-character which outweighs the effect of texture. They are usually light shallow loams and are liable to drought because of the porous nature of the underlying chalk. They are fairly easy to work when dry but become sticky and slippery when wet. If there is only a shallow topsoil it is advisable to break up the subsoil before planting. Chalk soils tend to puff up in frosty weather so that new plantings may be forced out of the ground and will need treading-in. Any attempts to acidify a chalk soil are usually very temporary and are not advised.

Peat soils – These have a high percentage of organic matter and consequently a high water-holding capacity. Alkaline peats make excellent soils once they have been drained, but acid peat occurs in regions of high rainfall, is difficult to drain and will support only a limited range of plants.

8.2.4 Soil reaction

The reaction of a soil may be expressed using a scale measured by the hydrogen ion concentration; the numbers on the scale are called pH and indicate the range of acidity. The pH of a soil may be estimated to 0·5 pH units by the colorimetric method using an indicator solution and barium sulphate. If a more precise measurement is required Test 9 (A) in B.S. 1377 gives the standard electrometric method of determining the pH of a soil within 0·1 pH units. Key points on the pH scale include:

pH 3   very acid sand
pH 4   very acid peat
pH 4·4   very acid loams and heavy soils
pH 4.7   organic matter not rotted by bacteria below this
pH 5·1   phosphates almost unavailable below this
pH 6·5   best for most garden soils
pH 7·0   neutral
pH 7·5   trace element deficiencies common in susceptible plants above this
pH 8·5   upper limit of pH on chalky soil.

In acid soils plant nutrients become more soluble and are quickly leached leading to deficiencies under bad management.

8.2.5 Soil examination

Preliminary site investigations will have determined the depth and quality of the topsoil and investigated the subsoil to a depth of 750 mm (approx. 2 ft 6 in) (see B.S. 4428 *General Landscape Operations* and B.S. 1377 *Methods of Testing Soil for Civil Engineering Purposes*). A complete record will also have been made of all existing vegetation and full ecological studies of each different plant community. These records will give a very good guide to existing site conditions and will be sufficient if planting areas are undisturbed by general landscape operations. On disturbed areas and where soil has to be imported further examination of planting areas will be necessary.

Examination of soil in the field.   A few simple tests will give the landscape architect a very good idea of the soil quality. Test holes made by digging or with a soil augur will show compaction or bad drainage. A profile to 1 to 1·2 m deep (approx. 3–4 ft) is needed to study natural conditions: a hole about 500 mm deep (approx. 20 in) will normally locate damage by machinery. Compaction may also be estimated in the field using portable gamma ray equipment to measure the penetration resistance of the soil.

Soil texture may be determined by a hand test on moist soil (see Appendix) and pH may be estimated by the colorimetric method.

Soil colour will give a good guide to the organic matter present, grey, dark grey or dark brown is usually due to decayed organic matter. A healthy topsoil will consist of bright brown homogenous material: dull grey colours and grey patches of matter indicate lack of aeration and periodic waterlogging.

Examination of soil in the laboratory. Soil analysis may be used to assess the quality of a soil in the laboratory and a general analysis will investigate total nitrogen, pH, lime requirement, available phosphorus, available potassium, organic matter, B.S. soil texture, as required. Extra tests for trace elements may be undertaken where the soil consultant has reason to suspect deficiencies or excesses; there is no satisfactory method of soil analysis for available nitrogen on open land.

The value of an analysis depends greatly on the method of collecting samples and since soil differences are numerous over quite a small area and only a small sample can be tested, the results can only indicate where deficiencies or excesses may exist. Skilled interpretation of the results is needed before any treatment is considered, taking into account the type of soil, climatic conditions, previous treatments and the plants which are to be grown.

There are a number of private consultants, research institutes and some seed firms who will carry out soil analysis; the A.D.A.S. will make recommendations for agricultural soils. These people will either collect their own soil samples or will provide detailed recommendations for collection.

8.2.6 Soil improvement
For landscape planting areas, soil improvement should be limited to the minimum needed to allow suitable plants to become established. Under natural conditions nutrients are recycled, by various biological cycles, allowing repeated use of the nutrients for plant growth. In a natural ecosystem there is usually abundant vegetation even on poor soils as a result of slow growth over many years. If this type of planting is to be copied, great care must be taken not to upset the soil balance by excessive cultivation or unnecessary soil additives.

In areas where intensive management will interrupt natural cycles or where the natural balance has already been destroyed, soil analysis will be of value in indicating preliminary and subsequent manuring programmes. For most crop plants fairly detailed soil improvements can be recommended but no real research has been done on the establishment of amenity planting and many of the traditional recommendations are now thought to be of

Plate 8.1. Ground cover planting of mixed evergreens and greys. Leaf forms and texture are contrasted as well. Designed by Peter Youngman, P.P.I.L.A.

Plate 8.2. The speckled stems of a grove of silver birch make a point of interest in an otherwise brown winter landscape.

143

Plate 8.3. The purple and grey of *Stachys lanata* backed by a group of *Macleaya cordata* with coral flower plumes.

Plate 8.4. *Gunnera manicata*. Great green plates nearly 2 m (about 6 ft) in diameter contrasting with the strong vertical emphasis of the weeping willow.

doubtful value. Good soil structure is probably the most important initial need so that roots can penetrate quickly to find essential moisture. This is especially necessary with container-grown plants where roots have to be encouraged to spread from the ideal growing medium of the container into the surrounding soil.

8.3 Planting design

8.3.1 Range of plants

From the very wide range of plants that will grow in the British Isles it should be possible to find species to suit any design requirement. Site conditions will limit the choice considerably and must be the main factor in plant selection for landscape work. Then from the material that can grow on the site the designer has to choose species that will give the effect required. This choice may be further limited by the availability of the plants in the numbers and sizes required and at a reasonable cost. The way in which the designer uses the plants will depend on the type of landscape and the quality of maintenance.

In 'wild' and rural areas it would be appropriate to plan for low maintenance requirements and new planting would be based on ecological studies of natural plant communities in the area. A natural ecosystem is built up over many years with new species establishing themselves and others dying out as conditions change. For landscape work it is not usually practicable to wait for a natural system to evolve and planting patterns are devised to imitate as far as possible the probable climatic climax vegetation of a habitat, using indigenous species or introduced species which have been accepted and fit into the pattern. Most communities grow in layers with trees, shrubs, sub-shrubs and herbs, although one or more layers may be missing; this pattern can be copied using a fairly wide range of suitable species in each layer to encourage a variety of wild life and minimise losses from disease. As in natural communities the use of one or more selected dominant species in each layer will avoid monotony and help define areas.

In gardens, and urban and industrial areas higher maintenance standards will be envisaged and planting design may be more contrived. The most effective planting

Plate 8.5. *Hypericum* is an ideal ground cover plant in deep shade, here making a pattern through the coursing of stone paving slabs.

Plate 8.6. The leaf of the *Acanthus* has been admired since the Greeks used it in the motif of the capital to the Corinthian column.

is usually achieved by using the fewest possible different plants to give the functional and aesthetic effect required. Material should still be chosen to suit the habitat but may be selected from a wider range of plants according to the sophistication of the scheme. The layered patterns of natural plant communities may be copied but often a garden-type planting with facers and fillers will be used: ground cover plants will take the place of the field layer and form a weed-suppressing carpet.

8.3.2 Influence of site conditions on choice of plants and planting

Climate. *Wind* – On windy sites it is more than ever necessary that plants should obtain a good roothold quickly and young vigorously growing material should be chosen. This applies particularly to conifers and ever-greens which are very liable to be blown over in later years if large specimens are planted initially. Small bushy plants may be planted in such a way that the head leans away from the prevailing wind and those that sucker easily may be planted deeply and pruned hard. Any taller material will need staking until well established and some form of shelter may be advisable, e.g. hurdles or low hes-sian screens.

Frost – Most landscape planting will use only plants of proven hardiness choosing particularly hardy species for known frost pockets. In special positions in areas of high maintenance some plants which are not quite hardy until established may be desirable, e.g. *Arbutus, Magnolia grandiflora, Phormium*: these are best planted in spring and may need winter protection at first. Frost damage may be intensified by bright sun on the frozen plant and susceptible species should not be placed where morning sun will reach them.

Shade – This may vary from complete lack of sunlight at all times to shade at certain times of the day or seasons of the year. The plants that can be grown will also depend on other associated factors that may limit growth. Lack of water is likely to be a problem in most shady places and larger plants may affect plants growing in their shade by the competition of their roots for nutrients and moisture and by water drip from their branches. Given sufficient moisture most evergreens and plants with green leaves except conifers will grow in shade; plants with grey or gold leaves require plenty of light if they are to thrive. Variegated plants are often chosen to lighten dark areas; those with silver variegations will usually do better than golden varieties. Flowering plants which are shade toler-ant tend to produce more foliage and fewer flowers when light is restricted.

Plate 8.7. The mirrored plane of still water makes an ideal background for the strong architectural shapes of marginal and deep-water plants.

Plate 8.8. The correct choice of plants in a public area is difficult; and doubly so when they are to be grown in pots. These well-filled concrete containers stood on the terrace at the Festival Hall.

Atmospheric pollution – Industrial atmospheric pollution may affect plants in several ways; it can restrict the light available, form choking deposits on the leaves, deposit detrimental substances on the soil, or weaken the plant with poisonous gases. Plants vary in their resistance to different sorts of pollution, and the source and type of pollution will give some guide to the choice of plants. Most conifers and evergreens are intolerant of pollution (there are exceptions); plants which are in leaf only for a short period of the year are usually resistant. In any area it is wise to plant a mixture of species since it is difficult to be sure which will survive best in any particular conditions.

Soil – Plants depend on the soil for anchorage and most of their nutrition and it is usually the main factor in the successful establishment and growth of a plant. In choosing plants to suit a particular soil all the characteristics of the soil have to be taken into account and the way in which they interact. Texture is important as it controls drainage, water storage and working properties and excessive wetness or dryness can outweigh other considerations. Plants vary in their tolerance of soil acidity and pH will give some idea of suitable species to choose, bearing in mind that many plants will tolerate greater acidity in a peaty soil than in a mineral soil. Most rhododendrons and ericacious plants prefer a pH between 4·5 and 6·0, H.T. roses 5·5 to 7·0 and most common garden

Plate 8.9. The controlled jungle. An exercise in differing plant forms, needing careful maintenance to ensure that no one species eradicates or smothers another. Designed by Clifford R. V. Tandy.

146

shrubs between 6·0 and 7·5. Although most plants have a preferred pH range many will grow over a very wide range if other conditions are favourable, e.g. beech has an optimum range of pH 5·0 to 6·7 but grows well on shallow chalky soils where good drainage outweighs other factors. It will be possible to select plants suitable for any soil except perhaps very acid sands where some soil improvement may be required in order to establish pioneer species.

Protection from people and animals – Young plants in rural areas will require protection from livestock and wild animals.

In urban areas domestic animals may be a nuisance but people are likely to do the most damage, by trespass or deliberate vandalism. Losses in newly planted areas are decreased when they are surrounded by chestnut paling until the plants are established; where this is not feasible it is essential that an area should be planted-up as quickly as possible, before the public is allowed near it. Planting in raised beds or in containers helps to prevent trespass, and larger sized plants tend to deter vandals. 'Plant collectors' are usually deterred if small plants, e.g. ground cover are planted under wire netting laid just below the soil surface and valuable plants, e.g. rhododendrons may be anchored by underground guys. Plants with built-in deterrents of thorns or prickles are useful to protect more vulnerable species, but they should not be used where they may catch passers-by or in play areas for children. Plants with single stems should be avoided in preference to those which produce several shoots from below ground level and quickly regenerate if broken down.

Litter may be a problem in some areas and spiky, open plants which catch and hold litter should be avoided. All plants tend to gather litter but smooth rounded forms will shed it more easily and it can be collected with less difficulty.

8.3.3 Choice of plants to suit design requirements

To choose exactly the right plant for a given design it is necessary to be clear about the role it is to play, so that a species can be selected which will not only fulfil its function but will express the intentions of the designer. This involves a detailed knowledge of the visual characteristics of a plant and of how these change through the seasons and through its life. Basically plants should be chosen to grow naturally into the mass and disposition required, without constant pruning and training. The mass may be achieved by using a single plant or more often groups of the same species which will grow together to form larger masses similar in outline to the single plant. Planting in groups not only helps to unify a design but there is evidence that many plants grow better in association. After defining the mass required the forms

composing it can be considered and the designer's idea amplified by choosing plants of suitable colour and texture.

Form – This is determined by the way in which the main stems or branches grow. This is easier to see in winter but it is also expressed by the internal shadows of summer foliage or of evergreens. It is this form which gives a plant its character and personality. Too many different forms in one group of plants can give a very restless effect. It is usually preferable to limit variety and to use very strong forms as focal points. It is especially important to choose suitable forms for planting in restricted areas, so that the character of a spreading or arching plant, for example, is not later destroyed by the need for drastic pruning.

Colour of foliage – This is more important than flowers or fruits which are usually only of interest during a comparatively short period of the year. In the soft light of the British countryside the more subdued colours seen against a background of restful greens are most appropriate. In smaller areas associated with buildings strong colours can be used more successfully to provide eye-catching accents.

Texture – This is a surface quality of a material and is less predictable than other qualities in plants. In the landscape, texture is, at near view, the result of the detailed structure of the plant growth, including the size, spacing, disposition, grouping and attitude of leaves and twigs. At greater distances texture depends on whole plants and masses of plants. The textural pattern is made by the play of light and shade on the plant mass. Glossy leaves and small leaves tend to give a finer texture because light reflections are more broken up. Large leaves appear coarse in near view and this is accentuated when the leaves are widely spaced. Uniformity of texture will tie together any planting and emphasis of texture should be related to emphasis on the plan. Texture is very closely related to scale; wrong textures can easily disturb the apparent size of an area. Texture is especially important in choosing plants for backgrounds, for example, close matt textures make the best foil for sculpture or for specimen plants.

Time – Plants are unlike other basic materials of landscape design in that they continually change with the seasons and through the years, and it may be some time before they reach a degree of development that matches the designer's vision of maturity. Only annuals and bedding plants reach their full potential in one season, other plants may require years in which to mature. Therefore it is important to consider the length of time that the site can be guaranteed to the plant. In most schemes, plants will be selected from quick-growing species for early maturity, together with slower-growing species that will not give much effect for several years. Many quick-growing plants are short lived, so only a temporary scheme should be based entirely on such species. Slower growing plants should always be included, either to take over from short-lived species after some years or to form the backbone of new planting. It is very expensive to buy slow-growing plants in large sizes but comparatively easy to move them on a site that is being redeveloped.

Planting near buildings – Growing conditions near buildings vary greatly according to the aspect and plants must be chosen to suit the amount of light and moisture available. Shrubs and herbaceous perennials may be planted as close to buildings as desired. Climbers may be used where adequate support can be provided; self-clinging climbers should be used only where the fabric of the building does not need painting and is suitably strong.

Access should be provided to the outside of the building for window-cleaning and other maintenance; either borders should be narrow enough to reach over or a small service path must be provided between the planting and the building.

The distance at which trees may be planted from buildings will depend on a number of factors, e.g. type of subsoil, climate of the area, foundations of the building. Poplars and other quick-growing trees should not be used. Slow-growing trees will not normally harm foundations when planted at such a distance from a building that they have room to grow to their natural size; problems may develop when trees are planted on shrinkable clays in the drier parts of England, unless the building has suitably constructed foundations.

8.4 Plant material

8.4.1 Sources of plants

Plants may be obtained from a wholesale nursery or from private nurseries such as those maintained by a new town or a parks department. The advantages of a private nursery are that the plants are probably grown with soil and climatic conditions similar to those on the site to be planted; also plants are more readily available and transport time and costs will be cut. The disadvantages of a private nursery are that unless requirements can be specified well in advance the range of plants may be very limited and is often restricted to plants which are easily propagated or of limited landscape use.

If plants are bought from trade sources it is usually possible to obtain the species required but it may be difficult to arrange deliveries when needed or at short notice. Also, the plants may have been grown under soil and climatic conditions very different from those of the area where they are to be planted permanently; plants grown in a light soil or in a warm part of the country may suffer a setback when moved to a heavy soil or a cold area. Similarly, imported plants will take time to adjust to our climate and should be grown-on for at least one year under skilled care in a nursery before being used for landscape planting.

On large-scale developments where work is spread over a number of years a temporary nursery may be established on part of the site and the required plants purchased and grown-on until their permanent positions are ready. In this way larger plants can be provided for moving quickly to suit the progress of the work. Such a nursery must be fenced and rabbit-proofed and skilled maintenance should be available.

8.4.2 Buying plants

Plants bought for permanent planting as part of a landscape scheme should comply with the requirements of the relevant part of B.S. 3936 – Nursery Stock: General. Some plants grown from seed do not come true and may show a wide range of seedling variation. This may be acceptable for certain purposes, but a nursery should state if plants normally propagated vegetatively have been grown from seed. Care should also be taken when buying plants which have been grafted or budded; the root stock may be short lived causing the plant to die after a few years or the root stock may sucker so vigorously that it causes maintenance problems.

8.4.3 Methods of plant production

Open ground – This is the commonest method of growing plants for sale and is suitable for most hardy plants. A good root system is ensured by regular transplanting, or by slacking or undercutting in the case of hedging plants. Material can be lifted during the regular planting season and supplied with bare roots or as root-balled material as indicated in B.S. 3936: Part 1. Bare-root plants are usually the cheapest form of plants obtainable and also save on transport and handling as no soil is moved; their disadvantage is that they need careful handling to avoid drying out and should be planted only during the main planting season.

Container grown – A very wide range of plants is now available in containers which allow material to be moved easily at any time of the year. The plants should be well established in their containers but not grown-on so long that the roots have become circled or kinked, leading to poor establishment and growth when planted out. The growing media should be noted; a compost with a high peat content may dry out in transit and be very difficult to wet before planting; very light compost or a granular medium may not hold together if the root system is not fully developed.

Pot grown – Certain plants are supplied in pots for ease and safety in transplanting. They may be species which have root systems that do not transplant readily or they may be small plants such as alpines which are pot grown for ease of handling. B.S. 3936: Part 1 notes trees and shrubs which should be pot grown.

8.4.4 Quality
The quality and condition of a plant is more important than its actual size. Nursery management aims to produce saleable plants in the shortest possible time and for woody material it is important to select plants with strong well-ripened shoots and a healthy root system.

Trees – Most species need a well-defined central leader if they are to grow into satisfactory specimens; exceptions are species with naturally branching heads or weeping trees. Multi-stemmed specimens are usually more satisfactory if produced by cutting back a young plant than by planting two or more trees to grow together. The branching of the head should show the character and natural growth of the species to which it belongs.

Shrubs – Whether open ground or grown in containers shrubs should have been spaced with room to develop naturally in all directions. They may, according to species, have been cut back or trimmed to encourage bushiness.

Conifers – Most species should be well-furnished evenly to the ground on all sides; there are exceptions, e.g. *Cedrus*. A single central leader is desirable for most conifers unless needed for hedging or if the natural form is branching.

8.4.5 Plant specification
The following information is needed by the nursery so that it may supply the correct material for a planting scheme.

Name of plant   This should be the full scientific name including genus, species and variety or cultivar, where applicable (following the *International Code of Nomenclature for Cultivated Plants*). Familiar plants may appear under new names as botanists reclassify, or discover an earlier legitimate name. To avoid confusion it is recommended that the scientific name should follow the nomenclature of *Hillier's Manual of Trees and Shrubs*, which provides a convenient list of names and descriptions available to both buyer and seller. Common names should be avoided as in many cases one name covers several species. This does not apply to forest transplants which are usually specified by an agreed common name and their seed source.

Size.   *Trees* – Form should be stated as well as size when ordering trees. Normal nursery stock will include the forms shown.

RECOMMENDED SIZES

Form	Height ground level to lowest branch		Min. stem circumference 1 m above ground level	
	Metric (m)	Imperial (approx.) (ft)	Metric (cm)	Imperial (approx.) (in)
Bush	0·3–0·75	1–2½	—	—
Half standard	1·1–1·4	3½–4½	6	2½
Three-quarter standard	1·5–1·6	5–5½	6	2½
Standard	1·7–1·8	5½–6	6	2½
Tall standard	1·9–2.0	6–6½	8	3
Weeping standard	min. 1·7	5½	6	2½

Tall standards should be specified for pedestrian areas and extra large nursery stock may be used where larger or more vandal-resistant material is required. Extra large standards are usually specified by height, spread and stem circumference; sizes might be in the range of 3·5–5·5 m (approx. 12–18 ft) high with a girth of 12–20 cm (approx. 5–8 in).

Shrubs, including conifers – For general planting the sizes requested should be within the range recommended in B.S. 3936. Plants of these sizes should transplant easily and grow away without special care. Very small sizes and rooted cuttings are not recommended for general planting because they give no immediate effect and are more likely to be damaged. Height should be specified in centimetres and the average diameter given for spreading shrubs; for pot-grown shrubs and climbers the diameter of the pot is specified; for container-grown stock the volume of the container should be given.

Quotations will normally be based on open ground or pot-grown plants according to species. If container-grown stock is required this must be stated.

8.4.6 Planting plans
Planting plans are needed to serve several purposes and time is saved if a single plan can be prepared with all uses in mind. A plan is needed which is:

(a) Easily understood by the client who may wish to approve the choice of plants;
(b) Accurate enough to prepare a detailed schedule of plants;
(c) Suitable as a working drawing for the planting foreman;
(d) Suitable for inclusion in the maintenance schedule.

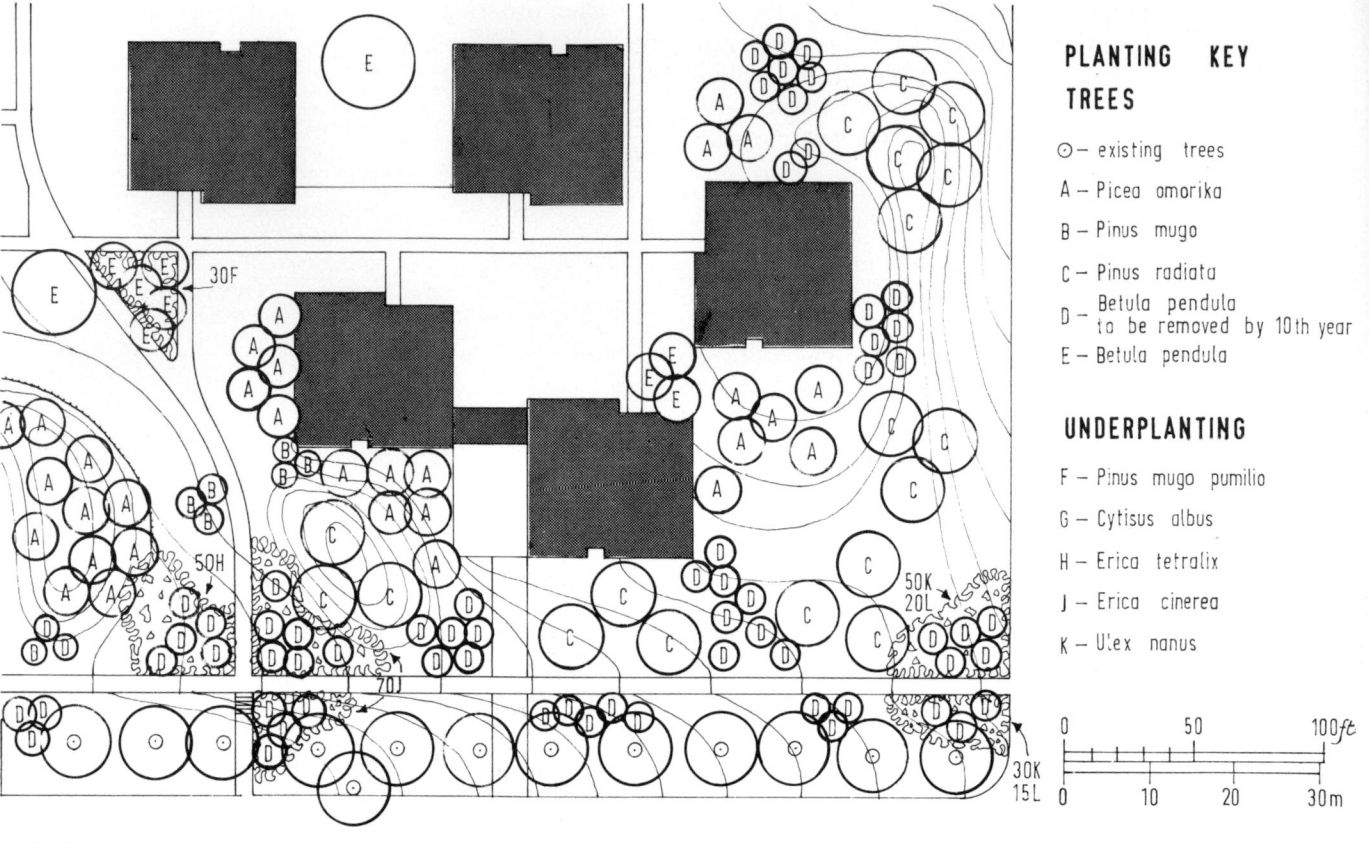

Fig. 8.1. A planting plan showing the use of a key to refer to planting positions.

The planting plan should show the name of each plant or group of plants, the number of plants in each group and the distance between plants within a group.

It is much simpler to consult or work from a plan where the plant name appears in full at the position the plant is to occupy, but often space on the drawing does not allow this and symbols have to be used. Planting areas which are normally viewed from only one direction, e.g. next to a building, should be so drawn and labelled that the plan can be read from that particular direction.

Any alterations in position or substitutions of plants at the time of planting should be noted on the planting plan, to help in identifying plants later; this is particularly important where plants die and have to be replaced. It is also necessary to have an accurate record of actual plantings to include in the maintenance schedule.

Scale of planting plans

For small areas and intricate planting	1:50
Shrub borders and less detailed planting	1:100
Tree groups and broad planting areas	1:200, 1:500, etc.

It may be helpful, both in planning and in laying-out plants on the site, to have the planting areas on a plan covered with a grid in suitably sized squares, e.g. 1 m, 5 m, 10 m, etc.

TABLE OF PLANTING DISTANCES

Plant	Distance apart in centimetres	Number of plants per square metre
Shrubs		
dwarf and slow growing	45–60	3–5
medium	100–120	1
vigorous	150–180	1 plant in 2–3 m²
Bush roses	45–60	3–4
Herbaceous perennials		
medium	60–120	4–11
vigorous	60–120	1–3
Ground cover and small herbaceous	20–30	11–25
Bulbs		
large – narcissus, tulip	15–30	11–36
small – crocus, snowdrop	10–15	36–50
		Number of plants per metre run
Hedging		
privet, quickthorn	25–45	2–4
beech, hornbeam	30–60	1½–3
yew, holly	45–75	1½–2

150

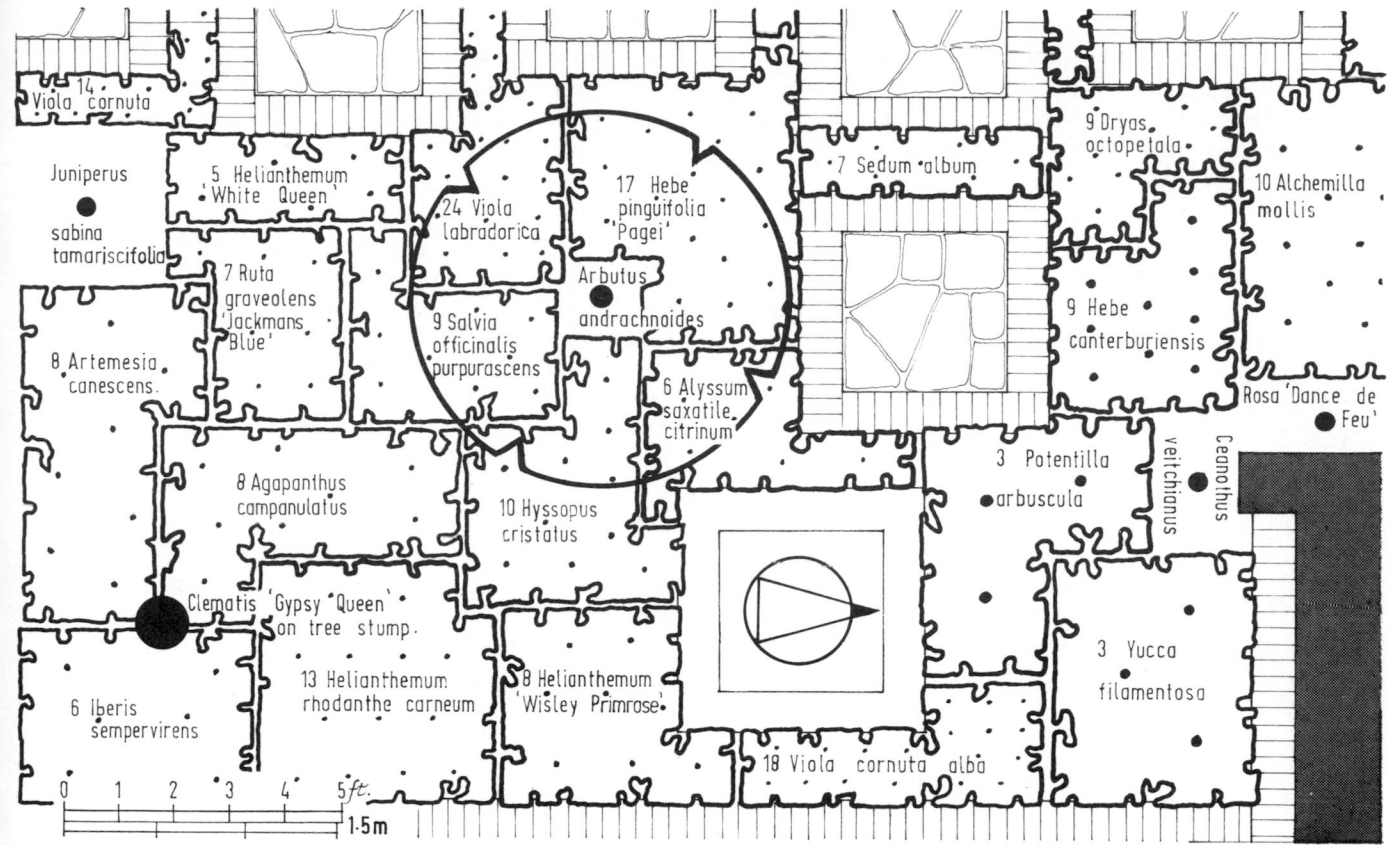

14 Viola cornuta

Juniperus
sabina
tamariscifolia

5 Helianthemum
'White Queen'

7 Ruta
graveolens
'Jackmans
Blue'

8 Artemesia
canescens

8 Agapanthus
campanulatus

Clematis 'Gypsy Queen'
on tree stump

13 Helianthemum
rhodanthe carneum

6 Iberis
sempervirens

24 Viola
labradorica

9 Salvia
officinalis
purpurascens

17 Hebe
pinguifolia
'Pagei'

Arbutus
andrachnoides

6 Alyssum
saxatile
citrinum

10 Hyssopus
cristatus

8 Helianthemum
'Wisley Primrose'

18 Viola cornuta alba

7 Sedum album

9 Dryas
octopetala

10 Alchemilla
mollis

9 Hebe
canterburiensis

Rosa 'Dance de
Feu'

3 Potentilla
arbuscula

Ceanothus veitchianus

3 Yucca
filamentosa

0 1 2 3 4 5 ft

1·5 m

Fig. 8.2. A planting plan showing plant names and quantities of plants to be used in each location.

Planting distances – Planting distances will depend on the vigour and ultimate size of the plant. It is desirable to cover all bare soil fairly quickly, particularly when using ground cover plants. If money is available plants may be put in more closely and thinned later, or quick-growing temporary planting may be included to give more effect in the early stages.

8.5 Ground preparation

8.5.1 General

The first principle of cultivation is to do no more than is needed and to do it at the right time. The initial preparation of planting areas should aim to bring the soil to a suitable physical condition and incorporate manures or fertilisers where necessary. Cultivations should provide a good root-run for plants without destroying the texture of the soil, and while maintaining sufficient consolidation for good anchorage. Water should be able to move freely and to be retained in sufficient quantity.

8.5.2 Cultivation

Areas where the topsoil has been stripped and the subsoil regraded or compacted should be cultivated with a subsoiler or ripper to loosen the surface and ensure free drainage. The required depth of topsoil can then be spread, taking care not to over-consolidate during spreading.

Areas which have been untouched by building operations can be prepared for planting by cultivating the topsoil to a depth of 250 mm (approx. 10 in). When the subsoil forms a hard or impermeable layer this should be broken up to a further depth of 250 mm (approx. 10 in) without mixing the two layers.

Cultivation may be done by hand or mechanically, whichever is the more economic for the scale of operations. Hand cultivation consists of digging or forking and raking. Mechanical cultivation may include ploughing, discing, harrowing or rotavating depending on the condition of the soil.

8.5.3 Weed clearance

It is much easier to destroy weeds while the ground is still bare of plants and future maintenance is simplified when the soil is substantially free from perennial weeds and weed seeds before planting is done. If possible, planting areas should be allowed to lie fallow for several months during the late spring and summer. During this

151

time weeds should not be allowed to seed and growing weeds should be controlled by cultivation or weedkillers.

Annual weeds are controlled by repeated hoeing or by a paraquat–diquat mixture applied to the foliage. Perennial weeds are a bigger problem since cultivation will spread the roots and propagate rather than destroy them. On small areas it is easiest to dig out the roots and burn them; on larger areas a suitable non-residual weedkiller may be used. For grass weeds, including couch grass, Dalapon may be used; docks, thistles, nettles, etc., can be controlled by repeated treatments with 2,4,5-*T*, or 2,4-D. Successful chemical weed control depends to a great extent on timing and weather conditions as well as to using the most appropriate weedkiller. It is wise to obtain advice on specific weed problems as they arise. In all cases it is essential that manufacturer's instructions are followed in detail and that all precautions are observed when using chemicals.

8.5.4. Drainage

Planting areas will not normally require special drainage since plants will be chosen to suit the existing conditions. It may be necessary to provide special drainage in certain cases, particularly on heavy soils or where the natural drainage has been impeded by building operations or landshaping. Drains will be required for individual plant pits in clay subsoil; planting areas excavated into an area of clay 'cut' in which water will be trapped; and areas where the ground water table lies within 1 m of the surface. Drains should be laid after ground shaping has been completed, before topsoil is spread.

8.5.5 Topsoil

Topsoil should be deep enough for plants to be planted with all their roots in this layer. Where topsoil exists on an undisturbed site it will usually be deep enough for suitable plants. Areas which have been stripped of topsoil will need the following minimum depths of soil after spreading and firming:

Ground cover and herbaceous plants	250 mm (approx. 10 in)
Shrub areas	400 mm (approx. 16 in)
Tree pits	600 mm (approx. 24 in)

Where there is insufficient topsoil on a site it will have to be imported, usually from grassland or cultivated areas that are being cleared for road building or industry. Imported topsoil should be free from large stones and rubbish, and free from pernicious weeds, e.g. couch grass, ground elder. When the soil is needed for growing a particular class of plants it may be necessary to specify texture – e.g. light, medium, heavy – and lime content and stone content if required. Topsoil should be chosen to complement the existing subsoil and to relate to any soil already on the site.

B.S. 3882 – *Recommendations and classification for topsoil*, should be used when importing topsoil and B.S. 1377 – *Methods of testing soil for civil engineering purposes*, gives details of tests for pH, soil texture and compaction if these are needed.

Topsoil that has been stripped and stacked on the site should have been sprayed with weedkillers or sown with Italian rye grass to suppress weeds. Soil that has been stacked for more than three years may have deteriorated physically and organically and should be examined before use.

8.5.6 Fertilisers, manures and soil ameliorants

Additives to improve soil structure are applied during the final cultivation before planting; fertilisers are probably best applied after root growth has started and the plant is ready to use the nutrients.

Most topsoil contains sufficient amounts of the minor plant nutrients although their availability may be affected by soil conditions. Nitrogen, phosphate and potash may not be present in sufficient quantity and can be applied in the form of fertilisers or manures.

Nitrogen – Should be applied to shrubs and trees with great caution. On soils with a reasonable proportion of organic matter natural sources will supply sufficient nitrogen. On soils which are deficient in organic matter a bulky organic manure or a slow acting nitrogenous fertiliser may be used.

Phosphates – Essential for seedlings and plants with a rapid growth cycle. They are unnecessary for trees and shrubs on most medium and heavy soils and are only of value on very poor acid sands and peats.

Potash – May be needed on sandy soils, chalky soils or acid peat. It will probably be deficient in soil that has been under lawn or grass cut for hay. Magnesium should be applied with potash as it tends to be deficient on soils where potash has been added. Farmyard manure will usually supply sufficient of both these nutrients, or sulphate of potash can be applied as indicated by the soil analysis.

Lime – May be used to modify the pH value and make a soil less acid. It is sometimes needed on very acid sandy soils to enable any fertiliser application to be effective. It is important in crop-growing and revegetating toxic sites but should be used with the utmost caution in general landscape work.

Peat – Supplies nitrogen in low concentration but is most valued as organic matter to improve soil structure. B.S. 4156 – *Peat*, specifies pH, moisture content, ash and particle size for peat suitable for landscape use.

Sand – Sharp river sand may be used with peat to improve texture of heavy clay soil.

8.5.7 Fertilisers and manures for planting areas

Material	Notes	Rate of application	Time and method of application
BULKY ORGANIC MANURES Various manures may be available locally and can be used to supply organic matter and some nutrients according to analysis.			
Farmyard manure	Should be well rotted or composted before use	1 cu m to 25 sq m (1 cu yd to 25 sq yd)	Mix with topsoil before planting, or apply as top dressing and lightly fork in during early spring
Spent mushroom beds	Contains lime and is not suitable where acid soil is needed	1 cu m to 50 sq m (1 cu yd to 50 sq yd)	Mix with topsoil before planting, or apply as top dressing and lightly fork in during early spring
SLOW ACTING NITROGENOUS FERTILISERS Hoof and horn	Coarse grades useful substitute for farmyard manure on soil rich in organic matter	70–140 g per sq m (2–4 oz per sq yd approx.)	Spread on surface after cultivation and rake in
Urea-formaldehyde	Mainly used for grass but suitable to encourage quick growth of shrubs	70–140 g per sq m (2–4 oz per sq yd approx.)	Apply as top dressing in spring
WATER INSOLUBLE PHOSPHATIC FERTILISERS Basic slag	Effective on most soils	70–140 g per sq m (2–4 oz per sq yd approx.)	Apply a few weeks after planting
Ground mineral phosphate	Effective on soils with pH 5·8 or less in wetter areas	70–140 g per sq m (2–4 oz per sq yd approx.)	Apply a few weeks after planting
PEAT Fine sedge	To increase moisture retention on light soils	3 kg per sq m (5½ lb per sq yd approx.)	Mix into top 150 mm of soil (top 6 in approx. of soil)
Sedge peat with a wide range of particle size	To improve drainage and aeration in heavy soils	3–6 kg per sq m (5½–11 lb per sq yd approx.)	Mix into top 150 mm of soil (top 6 in approx. of soil)
Coarse sedge peat	As a mulch	25 mm layer (approx. 1 in layer)	Spread on top of moist soil after planting
LIME Ground limestone or ground chalk	Safe and slow acting	Apply according to soil analysis	Work into top 150 mm of soil well before planting time (top 6 in approx. of soil)
COMPOUND FERTILISERS Slow-release inorganic fertilisers, e.g. Enmag	Nitrogen, phosphate, potash, magnesium released slowly over growing season	70–100 g per sq m (2–3 oz per sq yd approx.)	Spread on surface in spring or early summer and rake in

8.6 Planting and establishment of plants

8.6.1 Time to plant

Planting should normally be done during the recommended months, choosing periods when weather conditions are suitable. Planting should not be done when the soil is waterlogged, but frost and snow need not necessarily prevent planting if roots can be set in unfrozen soil. In very windy areas it may be desirable to provide temporary protection for valuable plants, particularly conifers and evergreens. As a general rule planting is better done during the autumn on light soils and in drier areas, while spring planting is better on heavy soils and in colder and wetter areas. Whenever possible planting should be arranged so that all the plants in one area are put in at the same time.

Type of plant	Planting season
Deciduous shrubs, roses	October–April (dormant period)
Evergreen shrubs and conifers	Early autumn or in late spring
Herbaceous perennials	September–October or March–April
Pot-grown plants and plants in containers	Throughout year if ground and weather conditions are favourable
Water lilies and marginal aquatics	Mid-March–early June
Narcissus and crocus	Early September–October
Tulips	October–November

8.6.2 Protection of plants while out of the ground

It is essential that roots should not be left exposed to frost or to drying winds. When it is necessary for plants to be left out of the ground the roots should be covered with damp sacking or other protective material. Trees and shrubs may be sprayed before lifting, using a proprietary wax or latex preparation to reduce transpiration. This treatment is particularly useful when moving evergreens and will assist towards their successful establishment. Plants that arrive and cannot be planted immediately can be stored for a short period in their packages, in a frost-free place. For prolonged storage during hard frost the packaging and ties should be loosened to admit air. When the ground is not hard-frozen it is best to heel-in plants until they can be put into permanent positions. An open trench deep enough to hold the roots should be made and the plants placed in it so that the tops lie at an angle of about 45°; the trench is then filled in and the soil trodden firmly over the roots.

Large bundles of plants should be opened before heeling-in so that all the roots are in contact with soil. It is important to make sure that all plants can be identified and that labels are not buried. Heeled-in plants should be watered when the soil is dry. It may be convenient to heel-in stock in several places near final planting positions. When needed for planting, the plants should be carefully lifted after removing the covering soil.

8.6.3 Planting, general

The ground should be prepared for planting and individual pits dug for trees and large shrubs before the plants arrive on the site, so that they will be out of the ground as short a time as possible. Positions for groups of plants should be marked-out and labelled. Where a large area is to be planted, the deliveries should be phased to avoid the need to heel-in plants which cannot be dealt with immediately. Trees and large shrubs should be planted before ground cover, and bulbs last of all to avoid disturbance. All plants in one group or section should be set out before planting is begun to ensure correct placing and distribution, but more material than can be planted within a short time should not be set out. After an area of planting has been completed the surface soil should be pricked over with a fork to prevent a hard crust forming and to leave the ground level and tidy.

Depth of planting. Most plants must be planted at such a depth that the final soil level will be where it was when the plant was previously growing in the nursery. This is particularly important on heavy soils where deep planting can kill susceptible plants. While it is safe to comply with this general rule there are certain exceptions; some plants will grow better when planted more deeply than in the nursery, e.g. heathers, lavenders, clematis, clumpy shrubs.

Planting bare-rooted plants. Most common nursery stock transplants readily, and can be lifted without soil attached to the roots for ease of packing and transport. A hole large enough to take all the roots without twisting or bending is dug with trowel or spade; broken or damaged roots are cut off and the plant is placed in the hole so that the roots are well spread and the plant is at the correct depth. Loose topsoil is carefully worked between the roots, each layer being firmed so that the roots are fixed and there are no air pockets. When the soil is dry the hole should be filled with water after the plant has been set and then partially filled with soil. The water will settle the soil around the roots and back-filling can be completed after the water has drained away. Firm planting is essential but care must be taken on heavy and wet soils that the ground is not over-compacted and the soil structure destroyed (see Fig. 8.3).

Fig. 8.3. Diagram showing points to watch in planting out a bare root plant.

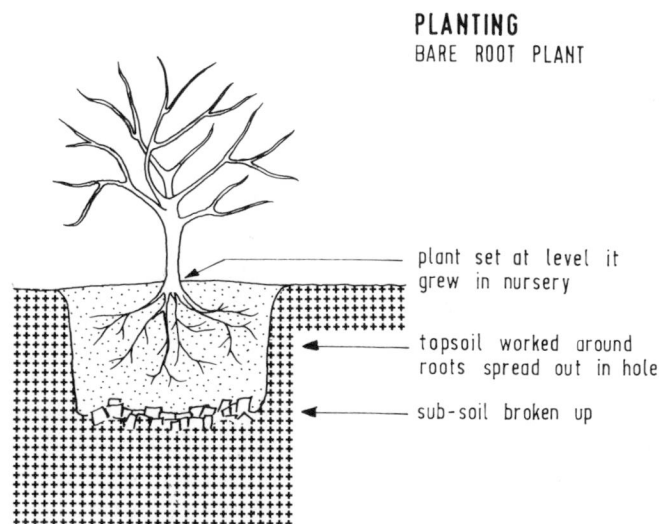

PLANTING
BARE ROOT PLANT

— plant set at level it grew in nursery

— topsoil worked around roots spread out in hole

— sub-soil broken up

154

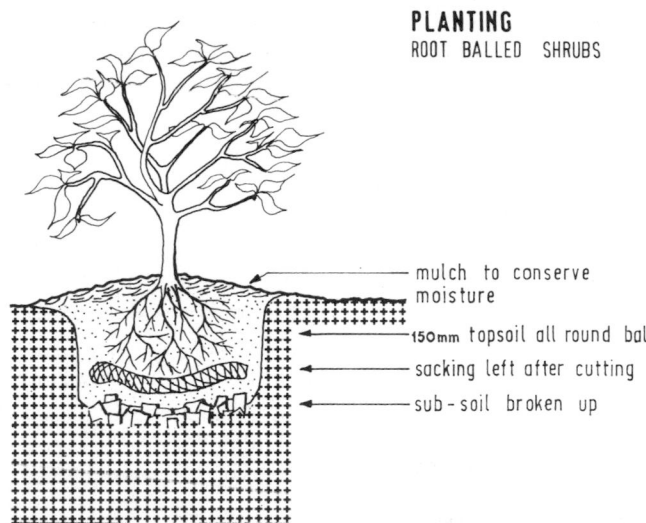

PLANTING
ROOT BALLED SHRUBS

— mulch to conserve moisture
— 150mm topsoil all round ball
— sacking left after cutting
— sub-soil broken up

Fig. 8.4. Diagram showing the planting out of a root-balled shrub.

Planting root-balled shrubs. Plants such as conifers and rhododendrons, which make a dense mass of fibrous roots, giving a root-ball, are lifted with the soil attached and the root-ball is wrapped in sacking or other protective material, to hold it intact and to prevent damage and drying out during transit. Such plants should always be handled by the root-ball and not by the top to avoid damaging evergreen foliage and to prevent strain on the plant. The root-ball should be soaked in water on arrival without removing the sacking. The plant is then put in a prepared hole at the correct depth, ties holding the sacking cut and any sacking that is easily removable cut away; plastic should be removed completely. When staking is necessary the stake should be driven into the ground at an angle (to avoid piercing the root-ball) with its head facing into the prevailing wind, otherwise guy wires may be used.

Planting pot-grown plants. The soil in the pot should be well moistened before the plant is knocked out of the pot, the young roots lightly loosened without disturbing the main soil-ball, and placed in the prepared hole in the normal way. When a plant has become pot-bound and the roots protrude through the bottom hole it is best to break the pot away to avoid damaging the roots.

Planting container-grown stock. The compost in the container should be removed from the container without disturbing the roots. Polythene containers may be slit at the base before placing in the prepared planting hole. The sides can then be slit and the polythene removed before careful backfilling with fine soil to ensure that the roots grow quickly into the surrounding soil.

8.6.4 Planting, particular types

Climbers and wall shrubs. Supports should be constructed, for all plants which are not self-clinging, before planting takes place. Plants should be set at least 15 cm away from the wall and their shoots tied loosely to the support to allow for any settlement of the soil.

Ground cover. Shrubs and climbers should have any stakes removed so that long shoots may be pegged out in the direction they are required to grow. Black polythene sheeting spread over the ground will control the growth of annual weeds. Small plants can be planted in holes in the sheeting which can be removed once the ground cover is established.

Naturalised bulbs. Narcissus and crocus are the most commonly used bulbs for naturalising in grass but many others may be grown successfully, particularly under trees where grass does not grow so strongly. Bulbs should be planted only where their foliage can be left to die down naturally and grass cutting can be postponed until the leaves are dead. Bulbs should be planted with a trowel or special planting tool to ensure that the base of the bulb is in contact with the soil and at the correct depth.

8.6.5 Out-of-season planting

It is not always possible to complete all planting during the recommended season and the wide availability of container-grown stock enables plants to be moved at any time of the year. Container-grown stock may be more expensive to buy and to transport but this may be balanced against convenience and possibly faster planting under summer conditions. Even using container-grown material out-of-season planting should not be considered unless there is an adequate water supply and maintenance staff are available to work as and when required. Given these essentials suitable weather and soil conditions are more important than the time of year. Plants with fibrous root-balls may be lifted from the open ground and will transplant well provided that they are only out of the ground for a short time. Plants with coarse straggly roots do not transplant so readily unless they can be lifted with the soil attached. Cold storage may be used to prolong dormancy in a wide range of plants but the material has to be selected and loaded into the store in a fully dormant state. This treatment allows planting to be delayed until May or June but the treated plants should be in the ground in time to grow and ripen their shoots before the onset of winter.

If the following precautions are taken failures will be minimised:

Spray trees and shrubs with an anti-dessicant before lifting and again after planting.

Plants should be out of the ground for as short a time as possible. It helps if material is available in a nursery area close to the site to be planted.

Choose a period of dull cloudy weather for planting. Water the soil round open-ground plants before lifting and water other plants in their containers.

Water plants into their holes to settle the soil.

When a period of drought follows transplanting the areas at the roots should be watered thoroughly at about weekly intervals. A mulch of well-rotted farm-yard manure, compost, damp peat or grass clippings applied on the surface around each plant after watering will help to conserve moisture.

Protect vulnerable plants from drying winds and direct sunlight by temporary shelters of wattle hurdles or hessian on supports.

8.6.6 Aftercare

Aftercare includes the operations which may be necessary during the first growing season after planting to ensure that the plants establish themselves quickly and begin to grow with minimum delay. (For care after the first year see section 8.7 on maintenance.)

Firming – Hard frost may loosen roots and cause plants to rise out of the ground. These should be firmed-in by treading the soil around each plant when the ground is not sticky.

Watering – When planting is done at the best time it should not be necessary to water plants in order to establish them; but when planting is followed by a drought then water must be supplied if the plants are to survive. The soil around the plants should be thoroughly soaked once a week during dry weather.

Evergreens are particularly susceptible to drought and drying winds. The soil round their roots should be soaked in March and covered with a protective mulch; watering should be repeated in a prolonged drought. During dry and hot weather a fine water spray should be given in the evenings until July.

Pruning – Damaged growths should be cut away, after planting. If roots have been damaged in transplanting and the root system seems inadequate to support the top growth, the main shoots may be shortened by one third to balance. Care should be taken that the shape and symmetry of each plant is not spoilt by cutting, especially with evergreens.

Some shrubs, including bush and climbing roses, large flowered clematis and *Buddleia davidii* cultivars grow best

when cut back hard to encourage growth from the base. Bamboos should be cut to half their height after planting and then old shoots pruned to the base as new canes grow.

Grafted and budded plants – Any suckers that appear should be removed by pulling or cutting so that no stump is left.

Hedging Plants	Initial Pruning
Quick thorn	Cut to within 10 cm (approx. 4 in) of ground level
Privet	Cut to within 30 cm (approx. 12 in) of ground level
Hornbeam, beech	Do not prune until 2 or 3 years after planting
Box, cotoneaster, berberis	Cut down by ⅓ of their height and trim back side shoots
Yew, conifers, holly	Shorten side shoots only; leave leaders until desired height is reached

Weeding – Weeds can be controlled by cultivation, by applying weedkiller or by supressing them with black polythene or a mulching material.

Hoeing at intervals of about 14 days throughout the spring and summer after planting will keep down weeds but needs to be done with care to avoid damaging surface roots. Paraquat–diquat mixtures will give a quick kill of weeds by attacking the foliage but they do not prevent further weed growth and precautions must be taken to avoid damaging the foliage of other plants. Residual herbicides applied to clean soil will prevent seed germination for up to eight months; in landscape work they are probably of most use in keeping weed-free areas round trees and shrubs until they become established and should not be used where self-seeding is to be encouraged. Residual herbicides are not suitable for all plants and their effect depends greatly on soil and weather conditions; they should only be applied where expert advice and supervision is available. Black polythene sheeting can be fitted round trees and shrubs to suppress weeds or it can be used as a continuous sheet as a base for ground cover planting. Mulches of weed-free material, e.g. peat, compost, ground bark, sawdust, will help to suppress weeds as well as conserving moisture. Loose mulches can increase the risk of frost damage to susceptible plants.

8.7 Maintenance

8.7.1 General
Plants are usually considered to be established when they survive the first growing season; but at the end of that period they may have made little new growth and their future care is very important if they are to grow to maturity and fulfil the designer's intentions. The maintenance of any planting should have been considered in the initial stages of design to ensure that it can be done with the manpower and machinery available. A maintenance schedule can then be prepared; this gives detailed guidance for the care of the planting after the initial establishment period. This schedule is essential if the maintenance staff are to produce the effect intended by the planner who may have no further contact with the scheme once it has been finished.

The maintenance schedule should include the following parts:

Plans showing details of the planting as actually completed, so that plants can be identified when labels become lost and any plants which may die can be replaced with the correct species. Where whole groups are unsatisfactory it may be necessary to replace with a different species to give a similar effect. The plan should also show which plants are intended as fillers to be allowed to die out or to be removed as the permanent planting matures.

Sections or elevations to show the intended shape and height of hedges and of any other planting that requires pruning to the form intended, together with details of any special pruning and treatment needed.

Recommendations for weed control, feeding, pruning and general management of planted areas.

8.7.2 Cultivation and weed control
There is no need to cultivate between plants except as a method of weed control; indiscriminate forking or digging may damage the feeding roots near the surface and hamper growth. Cultivation will also destroy self-sown seedlings of desirable species and may damage the underground runners of ground cover plants. On some soils it may be desirable to break up the surface crust, by hoeing or light forking to assist the penetration of rain water. Manures or fertilisers can be incorporated during this cultivation if required.

Regular weed control will be necessary for the first few years after planting until plants are established and the soil is covered by growing plants or leaf litter. If allowed to grow, weeds will use water and nutrients needed by the young plants and may eventually smother them. Weeds may be controlled by any one, or a combination of methods described in section 8.6.6, depending on the type of planting and the weeds to be controlled. The *Weed Control Handbook* is revised frequently and gives details of the latest recommendations for the chemical control of weeds.

8.7.3 Feeding
Feeding will depend on the type of planting and the site conditions, particularly the character of the soil. Amenity planting is not intended to produce a crop and any feeding should be limited to the minimum necessary to maintain health without producing excessive growth after the plants have filled the space intended. Ecological-type planting should not require any regular feeding except perhaps on very poor light sandy soils which may need fertilising until the plants are established and the soil has been enriched by natural leaf litter.

Plants that are clipped or hard-pruned regularly (e.g. hedges, roses) and quick growing bedding and herbaceous plants will require feeding by annual applications of bulky organic manures or compound fertilisers following the normal gardening practice for each type of plant.

8.7.4 Hedges
After initial pruning hedges have to be built up gradually by trimming the sides; the tops should not be trimmed unless recommended for the species (see Table in section 8.6.6). When the required shape and height is reached, all-over clipping at regular intervals will keep the final shape. Formal hedges are best trimmed with a slight batter so that the top is narrower than the base; this helps to keep them well furnished to the ground. Hedges which become bare at the base can be planted with ground cover, but if this is done initially it will prevent lateral growth near the ground.

Hedges may be trimmed with hand shears or a mechanical clipper; large-leaved shrubs (e.g. laurel, rhododendron) and informal hedges of flowering plants look better when trimmed with secateurs if time permits.

Overgrown hedges can be cut hard back to the main branch system in February–March: it is probably best to do this over two successive winters, cutting back one side of the hedge at a time.

Fast-growing shrubs such as *Lonicera nitida*, *Ligustrum*, will need clipping in May or June and at intervals of about six weeks thereafter.

Yew, beech and hornbeam and slow-growing plants can be kept fairly neat by clipping once a year in August but a neater appearance will result from two clippings, one at the end of May, the other in September.

Hedges of flowering plants should be clipped after flowering, for those that flower on older wood; shrubs that flower on the current season's growth need trimming in winter or early spring.

8.7.5 Shrubs

Shrubs growing in grass and borders edging on grass present a mowing problem, especially horizontally spreading types such as Juniper and Cotoneaster. Rotary mowers will cut close to the base of the shrub without damaging shoots but cylinder and gang mowers usually cause damage and prevent lateral growth. Underplanting with ground cover or edging borders with a wide mowing stone will help prevent damage, but a more natural effect may be obtained by using a rotary machine round shrub areas before mowing the main grass area.

8.7.6 Pruning

Pruning is a general term that covers several cutting operations, including shortening growths, cutting-out old and weak shoots, thinning. Most advice about pruning is intended for the gardener who wishes to grow a wide range of shrubs within a confined space and to produce quantities of good quality blossom. In landscape work the problem is usually to encourage plants to fill an area and the quality of the flowers is less important than the overall effect of form and colour. Therefore any pruning needs careful consideration to ensure that it will produce the required results. Because of the different aims of pruning, many plants which are pruned regularly in a garden need be given less intensive pruning when used as part of a landscape scheme. Hard cutting will produce bushy or vigorous growth and more flowers, but the natural habit of a plant may be lost and the year-round effect sacrificed for a short period of floral display.

The reasons for pruning include the following:

To remove dead, damaged or diseased growth.
To help bring out the character of a plant's natural form by selective cutting.
To prevent overcrowding and plants outgrowing their positions.
To maintain health by removing old and weak shoots and thinning others.
To increase quantity or quality of foliage or shoots.
To maintain the shape of hedges or topiary by clipping (see hedges).

Pruning should always be done to just above a bud, with no snags left. Quick-growing shrubs which tend to get leggy unless trimmed regularly will not usually stand pruning back into the old wood. These shrubs are better used as fillers, e.g. Cytisus, Cistus, Buddleia and can be removed once the permanent planting has become established. Shrubs that are out-growing their positions may be kept in check by removing complete branches rather than by overall trimming. If one third of the growth is cut back each year the size will be restricted but the natural habit of the plant retained.

Time to prune. Heavy pruning of deciduous shrubs is usually done in the winter months when other

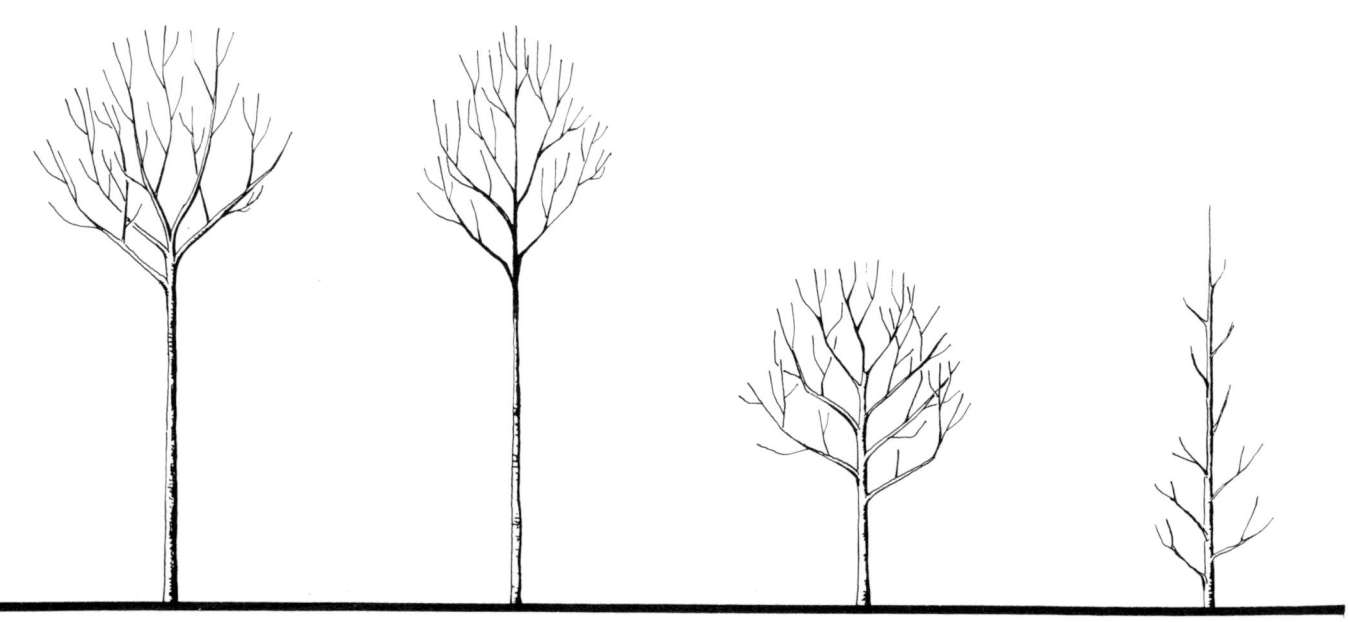

Fig. 8.5. Forms of trees.

standard with branching head   standard with central leader   bush tree   feathered tree

158

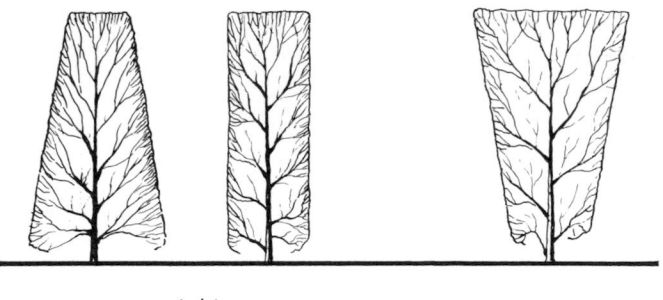

right   wrong

Fig. 8.6. The right and wrong ways to clip a hedge.

maintenance jobs are not so pressing. When time permits it is easier to identify and cut out dead and diseased growths when shrubs are in leaf and wounds heal quicker after spring pruning. Spring and summer time are also best for light pruning to encourage bushiness and to check over-vigorous growth. It is best not to prune evergreens in winter; this should always be left until spring or summer. Many shrubs, particularly evergreens, require no regular pruning provided they have space to develop naturally.

When necessary, pruning should be as follows:

Plant	Pruning	Season
Evergreens including conifers	Shape to natural form	April and throughout summer
Leggy and overgrown evergreens, e.g. yew, holly, box, etc.	Cut hard back into old wood	End of February or early March
Deciduous flowering shrubs, e.g. Philadelphus, Syringa, Rosa, Weigela	Thin every three years by cutting back old and weak shoots to base	Dormant season or after flowering
Ground cover, e.g. Vinca, Hedera, Calluna, Erica, *Hypericum calycinum*	Clip over to encourage bushy growth	April
Shrubs grown for foliage effect, e.g. Ailanthus, Sambucus, *Rhus typhina*	Cut hard back to within a bud or two of old wood	March
Shrubs for winter effect of coloured bark, e.g. Cornus, Salix	Cut hard back to within a bud or two of old wood	Late March, early April

8.7.7 Herbaceous perennials, biennials, annuals

For ease of maintenance select herbaceous perennials from robust species which are in flower or foliage for a long period of the year and need no support, e.g. Bergenias, Helleborus. Plants which die down completely in winter, e.g. Hosta, Polygonatum, are best associated with protecting shrubs or other plants with persistent foliage. Unless intensive garden-type management is practised it is best to leave dead flower spikes and all foliage to provide winter interest and ground cover; maintenance can be limited to removing obviously unsightly dead foliage in late winter or early spring.

Biennials such as Digitalis, Verbascum, Lunaria will naturalise if allowed to seed and dead flower spikes should not be removed until after seeding. Many plants normally grown as annuals or biennials for bedding, e.g. wallflowers, Nicotiana, forget-me-not will also naturalise in warmer areas if left in the ground; any weed control measures must allow for self-sown seedlings to develop.

8.7.8 Bulbs

Bulbs planted as permanent features in borders or naturalised in grass need very little maintenance and suitable species will increase by offsets and seeding. In borders, bulbs should be associated with other plants which will provide cover to hide the bulb foliage as it dies down, e.g. Narcissus among deciduous shrubs, tulips with Hostas, snowdrops with Tellima.

Bulbs naturalised in grass should be planted in areas which can be protected from public access from December, when the shoots begin to emerge, and where grass cutting can be postponed until the leaves have died down completely, usually some time in June.

8.7.9 Ground cover

One of the main purposes of using ground-cover plants is to reduce maintenance but extra careful attention is needed until the plants are fully established and a complete cover is achieved. Weeds are best controlled by a mulch but any deep-rooted perennial weeds must be removed by forking as soon as they are noticed. After establishment little regular maintenance is needed though some species, e.g. *Hypericum calycinum*, *Vinca*, may respond to hard cutting every other year in spring. Dead or damaged plants should be replaced to keep the cover complete, and in this context it may be easier to choose plants which can be divided on the site to fill gaps, rather than wait for a new plant to be obtained from the nursery.

159

Bibliography

Britain's Green Mantle, A. G. Tansley, Allen and Unwin.

Grounds Maintenance Handbook, H. S. Conover, F. W. Dodge Corporation, New York.

Manual of Trees and Shrubs, Hilliers, Winchester.

Plants for Ground-cover, G. S. Thomas, J. M. Dent and Sons.

The Pruning of Trees, Shrubs and Conifers, G. E. Brown, Faber and Faber.

Trees and Shrubs Hardy in the British Isles, W. J. Bean, John Murray.

Weed Control Handbook, Blackwell Scientific Publications, Oxford.

World of the Soil, Sir E. J. Russell, Fontana.

Landscape Design with Plants, ed. B. Clouston, William Heinemann.

9 Turf

IAN GREENFIELD

9.1 Soils

9.1.1 The soil and site preparation

The properties of the soil have their origins deep in geological history. While the differences between igneous, sedimentary and metamorphic rocks may appear largely academic, they do in fact greatly influence the nature and size of soil particles and therefore soil structure and drainage.

Quartz particles derived from igneous rocks form hard grains of sharp sand while silicates form the smaller silt and clay particles. The extreme forms of sedimentary rocks are the porous sandstones, the impervious clays and the alkaline limestones with a high calcium content, and in general the older they are, the harder they are. The metamorphic rocks are harder still.

When a pit is dug, the soil 'profile' usually reveals dissimilar layers, ranging from the topsoil down to the parent rock or in pedological shorthand, horizons A to D. While the upper part A is much modified by vegetation and other living organisms, C and D are little altered parent material; the intervening B horizon may be much influenced by minerals, notably iron, washed down from above; this iron may form a hard pan which hinders plant roots and drainage alike.

9.1.2 Soil texture and structure

An important feature of the soil, its ease of working, depends on its texture. This is a measure of the ultimate soil particles which are internationally defined in terms of size thus:

	Size (millimetres)
Stones and gravel	over 2·0
Coarse sand	2·0–0·2
Fine sand	0·2–0·02
Silt	0·02–0·002
Clay	below 0·002

In loams, sand, silt and clay are present in balanced amounts and thus allow easier working than heavy clays, but are heavier than sands (see also Chapter 1 – Survey, section on soils, and Appendix 2.2, Soil).

Soil structure differs from soil texture and describes the ability of the ultimate particles to form stable aggregates under varying conditions, particularly varying water supply. The crumbs of loams tend to be stable while those of clays are amorphous and in wet conditions collapse and become sticky. It is this factor rather than individual particle size, that makes clay soils 'heavy' and sandy ones 'light'.

9.1.3 Humus

Among the soil particles, plant and animal debris degenerates into humus, the organic constituent of the soil. Although this is degraded by microbes, insects, worms and fungi, it plays a vital part in maintaining soil fertility by improving crumb structure, retaining water, and making soils darker and therefore warmer. An important group of soil bacteria ('nitrifying bacteria') convert the unavailable proteins of dead creatures into nitrates and ammonium ions soluble in water and readily taken up by grass roots.

9.1.4 Soil minerals

The mineral elements nitrogen, phosphorus, potassium, calcium and magnesium must be plentiful in order to produce good crops, but turf, especially fine bent/fescue turf, requires less nutrients than do farm crops. The importance of these nutrients, other than magnesium which is seldom either deficient or excessive in turf, are shown by Table 9.1. The most common cause of mineral deficiency is leaching; much nitrogen, phosphate and potash, lime and magnesium, are carried out of the reach of plant roots by drainage water. Nitrogen may, conversely, be inadequate in badly drained soils where waterlogging discourages the nitrifying bacteria and fosters other bacteria that actually reduce the available nitrogen. Much soil phosphate is unavailable to plants, especially in heavy soils where a large fraction of it is in an insoluble form. Other elements required by the grass (sulphur, manganese, zinc, boron, copper, iron and molybdenum) are called 'trace' elements because the plant needs them only in minute traces. The commonest deficiencies are of iron, revealed by yellowing of leaves, and/or boron, shown by the collapse of growing points.

TABLE 9.1: PLANT NUTRIENTS AND THEIR EFFECTS ON GRASS SWARDS

Element	Normal Source	Effects of Deficiency	Effects of Excess
Nitrogen	Ammonium salts and nitrates, mostly in soil solution	Plants small, bright-tinted with pale older leaves	Soft flabby growth, a risk of mechanical damage and disease
Phosphorus	Organic and inorganic phosphates in soil, not all available to grass	Poor roots, weak bluish or purplish shoots, wearing badly	Encourages clover
Potassium	Potash salts in soil solution only scarce in peat, chalk or sands. Also in minerals, e.g. felspar	Growing points fail, shoots die back. Risk of disease	Seldom met with
Calcium	Limestone, chalk, soil solution. Plentiful except in very acid soil	Growing points fail. Leaf tips yellow or stunted	Causes iron shortage; favours weeds

9.1.5 Soil acidity

Under acid conditions the ions of potassium, calcium, magnesium and ammonium are replaced in the soil by those of hydrogen which affects soil fertility and the species of grass which will grow. Soil acidity can be measured both in terms of lime requirement (a high lime requirement indicating an acid soil and a low one, a basic one) or by the symbol pH. Some important figures are given in Table 9.2 and the reader will appreciate the importance of pH and its adjustment by the use of lime or, on acidic soils, by acid fertilisers like sulphate of ammonia.

9.1.6 The suitability of soils for turf formation

The ideal soil for turf formation is deep enough for roots to grow and spread, and drains freely allowing them ample moisture and air. This implies an open and well-defined crumb structure, and a texture that of a loam, neither sticky nor too friable. Humus should be plentiful. The pH, fertility and nutrients should be appropriate; fertility is well indicated by the population of earthworms which increases with fertility and alkalinity. 'Trace' elements must be present though only in small amounts, and toxic chemicals absent – this last condition being difficult to control in air-polluted industrial towns and on reclaimed derelict land.

The five main deviations from this ideal are corrected as follows:

Soil	Problems	Treatment
Clay and clay loams	Heavy, compacted, waterlogged in winter, crack in summer, earthworms	Difficult. If possible, cover with several inches of good loam, otherwise dress with sharp sand
Sandy soils	Inadequate humus and minerals; summer drought	Readily improved by working in compost or peat. Adjust pH with lime
Infertile heath	Mineral shortage, poor drainage; acidity	Break up 'iron pan' in subsoil to improve drainage; add lime, compost and fertilisers. Irrigate in dry weather
Chalky soils	Shallowness, alkalinity, excessive drainage	Break up subsoil, add sulphate of ammonia (or other acid fertiliser) and compost
Derelict land (slag heaps, etc.)	Debris, unweathered rock, sometimes acidity	This takes time. Clear the worst debris, break up the soil and allow to weather. Preferably import topsoil

9.1.7 Seed bed preparation

After levelling and draining the topsoil is evenly returned, to a depth of 150 mm (approx. 6 in) for normal landscape work, or for preference 300 mm (approx. 12 in) for playing fields or fine turf. While it is sometimes desirable to seed areas associated with building or engineering projects immediately best results are only obtained if the site is first allowed to settle, is dug or ploughed to 150 mm (approx. 6 in) depth in the autumn, and allowed to over-winter.

TABLE 9.2

Acidity	pH	Colour of B.D.H. Universal Indicator	Soil Suitable for
Very acid	5	Red	Heaths
Acid	5·5–6	Orange	Fine turf
Slightly acid	6–6·5	Yellow	Sports turf
Neutral	7	Green	Sports turf, many weeds
Alkaline	8	Blue	Chalk grass-land, weeds

In spring, further modifications may be necessary. Sandstones are improved with Keuper marl, gravels with manure, light soils with peat, green manure or sewage sludge, and heavy soils with sand. Cultivations such as harrowing and raking (alternately at right angles), mixes these materials with the soil, gives an even tilth, and kills weed seedlings. Analysis of soil nutrients and pH at this stage may reveal the need for fertilisers or lime. Weeds and insect pests may also require treatment. Successful fallowing should make weed killing with sodium chlorate 140–420 g per m² (approx. 4–12 oz per sq yd) unnecessary, but pre-emergence weed-killers may be used at this stage. Wireworms and other insect larvae encountered on ploughed up pasture and elsewhere, may be controlled by working D.D.T., B.H.C. or pest dusts into the soil surface, or by mixing $\frac{1}{2}\%$ lindane dust with the seed. Lead arsenate is less suitable as it may impair germination.

All these operations are designed to give a seedbed which is clean, free from weeds and their seeds, fine, moist, warm and above all, firm. In a well-tilled soil the particles approximate in size to wheat grains for the top few inches, grading downwards into a firm subsoil, well drained and aerated. 'Fluffy' seedbeds are bound to be disappointing.

9.2 Grasses

9.2.1 The grass

The plant family to which the grasses belong – the *Gramineae* – is one of the largest groups of plants, with over 10,000 species all told. It is, therefore, remarkable that all British turf needs are met from the 100 indigenous British species of plants clearly related to them.

The resistance of grass to close cropping by livestock due to its ability to provide a continuous foliage cover at ground level is its main virtue in the formation of good quality turf; in the perennial grasses it can be achieved in two ways. At one extreme, sheep's fescue forms compact tufts with many short erect shoots; at the other are the bent grasses with leafy shoots (stolons) creeping above ground, or couch grass with its whitish stems (rhizomes) ranging horizontally below ground level. Good quality turf contains a blend of tufted and stoloniferous species and the desirable fescues and bents can be found in grazed heathland as well as in well-managed lawns and greens.

In the more luxuriant meadows, the grass grows taller and it is here that cocksfoot, and meadowgrasses, ryegrass and timothy abound in nature. Though these are usually too coarse for use in fine turf, their vigour and productivity, especially when well fertilised, has suited them to agriculture and they may find a place in sports turf and extensive turf, especially in damper situations, or where a quick cheap attractive grass cover is the aim.

It is impossible to catalogue all the turf grasses, let alone all the wild British grasses, which, between them, can colonise almost any natural or man-made situation. Still less can all their English names be listed here, as some of them, like *Agrostis tenuis*, have as many as eight. Table 9.3 attempts to set out the most important of them, in order of their scientific names. The reader is advised to familiarise himself with the main scientific names, which will frequently be used in this text for reasons of clarity and brevity.

TABLE 9.3: COMMON GRASS SPECIES
(In order of their scientific names)

Scientific Name	English Name	Where Employed
Agropyron repens	Couch grass	A serious weed
Agrostis canina		
Subspecies *canina-fascicularis*	Velvet bent	Fine turf
Subspecies *montana-arida*	Brown bent	Fine turf
Agrostis gigantea	Black bent	Rough turf
Agrostis stolonifera – alba	Creeping or white bent	Fine turf, especially damp soil
A. stolonifera variety *palustris*	Fiorin	Rough turf or damp ground
A. stolonifera 'Emerald Velvet'		Rough turf; plant as stolons
Agrostis tenuis	Browntop common bent	Fine turf (important)
Aira, see *Deschampsia*		
Cynosurus cristatus	Crested dogstail	Cricket squares, playing fields (hard wearing–important)
Dactylis glomerata	Cocksfoot	Only very rough turf

cont. overleaf

cont.

Scientific Name	English Name	Where Employed
Deschampsia flexuosa	Wavy hairgrass	On acid soils
Festuca longifolia	Hard fescue	Playing fields
Festuca ovina	Sheep's fescue	Tennis courts, lawns (important)
Festuca rubra S.59	Red fescue	Playing fields (important)
F.r. variety genuina glaucesens	Cumberland marsh fescue	Fine turf
Festuca rubra FR10	St. Ives fescue	Fine turf, developed at Sports Turf Research Institute Bingley
Festuca rubra subspecies	Chewing's fescue	Fine turf and playing fields (important)
Festuca tenuifolia	Fine-leaved fescue	Cricket tables
Holcus lanatus	Yorkshire fog	Weed in fine turf
Lolium perenne S23 (There are other strains also)	Perennial ryegrass	Playing fields rough turf (important)
Nardus stricta	Moor mat grass	Weed in acid heathy places
Phleum pratense S50	Cat's tail, timothy	Playing fields on heavy damp soil
Phleum nodosum	Small timothy	Playing fields on heavy damp soil
Poa annua	Annual meadowgrass	Weed in fine turf, useful in urban turf
Poa nemoralis	Wood meadowgrass	Shady places
Poa pratensis	Smooth stalked meadow-grass, Kentucky bluegrass	Playing fields (important)
Poa trivialis	Rough stalked meadow-grass	Playing fields (important)
Puccinellia maritima and P. distans	Salt marsh grass	Poor constituents of sea washed turf
Sieglingia decumbens	Heath grass	Poor quality grass of heaths

9.2.2 Choice of seeds mixtures: general and fine turf

The main factors influencing the choice of seed mixtures are soil type and moisture content, climate, cost, the type and area of turf required, and the height of cut and foot traffic envisaged and the shade if any. The modern trend is to simplify the mixtures from 8–10 species down to 3 or 4, of which only one is stoloniferous, as grasses with this habit blend badly with each other. The best colour is obtained if species are used which mature at different seasons, the behaviour of grasses being as follows:

Bents	Best from July to October
Dogstail	Varies little with season
Fescues	Best from April to June; poor in winter
Meadowgrasses	Vary little with season
Ryegrass	Best in spring and autumn

Some fine turf mixtures (Table 9.4, column 1–3) usually contain 30% of *Agrostis tenuis*, but if it is scarce, as after the war, it can be replaced by fescue (columns 4–6).

Ryegrass is omitted except as an occasional 'nurse crop', to be eliminated later on by constant mowing and acidifying with sulphate of ammonia. Fertility must be kept low or fescues may be overrun by the bents.

TABLE 9.4: FINE TURF MIXTURES

Species	% Present					
	(1)	(2)	(3)	(4)	(5)	(6)
Agrostis tenuis	30	30	25	10	10	10
Chewing's fescue	70	30	50	70	90	60
S.59 fescue	–	40				30
Cumberland fescue			25			
Fine-leaved fescue				20		

9.2.3 Hard-wearing mixtures

Where short turf is subject to wear, dogstail comes into its own as seen in Tables 9.5 and 10.6. A lesser amount is required in tennis courts and hockey pitches, than in cricket squares.

9.2.4 Ryegrass mixtures

For reasons of suitability or cost, ryegrass is a major constituent of football pitches and other places where hard

TABLE 9.5: MIXTURES BASED ON DOGSTAIL

Species	% Present					
	Lawns		Cricket squares		Tennis	Hockey
	(1)	(2)	(3)	(4)	(5)	(6)
Crested Dogstail	40	35	20	15	25	10
Agrostis tenuis	10	5	10	10	30	15
Chewing's fescue	40	50	50	75	45	60
Red S.59 fescue				20		15
Poa species (see 9.2.5)	10	10				

TABLE 9.6: TENNIS COURTS AND HOCKEY PITCHES

| Species | Tennis Courts | | | | Hockey Pitches | | |
| | | | | | Wet | Medium | Sandy |
	(1)	(2)	(3)	(4)	(5)	(6)	(7)
Chewing's fescue	60	45	40	40	60	60	40
S.59 fescue	25		30		10	15	20
Fine-leaved fescue			10				
Agrostis tenuis	5	30	10	10	10	15	20
Dogstail	10	25		20	10	10	20
Timothy					10		
Poa species			10	10			
Ryegrass	useful on base lines			20			

TABLE 9.7: RYEGRASS MIXTURES FOR FOOTBALL, RUGBY, HOCKEY, AND OTHER PITCHES: VERGES AND LAWNS

(the last 5 are most suitable for rugby and football)

| Species | % Present | | | | | | | |
	(1)	(2)	(3)	(4)	(5)	(6)	(7)	(8)
Chewing's fescue	10	10						
S.59 fescue	30	15	10–30	10				
Hard fescue			5					5–15
Agrostis tenuis	10	5	10					
Ryegrass S.23	50	50			80–70	60–65	80	75
Ryegrass short-seeded			80–60	60				
Dogstail		15		10	20–30	10	20–30	10
Poa species				20		20–15	0–20	10
Timothy						10		

winter wear occurs on long turf (Table 9.7) and in extensive parks and outfields where cheapness is an asset (Table 9.8).

9.2.5 Seeds mixtures for special situations

Grass seed mixtures should be carefully modified for different situations and many of these are catered for above. Ryegrass and *Poa trivialis* cope best with shade, while the presence of toxic and acid chemicals in urban atmospheres kills or disfigures most perennial grasses so that *Poa annua* which establishes itself naturally, should here be encouraged; it may need summer watering. The most important modifications to suit situations are:

Situation	More Should be Sown	At the Expense of
Dry or light soil	Dogstail, *Poa pratensis*	Timothy, *P. trivialis*
Wet or heavy soil	Timothy, *P. trivialis*	Dogstail, *P. pratensis*
Shade	Ryegrass, *P. trivialis*	Most others
Chalky soil	Dogstail	Bents, fescues, or timothy
Acid or peaty soil	Fine-leaved fescue, wavy hairgrass or velvet bent	Most others
Dry, sandy heaths	*Poa pratensis*, fescues	Bents, fescues or timothy
Conifers	Wavy hairgrass	Most others
Urban situations	*Poa annua*	Perennials
Tennis base lines	Perennial ryegrass	Others in mixture

The following mixtures are suitable for shady places:

Heavy soil   50% ryegrass, 30% *P. trivialis*, 20% *Agrostis Stolonifera*.

Medium soil   50% *P. pratensis*, 25% each of ryegrass and either dogstail or sheep's fescue.

Towns   40% ryegrass, 30% each of *Poa trivialis* and *P. annua*.

Light soil   40% sheep's fescue, 20% fineleaved fescue, 10% S.59 fescue. 30% *Agrostis tenuis*.

Peaty heaths   40% wavy hairgrass, 30% each of S.59 fescue and hard fescue.

TABLE 9.8: RYEGRASS MIXTURES FOR PARKS, GOLF FAIRWAYS, AND CRICKET OUTFIELDS

Species	% in Mixtures								
	Cricket Outfields						Parks		Fairways
	Dry soils		Wet soils		S.59 mixtures				
	(1)	(2)	(3)	(4)	(5)	(6)	(7)	(8)	(9)
Chewings fescue	20	10					10	15	45
S.59 Fescue					40	40			
Agrostis tenuis	10	10	10	10			10	10	10
Ryegrass S.23	50	50	60	50	50	60	60	50	25
Dogstail	20	10	10	10	10		10	15	10
Poa trivialis			10	20			10	10	
Poa pratensis		20							
Timothy (see 9.2.5)				10	10	10			

9.3 Establishment of grassed areas

9.3.1 Sowing

Improved seed strains and site preparation methods have led to a steady fall in the prescribed seed rate over the last few years. Lawns, tennis courts, cricket squares and similar swards require 35 g per sq m (approx. 1 oz per sq yd) but on well-prepared extensive areas, 70 kg per ha (say 60 lb per acre) suffice.

A quick-acting fertiliser, evenly mixed and spread at 105 g per m² (approx. 3 oz per sq yd) and raked into the soil surface, 1–2 weeks beforehand, enables grass seeds to develop rapidly and is particularly useful where the small non-ryegrass mixtures are at risk from damping off. A good formula (parts by weight) is as follows:

		Analysis
Sulphate of ammonia	2	
Superphosphate	4	Nitrogen 5·4%
Bone meal	4	Phosphate 14·1%
Sulphate of potash	1	Potash 4·4%

Late summer, after adequate fallowing and cleaning, is the best time to sow, unless followed by an unusually cold, early or wet autumn. Mid-August is best in north Britain, late August or early September in the milder south, west and coastal districts. Less satisfactory are spring sowings, especially when the spring is late or May dry.

9.3.2 First-year management of turf from seed

When fine grass attains 25–50 mm (approx. 1–2 in) and rough turf 50–75 mm (approx. 2–3 in) the area is cleared of wormcasts and lightly rolled to firm the surface. 1–2 days later the top 12–20 mm (approx. $\frac{1}{2}$–$\frac{3}{4}$ in) of grass, not more, is removed by means of a side-wheel mower;

this encourages tillering. Regular and frequent mowing should then continue, the height of cut being reduced each time until the final height is reached, usually 12–25 mm (approx. $\frac{1}{2}$–1 in).

Coarse grasses have to be eradicated by hand, likewise the larger perennial weeds such as dandelions, docks and plantains. Annual weeds – chickweed, groundsel, fat hen, deadnettles, redshank and speedwells – unless very numerous as a result of poor site preparation, succumb readily under repeated close mowing. Only after six months can selective weedkillers and lawnsands be safely applied to fine turf.

Three months after a successful sowing, 1·5–2·0 kg per sq m (say 3–4 lb per sq yd) finely-sieved compost lightly worked in so as not to smother the grass, is beneficial. Nitrogen deficiency, revealed by weak yellow turf, is remedied by applying 18 g per sq m (approx. $\frac{1}{2}$ oz of sulphate of ammonia to each sq yd); spring sowings may need irrigation. Then bare patches should be reseeded and the edges clearly marked out.

9.3.3 Turfing

A common and quicker alternative to seeding is turfing, but it is more costly and by perfectionist standards not usually as good. A balanced sward is necessary; see section 9.2.2.

Turf beds need less preparation than seedbeds but should be well settled. Autumn or early winter is a better time to lay than Spring as in the latter case dry weather can hinder rooting. 70 g per sq m (approx. 2 oz per sq yd) of a fertiliser (bone meal 4 parts, superphosphate 4, sulphate of potash 1) raked in, should precede this.

Whatever type is desired, sown or turfed, it will be helpful to refer to *Specification* published by the Architectural Press.

9.4 Maintenance

9.4.1 Turf maintenance: machinery

Good turf maintenance results from good management – the ability to assess the labour, machinery and materials necessary to achieve good economic results. Labour and operations therefore must be undertaken with a proper understanding of the finances available and with a forward looking budget. Chemical fertilisers and sprays must be intelligently used and new techniques tried and where successful, adopted and worked into routine operations.

The capital outlay, and routine current expenditure, must be carefully judged beforehand, and before buying machinery one must consider:

Funds available for initial purchase.

Expected maintenance costs.

The labour available to handle it.

The turf itself – site, soil, size and quality.

9.4.2 Normal machinery requirements

This naturally depends on circumstances, but some idea of machinery needs may be gauged from *Turf Culture*, p. 201, by the author. In the next few years, one may expect this list to be modified a good deal, particularly as the agricultural tractor improves in versatility. The following fourteen machines can be operated with a standard tractor, though on smaller areas a 2-wheel universal tractor may suffice.

Plate 9.1. A CUSHMAN TURF TRUCKSTER – A basic turf truck to which can be attached a wide variety of turf maintenance equipment.

Plate 9.2. CUSHMAN TURF CARE EQUIPMENT – Transport and dump box, seeder-fertiliser spreader, articulated spiker, and top dresser module.

167

Plate 9.3. SISIS AUTO-CONTRAVATOR/LOSPRED – A hand-controlled machine being used to seed a football pitch (Celtic Football Club).

Plate 9.4. MOTOR MOWER – A machine with a large grass box. The operator sits on a towed seat. Ransomes Sims and Jefferies Limited.

Plate 9.5. ROUGH GRASS MACHINE – A heavy-duty side wheel machine being used for cutting a grass verge. Ransomes Sims and Jefferies Limited.

Gang mower with up to 7 units.
Heavy or light duty piercers.
3·6 m (approx. 12 ft) scarifier.
3·6 m (approx. 12 ft) tilther rakes.
3·6 m (approx. 12 ft) brushes.
1·8 m (approx. 6 ft) liftable roller or gang roller.
Rotovator.
Rotary or reciprocating screens.
Chain harrow.
Disc harrow.
Cartage of 1·5–2·3 cu m (approx. 2–3 cu yd) loads.
Spraying (units with 3·6–6 m (approx. 12–20 ft) boom).
Fertiliser distributors.
Plough.

9.4.3 Mowing

Mowing, the most important of all turf maintenance operations, can dictate the whole appearance, durability and well being of the sward. It should be done regularly and not too keenly – 'little and often' – so that only a modest amount of grass is removed at each cut. Once to twice per week is sufficient, and entails the removal of 12–20 mm (approx. $\frac{1}{2}$–$\frac{3}{4}$ in) at most, on each occasion, though the exact frequency can be modified by climate, season, grass species and fertiliser regime. Winter mowing, essential to prevent the sward becoming open and lank, must be carefully timed for dry, non-frosty conditions.

Mowing gradually eradicates many broad-leaved weeds, but also grasses such as ryegrass, given time. Turf is also much influenced by whether the clippings are boxed or returned; the latter produces a spongy sward and many earthworms especially on heavy soils, and distributes unwanted seeds, but in dry weather affords a valuable mulch. In rough work, the low budget and simple standards required favour frequent cutting without a grass box.

9.4.4 Choice of mower

Mowing machines fall into 8 categories according to their source of power and method of cutting:

(a) Hand mowers, driven by human effort. These have either a rear roller or two side wheels, and are respectively termed 'roller' and 'side-wheel' types.

(b) Cylinder-driven mowers, hand-pushed but with an engine to drive the cylinder.

(c) Fully driven motor mowers, powered by internal combustion engines.

(d) Heavy duty mowers, as (c) but with engines of $3\frac{1}{2}$ hp or more, capable of haulage as well as mowing.

(e) Machines powered by electricity, whether from mains or battery.

Plate 9.6. VERTIRAKE attachment used behind a tractor. H. Pattisson and Co. Limited.

(f) Rotary mowers, with the cutting cylinder replaced by horizontally rotating blades.

(g) Miscellaneous – including clipper-type scythes and general purpose engines.

9.4.5 Aeration and renovation

Aeration is second only to mowing in the production of healthy turf, a fact which is becoming increasingly realised. Correctly carried out and timed, it can promote free

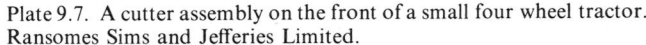

Plate 9.7. A cutter assembly on the front of a small four wheel tractor. Ransomes Sims and Jefferies Limited.

Plate 9.8. A gang-mower assembly towed by a tractor.

drainage under almost all conditions with but little inter-ference to the playing surface. Moisture, air and top dressings can penetrate the turf, roots and fibre are pruned, helpful bacteria develop and grass roots can penetrate deeper. As a result aeration can play a leading and relatively inexpensive part in turf renovation, especi-ally if this has to be done rapidly.

Aeration is achieved at two levels, surface and sub-surface.

Surface aeration. Some of the fine turf grasses produce excessive fibre which hinders green growth and root development. Once this exceeds a certain minimum, mowing fails to remove it and raking and scarification become necessary.

Spiked and smooth chain *harrows*, commonly 2·1 m × 1·8 m (approx. 7 ft × 6 ft) or 2·1 m × 4·2 m (approx. 7 ft × 14 ft) are useful on fairways, removing old matted grass, but their use on fine turf needs great care, and slitting gives better results. On a larger scale, a sports ground aerator with light metal wheels and tines, 150, 225 or 300 mm (6, 9 or 12 in) apart and capable of cutting 100 to 125 mm (4–5 in) deep, can be used monthly in winter, given suitable weather conditions.

Besides the above, *canes* are useful for scattering dew and wormcasts on fine turf; *mats* can work in top dress-ings, but are less good for this purpose than drag brooms

in wet weather; and *pricking* to a depth of 12 mm (½ in) rejuvenates neglected turf.

Subsurface aeration. It is seldom adequate to confine the attention to the matted turf surface; soil com-paction has to be avoided at all times by forking, spiking or slitting, and is most conveniently tackled as part of the autumn or early spring treatments, before applying top dressings. On a domestic lawn, the use of the ordinary garden *fork* at frequent intervals may suffice to remedy this.

Multipurpose aerators. Most of the above opera-tions and also rolling, are done using multipurpose equipment for which reference should be made to the trade literature. The frame which carries the tools may be driven by hand, mower or tractor.

Rolling and other mechanical operations. Much turf suffers from the over-use of the roller, especially when wet or in a vain attempt to level depressions. This compacts the soil surface, excludes water and air, inhibits grass root growth and admits weeds and moss. Aeration must therefore follow whenever rolling takes place throughout the season; this is especially true on heavy soils.

170

9.5 Turf dressings

9.5.1 Chemical treatment of turf fertilisers

The nutrients removed by cutting must be frequently replaced; of these (see section 9.1.4) nitrogen, phosphorus and potash (loosely termed N.P.K. after their respective chemical symbols) are the most vital. The analysis and rate of application of many turf fertilisers appear in section 9.5.2 and they may be classified as follows:

High-nitrogen fertilisers – Of these sulphate of ammonia is widely used, being cheap, readily taken up by the plant, and rich in nitrogen. Its acidity brings the turf to the optimum pH for fine grasses, eliminates many weeds and scorches moss – hence its use in lawnsands. Pre-sowing, 1·5 to 3·5 kg per 100 sq m (approx. 3–7 lb per 100 sq yd) should be applied. More recently urea of good quality (excluding biuret), near-neutral and non-scorching, has become a useful substitute, especially in the form of methylene–urea (38% N).

Alkaline nitrogenous fertilisers – These have a high nitrogen content but their alkalinity harms fine turf, except on very acid soils, and favours weeds and earthworms. Except for nitrochalk they take up atmospheric moisture and 'cake' in store; cyanamide is phytotoxic while nitrate of soda leads to sodium clay and *Ophiobolus* disease.

Low-nitrogen fertilisers – Organics but with little nitrogen slowly available to grass, these are mostly soil improvers and top dressings rather than fertilisers, they are used on seedbeds more than on established turf. The richest and best is dried blood which gives readily available nitrogen without scorch, stores well and blends with most other fertilisers.

Phosphatic fertilisers – As the raw material, rock phosphate, is mostly unavailable to grasses, it is usually modified before sale by treatment with sulphuric acid, giving superphosphate, or with phosphoric acid, giving triple superphosphate. Both these revert to the insoluble form, slowly in storage and more rapidly in acid soils rich in iron or aluminium. If applied alone they temporarily scorch the turf. Basic slag or bone derivatives are a useful source of phosphate for turf on acid or light soils, but unfortunately encourage clover. Quite different chemically is ammonium phosphate which is water soluble, rapidly available to the turf and may also scorch it.

Potassic fertilisers – Potassium sulphate and chloride ('Muriate') are both effective sources of potash, the sulphate being the safest for use on grass and the most pure chemically. Kainit contains sodium and magnesium salts as well as potash.

Other inorganic nutrients – These are not listed in the table. They can be supplied as follows:

Calcium	In lime, chalk, gypsum and some nitrogenous fertilisers.
Sulphur	In superphosphate, ammonium sulphate and sulphate of potash.
Magnesium	In Epsom salts, agricultural magnesium sulphate, kieserite, kainit and dolomite.
Iron	In chelated iron compounds.
Boron	In borax.

9.5.2 The main turf fertilisers

Fertiliser	Analysis	Rate of Application		Remarks
	% Nitrogen	(kg/100 m²)	(lb/100 sq yd)	
HIGH NITROGEN				
Sulphate of ammonia	20·6	1–2	2–4	Strongly acidic 2
ALKALINE-NITROGEN				
Nitrate of soda	15·5	1–2	2–4	Alkaline 2
Nitro-chalk	15·5	0·5–3	1–6	Mildly alkaline 2
Nitrate of lime	13	2	4	Alkaline 2
Calcium cyanamide	20·6	2	4	Strongly alkaline 2
LOW NITROGEN				
Dried blood	13	3–5	6–10	Use on light soil
Hoof and horn	7–15	6	12	Has 10% phosphate
Shoddy	up to 16	100	200	Use on heavy soil
Leather waste	6	20–35	40–70	For seedbeds
Rape meal	5·5	3	6	For sandy soils
Soot	4	3–6	6–12	Mildly acid 2
Sewage sludge	1–6	120–450	2–8 cwt	Sometimes alkaline
Malt culms	3·5	3–6	6–12	

cont. overleaf

Fertiliser	Analysis % Nitrogen	Rate of Application (kg/100 m²)	Rate of Application (lb/100 sq yd)	Remarks
Spent culms	3·5	0·5–1	1–2	
Farmyard manure	0·7	240–720	4–12 cwt	

	% (P_2O_5)			
PHOSPHATES				
Superphosphate	14–18	3	6	2
Triple superphosphate	47	0·5–1·5	1–3	
Basic slag	18	10–25	20–50	Alkaline
Bone meal, bone flour	21–25	5–10	10–20	Has some nitrogen
Ammonium phosphate	61	1–3	2–6	2

	% Potash			
POTASH				
Sulphate of potash	48	1–3	2–6	
Muriate of potash	50	1–3	2–6	
Kainit	14	2–6	4–12	

Notes:

1. To convert the above rates of application to oz per sq yd divide by 6, to cwt per acre divide by $2\frac{1}{2}$.

2. Where figure 2 appears in the remarks column, the fertilisers should be bulked with compost, sand or sterilised soil, 6 parts per part of fertiliser (10 parts in the case of soot).

3. See also Chapter 8 – Planting Techniques sections 8.5.6 and 8.5.7 for fertilisers and manures.

9.5.3 Choice of fertilisers

When buying fertilisers, consider the following points:

Cost per unit weight of nutrient – This can be deduced from the stated N:P:K analysis given by all reputable manufacturers.

Suitability for the purpose in hand – e.g. alkaline fertilisers will probably be inappropriate, and the nitrogen content must suit the time of year.

Compatibility – Although cheaper than buying a proprietary mixture of all three major nutrients, making up a compound fertiliser from its primary constituents needs care. Dried blood and potash salts blend quite well with other materials but others, e.g. sulphate of ammonia and superphosphate, inter-react with harmful results. A fertiliser compatibility table like that on page 331 of *Turf Culture* must be studied first, and then the ingredients thoroughly mixed under dry conditions (see also Appendix 2.3.1, Mixing of manures and fertilisers).

Although space does not permit a full discussion of the fertiliser requirements of turf, the following table accounts for most seasons and situations. It will be seen that the nitrogen content is reduced in the autumn to avoid flabby growth and disease, and potash and phosphate correspondingly increased.

9.5.4 Fertiliser analyses for season and situation

Purpose	% Nitrogen Inorganic	% Nitrogen Organic	% Phosphate Soluble	% Phosphate Insoluble	% Potash
SPRING					
Fine turf	4	3	6	1	4
Rough turf	4–6	3	6	1	6–7
AUTUMN					
Fine turf	1	1–2	6	6	6
Rough turf	1	1–2	9	3	12
Preseeding	4	1	10	3	5

Except for the last at 105 g per sq m (approx. 3 oz) they are applied at 70 g per sq m (say 2 oz per sq yd).

9.5.5 Other turf dressings

The following may also be useful:

Lawn sand (sand with 30–40% sulphate of ammonia, 15% sulphate of iron) at 105 to 140 g per sq m (approx. 3–4 oz per sq yd), acts as nitrogen fertiliser and weed killer.

Liquid fertilisers (e.g. 16:10:28) can be diluted and applied to greens.

Slowly released inorganic fertilisers, with nutrients

borne on a carrier.

Lime, on very acid turf. 0·1 tonne (approx. 2 cwt) of quicklime, 0·125 tonne (approx. 2½ cwt) of slaked lime, or 0·175 tonne (approx. 3½ cwt) of chalk or limestone are usually enough to raise the pH by one unit. Finely divided chalk is the kindest to the turf.

Top dressings, based on compost, improve the soil texture, the level, and the grass tillers. They are applied in the autumn, usually at 0·9 kg per sq m (approx. 2 lb per sq yd) occasionally at 1·8 kg per sq m (approx. 4 lb per sq yd), and must be thoroughly worked into the turf to avoid smothering it.

Charcoal or coke breeze, at 0·45 to 0·9 kg per sq m (approx. 1–2 lb per sq yd), help to lighten heavy soils.

Peat improves lawns on heavy and clay soils. It is then applied at 0·27 to 0·54 kg per sq m (approx. ½–1 lb per sq yd), but much more may be used in the preparation of seedbeds.

9.5.6 Fertiliser distribution

Even distribution of fertiliser is essential and while it can be achieved by hand, specially designed equipment is almost indispensable on larger sports grounds. The largest quantities, up to 5 tonne per ha (approx. 2 tons per acre), are spread by a tractor drawn spinning-disc distributor with a 250 kg (approx. 5 cwt) hopper, at 4 m.p.h. In most other models, the flow of material is regulated by a grooved roller or a canvas conveyor. These can sow fertiliser, seed (bulked), mowrah meal, etc., of differing texture. It is therefore advisable to check the actual flow rate of the given material by collecting it on brown paper, or a path, before applying it to large areas of turf.

9.5.7 Irrigation

The need for artificial watering of sports turf has been increasingly realised and several factors affect this need. Fine grasses are better adapted to withstand drought than are bents or annual meadowgrass; thin sandy soils need frequent irrigation in dry periods; and growing grass needs large amounts of water. Growth will always suffer if the groundsman waits for symptoms of drought before irrigating, and soil moisture should never be allowed to fall below half the field capacity. Irrigation equipment is likely to improve steadily in the next few years; for example the American practice of using remotely controlled golf-green watering units, may gain currency here. Irrigation water is, of course a useful vehicle for the delivery of chemicals to turf, and various fertiliser diluters can introduce accurately measured amounts of nutrients into it. Provided suck-back into the water mains can be avoided, the same methods can be likewise used for fungicides, insecticides, weed killers, and wormkillers.

9.6 Turf management

9.6.1 Different turf types and their management

The foregoing remarks apply to all kinds of turf, but according to its quality and purpose the various operations assume different degrees of importance. Sections 9.6.2 and 9.6.8 show how fine turf, rough-wearing turf, extensive turf and turf substitutes are treated in practice.

9.6.2 Fine turf establishment

Fine bent/fescue turf needs careful establishment to give a level surface, pleasing and uniform in appearance, with true running qualities. As found in golf, putting and bowling greens, and croquet and other lawns, it is usually flat, but may have gentle angles and undulations in golf greens and a 200–250 mm (approx. 8–10 in) central crown in crown bowling greens. Basic maintenance is the same for all.

Since Cumberland turf is increasingly difficult to obtain (see section 9.3.3), parkland and moorland turf may be substituted; the ousting of fescues by *Poa annua* and pearlwort may not always spoil the playing surface, but greens with excessive creeping bent may be slow running in wet conditions.

Turfing permits earlier play – autumn-laid turfs are usable by next June – but excellent results are obtained at low costs from New Zealand browntop/chewing's fescue sowings. Seeding requires careful management and takes a year to mature.

However turf is formed its site needs careful preparation. Golf greens require 200 mm (approx. 8 in) of good topsoil and a lengthy procedure must be followed when making a bowling green. A full 38 m (approx. 42 yd) square, or 41 m (approx. 45 yd) in crown greens, allowing for ditches and banks, is excavated and levelled on a 100 mm (4 in) peg placed in its centre, its height depending on the thickness of material to be laid. Drains in rectangular or herringbone pattern, with 100 mm (4 in) tiles for mains and 75 mm (3 in) for laterals should fall from near ground level at one end to 750 mm (2½ ft) at the other; overdrainage must be avoided.

Then a 100 mm (4 in) clinker layer (broken stone if well consolidated is also permissible) should extend to the ditches; after levelling, 50 mm (2 in) of fine ash is spread on top. The build up is completed by adding either 75–100 mm (3–4 in) of sandy soil or turfs boxed to 50 mm (2 in) or 150 mm (6 in) of light loam plus seed. Turfs, if used, are laid starting diagonally from one corner, or on crown greens from the centre, rolled, dressed with sharp sand, and levelled from a long flat block of timber.

9.6.3 Fine turf maintenance

The usual principles apply to all fine turf. Mowing is most important; hand-pushed roller mowers are best but special precision motor mowers are also suitable. Fine turf usually requires mowing at least once a week and a height of 5 mm ($\frac{3}{16}$ in) is the aim. On heavier soils a shorter cut, 2–3 times per week in the growing season, is necessary, but is less kind to the turf. During winter, a light topping is the rule, depending on conditions and grass growth; it should not take place in frosty spells or cold winds.

An American study of golf greens revealed compaction in only the top 50 mm (2 in); the resulting bad porosity is remedied there by using 150 kg (3 cwt) of krilium per acre and covering it with 100 mm (4 in) of a 7:1 sand/peat mixture, the sand being large grained.

Fertilisation, aeration and top dressing are similarly important. Spring treatment comprises raking, mowing at decreasing height, aeration and rolling with a roller 50 kg (1 cwt) or less. Cutting at 5 mm ($\frac{3}{16}$ in) and the use of sharp sand, gives as fast a surface as closer cutting and frequent rolling. The spring fertiliser and that for small booster doses should be mainly sulphate of ammonia; the more complicated autumn ones are applied at 50–100 kg (1–2 cwt) per acre with sharp sand or top dressing at 6 tonnes (6 tons). For formulae, see section 9.5.4 and also *Turf Culture* page 133.

Divots must be replaced and it is advisable to stagger the effects of wear, for example by moving the pins on golf greens frequently. Foot traffic in frosty weather harms greens and should be discouraged.

Fine turf needs protection against pests, diseases and weeds. *Poa annua* and pearlwort are common; plantains, daisies and other broad-leaved weeds may warrant grubbing by hand. Selective weedkiller application if decided upon, should not be delayed, and made a few days after fertilising and in settled non-drought conditions. Mat-forming mosses in otherwise well-maintained greens can be eradicated with mercury-based compounds, and earthworms can also seldom be tolerated. 'Switching' the dew reduces the risk of *Fusarium* disease but fungicidal treatment may also be necessary – before symptoms appear, if previous history shows that they are probable.

9.6.4 Turf subject to rough wear: winter pitches

Hardwearing turf falls into two categories with different management programmes, depending upon the time of year when it is used. This section deals with winter pitches for football and hockey; sections 9.6.5 and 9.6.6 deal with summer games such as cricket and tennis.

In a good winter pitch, with a firm even surface of close growing turf, the grass affords a cushioning effect against the compaction of the soil and injury to players following falls. Seeds mixtures as in section 9.2.3 should give an easily-managed hard-wearing sward, not necessarily fast growing which implies more mowing. From the outset, *football* pitches must be designed to endure 8–9 months play, often under bad conditions, for each of several subsequent years. Association football is more severe on turf than rugby. The soil must be a light medium, not heavy loam, levelled and well-drained. A First Division club may find it worthwhile to substitute large amounts of light soil for a heavy one, as did Tottenham Hotspur in 1952; smaller clubs can apply gypsum to advantage. Autumn play may follow a spring turfing, but after autumn turfing or seeding, a full year must elapse.

During the season, compaction due to play and rolling must be relieved by surface aeration and spiking, and applying sand. Rolling should be light and as infrequent as possible. Plantains, knotgrass and other weeds or bare patches may have to be removed. When play ends in April, the surface of muddy and compacted goal areas, etc., should be broken up with a disc harrow, or rotary cultivator set shallow, raked and forked. After dressing with gypsum and a fertiliser, it should be seeded with quick-growing ryegrass, or turfed from a turf nursery of similar soil type, and then kept well watered.

The whole pitch must be deep-pierced to 225 mm (approx. 9 in) using a slow moving tractor, and later pierced again to 100 mm (approx. 4 in). It benefits from a general fertiliser, and should be lightly rolled and topped with the mower – not allowed to run to hay – in the summer. The ideal height is 40 mm ($1\frac{1}{2}$ in) but 20 mm ($\frac{3}{4}$ in) where it also serves as a cricket outfield. As the summer closes, the height of cut should tend to 25–40 mm (1–$1\frac{1}{2}$ in) for association football, but 60–75 mm ($2\frac{1}{2}$–3 in) for rugby pitches. A fine surface is achieved by the use of a heavy roller before the association football season starts.

Hockey pitches need a firm level surface without minor undulations, to permit free-running of the ball. The soil must be well-drained and the grass kept short. A well-established bent/fescue turf is alone able to give the required clean resilient surface.

Divots removed during play must be quickly replaced. If it is necessary to roll in wet conditions to maintain an even surface, tining, slitting and dressings of sharp sand become vital. Frost presents a serious hazard and the use of electric warming wires should be considered if funds permit. Salt should never be applied to frozen ground as it destroys both soil structure and turf vigour. Renovation should begin early in April, obtaining a fine tilth and applying fertiliser. 50–100 kg per ha (1–2 cwt per acre) of grass seed should be sown per acre covered with 6–12 mm ($\frac{1}{4}$–$\frac{1}{2}$ in) of fine topsoil, raked and rolled and the seedlings mown when they reach 50 mm (2 in) high.

In summer the grass needs regular mowing at 25–38 mm (1–$1\frac{1}{2}$ in) with occasional top dressing and light rolling. Balanced fertilisers are preferable to sulphate of ammonia which produces quick flushes of growth. The height of cut should be reduced to 18 mm ($\frac{3}{4}$ in) as the playing season approaches, and earthworms eliminated.

On *polo* grounds there is a short playing season in spring and early summer. Hard true level turf should be established on loam soil from a non-ryegrass mixture; light soil is subject to undue wear and clay soil to 'poaching'. The grass should be kept to 25–38 mm (1–1½ in) rolled and spiked; weeds and ryegrass must be controlled as they cause slippery patches and erratic movements of the ball. As the season ends, levelling, renovation and fertilising are needed.

9.6.5 Summer sports turf: cricket

Cricket grounds consist of two sections, the wicket and the outfield. The latter needs a well-mown, 'fast' and accurate surface, with a gradient of no more than 1:60. Its mowing should start early in the year, with the blades set high at first and later lowered. Compaction, commonly due to heavy gang mowers, must be relieved by spiking and aeration. Otherwise outfields are managed as are other extensive areas. Wicket management however demands great skill. Recent losses in Test Match takings, estimated at £25,000, have been blamed on the wickets at Lord's and Headingley and the popular demand for 'fast' wickets continues. The pace and bounce throughout the match should encourage the batsmen to play shots. Fast bowlers need to be able to move the ball off the seam early on, and wrist spinners to turn the ball from the first day onwards; then sufficient wear should assist finger spinners from the second afternoon onwards.

The wicket is prepared on a 27 m (30 yd) square 'table' or 'cricket square', on excellently drained soil underlaid with ash or sharp stones. The top 75 mm (3 in) of existing soil may have to be replaced by the ideal heavy, water-retentive soil such as a heavy Surrey loam, or failing that by a 1:4 marl/lighter soil mixture, and the soil must be graded before seeding or turfing. A more simple way of making the soil heavier is by regular top dressing with heavy loam.

After seeding (see section 9.3.1) and management (section 9.3.2) the grass should be lightly 'topped' when 50–75 mm (2–3 in), lightly rolled, and gradually brought to the required shortness. If turf is used, springy or matted ones must be discarded. Maintenance begins in September on those parts of the square no longer required for play, with a general fertiliser, scarifying and raking, several close mowings, and a thorough 225 mm (9 in) spiking to allow dressings to penetrate. The equipment used must not cause undulations in the ground, and should make holes at 75 mm (3 in) intervals.

The worst areas may need returfing from a good turf nursery, but most of the square should be reseeded with 2·2 kg of seed per 100 sq m (5 lb per 100 sq yd) and covered with sacking or polythene. Top dressings of good loam, lime and sand are then worked in and levelled with a wooden lute and can be followed with a low-nitrogen fertiliser but bearing in mind that excessive organic matter makes the wicket matted or soft.

If the soil is still considered too light, the traditional autumn application of marl (0·45–0·9 kg per sq m (1–2 lb per sq yd) with up to 5 kg (10 lb) of loam) improves the surface. Control of earthworms and leatherjackets may also be necessary. In winter the square may need light mowing in dry weather. Fungal disease must be prevented by 'switching' the dew and by fungicidal treatment (see section 9.8). In February the turf should be well aerated and rolled – in different directions, to avoid ridges – using first a light roller, then a heavier one. From early March onwards, light mowing and aeration, if possible weekly, and at the end of the month a balanced fertiliser, develop a good wicket. Wormkiller may also have to be applied. As the first match approaches, particularly in the final fortnight, the pitch should be consolidated to a depth of 100 mm (4 in), with a roller of up to 2 tonnes (2 tons) weight, the last rolling being along the line of the pitch. Frequent raking and mowing, with the blades steadily lowered, encourages vertical growth, especially valuable on wickets for early play. Debris should be swept off. This is the ideal time to apply selective weed-killers; any watering must be completed in time to allow the top 75–100 mm (3–4 in) to dry out before play begins.

After play, spiking and light dressings of loam and a sprinkling of fertiliser should be given, bowler's footmarks returfed, and thin patches reseeded. Watering – copious in dry weather – must finish in good time and the sequence is then light rolling, heavier rolling, up to 1·5 tonnes (approx. 30 cwt), hand raking and final very close mowing, before the next match.

9.6.6 Tennis courts

These must have a true even surface giving an accurate bounce – 225 mm (9 in) of medium loam overlying 100–150 mm (4–6 in) of ashes give best results, and sandy soils need additional organic material. As the court must dry quickly and yet have negligible gradient, drainage needs careful attention. Courts are best oriented N.N.W.–S.S.E or failing that, North–South; their surroundings should allow the ball to be easily seen against the background, and in this respect trees and shrubs are preferable to open sky. At least 18 m (20 yd) of run back have to be allowed behind the base lines and similarly 3·7 m (4 yd) on either side. The seed mixtures in section 9.2.3 are suitable.

Base lines may be renovated in September using turfs of hardwearing species, of 18 g per sq m (½ oz per sq yd) of 50% chewing's, 40% dogstail, and 10% browntop. Rye grass with its power of rapid establishment may also be useful here. The whole court must be forked or aerated and treated with a phosphate- and potash-rich autumn fertiliser. The usual principles of winter and spring mowing should be followed; in April a general fertiliser rich in nitrogen but poor in organic matter which would give a spongy surface, is necessary. During the season, light raking, whaleboning, fertilising, slitting, rolling, frequent close mowing, and the usual measures against pests, diseases, earthworms, weeds, moss and drought may all be required.

9.6.7 Road and motorway verges

In recent years a large area of hard-wearing turf has been laid down on the *verges* of residential roads and motorways. The former of these sites present special problems such as the cutting of strips of turf intersected by paths, branch roads, drives and trees, and mowers have been considerably modified to meet them. Conventional motor mowers and gang mowers with easily raised cutting cylinders have been in use for some time, and more recently verge cutters have been developed with vertically rotating blades which cut the grass and direct the clippings downwards. Motorway verges receive similar attention although slope is here a more serious problem than obstacles. Grass growth retarding chemicals such as maleic hydrazide may be useful in these situations where grass quality is not a primary aim. New landscape problems on a grand scale have been presented by the development of our motorway programme. This has led to the development of hydraulic seeding, where seed is applied in liquid suspension from a special machine thus enabling the rapid treatment of large areas and the establishment of turf on all types of surface from fly ash to hoggin. In these situations grass may be replaced with grass/clover/black medick and other mixtures (Plate 9.4).

On *dog tracks* and *athletic tracks* the necessary short, even, weed-free turf has to be well kept and frequently renovated. Frost may be a serious hazard and dog tracks benefit from protection with straw or by electrical warming wires. The height of cut is 10–12 mm $\frac{3}{8}$–$\frac{1}{2}$ in) for dog tracks and 12–25 mm ($\frac{1}{2}$–1 in) for athletic tracks.

Racecourses, often sited on heaths where bents and fescues are indigenous, are ideally on light loam rather than sand or clay and form a fine matted springy turf. Their shock-absorbing quality is increased by keeping the turf fairly long – 50 mm (2 in) between meetings allowing longer growth just before the races, especially for steeplechasing – without letting it run to hay. After racing, and replacing divots, the course requires spiking, rolling, regular mowing and occasional fertilising.

Moles and rabbits may warrant removal.

Orchards and *cemeteries* pose few special problems if advantage is taken of rotary mowers tailor-made to these conditions; large gang mowers are likewise the obvious choice on *airfields*. Lastly their is the more difficult matter of establishing and maintaining turf on derelict areas despite debris, toxic chemicals, and infertile subsoil or shale. Given time, a fair humus may be built up by growing nurse crops of grey alder, willow, Corsican pine or birch; later on grass seed may be broadcast (not drilled) with fertiliser, on the cleared site. The low pH which must be adjusted to 6, makes alkaline–nitrogen fertilizers and lime much more valuable than on most turf, and legumes may also probably be included in the seeds mixture. Even then, turf cannot be expected to establish itself rapidly as on better sites.

9.6.8 Grass substitutes

While the superiority of turf is undoubted, there are a few situations where it may be preferable to replace it with artificial 'all weather pitches' or with fine greens composed of pearlwort, clover or yarrow, of aromatic plants like thyme, chamomile or pennyroyal. For details of these the reader is referred to pages 211–16 of *Turf Culture*.

9.6.9 The use of clover mixtures

In certain circumstances, clover may be better ecologically suited to a particular situation than grass, and can often be used to good effect. For example, for turf around factory premises, power stations, institutions, university parkland or campus, where maintenance and cutting may be carried out using a gang mower, and the length of grass is usually kept between one and two inches, the use of a mixture containing clover can be of particular value. In addition, clover confers a pleasant appearance, and supplies nitrogen, and also drought resistance.

Note: Department of the Environment specification for roads:

	For Verges, Central Reserves and Side Slopes
Perennial rye grass S.23	56
Red fescue S.59	18
Smooth-stalked meadow grass	8
Crested dogstail	10
White clover S.100	8
Total	100%

The nitrogen-fixing properties of clover can be valuable where one is faced with the problem of difficult soil and subsoil conditions, such as occur on high pH soils which are subject to boron toxicity as in the case of P.F. ash which is used as an embankment fill. The desirable properties of clover in obtaining nitrogen from the air together with the effect of its extensive root system, all help to produce a better soil structure under these conditions where grass species alone would not give the most beneficial results.

Examples of mixtures which can be used in such situations are given opposite:

	Grass on P.F. Ash Embankment on 100–200 mm (4–8 in) topsoil
Perennial rye grass S.23	40
Red fescue S.59	30
Smooth-stalked meadow grass	12
Crested dogstail	12
White clover S.100	3
Red clover S.123	3
Total	100%

9.7 The establishment of turf surfaces in difficult areas

9.7.1 Difficult sites needing special treatment

The construction and establishment of turf surfaces on areas which require significant treatment prior to the establishment of turf dictates a specialised approach. Assessment of the necessary treatments, grass seed mixtures, etc., to produce the correct turf for the required purpose involves chemical and physical analyses of the substrate, appropriate amelioration and ground preparation treatments, and the use of correct seeds mixtures in relation to post-seeding and routine turf management programmes.

9.7.2 Typical difficulties

The following are typical of difficulties:

Steep slopes/upland areas. These areas are particularly subject to water and wind erosion often causing impeded surface and sub-surface drainage and uneven turf due to the presence of boulders and gulley formation. Soils tend to be thin, of low nutrient status and frequently of low pH.

Colliery waste. Problems of soil stabilisation allied to 'finely textured soils' with little or no structure, prone to erosion, low in nutrients and devoid of nitrogen, and the presence of heavy metals toxic to plant growth, often characterise these areas.

Industrial waste areas. Sites such as those formed by pulverised fuel ash (PFA) are often toxic, having a high boron content as well as a high soluble salt concentration. They are frequently compacted, low in nitrogen, although often liberally supplied with trace elements, potash and phosphates.

Sandy and sand dune areas. These are particularly subject to wind and water erosion, and stabilisation either through the use of artificial binders, terracing or marram-grass plantings is necessary. Soil structure is often completely lacking as are nutrients.

Reclaimed land. In the vicinity of large urban conurbations reclaimed land formed by a mixture of unsuitable soil, clay subsoil, sewage sludge, industrial debris including car bodies, metal, wood, concrete blocks, etc. are often presented for turf establishment. These sites are frequently the result of many years tipping and require careful survey and treatment.

Damaged land. Most building projects cause serious damage to the surrounding land due to severe compaction, failure to conserve topsoil and its burial under unsuitable subsoil, damage to artificial and natural drainage systems both surface and sub-surface and the formation of unacceptable contours.

9.7.3 Adverse factors and their treatment

Wind and water erosion. Wind erosion can be severe on light, silty, sandy soils in exposed areas such as parts of the Fens, Suffolk and East Anglia. Windbreaks can be strategically established and ameliorants such as clay, peat and organic matter added to the soil surface to produce a stronger soil structure capable of resisting the effects of strong wind. In order to prevent water erosion, grading and land shaping should aim to channel water so that it runs smoothly and slowly to ditches rather than collect in ponds. The stabilisation of these areas by means of terracing and the use of chemical binders is well-known and is undoubtedly beneficial as is the planting of deep and tough rooting shrubs and grass species such as marram-grass on sand dunes.

Drainage. Of paramount importance is the free and unimpeded drainage of the site avoiding the presence of perched water tables and water-logged conditions. No plant, let alone turf, will grow on a poorly drained site and expert advice on the correct drainage system, both sub-surface and surface, is essential. The relieving of compaction by deep cultivations and the incorporation of coarse sharp sand, peat and organic matter is necessary to provide a fertile substrate. It is particularly important to relate drainage to the height of the water table and the clear running of ditches and outlets surrounding the site. The complete water regime balance needs expert consideration if good future management and financial saving is to be ensured.

Settlement. It is also particularly important to know what type of settlement is likely to occur and whether this will be uniform over the whole site.

Air. Similarly sites with free air circulation will be less subject to disease development in the future and the possibility of industrial pollution from surrounding factory areas also needs to be considered.

Debris. Apart from the above there is often the problem of removing quantities of foreign materials, old car bodies, boulders, concrete, wood, metal, etc., and whilst this can often be done by machine, hand picking may sometimes be required.

Ameliorants. Reference to the sections, concerning ameliorants, 9.1.6 and 9.1.7 show how soil texture and structure, whether it be predominantly sand or clay, may be improved by the use of the appropriate additions and cultivation techniques.

Analysis. Chemical and physical analyses to check the nutrient status as well as the presence or absence of heavy metals and other toxic materials as well as the pH is an essential part of the pre-seeding treatment.

9.7.4 Seed mixtures
Typical of low maintenance seeds mixtures for use in problem areas are:

Light sandy or infertile soils –
  40% Hard fescue
  30% Creeping red fescue
  20% Chewings fescue
  10% Browntop

Heavy clay soils or clay subsoil –
  60% Smooth-stalked meadow grass
  35% Creeping red fescue
   5% Browntop

Steep slopes, banks and verges –
  40% Creeping red fescue
  30% Smooth-stalked meadow grass

20% Perennial ryegrass
10% Browntop

9.7.5 Design for reinstatement
Having rectified the basic problems and produced a suitable substrate for turf establishment it then becomes necessary to consider the detailed use which is to be made of the area. It is dangerous to give blanket recommendations as each site requires specialist assessment and in the light of the technical appraisal the particular treatment, seeds mixture and management for the area can be prescribed.

Some landscape practices have built up specialist experience in connection with the establishment of vegetation on difficult sites. These practices have the range of expertise necessary to deal with many of the problems posed by difficult sites. Even so they often find it necessary to refer particular problems to associated specialists with whom they frequently work to help them deal with matters out of the range of competence of their own office staff. It is essential that specialist services should be used.

9.7.6 Establishment techniques
In addition to conventional seeding methods there are three broad classes of techniques that can be applied in the vegetating and stabilisation of difficult sites:

Hydraulic seeding (Hydroseeding);
Traditional or recently introduced turfing methods;
Natural colonisation.

9.7.7 Hydraulic seeding techniques
A variety of these have been introduced in the last ten years or so. No one method has emerged yet that can be clearly defined as a standardised procedure in the form of a hydroseeding specification for all sites. Innovations, modifications to equipment and improved techniques are constantly evolving. Broadly speaking, the following main techniques are used at present:

Wood pulp fibre method – For rocky slopes, embankments and sites with little or no subsoil or topsoil, shales, industrial wastes, etc. Single application of a combined seed, slurrified wood pulp and fertiliser mixture. Approximate mix – seed 10%, pulp 70%, fertiliser 20% (NPK 15:10:10 with the nitrogen in one of the slow release forms). Trace elements and bacterial innoculants for legumes may be incorporated. The mix is applied as a homogenous slurry in suspension in water. During 1978 costs ranged from 8 to 20p per sq m. Where erosion is a problem an additional application of plastic emulsions may be used at an additional cost of some 6 to 10p per sq m for areas of 10,000 sq m.

178

Fibreglass rovings method – Used for unstable slopes, sand banks, 'erosion risk' highway sites. This is a more specialised and costly method, only used for a localised area needing *immediate* stabilising treatment.

(*a*) Area pegged with steel pegs at 1 per 4 sq m. (approx. 1 per 5 sq yd) leaving 150–225 mm (approx. 6–9 in) exposed. Length of pegs determined by stability of substrate.

(*b*) Seed/water mix applied by hydroseeding at a recommended rate of 125–250 kg per ha (approx. 1–2 cwt seed per acre).

(*c*) Fibreglass rovings applied by hydraulic method evenly over area ensuring that the filaments cover the pegs. Rate may be around 625 kg per ha (say 5 cwt per acre).

(*d*) Final application of bitumen emulsion over the glass fibre to lock the filaments together. Rate of 4,500 litres per ha (approx. 400 gallons per acre).

A successful method, when conditions justify it. Costs are not available but they are considerably in excess of the first method.

Other methods – One alternative to pulp fibre is calcium sulphate (Gypsum). This forms a water retentive plaster capping on the surface and also has some beneficial effects on soil structure and stabilisation.

For shallower gradients, or level sites with difficult access and usually better soil conditions a straight water/seed/fertiliser mix can be used as an alternative to seed drilling. Other materials have been used such as chopped straw, peat and sawdust. These may either be a carrier for the seed and fertiliser or be used as a mulch after hydroseeding.

Hydroseeding seed mixtures – These may include grass and/or other herbs or may include seeds of woody species such as gorse (*Ulex europaeus*), broom (*Cytisus scoparius*). There is need for more research work in this respect on indigenous seed mixtures for these problem sites, and particularly to gain more information on pretreatment, seeding techniques and management aftercare.

9.7.8 Turfing methods

Localised areas of steep embankments and other gradients may be turfed to provide immediate ground cover and quick visual effects. Alternative techniques:

(*a*) Using traditional turves to B.S. 3969. Turves used on banks should be sufficiently tough and fibrous to withstand difficult handling conditions. Autumn or winter are recommended for turf laying unless irrigation is available. Grading should leave the surface slightly roughened. Smooth, polished surfaces should be avoided. Use 75–100 mm

(approx. 3–4 in) topsoil (if available), especially if the intention is to turf directly over stony subsoils or light porous soils.

Turf laying – Turfs should be laid diagonally or horizontally to stretcher-bond pattern, butt jointed, and secured by stout wooden pegs 200 mm (approx. 4 in) length or by 4 mm (8 swg) galvanised wire pins at least 200 mm (4 in) long. Work in peat or topsoil into joints after laying. On very steep slopes netting may be laid over the turfs and pegged down. (See also B.S. 4428 : 1969.) Use sprinkler irrigation after laying, if necessary.

(*b*) Some of the newer industrially produced turf types may be used. These are comparatively new to the landscape industry and are still subject to trial and use modifications.

'Tana' turf is produced to specified mixtures and qualities on a polystyrene foam mattress and plastic slurry media. The mattress and slurry are floated on a lagoon assuring a constant moisture level for germination and growth. The resultant turf is a third of the weight of traditional turf and extremely light to carry and lay. Pegging down and watering are important after laying.

'Grass carpet' is produced on extensive hard surfaces and in the growing media is incorporated stabilisation netting, allowing the turf, when ready, to be cut and rolled straight from the germination site for delivery. It is available to specified mixtures in sizes about 1 m wide and 5 m long. These are rolled out on site and pegged down as necessary. The incorporated netting aids stability. Other turf products are also being evolved. For further information write to the Sports Turf Research Institute, Bingley, Yorkshire, or the distributors and manufacturers.

9.7.9 Stabilisation and natural colonisation

Developments concerned with hydraulic seeding technology include the introduction and use of an increasing range of soil stabilisation preparations, including plastic or resin emulsions and latex compounds, e.g. Curasol, Permasol, Verdyol Complex, Huls 801 Stabiliser, Unisol 91 and others. These materials are superseding the use of bitumen emulsions as they are easier to apply and being largely colourless, do not create visual or physical contamination where drift occurs. The effect of these materials is either to produce a continuous film over the treated surface, or a binding adhesive to the surface particles to a depth of 10–12 mm (approx. $\frac{1}{2}$ in). Plant nutrients may be incorporated in these formulations which are then less readily leached from the soil. A wide range of unstable sites may be treated such as sand dunes, and P.F.A. sites and spoil heaps where dust contamination of nearby housing areas may be locally a nuisance.

Natural colonisation of these stabilised areas may occur without direct seeding, if sufficient natural propagules are present in the substratum. Where stabilisation is not a serious factor and there is an easier time schedule, many sites, particularly old gravel workings, former quarries and clay pits, etc., soon recolonise reasonably quickly with herb and scrub layers. Such areas can become excellent wild life habitats in as little as 10 years from the time of abandonment. Litter and refuse dumping are visually the main problems.

9.7.10 Aftercare and management of seeded sites

Whatever the seeding techniques, and even where some topsoil has been used, successful vegetation establishment will seldom occur without some maintenance in the years succeeding sowing. A maintenance schedule for hydroseeded areas should include:

Annual fertiliser dressings preferably in early spring, using a balanced slow release compound fertiliser, for at least the first two seasons following seeding, 250–500 kg per ha (approx. 2–4 cwt per acre). A very important item.

Re-seeding of bare areas or those places where seeding failed in the first instance.

Control of certain noxious weeds such as docks, thistles and ragwort if present in large numbers, using selective herbicides during maximum growth periods.

	Grass on P.F. ash
GRASSES	
Italian ryegrass	20
S.23 perennial rye grass	20
S.24 perennial rye grass	30
Rough-stalked meadow grass	15
CLOVERS	
S.123 broad red clover	5
Late flowering red clover	5
S.100 white clover	5
Total	100%

9.8 Calendar of turf management

JANUARY

Drainage: Check outlets and note where drainage is ineffective.

Top dressings: Under cover, screen, mix, and transport top dressing and compost.

Aeration: Use aerating machinery where ground conditions permit, and apply coarse sand to wet, muddy surfaces. Hand fork wet areas on sports grounds, especially goalmouths, and brush and harrow frequently.

Renovation: Although late, turfing is still possible in January, and sometimes necessary to rectify holes in football pitches.

FEBRUARY

Seeding: Cultivate and work spring seedbeds, add appropriate top dressings and fertiliser, and leave fallow.

Aeration: Continue aerating and brushing under suitable conditions, harrow and rake when the soil is drying off after a wet period. Improve aeration of golf greens on heavy soils with solid tine forks and sharp sand; on light porous soils replace the sand with loam.

Pests: If worm casts tend to smother grass scatter with a cane in dry weather, and apply arsenical or non-poisonous wormkilling preparations in dull mild weather.

Weeds: In dry weather towards the end of the month, apply lawn sand and other preparations to control pearlwort, daisy and clover.

Moss: If moss invasion is serious, examine possible predisposing causes. Control by combination of cultural and chemical treatments.

MARCH

Seeding: Make early spring sowings on well-prepared seedbeds; scarify and oversow thinly covered areas of established turf. Cover the seed with a fine layer of soil or sharp sand.

Fertilising: Apply general fertiliser at the end of March, or early in April.

Mowing: Mow with blades high, especially in cold and windy weather.

Rolling: Counteract effects of frost by rolling but only when the surface is dry. Roll cricket pitches lightly at first and more heavily towards the end of the month.

Aeration: Thoroughly rake all matted turf. Brush bowling greens, tennis courts and cricket pitches to distribute worm casts and top dressing.

Diseases: Apply fungicides to turf prone to *Fusarium* patch disease.

Pests: Tests for worms and leather jackets, and if necessary apply control measures.

Weeds: Use lawn sand, selective weedkillers, and other preparations to control daisies, pearlwort, clover and other weeds.

Moss: Continue treatment – scarify and apply moss control compounds.

APRIL

Seeding: Sow seed, rake in, apply thin layer of soil and roll if the weather is dry.

Fertilising: Apply the complete fertiliser if not done in March.

Mowing: Mow little and often, especially after warm showery weather, lower cutter blades at each successive mowing, except in cold weather.

Rolling: Roll periodically.

Renovation: Treat winter pitches by mowing, aerating, fertilising, scarifying, sowing 125–250 kg per ha (1–2 cwt per acre) grass seed, harrowing, covering with clean light loamy soil, rolling if dry, lay turf in goal areas.

Diseases: Apply fungicides for control of *Fusarium* and *Helminthosporium* diseases.

Weeds: 7–10 days after fertiliser treatment, and at least 3 days after mowing, apply selective weedkillers. Remove persistent weeds and coarse grasses by hand.

Moss: If not done in March, apply moss control compounds.

MAY

Fertilising: Apply supplementary fertilisers and water in during dry weather.

Mowing: Cut frequently with knives low. Prepare wickets by repeated raking, mowing and rolling until the surface is firm and true with the barest covering of grass. Cut newly-sown turf when 75 mm (3 in) high, using hand shears or a side wheel mower with sharp blades set high; avoid 'pulling' and early close mowing.

Diseases: Apply fungicides for control of Dollar Spot.

Weeds: Continue April treatment as necessary.

JUNE

Fertilising: Apply sulphate of ammonia and water in, if weather is dry. Examine and turn the compost heap.

Mowing: From June onwards until October, regulate the height of cut according to the weather – during drought raise the blades and cut without grass box.

Diseases: Apply fungicides for the control of *Corticium* and Dollar Spot.

Weeds: Continue selective weedkiller treatment except in drought.

JULY

Fertilising: Turn over the compost heap to destroy weed seeds.

Irrigation: Water before the effects of drought become obvious.

Diseases: If the weather is hot and humid, prepare to treat Dollar Spot, *Fusarium* and *Corticium*.

Weeds: Selective weedkillers may be necessary to deal with the second crop of weeds.

AUGUST

Seeding: Finally rake and roll the autumn seedbed; sow in favourable weather after the middle of the month.

Renovation: Prepare to renovate worn areas.

Diseases: In close, damp conditions apply fungicides to control *Fusarium, Corticium,* Dollar Spot, and *Ophiobolus* Patch.

Weeds: Prevent weed establishment on worn areas.

SEPTEMBER

Seeding: Take advantage of adequate moisture and warm soil to sow grass seed.

Fertilising: Apply autumn fertiliser with a large organic fraction and little or no nitrogen.

Renovation: Scarify, reseed, rake, cover with soil or sand, and roll to finish worn spots on cricket tables, bowling greens, and tennis courts.

Aeration: Use hand forks or turf aerators, and spike and hollow-tine tennis courts, bowling greens, and lawns followed by a dressing of sharp sand or compost, well brushed in.

Diseases: Continue to spray areas prone to disease with turf fungicides.

Weeds and Moss: Apply control measures.

OCTOBER

Drainage: Remedy defective drainage.

Turfing: October is the best month for laying turf.

Fertilising: After aerating, apply composts or other organic top dressings, or autumn fertilizers; apply also Nottingham marl to cricket pitches.

Renovation: Renovate and reseed bare patches on bowling greens, tennis courts, cricket pitches, and other turf which was still in use in September.

Aeration: Aerate with solid spikes or hollow tines.

Diseases: Continue preventive and curative fungicide treatment.

Pests: Apply worm control measures.

Weeds and Moss: Continue control measures in settled, dry weather.

NOVEMBER

Turfing: Complete the laying of turf.

Drainage: Carry out drainage operations while the weather remains suitable.

Fertilising: Apply winter turf dressing, as necessary, and on wet days, mix and screen compost indoors.

Aeration: Aerate by hand fork or machine.

Rolling: Lightly roll turf formed from autumn sowings, avoiding over-consolidation of clay soils.

Mowing: Machines can be brought in for overhaul as the need for mowing decreases.

Pests: Test for presence of leatherjackets and if necessary apply control measures. Continue treatment against earthworms.

DECEMBER

Turf nursery: Prepare the turf nursery for fresh sowing by digging over; add fresh soil, and well-rotted manure or sewage sludge.

Pests: Continue treatment against leatherjackets.

General: December is a good time for overhaul and obtaining details of new materials which have become available.

Bibliography

Turf Culture, Ian Greenfield, Leonard Hill Books, London.

Lawns, R. B. Dawson, Royal Horticultural Society, Penguin Books.

Lawns and Sportsgrounds, M. Sutton, Sutton and Sons Ltd, Reading.

Planning, Construction and Maintenance of Playing Fields, P. W. Smith, Oxford University Press.

10 Tree Planting

BRENDA COLVIN

10.1 Groups and specimens for functional or design purposes

10.1.1 Introduction

Trees play an all-important role in British landscape. For the landscape architect they are a material of design used not only for their beauty but also for their functional value as shelter, screens, backcloth; also for their power of absorbing smoke, dust and noise. They define and separate the open spaces, thus serving as do the walls and pillars of a building. Most of these functions call for collective use of trees, in belts, spinneys or woodland groups, rather than for single perfect specimens. Landscape architects often need to combine forestry and horticultural methods and require therefore a clear understanding of both systems. Only in rare cases is either system, undiluted, suited to the needs of landscape architecture. Modern methods provide further opportunities, such as the transplanting of mature or semi-mature trees, the use of larger nursery grown specimens, and of trees grown in containers which can be transplanted at any time of the year.

10.1.2 Types of planting

The landscape architect has now a wide and flexible choice of methods.

Traditional forestry – Small seedlings 150–375 mm high (approx. 6–15 in) closely planted with minimum ground preparation, and subsequent periodic thinning to produce timber.

Traditional horticulture – Nursery grown specimens of various heights from about 0·6 m–3 m (approx. 2–10 ft) in height. 'Feathered' if side shoots have been retained, or 'standards' for taller sizes on single stem, with side shoots removed.

Plate 10.1. Young trees of more than normal nursery size planted for a reasonably quick effect in an industrial setting. Bowater Paper Corporation, Northfleet office. Landscape architect: Brenda Colvin.

Nursery grown specimens – Of larger sizes, up to about 5 m (approx. 16 ft), specially prepared for quick effect, usually called 'advanced nursery stock'.

Mature or semi-mature trees – Transplanted after special root preparation, by means of new mechanical techniques.

10.1.3 Choice of type

The choice will be influenced by local conditions of the area: its size, soil type, the proposed management system and speed of effect required; it will also be influenced by the availability of plants and the cost of the initial planting and future maintenance. Plants must conform to existing soil and climatic conditions as well as to visual needs. The plantsman can either adapt the system to the site, or create artificial site conditions to the system required. The latter choice is suitable only to small plantations usually in urban situations. Further reference to this is made in section 10.8 under 'Choice of species'.

Traditional forestry systems prevail in large plantations where timber is a prime factor. Traditional horticulture prevails in parks and gardens where visual needs must be balanced with costs. Nursery-grown 'advanced size standards' are now available for plantations where speedy effects justify higher initial cost. Mature or semi-mature trees transplanted by special machinery after careful preparation may be available for transplanting, from sites to be cleared for development or other causes. Certain firms specialise in this costly operation but the failure rate has been high due to the need for long after-care. Its successes have been in areas where water supply and drainage has been adequate, but the subsequent growth rate of these trees is slower than that of nursery grown stock. The cost of transplanting trees rises steeply with the size and weight of the specimens. Forest-type planting of small trees spaced 2 m apart costs less per acre than any other landscape treatment (see section 10.9). It compares favourably both in initial cost and subsequent management with the establishment of agricultural grasses. However trees grown in established turf may be considered, among other methods combining one or more of the systems listed above. Although ultimate timber yields may still be a high priority in forestry practice, multipurpose planting is gaining favour even for economic reasons: it is certainly preferable for landscape projects where timber production may be of secondary importance. For landscape purposes a mixture of forestry and horticultural systems has many advantages; short-term and long-term effects can be planted at the same time, maintenance can be reduced if design and management are harmoniously related and a decision as to ultimate effect can be made at a later date (see 10.3.3).

10.1.4 Siting near buildings

Siting trees near buildings can be a difficult problem as shade is unwelcome in the case of old houses with small windows. In the case of modern buildings with large windows, shade may be an advantage. The difference is particularly marked in the case of schools where outdoor classes may be held on hot days only if shade is available near classrooms. Unwelcome shade may often be reduced by removing whole limbs or large overhanging branches of trees without spoiling the balance and appearance of the tree. Top-lopping increases the foliage density below the cut and ruins the shape of the tree (see 10.7.5 on tree surgery and 11.6.1 on care of mature trees).

Single specimens intended for this purpose need to be placed according to the angle of light at the hours and seasons when shade is welcome, bearing in mind that deciduous trees cast a significant shade only at the seasons when it is most needed. Car parks should be generously planted for this purpose. (See section 10.5.2 on protection of existing trees.) Quick effects are usually called for in landscape planting. Clients and architectural colleagues tend to press for immediate results even where these preclude slower but surer methods. The landscape architect may, therefore, seek some compromise to combine immediate effect with long-term value. Professional probity requires that long-term results are assured, and it is part of the landscape architect's duty to demonstrate to clients and colleagues all the issues involved. The rapid but sparse effect which we get by the use of mature trees is well justified in certain types of work, especially in urban housing and street planting, but such specimen trees can never take the place of dense woodland, either for visual or functional purposes.

Their value, indeed, is mainly ornamental – they tend to be inadequate as shelter or screens, and they fail to give the 'mass' needed as foil or counterpart to the voids or open spaces in a design. The transplanting of big trees should, in such cases, be done in conjunction with, and not as a substitute for, traditional planting. Temporary fencing around existing trees or groups is essential to prevent damage. In most cases it is best to enclose the contractor's working area to give protection to all surrounding vegetation to be preserved. Effective penalty clauses should be included in the contract, and the responsibility for maintenance of temporary fencing and replacement of damaged trees placed on the contractor.

New services should be sited to avoid damage to existing trees so far as possible. Detailed plans of services will influence siting of new trees and are therefore essential information for the landscape architect. The existing soil level must be maintained around trees to be preserved. Most tree species are liable to die if soil or rubbish is piled around their stems or over their roots. Equally they suffer from drought and starvation if their roots are cut,

Plate 10.2. Esthwaite: a Forestry Commission mixed plantation blends naturally with the countryside and indigenous trees.

exposed or unduly limited. Changes in the drainage conditions leading to excess or shortage of water damages mature trees more than young ones as the latter are more adaptable while still making vigorous growth.

10.1.5 Siting in the wider landscape – conservation value
Of the former forest once covering the British Isles relics in the form of hedges, shelter belts, woods and parks remain, and are a refuge for the wild life of the old forests. The older a hedge or plantation the richer its wealth of native vegetation and fauna. Extensive breaks between such groups, (whether of built-up land or arable cultivation) disrupts the pattern and prevents migration and spread of species. Shelter belts, hedges, verge planting beside road, rail or water ways form the basis of a green web of conservation linking town and country from coast to coast. The need to maintain and reinforce this network for reasons of conservation usually coincides with the visual needs of landscape and may influence the siting of major groups.

10.1.6 Hedgerows and shelter belts
With the use of bigger ploughs and harvesters, the sizes of fields in arable areas is increasing and many hedgerows are being destroyed. The Ministry of Agriculture and the Forestry Commission are concerned and have advised farmers and landowners to maintain trees where possible, as windbreaks, or as groups in the corners of large fields, to check the risk of wind erosion and to maintain biological balance, since much bird and insect life is lost along

with the hedges. Ground temperature is raised perceptibly by means of hedges – a point of importance in some areas.

In grazing districts, so long as animals are pastured in the open, the need for enclosed fields and shade trees remains and biological balance better assured than under modern factory farming systems. The landscape architect may appreciate the visual variety between the two types of landscape; he is also concerned to maintain biological balance and that traditional distribution of timber trees so characteristic of the British landscape. When we have few hedges and very large fields, the tree groups become outstanding features, and their siting and distribution an even more important element of the landscape. In such cases grouping is usually a key to success (Plate 10.3).

Most hedges contain numerous seedling trees, and traditionally the hedge cutter selected a few to replace those felled for timber or dying of old age. The machine hedge cutter is less sensitive and tends to cut everything regardless of future needs.

It has been estimated that one third of British standing timber consists of hedgerow trees and it should be realised that hedgerow timber, especially along country roads, has commercial as well as scenic value; the care needed to ensure continuity is well spent. To plant young trees in hedgerows is difficult and nearly always unnecessary. Selection and marking of natural saplings or groups, growing in the hedge is the best means of obtaining new trees where required, and this can be done by a woodman in anticipation of the hedge cutting holo-

185

Plate 10.3. Good standing timber in hedges in a field and wood pattern typical of many parts of the country before the ravages of elm disease.

Plate 10.4. Natural regeneration of beech trees in a Chiltern wood.

caust. A few metres of hand clipping, and removal of redundant growths on either side of the selected trees, before the hedge cutter arrives, will bring them to his notice and make it easier for him to follow previous instructions on the subject. The system has been found effective even without previous instruction.

Where no saplings are found and new trees are required, standards can be planted just alongside the hedge. Strong triangular tree guards and stakes (needing some attention for several years) should be supplied. Local types of trees should be chosen, and they should be planted far enough back to avoid slaughter by the hedging machine.

10.1.7 Natural regeneration

Foresters are growing more appreciative of natural increase and, with the advance of their own methods, are quick to observe and recognise tree seedlings at the earliest stages. Protection from rabbits and other damage may suffice to develop woodland of good quality and fast growth in areas where conditions favour natural regeneration, and such woods may be better adapted to the locality than man-made plantations (see Plates 10.4, 10.7).

The landscape architect can make use of many self-sown trees. By selection and trimming, small saplings, if left undisturbed, will make fine specimens sooner than transplanted trees. Such trees are less easily transplanted than nursery stock, and should therefore be preserved *in situ* where possible. The process of scrub clearance is often too drastic, and saplings are frequently destroyed even in areas destined for new planting, through lack of observation and care. The standard specification to 'clear all scrub and trees of less than 100 mm stem diameter' is short-sighted.

Tree cover is the normal climax for the British Isles. Any area below about 460 m (approx. 1,500 ft), protected from vandalism, grazing and other 'biotic' factors reverts to forest unless exposed to high gales or salt spray. If adequate protection, fencing and shelter is provided self-propagated groups make excellent spinneys and wood-

186

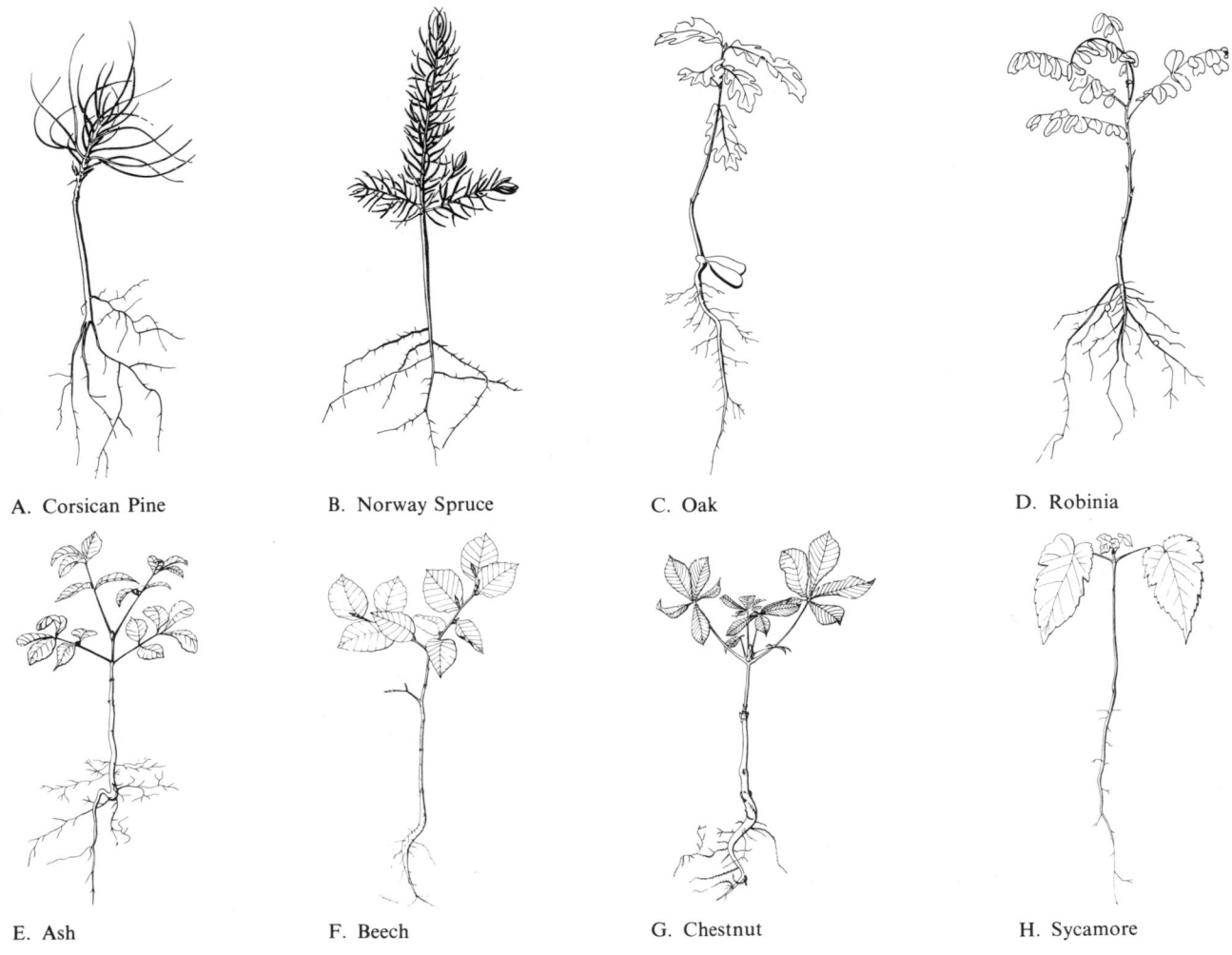

A. Corsican Pine   B. Norway Spruce   C. Oak   D. Robinia

E. Ash   F. Beech   G. Chestnut   H. Sycamore

Fig. 10.1. FOREST SEEDLINGS. Protection from rabbits and other damage may suffice to develop woodland of good quality and fast growth where conditions favour natural regeneration.

land. Under suitable circumstances economic timber may be produced sooner than by man-made plantations. In any case, for amenity and landscape where timber is of secondary importance, natural regeneration where it can be preserved *in situ* retaining existing contours, has great advantages which should be more often used. Cost of fencing can be set against cost of planting especially for quick effects. The minor disadvantage of an unkempt appearance in the early years, is largely overcome by good fencing, as proof of deliberate intention.

In many cases however some new planting may be necessary in addition.

10.2 Preparation of ground for new planting

10.2.1 Drainage

The following brief notes do not adequately cover this field. See Chapter 3, section 3.9 on drainage. Reference to a standard work on the subject, such as *Principles of Field Drainage* by H. H. Nicholson, is also recommended.

Many trees flourish in moist ground, but few can endure stagnant water at the roots, and a well-aerated soil is necessary for healthy growth. Plantations on porous formations such as chalk, limestone or sand usu-ally need no drainage, but the facts should be ascertained at the outset. Hardpans underlying sands can be trouble-some and should be broken, for the sake of healthy growth, by deep ploughing or by subsoiling. Clay and other retentive soils (unless overlying porous rocks near the surface) should be drained.

A high water table may defy improvement by drainage and such areas are suitable only for alders, willows and poplars.

Open ditches (and/or ridge ploughing) are more suit-

187

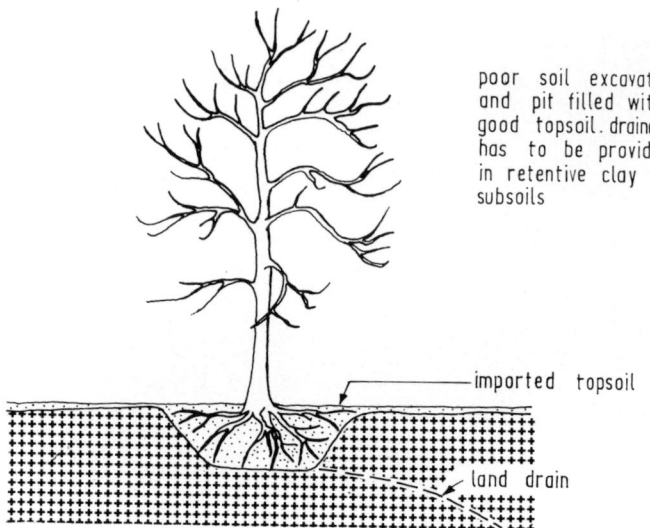

poor soil excavated and pit filled with good topsoil. drainage has to be provided in retentive clay subsoils

imported topsoil

land drain

Fig. 10.2. Tree planting in retentive clay subsoils.

able for woodland and hedgerow than covered agricultural drains, but for parkland planting of more open type normal pipe drains should be laid. Their depth depends on the soil profile. Normally they should be laid at the bottom of the topsoil. They may be useless if laid below clay.

Special drainage arrangements may be necessary in the case of stations prepared in retentive soils for trees whose roots require greater depth than the surrounding topsoil, as excavations in non-porous strata hold water and become bogs. Drains must in that case be as deep as the bottom of the pits (see Fig. 10.2) and the pipes covered with clinker or hardcore to the base of the topsoil (see also alternative treatment by mounding soil in section 10.2.9).

Planting positions and drainage layout should be related in all cases, and records of drainage kept for reference. Other underground cables, ducts and services of all kinds should also be related to, and recorded on planting plans.

10.2.2 Compaction of soil

On development sites, builder's vehicles and earth-moving machinery tend to compact the soil and to form hardpans, particularly in heavy retentive loams and on clay subsoils. Water will often lie on the surface of such sites giving an erroneous impression of a high water table and water-logged subsoil, but, unless the pan is broken, drought will follow in dry seasons, as water is unable to pass either up or down through over-compacted subsoil.

It is essential to ensure that the subsoil is friable and porous before planting on such ground. Deep cultivation by ploughing, mole drainage or subsoiling should be done to break up the subsoil and to ensure proper drainage conditions.

10.2.3 Damage to foundations and drains

Such damage by tree roots is liable to occur in soils of clay origin and in clay subsoils, where during periods of drought the roots seek moisture under these structures. Clay shrinks when dry and expands when moistened; it is this movement rather than any pressure of the root itself which causes damage. Where constant subsoil water is available, or where the soil is light and sandy, the risk does not exist. Roots do not penetrate sound waterproof drains, but may choke open land drains in heavy soils.

Fast-growing trees such as poplar and willow are not suitable for clay soils liable to shrink in drought. Research has shown roots twice as long as the height of the tree in such positions but in the moist situations to which such trees are adapted, such excesses do not occur.

10.2.4 Topsoil depth

Over normal subsoils, sufficiently loose and well aerated, 225 mm (approx. 9 in) of topsoil may suffice to establish most species, but depths up to 0·5 m (say 18 in) are preferable. So much depends on local conditions that no hard and fast rules apply. Trees have been successfully established on waste material without topsoil and in other circumstances depths of porous material of up to 1 m may be needed to overcome unsuitable ground conditions.

10.2.5 Preparation of ground – various situations

In existing woodland. Some felling of poorly grown or senile trees, and clearance of undergrowth should be done to provide space and light conditions for new groups. The removal of old tree stumps and roots is not customary, but can now be done by machines such as the Vermeer stump-cutter or the Myers–Sherman 'stump-gobbler' – both American machines. This makes it possible to level over the ground, so easing future maintenance.

Adequate drainage should be restored where damaged or choked. Little further preparation is needed for small seedling trees; for standards and specimens, pits should be prepared as described in section on standard and parkland trees (see 10.4.3).

Fertilisers are rarely needed in existing woodland soils at the time of planting, but light surface applications of general fertilisers in subsequent seasons will stimulate faster growth.

Trees planted in loose woodland soils must be well firmed in. Copious watering may be necessary in dry spring periods.

The above remarks apply equally to the replanting of areas recently clear felled.

10.2.6 In ploughed land

Well-drained ground which has been recently ploughed needs little or no further preparation unless weed growth is excessive. Freshly ploughed ground should be allowed to settle or disc harrowed, so that no air pockets remain below the surface. Clean ground may be kept weed free after planting by spraying with proprietary brands of weedkiller containing 'Simazine'. This is a potent and long-lasting compound and must only be used with expert supervision.

10.2.7 In grassland

Established grassland provides many problems as some form of treatment is usually necessary before planting. The usual methods are ploughing, screefing or spraying. Ploughing is very satisfactory on deep soils, but on shallow soils over chalk it may do harm by bringing up the chalk and mixing it with the shallow surface loam.

Screefing, that is scraping away the vegetation and top layer of roots so as to leave a bare patch of soil about 450–600 mm (approx. 18–24 in) square where the tree is to be planted, is often used when ploughing is impracticable, and on shallow soils. It does not suppress the growth of vegetation so well as ploughing, but the soil is not loosened and plants can be put in more firmly. There is thus less risk from drought.

Spraying with Dalapon can be very effective when carried out at the right time, but grasses vary considerably in their resistance to this chemical.

10.2.8 In moor and heathland

Ploughing of moorland or heath in preparation for tree planting adds to the cost but is becoming more general as many foresters believe it to be justified by better results, particularly in wet peaty highland where it is difficult to establish trees. Where necessary the application of a fertiliser such as triple superphosphate is becoming standard practice. Ploughing is done with a special deep plough and the ground is usually left with high ridges and furrows, in some cases adjoining (as in normal farming), in others spaced at wider intervals according to the tree rows (Plate 10.5).

The small trees are then planted on the ridge in the case of damp heathland on highland moors, in the furrow in dry eastern areas, or half-way up the furrow when in doubt. On peat moors the system of placing the root between the two soil surfaces (the normal ground on one side and the upturned turf on the other) enables trees to be established where planting on the flat unploughed land would fail. Small trees planted low on the ridge gain some protection from wind.

The ridge and furrow should be aligned to accord with drainage requirements, leading surface water to open ditches along the contours. In porous soils and dry areas they may be planned to reduce run-off and delay loss of surface water. The ridge and furrow system is well suited for forestry plantations on large areas, using very small seedling trees (Plate 10.5).

Plate 10.5. Deep ploughing on moorland.

10.2.9 Difficult sites

Difficult sites present special problems. When the subsoil or underlying rock material is porous – as in the case of chalk or limestone – no drainage is needed; it is only necessary to ensure sufficient depth of good imported soil – up to 1 m for trees. By this technique trees have been successfully established over pure chalk at the base of former quarries.

But in retentive clay or other non-porous material such tree stations must be individually drained. In these cases it is better to build up mounds of topsoil to give adequate depth and drainage above the impermeable strata, and to group trees on these mounds (Fig. 10.3). Shallow

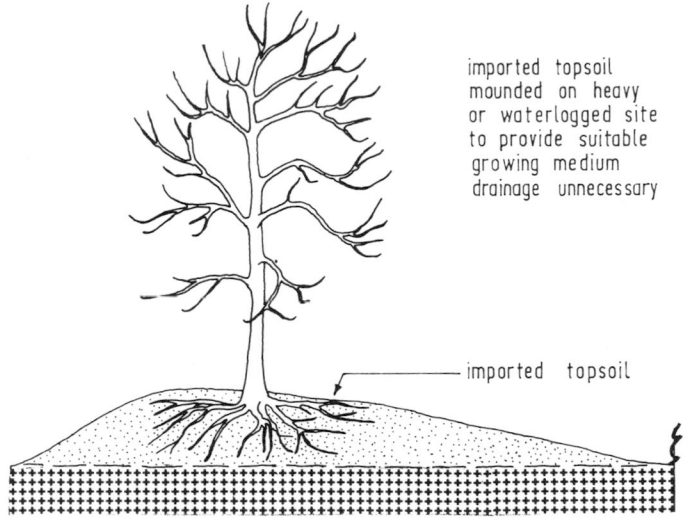

imported topsoil mounded on heavy or waterlogged site to provide suitable growing medium drainage unnecessary

imported topsoil

Fig. 10.3. Tree planting on a mound formed on a heavy or waterlogged site.

Plate 10.6. Planting on shale tip at Brayton, Cumbria. Forestry Commission.

it possible to establish trees which would otherwise fail; better root systems enable the trees to withstand high winds.

Too little is known as yet about the possibilities of tree planting without soil on difficult sites such as industrial waste materials, or in areas where soil or atmosphere, or both, may be polluted by industrial fumes. Research is still needed to enable such areas to be restored to health and balance. Many fairly good stands of trees have become established in unpromising situations such as colliery waste heaps, and where this can be achieved, eventual restoration of the soil will follow (Plate 10.6). On such difficult sites any vegetation cover is valuable; care should be taken to preserve even pernicious weeds if they are colonising unfavourable ground. In such cases, screefing and ploughing are to be avoided; instead, seeds, cuttings or young seedlings should be tried in mounds of topsoil, peat or whatever suitable medium may be available, added to the surface.

Young trees – especially when self-sown – are more tolerant of indifferent soil conditions than is usually supposed; when good topsoil is in short supply, almost any material of suitable pH value and texture may be added to eke out the supply. The texture should be well mixed and the material must of course be free of toxins. Ash, city refuse, sand, brickbats and brickdust, lime rubble and other waste materials can all contribute to a growing medium. Analysis will indicate special deficiencies and imbalance which can be chemically rectified. In such unfortunate conditions humus and soil bacteria may be deficient. All colonising plants helping to make good these deficiencies, however slowly, are useful, as are also peat, sawdust, wood shavings, straw, bracken and other organic materials if they are available.

drainage of the substrata may still be necessary but will be easier and less costly than individual drainage for each station. Mounding of additional topsoil above normal ground level may solve other problems also. For example, a low-lying site near the sea wall of an estuary, where the subsoil water is slightly saline, needs special treatment. Extensive mounds of topsoil, rising to 0·5 m or 1 m (say 1½ ft or 3 ft) above normal ground level make

10.3 Planting

The following grades of tree are normally available from growers:

    (a) Young seedling trees.
    (b) Normal nursery stock.
    (c) Advanced (extra heavy) nursery stock.
    (d) Semi-mature trees – (from specialist firms).

10.3.1 Young seedling trees

These are available from forest firms at low rates for large quantities. The supply is limited to timber producing trees, which seem very small to the uninitiated (150–300 mm, approx. 6–12 in), but the younger the transplant the greater its adaptability and its power of fending for itself in new and perhaps adverse circumstances. All plants should have been transplanted, however, at least once by the grower before sale so they are usually not less than two years old, and are normally sold for forest

planting when not more than three or four years old. The supply is usually limited to timber-bearing species, and may be home grown or imported. Firms should state which they supply, and specify if selected 'clones' are grown. 'Sturdy transplants having a high ratio of root collar diameter to shoot length' are recommended by the Forestry Commission which, incidentally, is sometimes willing to supply seedling trees for landscape work.

Shortages of certain young stock occur occasionally and in these cases imports from the continent may meet the need.

Transplanting helps to encourage a bushy root system and this can also be achieved by drawing a knife underneath the seed bed. This is known as undercutting. A plant grown in a seed bed one year, and then undercut and allowed to grow for a further year would be described in the trade as a 'two year undercut'. A plant grown in a seed bed for two years and then transplanted is called a '2 + 1'. A '1 + 1 + 1' refers to a three-year-old tree transplanted twice.

10.3.2 Normal nursery stock

Trees in a great range of variety for park and garden are supplied by growers of trees and shrubs at sizes ranging from 0·6 to 3 m (approx. 2–10 ft) high, but stocks are usually limited in quantity to one hundred or less of a kind. No single grower ever seems able to supply the whole list required for any landscape project and great insistence is required to obtain all the species and varieties correctly as specified. Substitutes are often offered, or wrong varieties supplied in the hope that 'mistakes' will pass unrecognised. The specification should guard against this as far as possible, but actual experience of nursery and planting work is invaluable to the designer and this knowledge is not easily acquired from books.

10.3.3 'Advanced' nursery stock

Standards specially grown on to heavier sizes, through wider spacing in the nursery, are available for quick effect in a wide range of ornamental species and varieties. They grow more quickly and suffer less from transplanting than the larger 'semi-mature' trees supplied and planted by specialist firms for 'instant' effect. Nursery-grown trees should have a well-developed compact root system as a result of frequent transplanting. Neglected trees and self-sown seedlings may have grown greater height for their age, but their straggling root system involves more risk in transplanting.

10.3.4 Semi-mature trees

These are usually transplanted by special machinery, and are supplied and planted only by firms specialising in this skill. The cost is high and can only be justified if survival is guaranteed and where instant effect is desired. Unless very good aftercare and copious watering can be assured, these large trees make little growth for some years, and the advanced nursery trees may overtake them during this period.

10.3.5 Size of trees for transplanting

In normal forestry where large areas are being close-planted, very small seedlings are usually found to become established more readily than older plants. This is particularly true where weed competition is not great. On bare stony windswept hillsides in Derbyshire for instance, sycamores of 150 mm (6 in) survive better than those of 375 mm (15 in) while losses among 750 mm (2½ ft) transplants amount to nearly 100%. On the other hand, in areas of coarse weed growth it may be better to plant trees less likely to be suffocated by grasses. In such regions the best results have sometimes been attained by saplings started

Plate 10.7. Natural regeneration of pine of different ages.

at 1 m (approx. 3¼ ft) high, whose tips reach above the surrounding vegetation. The degree of aftercare and weeding has a close bearing on this subject and these aspects must be considered in relation to one another. One of the forester's reasons for using very small plants – though not his only reason – is their low relative cost, but this is a matter of secondary importance in most landscape projects.

Under some circumstances forestry seedlings may be used in conjunction with larger trees. Advanced nursery stock, widely spaced, may be underplanted with small seedlings serving as speedy ground cover, with the intention of removing the latter as the canopy develops, or alternatively of retaining selected groups of seedlings to form a mixed association. In the latter case the final treatment will be determined by later management in conformity with the intention of the design.

Widely spaced standards of large size call for ground cover both for the sake of appearance and care of the ground until their canopy enables a normal woodland floor to develop. If grass is used for this purpose it will need cutting two or three times annually in the first few years.

10.3.6 Care of trees in transit and on arrival
Good packing and quick transport should be the responsibility of the supplier. Bundles of young trees should be opened, examined and 'heeled in' on arrival, and any complaints of dry or overheated roots should be registered without delay. The commonest cause of failures probably lies in wrong treatment between lifting and final planting. Plants tied up in bundles are liable to suffer irreparable damage from faulty aeration and moisture conditions. Once opened and laid in trenches with roots well covered by moist soil, the plants can await their turn without damage, but the shorter the period between lifting and planting, the better for the health of the trees.

10.3.7 Time of planting
Climatic conditions in the British Isles favour the winter season from October to March inclusive, especially for plants grown in open ground, although in wet seasons or high rainfall districts planting may continue into April, avoiding periods of hard frost or high wind.

Well-developed plants grown in containers may be transplanted at any time if proper care and copious watering can be assured, but except for the need to plant out of season, and for quick effects, plants grown in open ground are preferable.

Autumn planting avoids the risks of summer drought, but runs a higher risk of losses from severe frosts. In dry sandy soils the risk of drought following planting is considerable, whereas on heavy soils winter cold and damp are more to be feared. Special precautions requiring experienced supervision reduce the risks in either case if planting out of season is required.

10.3.8 Cold storage
Nursery stock of all sizes awaiting planting or transplanting can be successfully held in good condition under suitable cold storage conditions. This practice is widely used on the continent and increasingly so in this country by the Forestry Commission and others. It is well worth considering when site work and other factors lead to serious delayed planting into late spring or even early summer, the nursery stock supplier can be instructed to hold stock in cold store (if available), to avoid the undesirable consequences of late planting under conditions of emergent growth after prolonged 'heeling in' of stocks on site.

For further details read articles in the *Gardener's Chronicle/Horticultural Trades Journal*, 21 September and 7 December 1973.

10.4 New plantations

10.4.1 Trees
New trees may be required

- (a) for functional and visual reasons on all projects especially to improve conditions where trees are too few;
- (b) as understudies for existing mature trees to allow for future felling without loss of amenity;
- (c) as replacements for trees removed on account of unsuitability to new land use or because of disease;
- (d) in areas where former woods have been clear-felled;
- (e) on derelict and unsightly areas rendered difficult by industrial or urban misuse.

Woodland soils favour better tree growth than open land, even if cultivated, as the accumulation of humus and leaf mould favours the action of root bacteria. Some trees fail in soils lacking the associated fungi. Typical woodland species such as *Prunus avium* and *Acer campestre* rarely attain full potential character in open sites. Current research is testing which species are best adapted for reclaiming industrial dereliction.

10.4.2 Small forest trees
These are usually planted by spade. Special spades have been developed and these are useful where the ground is stony, hard or full of roots. The simplest method is a single 'notch'. Notching consists of making a slit with a spade, slipping in the young tree root before withdrawing the spade, and then treading the slit firmly together.

A skilled forester may, under favourable conditions, plant up to one thousand a day by this method. Variations are the T notch and the L notch. In these, two cuts are made at right angles to each other, and a flap of soil is levered up with the spade and the plant roots spread out underneath. The flap is then lowered and the plant well firmed in. These methods enable the roots to be spread out better, and also avoid the dangers of compacted soil, or the roots being left in an air pocket.

A mechanical tree planter can be used under suitable conditions and is capable of planting many thousands of trees a day (8,000 has been claimed). Two men are needed to operate tractor and planting trailer, but the machine is less subject to fatigue and uneven work than the human planter. The notches are regulated according to soil depth and tree root type, and any human tendency to shallow planting at the end of the day is obviated. It cannot operate in stony soil or in places where roots and rubbish are encountered, but will work well in many agricultural soils whether or not screefing and/or ploughing have been done previously. The distributors in Britain are Messrs Jack Olding of Hatfield, Herts.

10.4.3 Standard and parkland trees

Pit planting is the gardener's system suitable for larger transplant and standard trees. A hole is dug amply large enough to receive the roots without bending or confining them. Where grass is the existing ground cover, a thick turf is first cut, and after a hole of the required size has been excavated, is laid in upside down at the bottom of the hole to decompose and provide humus. Good quality loam with peat and a sprinkling of bone meal may be substituted for, or mixed with, the existing soil where this is of poor quality.

10.4.4 Cuttings or 'slips'

In moist situations, stem cuttings of willows and certain poplars may be used instead of rooted plants. Shoots should be about 750 mm (2½ ft) long and about 12 mm (½ in) diameter. The thinner leading shoot is usually discarded; it is less likely to make good growth. Three-quarters of the shoot should be below the soil, and kept moist until roots have begun to form. Willow cuttings are supplied by certain nursery firms at low rates, or wands may be cut from local plants.

In order to make a dense bushy growth, and to obtain the brightest bark colouring, willows may be cut back in the spring at regular intervals, to any desired height, thus making pollards or coppice forms. New shoots growing from buds below the cut will make annual growth from established root stocks.

10.4.5 Fertilisers

Additional fertilisers are sometimes applied, but experience indicates that subsequent surface mulching with organic material is better than use of rich compost at the time of planting. The young tree should begin to grow and make contact with normal soil moisture before stimulants are given; moisture in the early stages is more urgently needed than plant food. Slow release fertilisers such as bone meal can be safely given, however, where soil analysis indicates low state of nutrients in the local soil. See also Chapter 8.

A good all-round fertiliser for general use is:

4 parts superphosphate of lime
1 part nitro chalk
4 parts bonemeal (by weight)

This should be applied at the rate of 70 g per m² (approx. 2 oz per sq yd) and can be mixed with any organic mulch to make application easier. In exceptional conditions chemical analysis may be needed to enable corrections of balance, or to counteract deficiencies of trace elements.

10.5 Fencing and tree guards

10.5.1 Plantation fencing

Young trees need protection until thoroughly established against:

(a) Grazing animals, both domestic cattle, sheep, horses, etc., and wild rabbits, hares and deer.
(b) Human vandalism and carelessness.

The type of fencing must be adjusted accordingly. Deliberate aggressive vandalism is difficult to overcome but casual vandalism and trespass can be discouraged by high fences of close strands of strong barbed wire without horizontal timber bars. Post and rails make good cattle fences and look well in the landscape, but they invite trespass. In cases where some seasonal trespass by hunt servants, keepers and sportsmen is to be tolerated, stiles or bars should be provided. Gates or moveable panels in the fencing, necessary for maintenance, should be sited inconspicuously to discourage trespass.

Damage by contractors' vehicles and tackle in the course of development work should be avoided by the provision of fences in the case of established as well as young trees, although temporary protection may suffice for that purpose (see Plate 10.8).

With the exception of temporary fencing, it is false economy to erect fencing insufficiently durable or insufficiently high to give full protection. Above all, avoid easily climbable fencing where trespass is likely to occur.

Ornamental fencing, if required for special situations, must be designed to fulfil its functions also.

For general all-round use and to meet most types of hazard, the following specification is suggested.

(a) Fencing – stock proof (except for deer) without rabbit proofing – straining posts $1,800 \times 150 \times 100$ every 18 m set 600 mm in well-consolidated ground. 2 struts $1,600 \times 100 \times 50$.
Intermediate prick posts $1,700 \times 100 \times 50$ mm at 3 m intervals driven 450 mm into well-consolidated ground. 4 strands wire, alternately 12½ gauge barbed and 6 gauge plain. Top row barbed, spacing (from top of posts) 25, 250, 300, 300, 325 mm to ground.
(b) For rabbit proofing as above, but omit 1 strand barbed wire and add netting 18 gauge, 30 mm mesh, 1,050 mm high. Turn 150 mm under and bury in the direction of attack.

Plate 10.8. A mature oak requiring careful protection from surrounding development. Fencing should prevent change of level or compaction under the full extent of the branches.

10.5.2 Tree guards for specimen standard trees or groups of trees and shrubs

In parks or agricultural areas where fencing is of the type specified above, tree groups may be protected by similar means. Individual standards, or hedgerow and roadside trees may be enclosed by close set barbed wire supported on three posts making triangular guards. With the increasing use of mechanical hedgecutters, steel guards for hedgerow saplings may be necessary on industrial sites or where maintenance is liable to be carried out by men with no forestry training.

In urban areas tree guards may be of painted or galvanised metal. Many standard types are commercially available. All guards should be removed before the increase of stem girth approaches their diameter. Neglect of this obvious precaution has caused the death of many urban trees.

10.5.3 Stakes and ties for standard trees

Stakes for standards over 1·5 m high should be specified to suit the size of the tree. They should be stout enough to provide support until new roots are formed; say 75–100 mm (3–4 in) diameter they should be spiked at one end and driven 600 mm (2 ft) into the ground before planting the tree. In very windy sites two stakes per tree may be necessary. The length of the stake should equal that of the tree stem below the branching. If heavy standards are used in areas where vandalism is rife, the stake may be extended into the crown. Two or three adjustable ties per tree should be specified. Ties should be inspected and adjusted frequently to allow for expansion of stem diameter. Easily adapted ties are commercially available.

10.6 Shelter belts and screen planting

10.6.1 Shelter belts

In upland or coastal districts the wind shelter provided by tree belts can contribute materially to the temperature and 'amenity' of the leeward area (Plate 10.9). The width of shelter given depends on wind strength and ground form, but in broad general terms, on flat ground there is a fifty per cent reduction of wind velocity at a distance of ten times the height of the trees at ground level (Fig. 10.4).

The siting of shelter belts should be a preliminary aspect of design, considered at the master plan stage.

Belts of fairly open texture, breaking the force but not

194

deflecting the wind completely, are found to be more effective than complete dense growth, because the latter causes turbulence on the leeward side, as does a high wall. There are, however, means of overcoming this turbulence, such as a gradual lift, starting on rising ground with low shrubs, and increasing the height of the trees in the leeward rows, so that the wind is carried over.

It is useless to plant single standard trees in situations where wind or salt spray is prevalent. The principle of 'defence in depth' is essential in such cases, making possible an entirely different micro-climate in the sheltered area, favourable to crops and even to tender plants in frost-free coastal districts. Such conditions provide greater comfort and amenity for man and beast. Forestry Commission grants are available on request in certain cases for shelter belt planting, depending on the locality (see section 10.9.5). Wide belts, up to 100 m (approx. 110 yd), give better shelter than narrow rows; they offer better opportunity for renewal by means of rotational or selective felling. Single rows of trees are better than nothing but, if they are all of the same age, will become senile at about the same time. The principle of 'defence in depth' is applicable (see Fig. 10.6). Wide belts give better protection from noise, smoke, fumes and cold winds. They should be wide enough to permit a good mixture of height and texture. Shelter belts should relate to the ground plan and link visually so far as possible with neighbouring groups of important vegetation.

Shelter planting can be even more effective if related to ground formation as indicated in Fig. 10.6.

An effective screen for quick results on a comparatively narrow belt of about 15 m width is shown in Fig. 10.5.

Close planting encourages rapid growth in the early years but may need thinning at successive stages. When the ground is moist enough for willows, poplars and alders, dense and rapid growth can be encouraged by cutting back alternate rows in spring to form coppice growth at the height required. This is a good way of obtaining visual screens on narrow widths.

10.6.2 Hedges with shelter belts and trees
In nearly all cases a hedge planted on the windward side of tree belts increases the rate of growth of the screen in the early stages and ensures low cover in the long term.

Plate 10.9. Clydesdale. A view showing useful shelter plantations in exposed country.

195

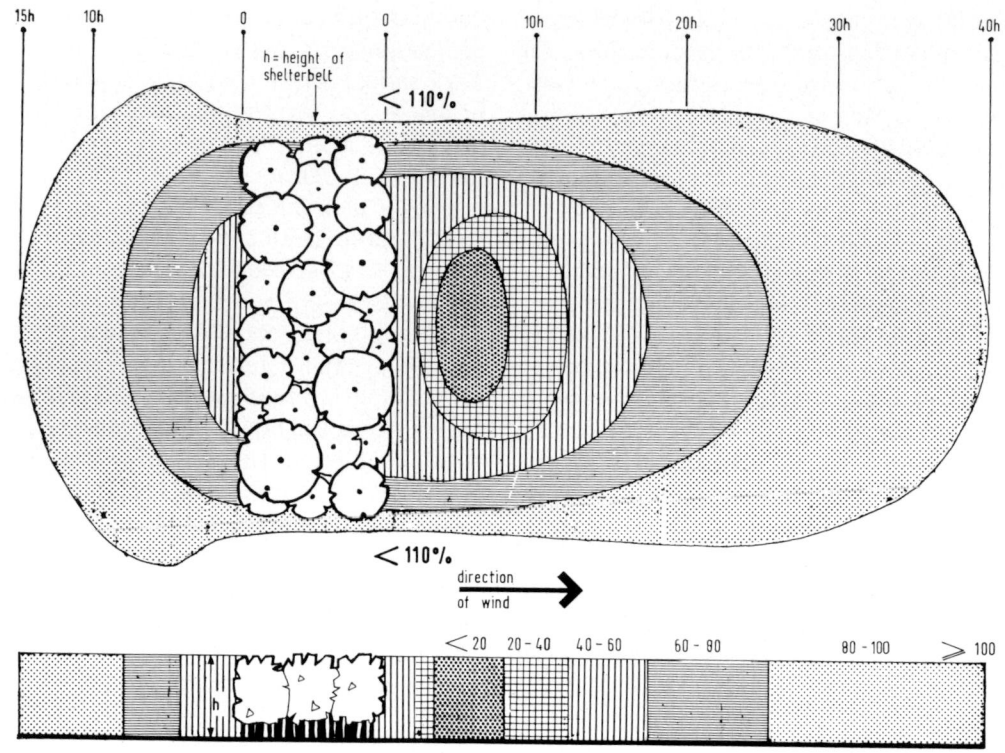

Fig. 10.4. Diagrams showing reduction of wind speed obtained from shelter belt protection (based on Forestry Commission Forest Record No. 22 – *Shelterbelts for Western Hill Farms*).

Screens which are allowed to become 'leggy' may defeat their purpose, as draughts develop near the ground. Thorn hedges are usually the most suitable.

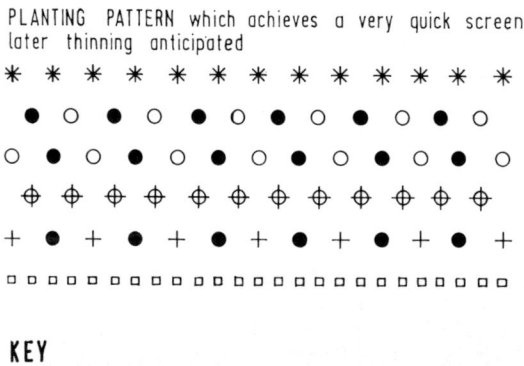

PLANTING PATTERN which achieves a very quick screen: later thinning anticipated

KEY

✱	— cotoneaster salicifolia	900-1200	[3' 0"-4' 0"]
●	— populus canescans	1800 standards	[6' 0"]
○	— ligustrum lucidum	600-750	[2' 0"-2' 6"]
⊕	— cotoneaster frigida	1200-1500	[4' 0"-5' 0"]
+	— prunus lusitanica	600-750	[2' 0"-2' 6"]
▫	— ligustrum ovalifolium	600-750	[2' 0"-2' 6"]

Fig. 10.5. Close planting for quick shelter and screening. To be thinned out at successive stages of development.

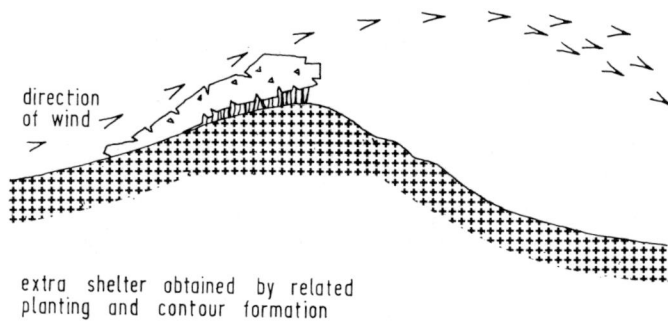

extra shelter obtained by related planting and contour formation

Fig. 10.6. Shelter planting. Additional shelter obtained by related planting and contour formation.

Hedge-laying, the traditional way of maintaining stockproof hedges, is now costly and although still practised in the home counties, machine-cutting is now in general use. Machines can cut a wedge-shaped hedge, wide at the base, which is stockproof and satisfactory for shelter and conservation, but the tendency to cut all saplings should be resisted. At least some lengths of hedge with their natural growth-forming groups in critical positions should be allowed for visual value and timber potential.

196

10.7. Maintenance and care of trees

10.7.1 New plantations

All new plantations require care and management. Maintenance for a stated period is usually included in the planting contract and should be specified in some detail. The period of contractor's maintenance should not be less than one year and in some cases it may be up to five years.

10.7.2 Long-term management

Responsibility for long-term management should be handed over on satisfactory completion of the contract period, to the authority concerned. The landscape architect, the client's representative or landscape manager and the contractor should be represented at a 'hand-over' meeting. Failure to ensure future care and maintenance of plantations involves loss of capital outlay. In some cases the client requires the landscape architect to make periodic visits to consult with the landscape manager for some years after completion to ensure implementation of the intention of the design.

10.7.3 Specifications for maintenance

Maintenance of new plantations of forest type – specifications should include:

Regular inspection;
maintenance of fences;
'treading-in' after disturbance by frost and other causes;
removal of weeds round small trees;
replacement of losses;
thinning and trimming at successive stages.

In the case of rabbit-proof fences repairs should include riddance of rabbits and hares which may have entered.

'Treading-in' is usually necessary more than once in the first season after planting.

Removal of weeds (by manual or chemical methods) is only necessary to prevent very small trees being choked by rank growth. 'Delapon' may be used with great care when the trees are dormant, to suppress rank grasses. Granular herbicides are available, and contact herbicides may be used with shields to protect small trees. After a few years their shade should suppress weed growth.

Replacement of losses or 'beating up' to ensure at least 90% of initial planting is usually included in the first year of maintenance contracts.

Thinning begins at the stage when mutual competition among the trees must be checked. Numbers are successively reduced to 50%, 25% or less of original numbers according to the species and rate of growth. Details of such thinnings, depending on many circumstances, should be determined in the light of developments.

Brashing, or trimming off the lower branches up to a height of about 2 m (approx. $6\frac{1}{2}$ ft) is usually carried out before thinning when the trees are about 6 or 7 m (about 20 ft) high.

Sometimes alternate rows only are brashed, but complete brashing is well worthwhile where landscape appearance is of importance. It lets in light and air, ensuring better development of the trees and of the ground flora.

High pruning is sometimes carried out on selected stems, and usually only those trees likely to form the final crop are pruned. This practice much improves the appearance of groups and plantations.

10.7.4 Care of young specimen trees and standards

A high standard of care promotes quick sturdy growth and good formation of specimen trees. The operations include:

attention to stakes and ties;
weeding, mulching and watering;
fertilising;
trimming.

Stakes should be renewed if necessary until the tree is wind-firm after which they should be removed. Failure to adjust ties to allow for stem growth can ruin the shape of young standards.

Weeding, mulching and watering are considered together; correct mulching should obviate the need for weeding and reduce the need for watering. The soil over the roots of newly planted standards should be kept free from grass and coarse weeds competing for moisture. Drought, before the roots are fully established, is accountable for many losses especially under urban conditions. Mulching consists of a litter of organic material laid over the roots, but not touching the stem itself. Straw, grass mowings, peat, garden compost or pulverized bark laid on the surface and thoroughly soaked by rain or copious watering will maintain soil moisture for many weeks and smother weed growth. Further watering may be necessary in the event of drought during the first spring and summer. If growth appears to be unsatisfactory, a fertiliser may be added to the mulch but is not necessary on good deep soils. Dry root conditions are the commonest cause of failure among transplanted trees.

Trimming consists of shaping the tree gradually to form a balanced head with straight clean stem up to the required height (to be determined by the design). A few small branches, especially the lower ones, may be removed each winter, by clean cuts leaving no stubs. It is not good for a young tree to be cut much at a time so

197

Plate 10.10. An open glade in established mixed forest. A pleasant feature in amenity woodland, or a suitable clearing for new planting to ensure continuity.

skill and judgment must be exercised. In the case of grafted trees such as copper beech or variegated maples, all shoots arising below the graft should be removed, but double or triple stems on trees such as willows, birch, sycamore and maple growing on their own roots can be very attractive. They can be induced by cutting a sapling almost to the ground once the root system is established, or by planting several in the same spot.

10.7.5 Care of mature trees: tree surgery

All dead wood should be removed, and misshapen or dangerous branches overhanging roads, buildings, etc., should also be cut away. The appearance of squalor and neglect given by dead wood and broken branches can be corrected and transformation brought about by skilled tree surgery. Some thinning out of redundant growth in the centre of the crown, and the removal of unbalanced branches may also improve the appearance and growth of the tree.

10.7.6 When to fell trees

To the forester, trees are a crop to be felled when the timber is at its best. The appearance of the tree at that stage, however, is just approaching its period of greatest beauty and will go on improving while its timber declines for perhaps another hundred years. Clients should be warned against the advice of timber merchants in this connection and reminded that landscape considerations may differ from those of economic forestry.

The safety factor often leads to the loss of fine trees. No expert can declare that any tree is 'safe' since storm or lightning may cause accidents. Nor, in this sense, is any wheeled vehicle 'safe'. Insurance against accident is the obvious remedy in both cases. Decaying and diseased trees should obviously be removed, but the landscape value of a sound tree continues long after the peak of its timber value and this gives time to plant and grow on young understudies to take the place of older trees threatened by senility.

Felling becomes necessary when the new annual growth fails to keep pace with dead or dying wood and the appearance of the tree declines. It may also be necessary to make room for new plantations or natural regeneration, particularly in woodland, where spaces can be cleared and replanted without loss of amenity. The decision whether or not to fell is more difficult in those cases of specimen trees, avenues and small groups where lack of space prevents new planting while the old trees remain (see Plate 10.10).

The landowner who forbids the felling of any single tree does a disservice to posterity, since so many plantations are of one age and therefore liable to complete

198

decay at the same stage. The need to ensure continuity is more important than short-sighted preservation of every individual tree; it is one of the landscape architect's special responsibilities, since many humans seem to think that trees are immortal.

10.8 Choice of species

10.8.1 Basis of selection
The selection of tree species and associated vegetation is in all cases influenced by ecological facts, whether we wish to create artificial conditions to suit the species or to use species natural to the situation.

10.8.2 Artificial conditions
Small sites in town gardens and parks or in any position closely related to buildings, can be artificially created to suit introduced or exotic plants – giving the designer a vast range of species available in commerce. But involving, as it does, constant care and attention, and special provision for irrigation and drainage, such a system is unsuited to broad-scale planting.

10.8.3 Ecological planting
The present tendency to design in harmony with existing local ecological conditions is due partly to the increasing scale of work, partly to our growing understanding of ecological factors, and not least to the realisation that the wealth of natural variety depending on local geology and climate has character and beauty which is lost if overlaid by the use of flamboyant horticultural introductions.

Plate 10.11. Woodland fringe. Typical low vegetation harbours wild life of every sort, and gives additional wind shelter inside the tree belt.

10.8.4 Woodland planting
The Forestry Commission publishes up to date information on species. Bulletin No. 14 *Forestry Practice* gives tables and advice on species suited to different soils and situations. A common forestry practice is to interplant between the trees of the final crop some quicker 'nurse trees' to encourage straight growth and to give protection and shelter in the early stages. Hardwoods such as beech or oak are slower growing than softwoods such as pine, larch and other conifers, and the latter give economic returns at an earlier stage than the deciduous timbers. They can be removed and sold as thinnings and this operation allows the final crop more room to develop. In pure conifer stands the thinnings may be of the same species as those selected for full maturity, but the risk of losses from disease or fire is reduced by using a mixture of species.

Plate 10.12. Married soldiers' quarters in a woodland setting. The natural setting is preserved so far as possible in the detail treatment of curbs, footpaths and 'street furniture'.

Young trees vary greatly in their requirement for light. Shade-bearing species suffer from too much sunlight and are best grown under light demanding species until they are well established.

10.8.5 Shelter belt planting
The above remarks apply also to shelter belts, but in this case the additional advantage of mixed species is greater; as timber production is of secondary importance, small trees such as thorn, privet and dogwood may be used on the windward side.

199

10.8.6 Trees in towns

Special conditions governing the choice of species for urban use include:

shade;
atmospheric pollution;
water supply;
root spread;
leaf fall.

The potential growth of the tree should be related to the area available, but it does not always follow that only small trees must be used in small places. The ultimate shape of a tree can be controlled to provide foliage at the level required, and in some cases a high canopy is more welcome than low foliage. This is most true in the case of car parks and streets, but it can apply also to gardens of dwellings, though light foliaged trees such as acacia (*Robinia pseudo-acacia*) and birch are usually preferred for the latter.

Fastigiate trees such as Lombardy poplar and others whose natural growth is narrow and erect are available but are visually boring unless grouped in association with contrasting forms.

Deciduous trees endure atmospheric pollution better than evergreens; most conifers resent town conditions. Common species most tolerant to smoke and other pollutants include ash, elm, alder, beech, willow, poplar, lime, sycamore, plane. Some flowering exotics such as magnolia, tulip tree and catalpa are also very tolerant. Grouping of trees separating neighbourhoods has great value in towns but single specimen trees in important positions play a significant role also, as foil and contrast to masonry.

Early care and attention especially to moisture conditions is essential until trees are thoroughly established. All town planting needs special care due to artificial surroundings. The commonest causes of failure are drought or stagnant water at the roots.

The risk of root damage to foundations and underground services was referred to in section 10.1.4. It should be emphasised that the trouble is caused by lack of moisture at the root, especially in clay soils.

Leaf fall has been blamed for car skids on roads. Tyre

Plate 10.13. Tapiola. Low rise housing in thin birchwood in Finland. Floor levels have evidently been determined relative to tree positions.

improvements have reduced this risk but trees with very heavy foliage should be avoided where they overhang traffic routes.

10.8.7 Trees in the rural landscape
In the countryside the need to use only the local species is especially important for practical and aesthetic reasons. Maintenance is reduced to a minimum, and the need to preserve the visual character of the locality greater. Even in the case of institutions or industries in rural situations which may require ornamental garden trees near the buildings the perimeter treatment should link them to their context: this may be by means of tree belts and hedges similar to those in the area. In bleak open country where there are few trees, tree plantations and gardens alike may be inappropriate so that the problem becomes that of designing ground modelling and low cover rather than planting bulky vegetation.

10.8.8 Rate of tree growth
Rate of growth of trees varies according to: species and favourable or unfavourable conditions of situation before and after planting. Some deciduous species grow as fast or even faster than forest conifers. Poplars, willows and alders in favourable conditions will outstrip pine, larch, and spruce from the time of planting, although growth will slow down sooner than that of the conifer.

Most of the hardwoods grow slowly when first planted, but speed up in the fifth or sixth years under favourable conditions. From then on they grow fast until nearing their ultimate height. At maturity growth slows, and in old age height may be lost as the young growths become vulnerable to wind and frost. The girth of stem continues to expand annually, so providing a rough indication of the age of a tree.

Accurate assessment can only be made by counting the annual rings which are clearly visible in sound timber after felling, and as the width of the annual rings vary according to climatic conditions they provide a record of the tree's history and of the climatic changes which took place during its lifetime.

10.8.9 Association of evergreen and deciduous species
A proportion of evergreen trees and shrubs is useful in many cases for shelter and colour in winter and as a foil to paler greens in summer. Of the few native evergreens the pines are the fastest growing and they all harmonise far better with our rural landscape than do most of the introduced conifers such as *Cupressus* and *Thuya* which strike an incongruous and artificial note in country areas.

Yew and holly (both shade-bearing when young) are slower growing but invaluable grown with deciduous trees. The typical association of yew with beech, and holly with oak are excellent visually, and appropriate both for practical and ecological reasons.

Yew, however, is poisonous to grazing animals under certain circumstances, and though cases of yew poisoning rarely occur when animals are feeding freely under natural conditions they do occur in enclosed pasture or where garden hedges adjoin roads. The action of the toxin is not clear, but the risk prohibits the planting of yew in places accessible to grazing stock.

Of the introduced evergreens, the Holm oak (*Quercus ilex*) is one that harmonises well visually with our native trees. Of introduced conifers, *Tsuga heterophylla* and *Pseudotsuga*, both faster growing under suitable inland conditions than the Holm oak, seem also visually better suited to our rural landscape than many of the more familiar introduced conifers. *Pinus radiata* is excellent in seaside or inland situations not subject to severe frost.

10.9 Costs

10.9.1 Rates per hectare
Variations depending on local circumstances and inflation make it impossible to give firm figures. The following assessments are to be seen as a relative guidance during 1978/9.

Forest planting may vary between £260 and £1,250 per ha (approx. £105–505 per acre) according to species used and size of plantation. Very small plantations or spinneys require more fencing per unit area and with a more choice selection of species, including perhaps evergreen shrubs and some standards for quick effect, they may cost up to £1,750 per ha (approx. £710 per acre) at 1978 prices.

The rates given relate to unfenced conventional forestry and amenity plantations respectively, but both in substantial blocks in rural conditions. For smaller plantings on urban or industrial sites and to a different

specification prices will vary considerably and unit costs for preparation, planting and fencing rather than rates per hectare may have to be used for accurate estimating purposes.

10.9.2 Rates per tree
Nursery tree prices depend on the size of the plants, both in original cost and preparation of ground and planting. Species vary also in regard to supply, and this in turn relates to the ease of propagation, and the time taken before they reach saleable sizes. As a very rough guide 1·8 m (approx. 6 ft) standard hardwood trees cost from £1·75–8·75 per tree (at the per 100 trade rate) unplanted or approximately £11·00–16·00 per tree including preparation, supply, planting, staking, tree guard, feeding and mulching and a replacement guarantee for one sea-

son after planting (again 1978 prices).

The cost of mature or semi-mature trees is very high and so dependent on size and distance that individual estimates are essential. Firms specialising in the transplanting of these may in some cases guarantee their success, but the rate of failure is high unless copious watering and aftercare is assured until the trees are fully established.

10.9.3 Fencing, tree guards, stakes and ties

Fencing is usually essential for forestry plantations, shelter belts, tree groups and areas of natural regeneration for protection until fully established. The cost depends on the type of fencing; also on whether or not rabbit wire is needed as well.

Recent costs for fencing with rabbit wire have been £1·50 per linear metre (spring 1979).

Standard wire tree guards suitable for built-up areas are available from commercial firms at a cost of approximately £7·50 per tree guard.

Stockproof tree guards are needed in fields used for grazing; in practice these are usually designed and specified to suit local circumstances.

Stakes of 2·5–3·0 m high and × 100 mm (approx. 8–10 ft and 4 in) diameter, for well-grown standards, cost from £1·10–1·70 per stake.

10.9.4 Preparation of ground

Deep cultivation on compacted ground for single tree stations is costly and on clay soils may call for individual drainage for each station.

For groups, or belts of trees, the whole area should be cultivated to a depth of not less than 450 mm (approx. 18 in).

On compacted or badly drained sites it is advisable to build up levels over the whole plantation area with good topsoil to about 450 mm (approx. 18 in) above surrounding ground level.

10.9.5 Government grants for tree planting

The Forestry Commission has revised its grant aid towards the cost of tree planting. This took effect from 1 October 1977 and now comprises:

(*a*) The Dedication Scheme (Basis III) giving outright payments of £100 per ha (£225 per ha for approved broadleaved schemes) for areas of 10 ha or more. Management grants of £3 per ha per annum are given for conifers under 25 years old and broadleaves under 50 years old.

(*b*) Transitional arrangements for Basis III dedications of less than 10 ha exist.

(*c*) The Small Woods Scheme was reintroduced in October 1977 following concern about the loss of woods 'whose importance lies not only in their aes-

thetic, nature conservation and amenity value but also the significant contribution they make to the country's timber resources'. Grants of £300 per ha for areas of 0·25–3 ha and £250 per ha for areas of 3–10 ha are made. Grants cover planting and 5 years maintenance. Details of the grants are set out in the forestry Commission's booklet *Advice for Woodland Owners* dated August 1977.

Countryside Commission. Grants under Section 9 of the Local Government Act 1974 enable the Countryside Commission to make available funds for planting as part of their statutory obligation 'to offer assistance towards expenditure conducive to the purposes of the National Parks and Access to the Countryside Act 1949, and the Countryside Act 1968'.

The Commission have published two pamphlets setting out financial assistance policies to local authorities and other public bodies (CCP78) and to private individuals and other bodies (CCP79). These are concerned specifically with the Commission's policy toward financial assistance for amenity tree planting in the Countryside and for landscape management, and supercedes CCP91 'Grants for Amenity Tree Planting', November 1975. This revision was made necessary by the modifications to the Forestry Commission's grant policies for small woods (from 1 October 1977). 'Grants will normally be in the range of 40–60% of acceptable costs and will not exceed 75% of such costs.'

Ministry of Agriculture. Tree planting may be eligible for grants in the following circumstances. Planting and improvement of hedges and shelter belts (as well as their removal) may be eligible under the 'Farm Capital Grant Scheme 1973 (Item 13)' where the scheme forms part of a hill farming enterprise (defined as in a 'less favoured area'). Grant eligibility (up to 50%) relates to the income from the farm enterprise and the decision lies with the Ministry's Divisional Offices. See pamphlet FCG1 (revised February 1977). The Ministry will grant aid towards screen planting for new agricultural buildings where it is required as a condition of planning approval at the same rate as the grant given on the new buildings.

Under an E.E.C. directive the 'Farm and Horticultural Development Scheme' makes grants available from the Ministry of Agriculture for shelter planting on both upland and lowland areas at variable rates. These range from 10% in general agriculture to 50% in 'less favoured areas' and 30% in horticulture but are conditional upon achievement of the improvements set out in the development plan for any specific enterprise.

Department of the Environment Derelict Land. Under Section 8 of the Local Employment Act 1972 and Section 9 of the Local Government Act 1966, local authorities are empowered, but not required, to reclaim derelict land. Grants vary from 100% in Development Areas, Intermediate Areas and Derelict Land Clearance Areas (so designated by the Secretary of State for Industry), to 50% in all areas which in practice means areas not covered by the higher grant or National Parks or Areas of Outstanding Natural Beauty where a 75% grant is payable under Section 97 (1) (*c*) of the National Parks and Access to the Countryside Act 1949.

Derelict land is that which is 'so damaged by industrial or other development that it is incapable of beneficial use without treatment' (see Chapter 12). In practice tree planting is likely to form part only of the reclamation scheme which will also include major earthshaping and grassing. Grants are summarised in the DoE Circular 17/77 'Derelict land' dated 3 March 1977 and the Explanatory Memorandum PRM3/802/81 for the 1966 and 1972 Acts dated January 1976.

Operation Clean Up. In September 1978 the Secretary of State for the Environment announced his new environmental scheme for inner cities. He stated that 'the kind of projects I have in mind include the clearance of rubbish from vacant and waste land, provision of top soil and grassing vacant sites, planting trees and shrubs on vacant land ...' District Councils have been invited to operate the scheme drawing as much as possible on local communities including voluntary bodies and the Special Temporary Employment Programme of the Manpower Services Commission. Total expenditure of £15 m over $3\frac{1}{2}$ years is planned which will attract grant aid of 75%.

11 Maintenance and Conservation

TOM WRIGHT AND JOHN PARKER

11.1 Introduction

11.1.1 Definition

The main objectives of this chapter are well summarised in a definition of landscape management and landscape maintenance evolved by a group of 'professionals' asked to look more closely at these fields by the Landscape Institute.

'Landscape management is the role of professionals, ensuring that the *long-term* objectives of both designer and user are achieved so that the landscape evolves and matures to their satisfaction. Landscape management concerns both the use of the land and the growth of physically and visually acceptable relationships between the land and its living communities. This calls for closer consultation between designers, managers, and land scientists. Landscape management may involve some design procedure and a keen appreciation of landscape design. *Landscape maintenance*, an important aspect of management, concerns the routine care of land, vegetation and land surfaces, as intended by the manager or designer.'

11.1.2 Background

Until the second decade of this century, it is probably true to say that the majority of the British landscape was managed as an accepted tradition and responsibility by landowners and their tenants. Apart from the cities and urban areas, the landscape was largely in the hands of these landowners with a firm control over the whole visual appearance of the countryside. A reasonably stable and well-ordered hierarchy of estate staff and craftsmen managed and maintained these estates, the staff being drawn invariably from local stock and families and frequently generations accepted life-long employment with one establishment.

The intensification of Britain's industrialised society and the associated rate of change of landscapes with more pressure of housing, industry, roads and communications, has led to the insidious degradation of many urban environments, and a lack of the skilled staff to maintain them. Not even the agricultural landscape has escaped these effects. A reaction to these 'mounting assaults' on the landscape has grown rapidly in recent years and there is now a strong call for conservation and protection of environmental quality and a rehabilitation of those areas damaged in the past.

Landscape management and maintenance objectives, must therefore involve some concern for the conservation and welfare of the landscape. This underlies much of what follows in this chapter.

11.2 Maintenance policies

11.2.1 Maintenance objectives

Not all landscape areas, which are to be maintained, will have been consciously designed at any one time. Two main categories are distinguished in this respect:

(a) Natural, semi-natural and rural landscapes slightly or substantially modified by man's activities but still strongly dominated by the characteristics of the natural environment of the particular area or region (see also section 2.3). Design in these areas must always be closely related to the natural qualities and association of the area or region, i.e. sensitive use of local building materials, indigenous plants, etc. Maintenance will usually be within the framework of the existing land use.

(b) Designed landscapes, creating new environments conceived by the designer and frequently created in rehabilitated or reclaimed areas, large housing or industrial projects, etc. Here the designer may be free from constraints imposed by the natural environment, and he can evolve schemes which may be of low or high maintenance depending upon many factors (see section 2.3).

Wherever possible the designer or manager should attempt to broadly classify the type of landscape involved in terms of its 'welfare' and management. He should cultivate an awareness or 'feel' for landscape, and develop an instinctive skill in specifying the right balance of maintenance for each category proposed.

Standards of maintenance

The standard should be appropriate for the design, its use and be practicable for the staff who will maintain it. Excessive deviation from the standard agreed upon will seriously impair the visual, functional and possibly ecological qualities of any scheme.

11.2.2 Categories of landscape

Extensive natural or 'wild'.   Examples would include National Parks, areas of outstanding natural beauty, areas of great landscape value, heritage coastlines, etc.

Management policy – Ownership of much of this land will be in the hands of a number of landowners including private individuals and companies, extractive industries, Forestry Commission, Nature Conservancy, Department of the Environment, local government, etc. Management policies and their implementation will largely be the responsibility of these landowners. Statutory planning, staff suitably trained and experienced officers and the new National Park officers are key people to see that the management policies set for this category of landscape are followed. Guidelines for techniques of policy formation are as follows:

Appraisal – A thorough appraisal and understanding of the essential qualities of an area or region in terms of topography, vegetation, wildlife, farming patterns, traditional industry, etc.

Discussion – Good public relations work with all inter-ested parties including the landowners and the potential or actual users such as the recreational groups, ramblers, anglers and the Naturalists Trusts, etc.

Management plan – The preparation of an overall plan, agreed as far as possible by all parties concerned and having as its principal objectives the short- and long-term management of the whole region or area in question bearing in mind such important factors as changing land uses. and farming systems, pressures for resource exploitation (including water) and recreation. Key points in this plan would cover the following:

(*a*) Indigenous tree cover.
(*b*) Hedges and hedgerow trees. Worked out with landowners accepting the needs for change while retaining an overall 'feel' for the enclosure pattern of the area. Retention of key hedges, hedgerow trees and such related factors as stone walls, particularly along footpaths.
(*c*) Small woodland areas, copses, spinneys.
(*d*) Heath, open moorland.
(*e*) Streams, water courses, and ponds.
(*f*) Road verges policy for limited cutting where necessary to maintain the rural character of the road network (see bibliography).
(*g*) National Nature Reserves, Areas of Special Scientific Interest (see 11.9.2).

Major developments – such as extended mineral workings, recreational centres and forestry and many others – should always be the subject of careful landscape study followed by professional design treatment. At all times

Plate 11.4. Standards of maintenance. An area with transition from mown grass to woodland fringe. Success depends upon the right maintenance standard.

Plate 11.5. Standards of maintenance. Traffic island planting of the floral impact type, increasingly difficult and expensive to maintain.

planned facilities such as car parks, picnic sites, ancillary buildings associated with developments should be carefully scrutinised and sited. The management staff should be involved in this stage. They should also advise on general matters in their region concerning construction and colour of farm buildings, fences, gates, stiles, footpath signs and many other detailed features that will help to determine the qualities of the area.

Special problems in this category. Policies could be seriously affected by:

Changes in farming systems. Abandonment of the more remote hill farms. Lack of grazing leading to hill pastures reverting to scrub with possible loss of amenity and access.

Intensification of land-use activities. Ploughing of moorland and 'open' countryside. Farm amalgamation (loss of buildings, walls, etc.). Forestry planting.

Plate 11.6. A traffic island with planting showing a contrasting attitude to design and maintenance in an urban situation similar to that in Plate 11.5.

Major national priority developments. Extractive industries, reservoirs, service training areas.

The key to meeting these problems and coping with the long-term management of the category lies with good, well-trained and experienced staff who can successfully co-ordinate the interests of all those involved, and with sufficient vision to determine the objectives and see that they are carried through.

Extensive parkland, woodland, commons and heathland.

Examples would include Green Belt public open spaces, estates under private and public ownership, historic forests and open spaces such as the New Forest, Sherwood Forest, Malvern Hills.

These are usually smaller in scale than the 'wild' category above and more accessible to visitors due to their location near large centres of population or in heavily visited tourist areas. There are greater problems of excessive pressures from over use. Generally there would be fewer individual owners than in section 2.3.1 and with more land under public ownership, thus offering more scope for comprehensive management techniques.

Management policy
Appraisal – Identify the essential characteristics of the area and its outstanding qualities, i.e. woodland, heath, open grassland, historic parkland. Formulate policies and standards of maintenance to perpetuate these characteristics or to modify them by general agreement with all interested parties according to current or proposed changes of use.

Key points to note:

(a) Woodland and tree cover (see also 11.9.5).
(b) Management for public access, conservation, economic returns. Establish priorities here.
(c) The durability of woodland and especially the underlying soil and herb layer to public use and relate them to determining zones for car parks, information centres, riding, walking, etc. A woodland of sufficient size may be zoned into *'tranquility' or 'reserve' areas* for wildlife and ecological studies where public access is limited; *public access areas* where felling and clearing zones can be precisely planned and possibly *economic areas* primarily intended for timber production. In woodland under private ownership the planning authority and management staff should be fully aware of the insidious changes that can soon affect the quality of landscape, i.e. indiscriminate felling, change of land use and other encroachments into woodland. In the care of woodland under public ownership the management may be vested in tradi-

tional trusteeship or a Parks and Recreation Department of a local government authority. Management standards here can easily deviate from the optimum. Excessive maintenance may erode the natural charm of woodland.
(d) Grassland management (see (b) above).

Agricultural, pastoral.
This category almost falls beyond the scope of this chapter. The maintenance of predominantly agricultural land for the prime functions of food production is obviously in the hands of the farming community who will determine a level of maintenance to suit their resources, farming systems and particular personal interests.

If one accepts the definition of landscape management as quoted at the start of this chapter, however, it is in the interests of the landscape designer and the manager to regard the farmer as a custodian of the landscape in his particular ownership or charge, and therefore to encourage him wherever possible to maintain and perpetuate visually pleasing and biologically diverse landscapes. Undoubtedly the key to the visual and ecological qualities of much of Britain's future landscape rests with the farming community.

Considerable research and developments are now in progress in new aspects of public access to the agricultural landscape. This is beyond the scope of this section although the influence of this expanding side of farm enterprises could have important effects on the farm landscape and its management.

Urban open space, parks and sports grounds.
In all these areas the labour inputs, and therefore costs, are likely to be much higher. Details of design and the degree of formality can considerably alter the costs and it is most important that the standards of maintenance are appropriate (see Plates 11.4–11.6). Excessive maintenance can induce too much formality and inhibit variation. Too little can suggest neglect and encourage abuse. Maintenance costs can be considerably reduced by careful detail design as indicated below.

Trees.
Groups in mown grass should be planted so that there is not less than about 3 m (10 ft) clear between trees to allow easy mowing. This does not necessitate trees in straight rows however.

Shrubs and planted areas.
Aim for massed planting using short-term 'fillers' if necessary. Create grass to border curves or shapes to suit mowing patterns.

Grass.
Avoid excessive proportion of edge to be trimmed. Do not create too many narrow strips or inaccessible grass areas for mowing. Minimum area of

Plate 11.1. Maintenance and design. Steps in grass banks with no mowing strips invariably become neglected.

Plate 11.3. Good grass-to-hard surface detailing. Reduced mowing regime also allows a more attractive sward in this setting but loose stones could seriously damage mowers if they are kicked into the grass.

grass in a courtyard is probably 100 sq m (say 120 sq yd) for rational maintenance. Avoid breaking up grass areas with too many obstructions.

Allow mowing strip detailing beside borders, avoid obstructions, etc. Manhole covers not less than 20 mm (approx. $\frac{3}{4}$ in) below finished surface.

Do not create excessively steep banks or gradients making immediate mowing problems.

Mowing access. Grass areas protected by fencing, trip rails, etc., should allow for a gate or removable bar not less than 3 m (approx. 10 ft) wide for gang mowers or 2 m (approx. 6$\frac{1}{2}$ ft) wide for motor mowers.

Allow for use of load-bearing grass-sown blocks in areas where excessive wear is likely, e.g. car parks.

Allow for clearly defined zones of grass cutting at different heights if the opportunity allows. Transition areas from close mown to woodland, tree groups or hedgerows can be left longer as more informal margins, with the possible establishment of conservation grassland area etc. (see section 6.3). Always relate grass seed mixtures to soil, site and use and keep fully up to date with introductions of low maintenance strains etc. (see Chapter 9).

11.2.3 Economics and resources
Maintenance costs. Maintenance of landscaped areas and open space is expensive in that it is a continuous charge carrying on from year to year. As a result even small savings on a yearly basis will create long-term savings whether they are brought about by careful attention to detail and improved management or by alterations in detailed layout and design. The cost of maintenance is usually higher for newly established areas but thereafter the cost depends on the standard required, the intensity of use and wear and, to a lesser extent, the soil type and climatic conditions. However, whatever the maintenance requirements are, economic maintenance requires adequate resources of manpower, technical ability and equipment and the necessary financial capital to provide them. Economic maintenance also requires that the organisation of the work is on a sufficient scale to make proper use of qualified manpower and expensive labour saving equipment.

As most maintenance work is labour intensive, wages form a major part of the costs as shown in Table 11.1.

TABLE 11.1: TYPICAL PROPORTION OF COSTS IN A LANDSCAPE MAINTENANCE ORGANISATION

Wages (includes National Insurance, etc.)	71·0%
Machinery and transport (purchase, repairs and fuel)	15·0%
Materials (seeds, fertilisers, weedkillers, etc.)	3·0%
Depot upkeep (garages, etc.)	2·0%
Small hand tools (spades, forks, etc.)	1·0%
Hired equipment	1·0%
Protective clothing	0·5%
Misc. expenses, advertising, telephones, etc.	0·5%
Management and supervision	6·0%

Plate 11.2. Maintenance and design. Steps with a mowing trim.

Management and manpower resources. The management of landscape maintenance requires a wide range of knowledge and experience that combines technical expertise with managerial ability and an essential aesthetic appreciation of the landscape art. Historically, many of the managers have been primarily horticulturalists orientated very much towards the care and growing of plants. The increasing need for sophisticated management of labour and machinery and the growing public awareness of environmental matters have created a demand for more specialised training for landscape managers. A number of courses specifically aimed at amenity horticulture have developed in recent years and these courses are providing some formal training in the relevant disciplines. These courses, however, will only be of value if it is recognised that the management of landscape maintenance requires the services of a professional qualified person who can work in partnership with the landscape designer.

Much of the manual maintenance work can be carried out by semi- or unskilled men provided they are given adequate technical supervision. Some operations, e.g. pruning and herbicide application, do however require higher levels of skill and experience and it is therefore usually sensible to group the personnel together into small teams, each under the control of a chargehand or foreman and those teams in turn being under the day-to-day supervision of an area foreman or supervisor. In this way it is possible to make full use of the skills and aptitudes within the workforce and also provide some career and promotion prospects for the individual workers. Manpower requirements per area will obviously depend very much on the type and standard of maintenance as well as the management organisation and some indications of these requirements are given in section 11.5.2.

Economies of scale. It can be seen therefore that small maintenance organisations will have difficulty, first of all, in justifying a properly qualified manager and secondly being able to make economic use of essential skilled workers. The minimum viable size for a mainten-

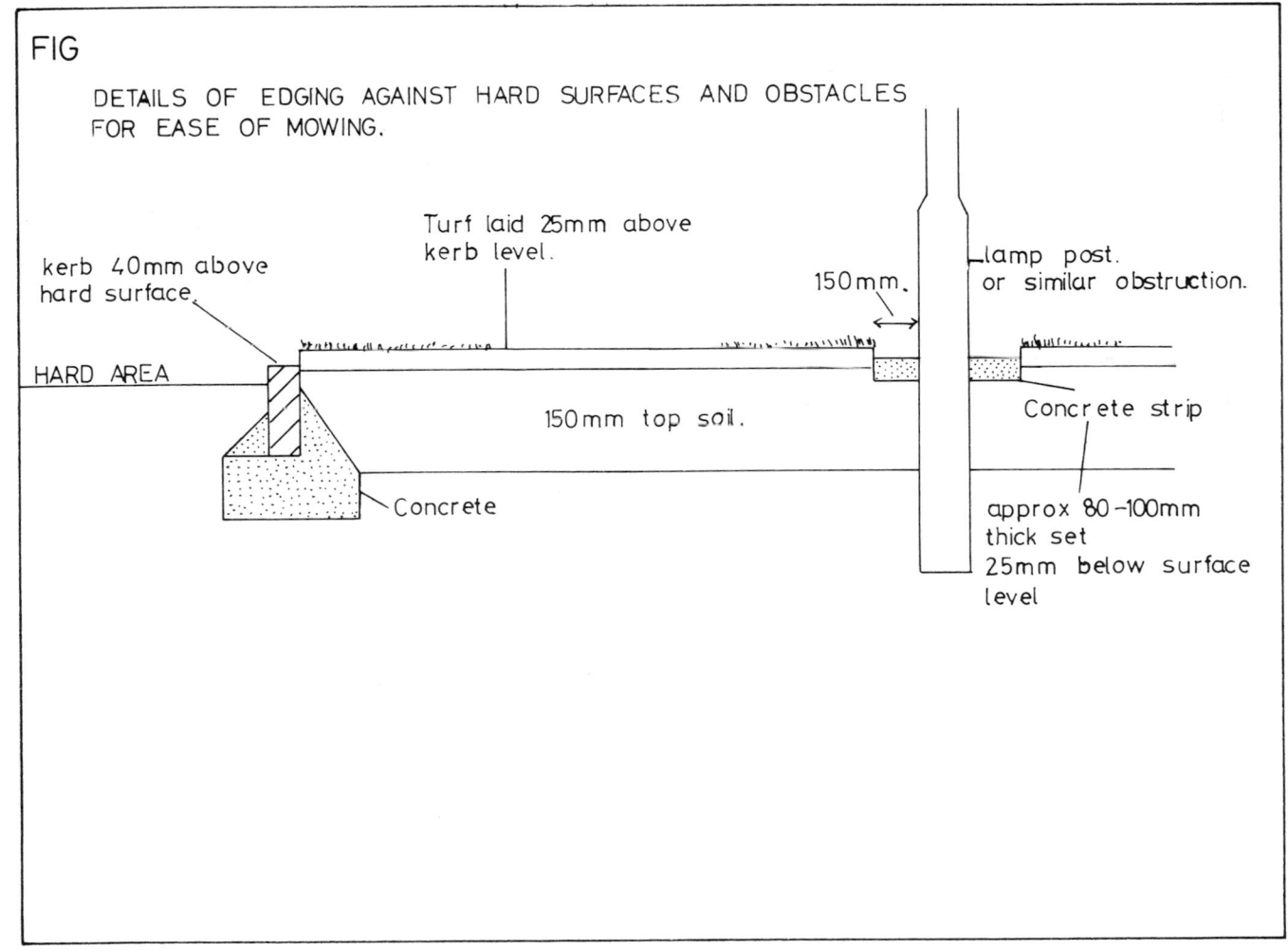

Fig. 11.1. Details of edging against hard surfaces and obstacles for ease of mowing (see also Plates 11.1–11.3).

ance organisation will depend very much on the type of work that is undertaken and also whether it is combined with design and new construction work but about thirty workpeople can probably be regarded as a minimum for a satisfactory independent maintenance organisation.

Machinery and equipment resources. For small volumes of work it is often difficult to justify some of the more expensive labour-saving equipment and so a large organisation has the advantage of being able to make more economic use of, for instance, tractor-powered gangmowers that can mow in excess of 100 acres (approx. 40 ha) of grass as a weekly cutting schedule. Other items of equipment are capable of covering even greater areas and can rarely be fully utilised even in very large organisations. For example a tractor mounted with a sprayer can apply selective weedkillers to many hundreds of acres of playing fields and so for small organisations it is probably better to employ a specialist contractor for this type of work. The lists below indicates the basic machinery needs for the particular types of maintenance (1978 costs).

TABLE 11.2: EQUIPMENT FOR LARGE GRASS AREAS INCLUDING PLAYING FIELDS

	Approx. capital costs, 1978
Tractor (approx. 40 b.h.p.)	£5,100
5 unit gangmower + carrier	£4,600
Tractor-drawn spiker	£700
Tractor-drawn gang roller	£800
Tractor-drawn harrows	£250
Tractor-mounted fertiliser spreader	£400
Tractor-mounted sprayer	£1,000
	£12,850

The tractor and gangmower would normally be sufficient for 40 ha (approx. 100 acres) of grass cut once a week at the height of the season but could cope with a larger area on a single site where there was no travelling required between cutting. A gang carrier can be dispensed with where there is no need to travel between sites. The other tractor mounted and trailed equipment would

TABLE 11.3: EQUIPMENT FOR ROUGH GRASS AREAS, ROADSIDE VERGES, ETC.

Tractor (approx 40 b.h.p.)	£5,100
Tractor mounted flail mower (rear or side arm mounted)	£3,000
Rotary mower (pedestrian operated) 450–600 mm (approx. 18–24 in)	£500
Knapsack sprayer	£50
Hand tools	£50
	Total £8,700

TABLE 11.4: EQUIPMENT FOR AMENITY LAWNS AND BORDERS

Large cylinder motor mower, 750–900 mm cut (approx. 30–36 in)	£800
Small cylinder motor mower, 450–600 mm cut (approx. 18–24 in)	£350
Small rotary mower (Flymo type where there are steep banks)	£150
Knapsack sprayer	£50
Electric hedge trimmer and generator	£350
Wheelbarrow or hand truck	up to £100
Fertiliser spreader	£40
Hose pipes and sprinklers	£50
Hand tools	£100
	Total £1,990
Van or light truck (for transport to small sites)	£2,800

not be used as intensively as the gangmower and should be sufficient for at least 80 ha (approx. 200 acres).

The tractor with a rear-mounted flail mower 1·5 m (approx. 5 ft) cut should be able to roughcut about 8 ha (approx. 20 acres) per week and so could maintain up to 100 ha (approx. 250 acres) annual cutting cycle. The side arm mower with a smaller width of cut has the advantage of being able to mow steep banks, if it is necessary, but has a slower mowing rate. The tractor mounted equipment cannot work in confined spaces or mow close to tree trunks, sign posts and other obstacles so it is essential for there to be a follow-up mowing with a small rotary mower.

The large cylinder mower is only necessary for 'extensive' lawn areas and the smaller may only be necessary to deal with a complicated layout where the larger machine would be difficult to manoeuvre. It is however usually an advantage to have at least two mowers available to provide a reserve in case of breakdown. This equipment would be sufficient for a pair of men working as a team, either on a large single site or looking after a number of smaller sites.

Details of equipment for fine turf areas such as tennis courts, bowling greens, etc., will be found in Chapter 9 on turf maintenance.

Garaging and depots. When a new organisation is being set up it is essential to budget for garage and depot facilities that will provide secure undercover storage space for machinery and vehicles and proper rest and mess facilities for the staff. A typical depot will need to include the following:

Heated mess room for staff with cooking and washing up facilities.
Locker space for each man's personal clothing, etc.
Drying space for wet clothes.
Toilet and washing facilities (with hot running water).

Storage space for seed fertilisers, stakes and other horticultural sundries.

Lock up cabinet for store room for herbicides, fungicides and other poisonous chemicals.

Storage bunkers for peat, sand, topsoil, etc.
Covered bunker for sifted topsoil for top dressing.

Storage space for goal posts, nets and other sports equipment.
Garage space for tractors, vehicles and equipment.
Wash-down area for cleaning tractors and equipment.
Lock-up bunker, away from the main buildings, for petrol in cans, lubrication, etc.

Loading ramp.
Heeling in ground for plants.

A precast concrete construction similar to that used for agricultural buildings can often be used with exterior cladding to suit the surroundings and or planning conditions. Alternatively, the facilities can sometimes be incorporated with pavilion and changing facilities. A building with about 120 sq m (approx. 1200 sq ft) will provide an area depot for a team of around four men and include garage space for a light truck and tractor and gangmowers. A larger central depot will give economies in the provision of mess and toilet facilities but may involve the workmen in considerable extra travelling to their sites.

11.2.4 Public relations and maintenance

There is undoubtedly very considerable scope for harnessing the enormous potential of communities for assisting in many ways in the welfare and management of landscape and this is especially important at the present time of shortage of maintenance staff and limits of financial resources. The following are suggested as some techniques which should be more fully exploited for this purpose.

Schools and school children. Close liaison with Parks and Recreation Departments, Forestry offices, and local government offices to initiate a stronger first-hand involvement of teachers and children with the care of the landscape. Fundamentals could begin with the provision of children's gardens by the local authority with suitable enthusiasm and initiative. Brooklyn Botanic Gardens, New York, have operated such gardens for many years for all classes of children with great success. Volunteer wardens come from Botanic Garden staff and local individuals, with tools and seeds mainly provided for the children by the local authority.

There could be more widespread involvement of children at schools with planting programmes and subsequent maintenance of areas of parks, local woodlands, etc. This needs to be accompanied by visits to schools by Parks Officers providing lectures on the problem and techniques of looking after the landscape. Parks might have 'Children's Days' when parents are also invited to be associated with community responsibility for particular areas.

Youth movements, Conservation Corps and student involvement. Greater co-ordination and increase in these activities of the already excellent work of these movements to help with work in all categories of landscape maintenance.

Adult groups and amenity societies. Following the U.S.A. example, much greater involvement by horticultural societies and garden clubs in the 'welfare' of landscape 'outside the garden fence'. In the U.S.A. these clubs provide valuable practical assistance and funds to raise the general quality and standards of maintenance of urban environments. Rural amenity societies could also assist with conservation and 'clean up' work in areas with which they are closely concerned. Lecture programmes to these societies are also needed.

11.3 Maintenance practice

11.3.1 Maintenance contracts (see also 11.3.2)

Maintenance and particularly long-term management is far from easy to specify or enumerate to the contractor and the client. For many the conclusion of a lengthy and possibly expensive contract ends with the seeding and planting, and insufficient thought is often given to the importance of subsequent maintenance. Alternatively, maintenance may be by direct labour provided by the authority or department who has taken over responsibility of the site or region.

Maintenance clauses. These are an essential part of the main contract. This is normal and should cover at least one or, if possible, two planting seasons after the completion of seeding and planting. Careful writing of the maintenance clauses can help to emphasise the importance of this end of the contract and oblige the contractor to agree to a schedule of work. Supervision is important throughout the period, preferably by the designer or agreed responsible staff.

Schedules and management plans. These may be written on a yearly or longer term basis and are one way of dealing with the maintenance of given sites. Standards of maintenance intended by the designer or manager can only be achieved on the ground by drawing up of carefully compiled maintenance schedules.

Maintenance schedules. These should cover every aspect of the maintenance operations for a given period of time, and should be readily understood by the responsible maintenance supervisor. (An example of a maintenance schedule is shown in Table 11.5):

Management plans. For longer-term management the preparation of a management plan is strongly recommended for all sites. This may take the form of a clearly presented plan and accompanying report, the two together embodying the main objectives of the designer and manager. Such a plan should reduce the chances of serious deviation from the original objectives, by presenting a continuity of management proposals, for the succession of maintenance staff to follow.

11.3.2 Organisation of maintenance

Direct labour or contract. A considerable amount of grounds maintenance is carried out by direct labour organisation varying in size from the single privately employed gardener to the large work forces employed by local authorities. Contract maintenance generally operates on a relatively small scale with, for in-

TABLE 11.5: EXAMPLE–MAINTENANCE SCHEDULE

DIVISION   SITE
SUMMER PROGRAMME I   PERIODS 1–4   APRIL TO JULY

Operation	Location	Quantity	Time Allowed	1					2					3					4				
				F	1	2	3	4	F	1	2	3	4	F	1	2	3	4	F	1	2	3	4
1. Mow and box off lawns				3					4					4					4				
2. Cylinder mow lawns				3					4					4					4				
3. Rotary cut rough grass				1					1					1					1				
4. Rotary cut rough grass									1					1									
5. Rotary mow round fence lines and trees									1					1									
6. Flymo banks				2					2					2					2				
7. Mow C/P cricket strip				3					4					4					4				
8. Clip border edges				3					4					4					4				
9. Hand cut long grass									1					1									
10. Set out running track																							
11. Re-mark running track																							
12. Mark for Sports Day only																							
13. Set out ... rounders				1										1									
14. Re-mark ... rounders				1					4					3					4				
15. Spray roses with fungicide									1					1					1				
16. 'Dead-head' roses																			1				
17. Weed and tidy ground cover				1					1					1					1				
18. Take down goal posts				1																			
19. Spray fence and building lines and tree bases				1																			
20. Check tree stakes and ties				1																			
21. Recut kerb edges														1									
22. Hand hoe new borders				2					2					2					2				
23. Hedges																							
24. Site allowance per man visit																							
25.																							
26.																							
27.																							

stance, small suburban 'jobbing' gardeners but with some larger organisations operating in conjunction with landscape construction work.

There have been few attempts to make strict cost comparisons between direct labour and contract work but it is unlikely that there would be major differences, given equal conditions. Under certain circumstances there are clear advantages for using contractors and many organisations make occasional use of contractors even though they normally rely predominantly on direct labour.

The advantages of a direct labour organisation are:

(a) The staff and machinery are under the direct control of the employer who can quickly direct the organisation in case of emergency or altered priorities.
(b) Direct labour is probably more economic for work that is difficult to predict in advance or to specify and measure accurately, e.g. clearing storm damage or preparing for sports events.
(c) Staff can be encouraged to develop pride of site and job satisfaction.
(d) A large direct labour force will provide job security, training, experience and career prospects within the organisation.

The advantages of a contract system are:

(a) The employer is freed from the responsibilities of staff employment although he pays for this indirectly.
(b) A contractor can often achieve quicker results because of greater flexibility with wage and bonus rates.
(c) The employer does not have to provide capital for equipment and depots.
(d) Because the contractor will work for a number of employers he will be more economic where a single employer might have insufficient work to justify a maintenance organisation or the purchase of specialist equipment.

Maintenance contract arrangements.　　　Few contractors have spare capacity at the height of the season and they are therefore not usually willing or able to tender for short-term work at economic prices and a term contract is usually preferable for a season or several years. This is particularly important for large contracts where the contractor will need some security to justify his capital outlay both in equipment and manpower. Contracts covering more than a season will need to have a fluctuation clause to cover the cost of wage and price increases.

For economic maintenance it is important to award the maintenance contract on the basis of competitive tenders and the tender form must be based on a precise description of the maintenance work required. The description will need to include a plan of the areas, a schedule of operations and frequencies and a bill of quantities. The conditions of the contract will follow those normally used for construction works but is particularly important to have precise conditions regarding the safe use of chemicals and machinery on areas where the public have general access.

Seasonal work load.　　　There is considerable variation in seasonal work load for grounds maintenance and for individual features the winter work requirement can be as little as ten per cent of that required at the peak of the growing season. Fortunately, the combination of features will usually provide a more even distribution of work but there still remains a problem of coping with the peak or 'harvest' periods just as there is in other branches of horticulture and agriculture.

The problem can be eased by allowing staff numbers to run down during the autumn/winter period by natural wastage, and altering the methods of maintenance to avoid work in the main growing season, e.g. defer hedge-cutting to autumn or winter (with or without growth retardant sprays).

The extent of the remaining seasonal 'peak' will depend on the standard and type of maintenance but it can only be effectively dealt with by overtime working or the employment of casual labour. Overtime working is usually more effective as it uses the skilled men already employed and gives them an opportunity of extra earnings. Overtime cannot however be expected to cope for extended periods with more than about a ten per cent increase in the seasonal work, i.e. about four hours overtime per man over the whole workforce.

Seasonal workload problems are substantially eased if the direct labour or contract organisation is also employed on new capital works. Thus parks department responsibility for planting on new local authority housing sites can help. In new towns and on new university campus sites it is possible to plan for an economical mix of capital and maintenance works. Relatively heavy winter planting programmes balance the heavy peak summer maintenance periods.

Manning levels.　　　In order to fix manning levels it is essential to make an estimate of the peak work requirements for each site based on:

(a) A specification of the main operations and methods required to achieve the required standard of maintenance, e.g. mowing, clipping, spraying, etc.

(b) Measurements of the areas to which the various operations apply, e.g. area of lawns and borders, lengths and heights of hedges.

(c) Unit labour rates for the operations (if possible obtained from work study measurements) including rest times and times for preparation and putting away of equipment.

(d) An allowance for unpredictable and non-routine work (say ten per cent).

Before accepting the inevitability of this peak further efforts should be made to secure a more even spread of work.

The adjusted estimate will then provide a figure for the average number of man hours required to maintain each site during the peak season and this information can be used to build up a schedule of sites to be maintained by each man or team (as shown in Table 11.6) and thus arrive at manning levels for a geographical area.

Maintenance to standard. If the grounds staff are encouraged to take an interest in 'their' sites and encouraged to be flexible in their working to make best use of weather and soil conditions, they will inevitably develop an interest in the overall standard of maintenance. In so doing there is a likelihood that they will seek to impose their own standards. In some areas these standards may be aesthetically undesirable or be higher than the employer is willing to afford.

Grounds staff training. As a labour-intensive industry landscape maintenance depends very much on having a properly trained workforce but it has in the past depended to a large extent on being able to recruit men who have been trained by long experience in the large private estates. This source of staff is now considerably

TABLE 11.6: EXAMPLE. TEAM WORK SCHEDULE 1974 SEASON

Team area: Newton/Stanton Site	Chargehand: J. Brown Total number of men: 3
Site	*Average man hours per week April–Sept.*
Coronation gardens	19
Newtown sports centre	10
Newtown playing fields	12
Newtown library gardens	2
Wayden recreation ground	8
Langley playing fields	11
Stanton estate verges	8
Stanton roundabout	2
Stanton recreation ground	6
Ogden old people's home	17
Sub-total	95
Travelling time (3 men)	10
Wet weather and depot time (3 men)	15
Total	120

reduced and in the absence of an outside supply, organisations must make arrangements to train their own staff and any large organisation (say 100 men or above) should employ a person with specific responsibility for training of staff.

Proper training costs money and organisations must be prepared to bear the costs if they are to develop and maintain a properly trained workforce. In the long term it is likely that these costs will be largely repaid by better job satisfaction for the staff and lower staff turnover and by more effective working.

11.4 Machinery and equipment

11.4.1 Labour and machinery costs
Next to labour, machinery costs are usually the biggest single cost in grounds maintenance work, but the use of labour-saving machinery will significantly affect the actual labour requirements.

For many areas mowing equipment is the most important but there is a whole range of other mechnical aids, in common use, e.g. hedge-cutters, chain-saws, sprayers and cultivators. In many cases these machines do not, by themselves, make great savings in time but they do help to eliminate much of the hard physical labour in the work and at least the younger employees will expect to be equipped with a comprehensive range of machinery.

Organisations covering a large geographical area will also need to provide vehicles for the transport for men,

materials and machinery as well as tractors for field-scale operations.

11.4.2 Choice of equipment
A large number of firms are manufacturing machinery for grounds maintenance work and are constantly increasing the range and choice by the development of new and more sophisticated types. In large organisations it is therefore advisable to have one staff member with special knowledge and the responsibility for the choice and purchasing of vehicles and equipment and for the subsequent management of repair and replacement policies.

Because of the wide range of equipment that is available and the many different circumstances in which it could be used, there is little value in recommending any particular types but in making a choice of machinery these factors will need to be considered.

Area or volume of work. For expensive items of equipment there is little value in buying a large-capacity machine unless it can be used to the full. The manufacturers will often quote a rate of working for ideal level conditions but the effective capacity must take account of:

Lost time through wet weather, etc.
Travelling time from site to site.
Operator's time.
Downtime for routine servicing, breakdown and repair.

The extent to which a machine can be used will also depend on how much work can be made available for it without excessive transporting from site to site and without expecting staff to spend undue time on a single monotonous task, e.g. mowing large areas with a small machine. Table 11.7 indicates the likely capacity and operating costs for various types of mowing equipment.

Manœuvrability and size. It is often very difficult to use large heavy machines in small areas particularly if the landscape design is complicated. Where there are small raised or sunken areas or quandrangles it is often more convenient to use light, hand-powered mowers. The use of large machines in small areas can often cause considerable damage and counteract the labour saving advantages, for example by badly marking turf or breaking the bark away from trees. Changes in design can often facilitate the use of larger machines but these changes must not be allowed to alter the overall design concept merely for the sake of convenience of maintenance.

Noise and operator comfort. Long-term excessive engine noise can cause permanent hearing damage to the operator as well as increased fatigue. A noisy machine can also be a distraction and annoyance to other people, e.g. in offices and classrooms. Regulations are now in force to limit the noise levels in agricultural tractor cabs. Long-term exposure to engine and wheel vibrations in tractors is known to cause spinal injuries but these effects can be limited by antivibration seats. Engine vibrations from hand machines such as chainsaws can cause 'white fingers disease' and so antivibration handles are important for machines in continuous use.

Safety. All moving parts must be adequately guarded and rotary and flail mowers guarded to prevent stones and other objects being thrown out. Agricultural guarding regulations apply. On–off switches for engines should be clearly marked and easily accessible. Machines for use on banks must be fitted with an over-run preven-

TABLE 11.7: COMPARATIVE PERFORMANCE AND ESTIMATED OPERATING COSTS OF GRASS MOWING EQUIPMENT

Machine	Capital Cost 1978 (£)	Average Life (Years)	Running Cost per Year (fuel, depreciation and repairs) (£)	Cost per hour† (£)	Cutting Rate ha per hour (acres/hour)	Costs, £ per ha (per acre)
500 mm (20 in) cylinder mower (cuttings boxed off)	300	5	190	3·23‡	0·07 (0·17)	46·00 (19·00)
500 mm (20 in) rotary mower	150	2	195	3·25‡	0·05 (0·13)	65·00 (25·00)
650 mm (26 in) rotary mower	650	6	295	3·58‡	0·07 (0·17)	51·00 (21·00)
900 mm (34 in) cylinder mower	800	8	310	3·63‡	0·13 (0·33)	27·00 (11·00)
Triple motor mower 2·1 m (7 ft) cut	3,900	6	1,450	5·02§	0·6 (1·5)	8·32 (3·35)
Tractor-hauled gangmowers, 3 unit 2·1 m (7 ft) cut	1,400	10	350	4·38§	0·6 (1·5)	7·30 (2·90)
*5 unit 3·5 m (11½ ft) cut	4,600	10	860	4·75**	1·2 (3·0)	3·95 (1·60)
*7 unit 4·8 m (15 ft 8 in) cut	6,200	10	1,180	5·11**	1·6 (4·0)	3·20 (1·30)

* Including carrier
† Including labour cost at £2·60 per hour and tractor at £1·20 per hour where applicable
‡ Based on 300 hours use per year
§ Based on 600 hours use per year
** Based on 900 hours use per year.

tion device or a proper braking system. Safety cabs or frames are a legal requirement on agricultural tractors and are a wise addition to all tractors used for landscape maintenance and construction.

Ease of adjustment and servicing. It is essential that routine adjustments can be carried out as easily as possible using a minimum of tools, as if adjustments are difficult they are likely to be left undone.

Repair facilities and replacement policies. Even high quality long-life machines will still require overhauling by skilled mechanics. Where proper overhaul facilities are not available it may be preferable to buy cheaper short life machines and replace them at more frequent intervals.

Life of wearing parts and cost of replacements. The cost and life of wearing parts and engines should be assessed as accurately as possible as these costs can be significant, particularly for machines like rotary rakes and spikers.

Operator preferences. If an operator believes a machine to be a good one he will usually get the best out of it. Conversely, an operator will complain about even a good machine if for some reason he believes it to be a bad machine. Therefore whenever there is a choice between two very similar machines, the operator's preference should be given a high priority. It is in any case a good thing to involve the operator in the decision process as much as possible as he can give valuable advice on the comfort and ease of operation aspects.

11.4.3 Replacement and repair policies

The longer a vehicle or machine is kept in service, its capital cost per year or even month of use, is reduced. Also there will be a general increase in the costs of repair. This is expressed in Fig. 11.2.

The ideal time to replace a machine is when the minimum average annual cost point is reached and to determine this point, it is obviously essential to keep records of the costs of repairs and overheads, so that a soundly based replacement policy can be developed.

The graph of repair costs will, naturally, vary considerably depending on the way in which the equipment is used and so a detailed pattern of average annual costs will be unique to any one organisation and will need to be reviewed regularly to take into account any changes in

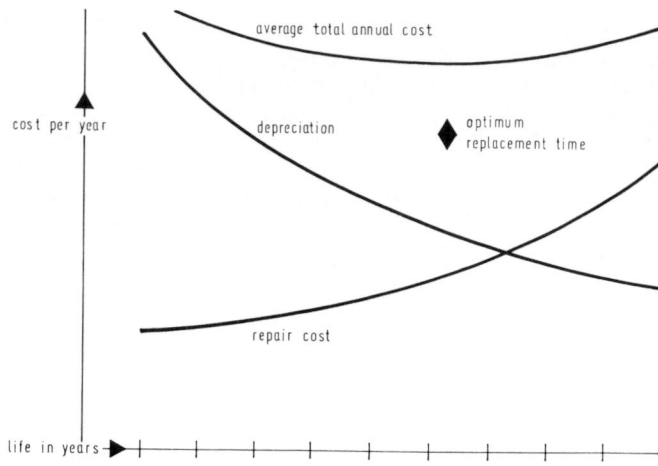

Fig. 11.2. REPLACEMENT – Graph illustrating depreciation, repair costs, and optimum replacement time before rise of total annual cost.

general policy that may influence the equipment use.

Once the basic data have been collected they can be used in alternative ways as shown:

(a) To decide on a replacement life for a particular type of machine and thereafter agree on a replacement programme for all these machines when they reach that age. This is the simplest method to operate particularly for advance budgeting but it does not take into account hardly used or carefully used machines which may either be long past replacement point or still be in good condition for further efficient use.

This situation can to a certain extent, be overcome by examining the machines at the time of replacement and retaining those still in good condition, either as a reserve or on the 'active' list until they require major overhauls.

(b) The inspection of each machine at the start of the overhaul season and to estimate the cost of overhauls and repairs anticipated for a future season's use. If this estimate will increase the average annual cost above the minimum for that type of machine, then it should be replaced in readiness for use at the start of the next season.

The disadvantage of this system is that it involves much estimation work, detailed dismantling and inspection of machines merely to establish the extent of repairs needed. However there is evidence to suggest that such individual decisions on machinery replacement can reduce annual operation costs.

216

11.5 Rates and costs of landscape maintenance

11.5.1 General labour costs

Labour costs are changing so rapidly, and therefore the rates expressed in man hours are considered to be a more accurate gauge of the costs, if they are multiplied by the current hourly rate for the particular grade of staff involved.

A series of rates are given for some of the landscape categories and other areas referred to in section 11.2.3.

The average limit for one man's performance in terms of hectares is also shown as this can be an important factor.

It is only possible to give firm maintenance estimates to specific areas when the various site conditions have been defined although it is possible to indicate the relative costs of maintaining the different components that are included in landscaped areas. Section 11.5.2 shows these relative costs in terms of man hours per year.

11.5.2 Annual labour requirements

Landscape category	Approx. man hours per year	
	Small units	Extensive units
1 *Fence lines.* Annual weed spray and rotary cut long grass.	3 hr/100 m	11 hr/1,000 m
2 *Hedges.* Formal hedge cut 4 times a year, e.g. privet.		
1·5 m high (approx. 5 ft)	8 hr/10 m	50 hr/100 m
2·5 m high (approx. 8 ft)	13 hr/10 m	95 hr/100 m
Hedge cut once a year, e.g. beech.		
1·5 m high	2 hr/10 m	18 hr/100 m
2·5 m high	4 hr/10 m	30 hr/100 m
3 *Large grass areas*	up to 0·5 ha	over 1 ha
Playing fields – mown up to once a week (24 cuts/year) with 5 unit tractor trailed gangmower (excluding travelling to and from site).	24 hr/ha	14 hr/ha
Rough grass cut with tractor mounted flail 4 times a year.	20 hr/ha	17 hr/ha
4 *Lawns and grass banks*		
Large lawns cut up to once a week with a 900 mm (approx. 36 in) cylinder mower.	11 hr/100 sq m	34 hr/1,000 sq m
Ditto with cuttings boxed off.	13 hr/100 sq m	45 hr/1,000 sq m
Smaller lawns cut up to once a week with a 500 mm (18–20 in) cylinder mower.	14 hr/100 sq m	70 hr/1,000 sq m
Ditto with cuttings boxed off.	17 hr/100 sq m	80 hr/1,000 sq m
Rough grass cut up to once a month with a hand-propelled rotary mower up to 500 mm (18–20 in).	4 hr/100 sq m	25 hr/1,000 sq m
Steep banks cut with a small rotary mower up to once a month.	8 hr/100 sq m	50 hr/1,000 sq m
Steep bank with grass controlled by one cut and two sprays of maleic hydrazide.	—	24 hr/1,000 sq m

NOTE
The hours shown for the smaller quantities are for isolated amounts and reflect the additional time that is used to prepare and put away equipment and tools for small amounts of work.

	Approx. man hours per year
5 *Shrub borders.* Light digging in winter and sprayed with simazine.	15 hr/100 sq m
Light digging in winter and hand hoed.	33 hr/100 sq m
6 *Ground cover* (established). Summer hand-weeding and clip and tidy in winter.	8 hr/100 sq m
7 *Annual bedding.* Spring and autumn replanting with hand hoeing in summer (excludes provision of plants).	80 hr/100 sq m
8 *Amenity woodland.* Established (excluding major felling).	up to 50 hr/ha
Newly planted (or tree screens).	up to 50–100 hr/ha
9 *Extensive parkland with woodland.*	
Without grazing animals.	say 90 hr/ha (up to 20 ha/man)
With grazing animals (excluding care of animals).	say 50 hr/ha
10 *Road verges* (grass cutting). Rural roads (four cuts a year with tractor mounted flail).	12 hr/km of road (mainly summer work up to 80 km/man)
Urban roads (12 cuts per year with pedestrian mower).	75 hr (up to 15 km/man)
11 *Urban recreation grounds*	300 hr/hectare (4 ha/man)
12 *Sports Grounds*	370 hr/hectare (up to 3 ha/man)
13 *Building surrounds.* Lawns, shrub borders, etc.	850 hr/hectare (up to 2 ha/man)
14 *Municipal gardens.* Lawns, borders, summer bedding, etc.	3,000 hr/hectare (up to 0·5 ha/man)

11.6 Maintenance and conservation techniques

11.6.1 Trees

These are considered here as individuals or when used in small groups for amenity purposes.

Indigenous broadleaf trees. Check with local authorities for any T.P.O. or conservation area restraints.

Arrange regular safety inspection by trained staff or tree specialists under contract. Protect trunks and lower limbs from damage by horses and cattle in grazed areas and parkland. Discourage ploughing or deep cultivation within an area equal to at least the canopy spread beneath the tree.

Diagnosis of poor growth is usually shown by 'stag heading' and die back on poor growth in the crown. Possible causes:

Over maturity – Root/crown relationship affected by alteration of water table particularly in urban and newly developed areas, from drainage schemes, excessive run-off from hard surfaces, etc. Existing trees on the edge of new reservoirs or lakes may die from excessive water-logging of the root system.

Pest and diseases – Consult local Forestry Officer or Tree Specialist.

Compaction – This is most likely to occur when trees are in development sites and inadequate protection has caused contractors' vehicles to severely compress the soil above the tree root system. Ripping, aeration and feeding may help.

Spillage of oils, chemicals, etc. – Farm effluent accumulation. There is no remedy if damage has gone too far. Localised dumping of road salt, especially in roadside laybys near trees can be very serious

Subterranean gas leakage – Regular inspection of all trees should detect some of those symptoms or causes of

Plate 11.7. Tree maintenance. Unploughed zone beneath mature trees in ploughed pasture. This shows the minimum that can safely be left.

damage before it is too late. Large-scale surveys can be carried out with the aid of aerial photographic interpretation, using infra-red techniques to analyse tree health.

Flowering trees. These are widely used in urban areas and private gardens, and include Japanese Cherries, ornamental *Malus* (Flowering Crab Apples), *Laburnum* and others. In the context of the indigenous trees, this group provide relatively short-term attractions for the appropriate settings. Trees that associate well with man's living and working environment, they generally establish well and thrive in urban environments with remarkable resistance to atmospheric pollution and other unfavourable factors. Maintenance is an increasing problem after some 30–40 years when the trees have generally reached their middle or later life. Almonds and cherries are very prone to bacterial canker and other dieback conditions. Renewal must be envisaged after this period, although some species of cherries and other flowering trees may have a much longer life.

Many trees in this group are grafted or budded on rootstocks either at ground level or on stems, and disparities in the growth rates of stock and scion variety can cause unsightly overgrowths or swellings. Suckering can be a problem with ornamental plum varieties grafted on to plum rootstocks.

Conifers. The majority of conifers used in planting schemes have been introduced from temperate regions of such countries as in N. America, Europe and Asia. The finest specimens of the American and Asian conifers are to be found in the cool west and north-west of Britain, and in sheltered valleys on lime-free soil elsewhere. The European pines are the most adaptable to the urban and developed landscape as long-term trees, although many others have value as hedging, screening and decorative planting.

With the exception of yew (*Taxus baccata*) and redwood (*Sequoia sempervirens*) and a few others, little or no regeneration occurs of side or basal growth if conifers are cut hard back or felled. Many of the hedging species such as Lawson cypress (*Chamaecyparis Lawsoniana*) gradually thin at the base and little can be done to remedy this. Clipping and pruning of conifers is best done in early spring or summer and hard cutting back is not recommended as a general rule.

Conifers benefit from a basal mulch and until well established avoid grass or weed growth competition.

Atmospheric pollution can be detrimental and excessive drought with conifers growing in containers or 'rain shadows' of buildings can be disastrous. Spreading and rounded shaped species are liable to disfigurement in heavy snowfall. The American and Asiatic species have

Plate 11.8. Hedgerow pattern. An example of a vestigial tree and hedgerow pattern on an intensive farm that needs rationalisation.

Plate 11.9. Hedgerow management. An infrequently trimmed belt of native species. Note good flail treatment of verge beneath and the contrasting effect on the opposite side.

a limited life span in adverse sites and thin and brown rapidly from the base, generally looking poor and stunted.

11.6.2 Rural hedgerows and hedges

Hedgerow management can be important for the following reasons:

Maintenance of stockproof barriers on farmland (the original primary reason for enclosure). Now it is less important with increasing field sizes, temporary leys, fencing etc.

Local shelter for stock and also for walkers or farm staff especially where the footpaths run beside hedges.

Wildlife conservation, game conservation, visual amenity and to provide farm timber.

Despite continuing losses of hedgerows from the landscape there still remains a tremendous number of hedges in the British Isles and estimates put this at more than 500,000 miles. The recent controversy between conservation interest and the necessary economic return farmers are seeking from all land has led to some encouraging compromise hedgerow policy experiments (see bibliography). The following guidelines are suggested for a hedgerow policy that might be worked out with a farmer on lowland with a normal stock or arable enterprise:

Hedgerow survey. Assess visual, physical and ecological characteristics of the hedges on the farm. Students or school children could be enlisted for this survey, which would include notes on the plant spcies, estimate of wild life and record of the management regimes. Hedgerow trees would be an important part of the survey, where present.

Hedgerow pattern. Relate the hedgerow pattern to the owner's proposals for middle- and long-term management programmes for the farm. Agree on 'key' hedges that should be retained and those that could be grubbed out. Look for possible sites for new hedges or strengthening of old or 'gappy' lengths.

Hedgerow trees. Encourage hedgerow trees wherever possible.

Hedgerow-cutting regimes. Much of lowland Britain was traditionally enclosed with thorn and mixed hedges laid at intervals and hand pruned annually to create a thick barrier usually not higher than 1·2–1·5 m (approx. 4–5 ft) in height. The present face of the British lowland countryside is changing fairly rapidly, partly due to hedgerow loss, but also due to hedgerow management practices.

Hedges allowed to grow with little or no pruning form 5–6 m (approx. 16–20 ft) belts, particularly when the dominant species is thorn or hedge maple. Such hedges are of good value as visual elements, and for shelter and conservation. After a number of years however such hedgerows develop into a line of spreading tree forms with limited barrier effect. This should be foreseen by the landowner and manager.

If hedgerows are partially managed by side trimming only this may create tall straight hedges which may be topped occasionally, or when the side cutting only extends to 1·5–1·8 m (say 5–6 ft) the upper parts of the hedge can be encouraged to spread out into a canopy giving a 'pleached' effect. This probably happens by accident on some roadside hedges when the cutting machinery has limited height of cut.

Hedgerows may be cut once or twice annually using one of the following techniques:

Plate 11.10. An overgrown hedge massacred by the flail mower. Such treatment cannot restore a hedge in this condition. Severe cutting back, some planting and selection of a few existing trees is recommended.

Tractor-mounted flail mower, which is being increasingly used. Once hedges have been 'cut' with these for several years a reasonably compact and satisfactory appearance develops. Overgrown hedgerows and irregularly cut thickets can look appalling after the initial 'bash and mash' of the flail.

Tractor-mounted cutter bar which makes neater, straighter-sided hedges. More suited for overgrown hedges and thick scrub.

Tractor-mounted rotary saw for heavier work, hedge tops, overhanging branches, and less manœuvrable than the flail.

Hand-cutting is now largely abandoned on grounds of economics. Hand-laying is still practised in some areas, with mechanical management in the intervening years.

Road and boundary hedges and those alongside footpaths and bridle tracks may have to be trimmed twice yearly, in June or July and again in winter. Other hedges can be cut once a year in the winter months.

Hedgerow species and management. For new farm and open country hedges the following species are recommended for foundation planting (depending on soil and regional limitations) that respond well to consistent management:

Thorn (*Crataegus monogyna*)

Field maple (*Acer campestre*)
Hornbeam (*Carpinus betulus*)
Myrobalan plum (*Prunus cerasifera*)
Holly (*Ilex aquifolium*)
Beech (*Fagus sylvatica*)

Diversity can be created by adding the following:

Hazel (*Corylus avellana*)
Goat willow (*Salix caprea* and other species)
Dogwood (*Cornus sanguinea*)
Dog rose (*Rosa canina*)
Wild privet (*Ligustrum vulgare*).

11.6.3 Turf and grass

Lawn and sportsfields turf is covered mainly in Chapter 9. This section deals primarily with the more extensive grass areas managed to more 'natural' conditions to meet the outfield needs of much landscape work. Manpower, fuel and financial restrictions will probably have significant effects on the maintenance standards of amenity grasslands and with increasing public interest in the establishment of conservation habitats for plant and animal life associated with public open spaces, banks and road verges, this section concentrates on techniques for creating specific grass or turf zones each with a certain objective in view. The following tree main zones can be identified.

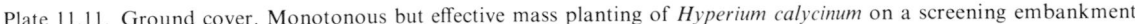

Plate 11.11. Ground cover. Monotonous but effective mass planting of *Hyperium calycinum* on a screening embankment.

Plate 11.12. Ground cover. Attractive cover of *Mahonia aquifolium* in an urban park.

Intensive use, public areas, close-cut zones – Associated with buildings, approach drives, schools, visibility and walking areas etc. Traditional reasonably close mown turf 20–25 mm (approx. ¾–1 in) giving a well-groomed, smooth sward effect, needing 25–30 cuts per year (see Chapter 9 – Turf).

Objective is functional, visually complementary to high maintenance buildings, hard surfaces, ornamental areas, etc.

Intermediate zone – Grass is maintained as far as is possible to 100–125 mm (approx. 4–5 in) by using flail or rotary cutting equipment set to 100 mm (approx. 4 in); needs only 4–6 cuts per season depending on soil, site, etc., beginning in early May. Objective is more informal, natural paddock appearance, reduced maintenance, suited to road verges, embankments, parkland, edging zones between smooth grass and trees/shrubs or hay meadow grassland.

Consistent cutting over the years can slowly build up a reasonably interesting diverse flora, although seeding is restricted by the cutting regime.

'Natural' or 'wild' grassland zone – This may have the attractive meadowland effect with a mixture of grasses and flowering herbs associated with permanent 'hay meadow' pastures and traditional farming. There is considerable interest in re-creating or establishing this type of grassland in appropriate settings and circumstances in historic parkland and country parks, road verges and extensive public open spaces.

Objectives are low maintenance and conservation of a wide range of plants. Guidelines for establishing such flowering meadows are shown on p. 223.

Plate 11.13. Grass on a rural road verge. Three flail cuts per year for visibility strip with the uncut area left to develop attractive flora and ultimately scrub.

222

(a) Choose grass mixtures of mainly short seeded finer species such as fescues and bents. Include legumes such as clovers, trefoils and vetches (depending upon availability). In established grass areas, where coarse tussock grasses such as cocksfoot (*Dactylis*) and Yorkshire fog (*Holcus*) may be dominant, the cutting regimes for 'Intermediate Zones' for 2–3 years will gradually reduce them. Alternatively, an application of the herbicide 'Dalapon' in early spring can reduce these coarse, invasive grasses.

(b) Maintenance. The most critical and difficult aspect. Two cuts per year as follows:

Mow with tractor mounted cutter bar or auto-scythe in late June or early July when seeding of all species is occurring. Remove all cut material as hay or organic waste. This aspect is the most important and probably the most problematic part of this regime. A forage harvester might be used with associated trailer to remove mowings, if practicable and so prevent a build-up of fertility which will limit diversity.

Repeat mowing or cutting with a flail or rotary cutter to 100–150 mm (approx. 4–6 in) in August and September. Spot treat with herbicide, areas or specimens of noxious weeds such as docks, thistles and some but not all nettles. Coarse tussock grasses can be spot controlled with Dalapon or Paraquat or growth retardants.

Introduce seed of other meadow species if and when available, preferably from local sources. Excessive trampling, irregular cutting, failure to remove cuttings will all tend to reduce the diversity and appearance of these critically managed meadowlands which are not recommended in intensively used areas, or very small pocket-scale habitats. Delayed first cut can create a fire hazard if left after July. Litter accumulation can be a problem.

Growth retardants and grass maintenance. There is considerable potential for using maleic hydrazide (and probably newly introduced materials with a similar mode of action) in grass maintenance programmes. Maleic hydrazide has been available and in use for over ten years now but for a number of practical reasons, its application is still limited and controversial, but high costs are quoted by some authorities as the main limiting factor.

Timing of application – This is very critical; usually applied when the grass is in first spring flush, in early April. Where coarse fast growing grasses such as rye (*Lolium*) and cocksfoot (*Dactylis*) are widespread, it is advisable to cut first to 75–100 mm (approx. 3–4 in) in

Plate 11.14. Trunk road on the fringe of an urban area. Scalloped bays of turf mown five to six times annually between groups and thickets of native and exotic species.

Plate 11.15. Motorway verge. Grassland merging to new woodland. Visibility strip flail cut three to four times annually. Native species established in unmown herb and grass layer. A recommended system.

223

March and then spray in early April.

Dosage rate – Follow maker's recommendations accurately or grass can be scorched with excessive rates. Weather after application is critical as heavy rain after application can greatly reduce the effect of this material.

Effects appear to be accumulative over the season. It may be necessary to cut herbage later in the first season of application or apply a second spray. In subsequent years one application only may be sufficient in early Spring. Differential effects on grass species and herbage may be expected so that an even smooth low growing sward is seldom achieved. Long-term effects seem to show the gradual suppression of coarse grasses and vigorous perennial herbs, and the encouragement of finer 'bottom grasses' and low growing herbs. Selective herbicide may need to be included in the mixture for immediate control of broad-leaved 'noxious' weeds such as docks, thistles and ragwort.

Main areas of potential uses include steep banks, gradients, road verges, extensive intermediate zone grassland, difficult sites such as cemeteries, bases of obstacles in grass, etc. Maleic hydrazide is of little use for close mown grass control, particularly if the surface is subject to wear.

11.7 Herbicides and landscape maintenance

11.7.1 Herbicides and the public
Many people regard herbicides and other agricultural chemicals, purely as dangerous chemicals that are a threat to themselves, wildlife and the environment in general. While it is true that some herbicides, along with many other chemicals in day-to-day use, can be dangerous if they are misused, they are extremely valuable for modern food production and agriculture and can also be of significant value in landscape maintenance. There is also a popular misconception that *all* herbicides are poisonous and dangerous. Although for their own safety, it is probably a good thing that the lay public have this view, the modern herbicides have widely differing properties and so whenever complaints are made against their use, it is essential to identify the active chemicals that have been used.

11.7.2 Safeguards for use
As the modern herbicides are generally very powerful and effective, they can easily be abused and cause considerable damage to cultivated or desirable natural plants, either through ignorance or deliberate misuse. It is therefore essential wherever herbicides are used that:

(*a*) The appropriate chemicals are chosen by a properly qualified person who understands their mode of action and properties.

Plate 11.16. Hard surface areas where the use of herbicides is essential. (Acknowledgement, Geigy Agricultural Chemicals.)

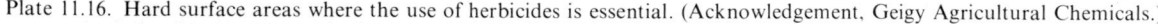

TABLE 11.8

Situation	Active Chemical	Notes
AREAS REMOTE FROM TREES AND SHRUBS		
e.g. Factory surrounds	Diuron	
Around industrial plant	Manuron	
Railway sidings	Sodium chlorate	
Car parks	Aminotriazole/ Atrazine	Persistent control of up to 12 months from
Foundation bases	Dichlobenil/ Chlorthiamid	one application
CLOSE TO TREES AND SHRUBS		
e.g. Roadside gulleys and pavements	Simazine + amino- triazole	
Pathways	Dichlobenil	
Fence lines	Chlorthiamid	
Mowing strips	Paraquat + Diquat	Quick kill but no residual effect
ROSE AND SHRUB BORDERS		
(Persistent control 1 application per season)	Simazine	Will not kill established weeds.
	Simazine + Aminotriazole	
	Dichlobenil	
	Diuron + Paraquat	Must not be sprayed on to shrub foliage.
NEWLY PLANTED TREES AND SHRUBS		
	Paraquat + Diquat	Must not be sprayed on to shrub foliage No residual effect, may need up to 4 applications per season.
LAWN AND PLAYING FIELDS		
	2,4 D M.C.P.A. Mecoprop Dichlorprop	Controls clover and chickweeds.
IN OR NEAR LAKES AND WATERWAYS		
(see note below)	Dalapon Paraquat	Emergent weeds
	Chlorthiamid Diquat Dichlobenil	Floating weeds

Plate 11.17. *Accurate control of herbicides can be achieved with suitable equipment and trained staff. There is no need for spray drift damage.*

(b) The operators are properly trained and experienced in the application of weedkillers and are fully aware of the possible damage to themselves, other people, domestic and wild animals and plant life.

There are a number of general safety rules that apply to the use of all agricultural and horticultural chemicals and specific precautions for individual chemicals are published by the Ministry of Agriculture, Fisheries and

NOTE 1. Application of weedkillers to water courses may endanger fish and lead to illegal pollution and the appropriate river authority must be consulted. See also the Code of Practice for the *Use of Herbicides on Weeds in Watercourses and Lakes*, published by the Ministry of Agriculture, Fisheries and Food.
NOTE 2. Some trees and shrubs are susceptible to the more commonly used herbicides such as Simazine or Paraquat even where correct rates of application are used. Lists of susceptible species are given in the current edition of the *Weed Control Handbook*.

Food under the Pesticides Safety Precautions Scheme. In addition the Ministry publish a list of approved agricultural chemicals to assist users and advisers in the selection of suitable chemicals.

11.7.3 Herbicides for landscape work

The range of chemicals available for landscape maintenance work is constantly expanding as new chemicals are developed but detailed information on herbicide use is contained in the latest edition of the *Weed Control Handbook*. In addition changes in the price structure due to alteration to licensing and manufacturers' agreements can have a significant influence on the final choice for any particular use.

There are three main types of herbicides that are used for landscape work.

(a) Contact herbicides – foliage applied, e.g. Paraquat or Diquat that kill all green tissue on contact.

(b) Translocated herbicides – foliage applied. These include most of the selective weedkillers such as 2,4 D and M.C.P.A. that can be used for killing broad leaved weeds in turf.

(c) Residual herbicides – soil applied. These usually remain active in the soil for some time, up to a year, and are taken up into the plant via the root system. They are usually total weedkillers but can be used as selective weedkillers at low doses, e.g. Simazine.

A selection of commonly used herbicides is given in Table 11.8 but more detailed information should be obtained from the references given and from trade literature on the use of special formulations.

11.8 Plant pests and diseases

11.8.1 Introduction

Incidences of serious pest infestations and disease epidemics of plants, mainly occur where large-scale production of mono-crops has been in practice for a considerable period of time.

In the agricultural and horticultural industries there is a continual need to carry out regular pest and disease control programmes on crop plants. Chemicals are normally used for this control although there is increasing interest in using natural predators and organisms to achieve what is termed biological control.

In landscape maintenance, where mature or established plantings are usually of a very diverse age and species structure, there is much less likelihood of a serious pest or disease problem. A notable exception has been the Dutch elm disease outbreak which has been disastrous in some areas (see 11.8.3). Also in extensive forestry plantations, and woodlands, grey squirrels can build up to devastating numbers, and plagues of leaf-eating larvae of some moth and sawfly species can occasionally defoliate areas of plantations.

It is strongly recommended that a specialist from the Ministry of Agricultural Development Advisory Service be approached in the first instance with plant pest or disease problems of a general nature, and such specialists as the County Forestry Officer, or regional Horticultural Colleges or Institute staff for more specific problems.

11.8.2 Pests

A brief guide to the more commonly occurring types of pests and damage likely to be met in general landscape maintenance follows with notes on control measures (p. 227).

11.8.3 Plant diseases

Reference to *Pathology of Trees and Shrubs* by T. R. Pearce is strongly recommended for detailed studies of the major diseases and other damaging agencies (fire, wind, frost, waterlogging) of trees and shrubs, and to the relevant Forestry Commission leaflets.

The most commonly occurring are briefly summarised here.

Armellaria root rot. Honey fungus. *Armellaria mellia.* A widespread, sporadic and locally serious root disease attacking trees, shrubs and even some perennials. Trees or shrubs infected usually show poor growth symptoms or die suddenly in full growth. Infection comes from dead stumps by extensive 'bootlace' or rhizomorphs travelling through the soil. It is common in gardens and orchards.

Control is difficult. Eradicate stumps and sources of infection. Soil injection with strong fungicidal chemicals is possible. Active reasearch in progress. There are some promising results now with 'armillatox' (Forestry Commission leaflet No. 6).

Fomes. Root rot. This is primarily a forestry disease and mainly serious in conifers (Forestry Commission leaflet No. 5).

Dutch elm disease. *Ceratostomella ulmi.* The outbreak of this disease and its rapid spread through first the lowland counties of southern and central England is well documented by the Forestry Commission.

Control measures have been widely investigated and the injection method using the fungicide 'Benlate' has only given limited control. Resistant elm species and varieties

Group	Damage	Control
ANIMALS		
Grey squirrel	Severe damage to young and establishing trees.	Consult Forestry Commission. Trapping, shooting.
Rabbits/hares	'Barking' of young trees, winter damage to newly-planted trees/shrubs.	Plastic tree guards. Repellent paints.
Bullfinches/small birds	Usually widespread stripping of flower buds. Rosaceous trees and shrubs and wide range woody, amenity plants. Usually late winter, early spring.	Difficult on large scale Netting, repellents
INSECTS AND OTHERS		
Leaf-eating larvae of some moth and saw-fly species. 'Tortrix' moths especially widespread.	Occasionally extensive de-foliation of some trees – oak, willow and shrubs, roses, etc. Forestry Plantation.	Not usually economic or desirable on a large scale. Natural predators usually take control in due course.
LEAF-SUCKING PESTS		
Especially aphids (greenfly), blackfly and red spider mite	Seasonal and localised 'build up' of aphids on trees, especially some species of lime (sticky honeydew effect), plum trees, and serious on honeysuckle and amenity and crop plants. Red spider can cause yellowing and premature defoliation of some trees especially limes and shrubs in dry, warm summers.	Natural predators such as birds, ladybirds, hoverfly larvae usually efficient control in large-scale landscape areas. Use systemic insecticides in garden and small-scale areas where feasible and the infestation severe enough. Plant aphid-resistant limes.
SOIL-BORNE PESTS		
Chafer grubs, wireworms, leather jackets, cutworm, etc.	Occasionally serious on newly planted annuals and softer plants.	Soil applied pesticides only where situations really demands this.

are being considered and there is the distinct possibility that this epidemic will eventually die out, allowing regeneration of elms from resistant hedgerow suckers and a policy of re-planting (Forestry Commission leaflets Nos 19 and 57).

Bacterial canker and canker diseases.   Widespread incidence of canker diseases is due to a number of pathogens, and particularly serious on some species of poplars (Balsam group), willows and ornamental cherries and other *Prunus* cultivars. They cause dieback and ugly cankers on trunks and lateral branches and eventually are fatal in many cases.

Select resistant species. Regular tree surgery is important wherever disease is noticed.

Fire blight. *Erwinia amylovora*.   A bacterial disease that was first detected in east Kent in 1948 on Laxtons Superb Pear trees. It subsequently spread to many parts of east and south-east England infected many woody members of the Rosaceae family, but particularly commercial pear and apple varieties and such genera as *Cotoneaster*, *Crataegus*, *Sorbus* and *Pyracantha*. The Fireblight Disease Order of 1958 made this disease notifiable.

Symptoms are a scorching and die back of twigs and branches and flowering shoots during the current season. Substantial die back occurs and cankers are formed on the infected branches. Dead leaves do not fall. A complete kill of trees and shrubs can occur. There is no real control for the disease. Cutting out infected wood is essential and the removal and burning of all diseased material.

The initial concern over the rate of spread of this disease has been followed by a more realistic view, since there now seem to be only sparodic outbreaks, mainly in the south and east of the country. Any suspect cases should always be referred to the local A.D.A.S. office.

Coral spot. *Nectria cinnabarina* **and related species.** This seems to be increasing in incidence and causing more significant damage. It is die-back disease of twigs and branches, associated more often with dead or dying tissues as a secondary infection. Evidence now points to coral spot becoming a primary pathogen causing damage or even death of trees and shrubs. The bright orange pustules that are dotted all over diseased areas are clear symptoms, usually seen in late winter or early spring. Regular maintenance and prompt cutting out of diseased tissue may effect a cure. Paint over all pruning cuts as a precaution. The damage resulting from flail mowing of overgrown hedges may help to spread this disease.

Fungi causing decay and stain in living trees. Saprophytic or parasitic fungi attacking the dead heart wood of trees. Infection is determined by the age and health of the tree, and a regular tree surgery programme should reduce entry of these pathogens into the tree. See diagram p. 51. Peace: *Pathology of Trees and Shrubs*, 'The methods by which decay enters a tree.'

Water mark disease. Of cricket bat willows particularly in Essex and Hertfordshire has similar external symptoms to Honey Fungus attack (see Forestry Commission leaflet No. 20).

11.9 Conservation

11.9.1 The need for conservation

Conservation in the context of this chapter is seen as the management of wildlife as a natural resource. The Nature Conservancy Council's definition of 'wildlife' is 'the sum total of the animals and plants ... excluding domesticated and captive animals and introduced plants grown for home purposes'. Such wildlife can therefore be regarded as a highly important renewable biological resource which must inevitably overlap with other categories such as forestry, and agriculture.

Although the whole business of conservation is now an emotive and popular trend, it is necessary to present serious and logical justifications for any policies or techniques for the role of conservation in landscape, particularly when insensitive clients or strong economic pressures are involved.

An excellent summary of the justifications for conservation of wildlife is contained in the 'Sinews for Survival' Report following the Stockholm Conference for 1972. They are:

'(*a*) As a contributory component of ecological stability and as a monitor of environmental pollution.

(*b*) For the maintenance of genetic variability and the provision of a source of renewable biological resources.

(*c*) For the needs of scientific research into the environment.

(*d*) For its cultural and recreational value and as a component of the aesthetic quality of the landscape.

(*e*) For environmental education.

(*f*) For the economic value of its resource, scientific and recreational components.

(*g*) To provide future generations with a wide choice of biological capital.

(*h*) For moral and ethical reasons.'

11.9.2 Agencies for conservation

There are a number of important groups concerned with various aspects of wildlife conservation, but probably the two most important ones are as follows:

The Nature Conservancy Council. Until recently the Nature Conservancy, established by Royal Charter in 1949. It establishes, *manages* and maintains nature reserves in Great Britain, providing scientific advice on the conservation and control of the natural flora and fauna. The two broad categories of nature reserve are the *National Nature Reserves* (N.N.R.) which are important areas of biological and scientific interest, owned or leased by the Nature Conservancy Council, and the *Sites of Special Scientific Interest* (S.S.S.I.) which are frequently under private ownership with advisory and other links with the N.C.C.

It should be emphasised that the Nature Conservancy Council's main objective is the management of these reserves as ecosystems for wildlife rather than recreation or public use, and where a National Nature Reserve coincides with a popular public 'beauty spot' additional management problems are involved.

Society for the Promotion of Nature Reserves. This voluntary organisation founded in 1912 is now the principal central co-ordinating body or association for the County Conservation and Naturalists Trusts. These Trusts are playing an increasingly important role in the conservation work of counties where they exist. Their officers should always be consulted when any matters needing expert local information and advice arise.

Full particulars of these two organisations with regard to office addresses and telephone numbers are given in the *Countryside Information Directory* published annually by the Countryside Commission. This useful Directory contains information on many other important groups who are actively concerned with the countryside and its management.

11.9.3 Conservation and the landscape architect

Discerning and enterprising landscape architects and professionals in related fields are in an important position to influence or demonstrate conservation principles and practices to many clients with whom they work both in the public and private sectors.

Reference has already been made in this chapter to the importance of a sensitive knowledge of a site or region in order to conserve its important qualities and the following are further guide lines for integrating conservation of wildlife into landscape projects.

Plate 11.18. Conservation areas on a University campus. Herb layer of remnants of oak/chestnut coppice returning under enlightened management. This flora includes cow wheat (*Melampyrum prateuse*) food plant for the scarce Heath fritillary butterfly.

Existing sites. *Survey* – Careful appraisal of all natural features. Close consultation with local naturalist group, etc. Detailed ecological survey. Check for any 'designated' habitats during the initial consultation. Notes on existing and potential conservation value of the site or vegetation type. Existing management or lack of it should be assessed.

Design – Integrate important areas or features for conservation into the design, i.e. as existing hedgerows retained for car park screening, wet habitats, water courses retained or enhanced as features; diverse grassland habitats retained.

Development – Ensure that all features or areas for conservation are adequately protected before contract work begins. Retain close liaison with the contractor who will probably need the relevant clauses in the contract specification dealing with the retention of 'conservation areas' *carefully explained to him*. An area of scrub and brambles may be very important for its fauna and flora, but may be an untidy mess to the contractor.

Maintenance: see also 'Habitat management' – Probably the most important and the most critical part of the whole business. Management of any area for conservation involves the maintenance of a delicate balance between a well-cared-for landscape and an apparently neglected one. Excessive 'tidying up' of woodland ground flora, shrub layer, cleaning out of hedge bottoms, close cutting of extensive grass areas, and use of herbicides, are all important and all too frequently applied management practices that can wreck all hopes of promoting wild life and interest to a given area. Here carefully planned objectives, discussions with the managers and close supervision during the early stages become essential factors in determining the success of a scheme.

Planning new sites. The opportunity of incorporating less intensively managed areas in any scheme should always be taken. Large sites for hospitals, university campus development, and power stations in rural locations are all cases where 'outfield' land may be protected during the construction period and then deliberately left in a semi-wild condition. The Central Electricity Generating Board has adopted this low cost maintenance policy in appropriate locations. (Examples in the C.E.G.B. Midland Region include Drakelow Power Station and the ash disposal site at Peterborough. In both cases field studies are encouraged.)

229

Plate 11.19. Conservation on golf courses. Well-designed and managed golf courses offer excellent conservation habitats.

Similar opportunities may occur in association with large-scale playing facilities. In this category golf courses are especially interesting examples. Courses developed on hilly or upland marginal land, or on historic estates, exploit the natural features and usually retain indigenous trees, woodland, scrub and grassland. Zones of grass-cutting regimes between the close main 'fairways' and the 'rough', where consistently carried out without the use of herbicides or excessive doses of fertilisers, can favour the development of a rich grassland flora and associated wildlife. Scrub, and woodland, and natural streams and wet areas are regarded as 'hazards' to the game and at the same time create very effective visual landscape features. Golf courses also lend themselves as wildlife habitats. They cover considerable areas of land, with woodland, copses, water courses, and extensive areas of grassland. The disturbance factor to wildlife is limited and a very diverse range of habitats are invariably found on the larger courses.

11.9.4 Educational value of conservation

This is undoubtedly the most important aspect in achieving the ideas of conservation in the future.

The present valuable work of the agencies referred to earlier in this section together with Field Studies courses, local Education Authorities and schools is doing much to promote interest and understanding of nature in the countryside. There is still far too little being done to demonstrate the importance of nature conservation in urban and suburban environments. A large scale public

relations exercise is first needed to show to public (including the rate payers) and management staff what could be done. There are undoubted problems in changing maintenance standards in high density areas to encourage wildlife other than the two-legged species. 'Long grass collects litter and is a fire hazard' is the usual objection. A realistic approach is needed here. Designers, maintenance staff and conservation specialists must evolve a policy together with the full participation of the public.

Schools and colleges may have extensive surrounds where pilot conservation projects could be initiated. Universities or botanic gardens could also assist with such schemes. At Kew Gardens, 'conservation areas' have been established where the public are clearly told of the objectives, and the maintenance staff, too.

Country parks also offer considerable potential for practical research into discovering systems and techniques for reconciling wildlife interests with public use. Any projects should be clearly demonstrated to the users and suitable notices erected to invite the co-operation of the public.

11.9.5 Conservation techniques

Woodland. When management is based upon ecological and geological principles wildlife communities will develop with the trees. Sustained forest management must be so based. Eighty per cent of the wildlife in Britain is of woodland origin. Measures for improvement of

230

woodland habitat fall into five classes, plant diversity, structural diversity, other habitats, water, shelter.

Plant diversity – needs the following:

(*a*) A wide variety of species including shrub and herb layer.

(*b*) Broadleaf species included among conifers.

(*c*) Conifers in broadleaf woodlands to give shelter and variety.

(*d*) When converting broadleaf to conifer, broadleaves left as single trees; as margins to roads, rides, glades, water courses and around ponds; as groups or clumps, together with shrub and field layer.

(*e*) In conifers, encouragement of natural regeneration of broadleaves.

(*f*) Concentration on native species in amenity planting.

(*g*) Insect fauna, associated with oak, birch, willow, elm, Scots pine, aspen, alder, beech, hawthorn, hazel, blackthorn. Less on introduced species, e.g. larch, spruce.

(*h*) Protection of the field layer from trampling.

Structural diversity – can be retained or achieved by:

(*a*) Retaining or creating canopy, under-storey, shrub and field layer.

(*b*) Maintaining diversity by wide distribution of age classes when there are few species in the woodland.

(*c*) Mixing with broadleaves wherever possible.

(*d*) Heavy thinning to promote field layer.

(*e*) Small felling coupes scattered in time and place.

Other habitats – to be kept or provided:

(*a*) Large old trees such as oak, beech, elm, Scots pine, left on edges. Some old trees may be left to die provide: standing dying wood, standing dead wood, large fallen logs. These are all special habitats. Small logs stacked in shade give habitats for insects, hence food for birds which also nest in old trees.

(*b*) Flowers and fruit. Crab apples, berried trees and shrubs, etc., are valuable as a habitat and as food.

(*c*) Fungi. Most of these are harmless in the forest.

(*d*) Paths, rides and glades. Avoid long, straight rides which act as wind tunnels. Create curves and bends inset into the forest, and keep margins, shrubby. Retain front hollows as glades.

Water – This is a vital habitat, often lost in development projects. Try to adopt principles as follows:

(*a*) Maintain existing streams and ponds.

(*b*) Construct ponds and small lakes with shelving sides and islands.

(*c*) Keep some open margins with scattered native vegetation.

(*d*) Avoid conifers on water edge.

Plate 11.20. A dead tree as a habitat on a farm. Note also the public footpath left unploughed by the farmer.

Plate 11.21. Extending an existing copse on a farm. This marginal area was fenced by the farmer and then planted with indigenous species by a student conservation corps.

(e) Prevent unnecessary drainage. Leave some bogs, frost hollows, etc.

Shelter and quiet for wildlife –

(a) Remember the amelioration effect of woodlands on climate.

(b) Avoid forest operations during breeding season, especially April, May.

Pesticides and poisons should be used selectively, sparingly and sensibly and according to instructions. Unused pesticides must be sorted carefully and used containers and residues disposed of to tips or sites where they will not cause damage.

What is apparently ecological untidiness is sometimes a necessity. Avoid urban park-like vegetational tidiness. Leave islands and margins of scrub, brakes of bramble and thorn, piles of rotting wood, dead trees. Do the minimum work to get the new crop through. Money thus saved can be spent on positive conservation measures.

Costs need not be great. There has been little systematic or costed investigation, but indications are that there is no dramatic difference in cost between materialistically based and ecologically based management.

Wildlife notes – Out of the 100 or so species of birds that breed in woodland 32 have nested in conifer. All 29

species of mammals are found in conifer as well as broadleaved woodland. Butterflies are insects of glades and felled areas. They depend on the herb and shrub layer. Some depend on oak, elm, willow, etc. Provided food plant is present they will exist in conifer.

Woodland herb layer. A rich and biologically important layer especially with deciduous oak and beech woods, but equally very fragile under excessive pressure from visitors, or mismanagement of the woodland.

Visitor pressure – Positive deterrents such as fencing or notices but preferably more subtle deflection with barriers of woodland, coppice or shrub, bramble areas, careful planning of pathways, trails and other drives to lead people away from vulnerable areas.

Management – Herb layer vegetation can suffer from excessive scrub and coppice development which suppress the more light-sensitive species. Rotational coppice management, the creation of glades or clearings beneath the main canopy and the zoning of scrub areas can encourage and maintain the rich bluebell, moss, anemone and other associations of species of woodland. Birdlife is also maintained in scrub areas.

232

11.9.6 Wetlands

Existing ponds and ditches are very important since the wildlife has usually achieved a stability and variety over the years. On many farms and estates the only open water life is in open ditches and streams and old ponds. Such habitats are rapidly disappearing from the landscape. Retain these wherever possible. Schools can help with studies of such habitats, if this is feasible.

New ponds – Check for water table with a test hole. A lining is usually necessary with low level of natural water. Butyl sheeting easier than clay puddling. The catchment area around ponds should be as extensive as possible. Investigate possibilities of damming streams. Consult River Authority. Make pond-edges irregular with projecting spits and bays with edges for vegetation zones. Introduce vegetation from local ponds if possible, together with wildlife. Assistance from schools, local Naturalist Trusts. Allow time for the new habitat to stabilise.

Management of ponds – Keep water level as stable as possible. Avoid heavy shading from overhanging trees, especially conifers. Use alder, willow and other trees on north side if possible. Fence out farm stock (trampling, punctured lining) and protect areas that are vulnerable or establishing from excessive public use. Periodic clearance of silt and mud on a phased basis may be necessary to avoid excessive disturbance, including removal of rubbish and debris. Create marginal habitats with native species that are generally prolific, once established. A local supply may be found that can be used in consultation with all concerned for a new habitat.

Management of ditches – Mechanical ditching equipment may give effective drainage, but tends to create straight-sided channels poor as a mud and fresh-water habitat. Allow as much irregularity as possible. Shallow sloping sides, occasional trees and overhanging banks and slower moving flow areas for richer plant life. Phase ditching operations over the years to allow one stretch to re-colonise before another is started. Also conservation groups or similar organisations may be used for very sensitive areas. Use streams and water courses as planting habitat for indigenous trees like willow and alder, and associated herbaceous species. Avoid the excessive introduction of willow and alder species into some wetland habitats as these can have a marked effect on lowering the water table and slowly drying out the area.

11.9.7 Grassland (see 11.6.3)

11.9.8 Establishment and maintenance of indigenous vegetation

Increasing justification for this concept, where development in rural areas and some categories of landscape considered in 11.2.3 call for restoring open spaces associated with these developments (i.e. power stations, motorways, country parks) to a natural or semi natural vegetation.

Three main techniques are possible to achieve this:

Natural colonisation. Not generally satisfactory on those sites where imported topsoil, lack of natural local source of propagules (seeds) and perhaps the need for rapid vegetation cover due to erosion (or local opposition) demand a reasonable quick and effective landscape re-vegetation process. In some cases, however, where natural sources of seed or vegetative material is known to be present, areas can be left to develop a plant community, perhaps with some control of undesirable 'weed' species.

Seedlings with carefully selected seed mixtures. A range of grass/legume mixtures are available to suit most soils and sites, but the availability of seed of many indigenous species is very poor indeed at present. To re-create the habitat vegetation, select the nearest basic grass/legume mixture to suit the site and then either by suitable management or over a period of time other natural species will usually develop. In addition, one may arrange for collection of seed of species required by school children or conservation groups and introduce these in zones into the establishing seeded mixture. It is important to notify or consult with the local Naturalist Trust or Nature Conservancy Office before introducing indigenous species to any particular area. A mixture used in Kent for a chalk highway cutting is given in section 11.10.2. Most of this was supplied by a British seed company and the establishment results are so far most encouraging. Hydro-seeding techniques were used to apply this mixture.

Planting of indigenous vegetation. Some techniques noted that are achieving considerable success.

Turfs. Turfs of local vegetation – For limited areas that have created disturbance of habitat; vegetation of the same habitat, i.e. chalk downland/heather, can be lifted with approval of all parties as 200–300 mm (approx. 8–12 in) square turfs and planted at suitable spacings over the area to be recolonised. Such turfs can form the basis of the new vegetation. Not recommended for very large areas on cost grounds alone. Establishment depends upon good growing conditions following planting. Drought can be disastrous. Avoid introducing topsoil from unrelated sites.

Chopped or stripped turf – Turf stripped from the original or adjacent site can be spread back as broken sods while still fresh over the areas to be colonised. Avoid fresh topsoil. Success depends on season, type of vegetation and subsequent management.

Hand planting – Of 'ecological' selections of trees, and shrubs and herbs into a seeded grass/herb mixture or clover mixture or clean land. Choice of species is important and the availability can again be a problem here. It may be necessary to develop a contract with a local nursery or horticultural establishment, to propagate and grow on required species of native plants for planting out. Always consult with the regional Nature Conservancy Council officer, and the local Naturalist Trust before embarking on these techniques.

11.9.9 Management of these vegetative areas

Remove undesirable weed species by hand digging or localised herbicide treatment.

Follow a consistent maintenance policy of cutting to favour maximum development of the vegetation communities.

Co-operate with local Naturalist Trusts or schools or colleges, etc., to maintain regular observations of the wildlife of the new habitat as it develops.

11.10 Some conservation data

TABLE 11.9

Taxon	Number of Species			
	Total British lowland terrestrial species	Total breeding in hedges	Commonly breeding in hedges	Confined to hedges
Mammals (less bats)	28	21	14	0
Reptiles	6	6	1	0
Birds	91	65	23	0
Butterflies	54	23	15	0
Mecoptera	4	3	3	0

TABLE 11.10   INSECT SPECIES ON TREES

Species	Number of Insect Species
Oak (*Quercus*)	284
Willow (*Salix*)	266
Birch (*Betula*)	229
Hawthorn (*Crataegus*)	149
Poplars (*Populus*)	97
Apple (*Malus*)	93
Pine (*Pinus*)	91
Alder (*Alnus*)	90
Elm (*Ulmus*)	82
Hazel (*Corylus*)	73
Beech (*Fagus*)	64
Ash (*Fraxinus*)	41
Spruce (*Picea*)	37
Lime (*Tilia*)	31
Hornbeam (*Carpinus*)	28
Larch (*Larix*)	17
Fir (*Abies*)	16
Holly (*Ilex*)	7

11.10.1 Hedgerows and wildlife

Birds.   The Monks Wood B.T.O. Common Bird Survey shows that hedges on average support one pair of birds per 100 yards of hedge-length in England and Wales.

11.10.2 Seed mixtures

One mixture used for a freshly cut chalk embankment in Kent, by the Estates and Valuation Department, Kent County Council.

Sheeps fescue	*Festuca ovina*	$12\frac{1}{2}\%$
Creeping red fescue	*Festuca rubra*	$12\frac{1}{2}\%$
Smooth stalked meadow- grass	*Poa pratensis*	$12\frac{1}{2}\%$
Brown top	*Agrostis tenuis*	12%
Sain foin	*Onobrychris viciifolia*	15%
Kidney vetch	*Anthylllis vulneraria*	15%
Viper's bugloss	*Echium vulgare*	1%
Burnet	*Poterium sanguisorba*	4%
Bird'sfoot trefoil	*Lotus corniculatus*	5%
Wild white clover	*Trifolium repens*	5%
Red clover	*Trifolium pratense*	5%

Observations by students from Wye College, University of London, on a similar mixture used on chalk embankments, show that over the years the legumes and particularly the kidney vetch and other species like burnet establish well. Grasses tend to disappear slowly on the steeper banks. Vegetation in these areas has never been cut due to the gradients and the attractive visual qualities of the plant communities.

11.11 Conservation and the future

This chapter is essentially concerned with the short- and long-term welfare of the landscape and a number of techniques and guide-lines have been outlined to achieve certain management objectives. Conservation of wildlife and the associated habitats are constantly referred to throughout the chapter in the context of maintenance and management. As design and management may involve long term effects on the landscape the future role of conservation must also be taken into account.

Changes in public awareness. The work of conservation groups, Friends of the Earth, schools and amenity societies, etc., has done much to generate an awareness of the need for conservation, and action groups are already achieving considerable impact with projects and 'reserve' operations. Landscape architects, managers and those with authority and responsibility for landscape must assist with the generation of this awareness, and equally important the harnessing and directing of this public energy flow once induced, into beneficial and practicable projects.

There is no doubt that there has been a tremendous change in attitude to conservation, and the protection of the countryside and its wildlife during the last few years.

Recreation pressures. One of the greatest challenges facing designers, managers and consultant natural scientists today is the reconciliation of public use of landscape with the protection of attractive habitats and wildlife.

Future policies must be concerned with management plans allowing for conservation zones, rotational use of pressurised areas, restoration of habitats, more public education and participation, and far more research into many aspects of this important field.

Changing agricultural practices. The key to much of the present and future visual and physical qualities of rural Britain, and to a lesser extent the rural/urban fringes, lies with the farming industry. It is presumptuous of idealists, planners and designers to expect a primary industry to make great concessions to amenity interests without some sort of financial recompense. Many farmers are indeed sensitive to wildlife, trees, hedgerows and all the elements of the British countryside. They are also, for the most part, heavily involved with making a living from the land. This clash of interests is well summarised in Sir John Winnifrith's chapter in that enlightened report *Farming and Wildlife. A study in compromise* which covered the proceedings of a first attempt at getting to grips with the problem at Silsoe in Bedfordshire. Elsewhere the Countryside Commission has sponsored a series of demonstration experiments to further the principles put forward in *New Agricultural Landscapes*.

Future responsibility for landscape. There are already signs of a greater willingness by the many professional and commercial groups with landscape responsibilities and interests, to work more closely together with common policies and objectives. Clearly a more defined and recognisable profession of landscape management will have to emerge, and the future for a balanced healthy landscape undoubtedly lies in the hands of well-organised multi-disciplinary teams working closely with government and industry on the one hand, and able to build a good public relations image on the other.

Bibliography

Farming and Wildlife. A study in compromise, D. Barber (ed.).

The Pruning of Trees, Shrubs and Conifers, G. Brown.

Grounds Maintenance Handbook, H. S. Conover, McGraw-Hill Book Co.

The biotic effects of public pressures on the environment, E. Duffey (ed.), Monkswood Experimental Station, Symposium No. 3, The Nature Conservancy, 1967.

The Scientific Management of Animal and Plant Communities for Conservation, E. Duffey and A. S. Watt (ed.), Blackwell Scientific Publications.

A Study in Countryside Conservation, East Hampshire A.O.N.B., Hampshire County Council.

Horticultural Pests. Detection and Control, G. Fox Wilson, Lockwood and Sons Ltd.

Hedges and Hedgerow Trees, M. D. Hooper and M. W. Holdgate (ed.), Monkswood Experimental Station, Symposium No. 4, The Nature Conservancy, 1968.

Approved Products for Farmers and Growers (Annual Guide to Chemicals for all aspects of these industries), Ministry of Agriculture, Fisheries and Food. (Leaflets on relevant topics of this chapter especially pests and diseases of many plants.)

Pathology of Trees and Shrubs, T. R. Peace, Oxford University Press.

Pesticides. A code of conduct. The Joint ABMAC/Wildlife Education and Communications Committee.

'Birds and Landscape', A. Rackham, *ILA Journal*, Nov. 1972.

Road Verges, Symposium proceedings, Monkswood Experimental Station Report, The Nature Conservancy, 1969.

Wildlife Conservation in Woodlands, R. C. Steel, Forestry Commission Booklet No. 29, H.M.S.O.

Hospital Grounds' Maintenance, P. Thoday, University of Bath.

Landscape for Living, U.S. Department of Agriculture, Year Book of Agriculture, 1972.

Biological Management and Conservation, M. B. Usher, Chapman and Hall, London.

Road Verges. Their Function and Management (1969).

Road Verges in Scotland. Their Function and Management (1970).

Road Verges on Rural Roads. Management and other Factors (1973), J. W. Way (ed.). All from the Monkswood Experimental Station, The Nature Conservancy.

'Landscape Management and Site Conservation at Heriot-Watt University, Scotland', A. E. Weddle and J. Pickard, *ILA Journal*, May 1971.

Weed Control Handbooks, *Vols I and II*, Weed Research Organisation, Blackwells Scientific Publications.

'Planting Design and Management of Wildlife Interest', Techniques No. 15, A. E. Yarrow, *ILA Journal*, May 1973.

'Site Conservation: A New Approach', O. L. Gilbert and A. E. Weddle, *ILA Journal*, August 1974.

New Agricultural Landscapes, The Countryside Commission.

12 Professional Practice

GEOFFREY COLLENS

12.1 The client

12.1.1 Different types of client

Although clients now include local authorities and government agencies there remain many private companies, organisations and individuals who seek landscape advice. After a decline in private garden design over a considerable period, there has been a certain revival in this type of commission in the last few years, together with the increase in larger scale work.

12.1.2 The main classification of clients

Private persons who wish to have gardens designed.

Local authorities who commission parks or reclamation schemes and seek advice on roads, siting of buildings and housing estates. The main types of local authorities are now county councils, city, metropolitan district, non-metropolitan district or parish councils. In Wales parish councils are called community councils.

Government agencies such as the Property Services Agency/Department of the Environment, the Forestry Commission and New Town Corporations.

Nationalised industries, national and local supply boards and their agencies, such as the Central Electricity Generating Board, local water boards and regional health authorities.

Industrial concerns, private companies and developers who commission work concerned with commercial, industrial, reclamation, recreation and housing schemes.

Amenity societies who often ask for landscape advice in connection with their particular local problems.

Architects, engineers, town planners or members of other professional bodies who require the technical advice of a landscape architect and seek his collaboration as a consultant to themselves rather than to their client.

Some of the above clients may also need the advice of a landscape architect to help with planning inquiries at which he may be required to act as an expert witness to support their case or to oppose development proposals to which they object. In many cases the clients also employ landscape architects as members of their technical staff, sometimes using them as liaison officers between outside consultants and their employers. For example the Department of the Environment, the Ministry of Transport, the Central Electricity Generating Board, the New Town Corporations, County Council Planning Departments, city authorities, and several local authority parks departments have their own staff of landscape architects.

12.1.3 Serving the client

A different response is needed for service to each type of client depending on the nature of the commission and the type of work required. Most private individuals like personal service with a minimum of letters and paper work and they often expect the advice of a landscape architect to include detailed explanations of schemes and of the plant material to be used. Committees and other similar clients often ask for more written material and regular reports but seldom require detailed explanations of projects once the basic designs have been agreed.

Private clients, both large and small, are usually in a hurry for a scheme to be produced and carried out. These clients sometimes include those on whom pressure has been brought to bear, by planning authorities for example, to produce an acceptable development proposal which includes landscape treatment and who would not otherwise commission landscape designs.

Most local authorities and government agencies commission landscape architects in good time to work to a reasonable predetermined programme. However, there are still isolated cases where the landscape architect is brought in at the end of the planning stage and sometimes when the project is nearing completion, and is expected to finish off the job in a seemly manner. In these unfortunate cases it will often be found that financial provision for landscape work is inadequate. It should not be automatically assumed that work commissioned in conditions which are far from ideal will necessarily turn out unsatisfactorily and in the interests of good landscape, the designer should attempt to do the best possible with limited time and resources.

12.1.4 Commissioning landscape work
In some local authorities the technical officer may have a complete say in the way the project is designed and handled with his responsibilities delegated to him by the relevant committee, but in some cases he is an intermediary and will have to submit all major issues to his committee for a final decision. He is usually an engineer but might be an architect, planner or an estates officer. The technical officer may present consultant's schemes to the committee and it is quite usual for the consultant not to meet the committee members and to deal almost exclusively with the technical officer. But some direct contact with the committee is nearly always helpful. It is particularly desirable for the consultant to meet the committee when a scheme is presented for approval. Many committees now put their schemes through public participation procedures in which the designer of the scheme in question should take an active part.

12.2 Briefing and conditions of engagement

12.2.1 The brief
The employer should start by setting out his requirements as a basis for discussion with the landscape architect who will refine these user requirements into a more explicit brief. The formulation of the programme is a two-way process, as the client does not always know exactly what he wants and needs to be guided by the landscape architect. The designer will find it almost impossible to produce a good scheme based upon a bad or confused brief, and it is essential that at this early stage the basic functional needs should be analysed and clarified so that time is not wasted in producing impractical sketch designs. A few large employers who commission schemes of a repetitive nature have evolved standard briefs and terms of reference within which a consultant can work. Others commission feasibility studies to help clarify the brief and its elements.

12.2.2 The Landscape Institute conditions of agreement
The landscape architect is a skilled professional person qualified by examination before becoming a recognised practising member of the Landscape Institute. He works within a strict Code of Professional Conduct, but the Institute does not have a Royal Charter to give standing to its members as do the R.I.B.A. and T.P.I. Nor is there a Registration Act to restrict use of the professional title 'Landscape Architect' in the way, for example, the term 'Architect' is limited to those on a statutory register.

The landscape architect advises clients on all matters concerning the design and implementation of landscape work from the initial conception at sketch plan stage to the final certifying and checking of accounts on completion. He will advise on the approximate cost of the work, the most appropriate contract method, and the most suitable basis for assessing the fee. He is able to obtain and advise on estimates received from contractors and as to their suitability, as well as supervise the work during construction.

In the event of the client not knowing of a suitable landscape architect he may write to the Registrar of the Landscape Institute explaining the nature of the work and asking for suitable nominations.

12.2.3 The Landscape Institute nomination committee
The Registrar of the Institute will refer the client's enquiry to the nomination committee; this committee is composed of senior experienced members of the profession who are in no way concerned with private practice. Normally the prospective client would be sent a list of several names from which he can make his own final choice. When several landscape architects are being considered by a client for one particular project it is not ethical for any landscape architect to attempt to secure the work by any other means than by his own competence for the work in question.

12.2.4 The Landscape Institute scale of fees
There is a scale of fees prescribed by the Landscape Institute for most classes of work which is from time to time adjusted by the council as may be necessary. This scale (see *Conditions of Engagement and Scale of Professional Charges*) lays down the *minimum* fee which any member of the Institute will charge for his services. It is important for any client commissioning work to be certain that the landscape architect he appoints has the resources to cope with the scope of the work under consideration. It may well be that the fee required would be in excess of the prescribed minimum where very experienced practitioners are commissioned.

The Code of Practice does not permit members to charge less than minimum scale. This rules out attempts by clients to seek reduced fees and prevents undercutting of fees by members to secure the commission, and should there be any doubt as to the exact method of fixing the fees, members and clients are advised to contact the President of the Institute who will obtain a ruling on the matter. There are many landscape works of a direct contract nature about which there need be little doubt in assessing the approximate final cost and the scale fee which would then be charged as percentage on the contract. This applies to sports grounds, public and private gardens, parks, etc.

Landscape architects by virtue of their own wide knowledge and design ability are more and more employed in a consultant capacity where there need be no contract work at the disposal of the landscape architect. This may apply to engineering, architectural, conservation, town planning and constructional developments carried out in association with other professions. In these and other similar cases the only reasonable method of fixing the fee is on a time charge basis, and the method of assessing this is clearly stated in the scale. As the time spent on schemes of this type can vary considerably according to the complexity and intricacy of the work it is generally not possible for the landscape architect to assess his total fee at the outset. The time-charge method has proved by usage and experience to be satisfactory and much work has been carried out for both government departments and local authorities who have been satisfied with the arrangement. If, however, for reasons of cost planning the client at the beginning would wish to exercise a more rigid control it is suggested that a ceiling figure is agreed or the work is programmed according to financial stages, and the landscape architect should inform the client when so much time has been spent, and the amount of fees due.

12.2.5 Formal agreement
In some instances a client will enter a formal contract with the landscape architect and this will incorporate the fee basis to be adopted, together with the intervals at which payment will be made and other appropriate terms of reference. If the fee basis changes during the course of the contract a further written agreement will have to be signed by the client and the landscape architect to cover the amendment. In the absence of a signed contract the scale of fees should at least be confirmed in a letter before work commences.

12.3 Landscape reports

Reports are usually required only on larger schemes for local authorities or public bodies. Private clients do not often require reports of any size or frequency as they are usually keen to get on with the actual planning and construction work with a minimum of paper work beforehand. Reports for private clients are sometimes produced however where the employer wishes to carry out the work himself over a period of time and needs a book of guidelines.

12.3.1 Preliminary report or feasibility study
This will probably need to include most of the following items:

Assets of the site recorded (see also Chapter 1 – Survey and Analysis).
Special features influencing the design assessed, such as good vistas, worthwhile trees, existing streams and ponds and outcrops of rock.
Impact of buildings on their surroundings.
Change in natural landscape brought about by the development.
Description of existing site character.
Topography, climate, microclimate, soil, ecology.
Maintenance problems.
Basic siting considerations.
Drawings, photographs, diagrams, montage presentation should also be included where appropriate to provide explicit information.

12.3.2 Main report
This will cover all aspects of the scheme starting from an analysis of user requirements (see also Chapter 2 – Site Planning).

The main reasons for the landscape scheme will be described together with some details of the methods and programming of work by the landscape architect.
Descriptions of the type of planting and plant material will be needed.
Any off-site planting recommended should be the subject of a separate chapter.
A note on maintenance should give guidance to the client on this vital aspect.
The programming of work needs to be stated indicating the relationship to planting seasons.
If appropriate, recommendations should be made on immediate work to be undertaken, such as the establishment of tree nurseries.
Approximate cost figure for the total job must be given, together with any other statistics which are necessary.
Special details applicable to the site can be described and illustrated.
Perspectives should be included to illustrate the plans and to show the character being aimed at, and diagrams, site views and photographs of models are all helpful illustrative material.

It may be necessary to include details to specify amongst other things, surfaces, levels, grading, earth modelling, car park positions, rearrangement of roads and paths if desired, fencing recommendations, siting and design of external lighting, street furniture, water features and sculpture, if appropriate.

12.3.3 Number of reports

The final report will contain many proposals which are subject to eventual modification and everything will be detailed more exactly in the working drawings which follow the production of the report. Where a report is required in quite a small scheme, this will be a single document which is simple and brief. A preliminary report followed by a final version are all that is required in normal circumstances and intermediate documents are only necessary when the programme is so long and problems so complex that further reports covering special aspects are needed. Reports are favoured by all types of clients because they form an easy and attractive means of reference to the cardinal points of any project and can be referred to more quickly in a bound volume than in bundles of separate drawings.

12.4 Landscape drawings, specification and bill of quantities

All design work will be based directly on the site survey and an analysis of the client's requirements, and from this information working drawings will be made. There are advantages in preparing the design at the scale that will be used for working drawings, but in most cases this will involve more detail drawing than is necessary to indicate the suggested design, particularly if several alterations or amendments may be considered.

12.4.1 Working drawings

All working drawings should be set out direct from the original survey and grid and not from the sketch design drawings, to ensure a proper degree of accuracy. Working drawings for all constructional details should follow the current landscape and architectural practice of presentation and notation and the British Standard for drawing office practice. Working drawings for large site work may have to follow civil engineering practice in showing sections and relating plans to grid or chainage lines.

For very large sites a map notation may be necessary and on most sites it will be essential to have a key master plan which indicates areas with special detailing set out separately on drawings at a larger scale. All site plans must have a scale and a North point on them.

Working drawings for planting plans must clearly show what is intended by containing a plant list on each planting plan. The scale of the plan should be large enough to show the actual names and positions of plants as this is the clearest system for a contractor to follow on site (see also Chapter 8 – Planting). Alternatively a key system can be used with key numbers placed against each plant on plan. The plant list must be on the planting plan and not on a separate sheet and should be written in a form similar to part of a bill of quantities containing the key number, the quantity, the Latin generic name, planting size and any special notes such as 'half standard, feathered, clean stem to 2 m'. The common name may also be shown if the drawing is to be used by the client or others to whom this might be helpful. The plants listed should be varieties which are grown commercially and a requirement that stock should be from a nursery close to the site, although theoretically desirable, is often unreasonable in practice.

All working drawings should be fully dimensioned but the setting out of the plants might be made approximate, subject to staking out and checking on the site at the time of planting. If this is the case the procedure to be followed must be clearly defined in the specification so that the contractor fully appreciates that planting positions must be staked out for the landscape architect's approval before planting operations commence. All drawings should now be in metric dimensions to recognised metric scales.

12.4.2 Bill of quantities

All except minor contracts should have a bill of quantities if put out to tender as this ensures that all contractors tender on an equal basis and simplifies the making and pricing of variations during the course of a contract. Even negotiated contracts benefit from the use of proper bills of quantities. Part of the bill will consist of the plant schedule used on the planting plans. For substantial contracts a quantity surveyor should be engaged to prepare bills and to give a full service from preliminary cost plan to settlement of the final account.

Although there are many different ways of setting out the planting portion of the bill, there are some advantages in arranging for the price of each plant specified to include the complete cost of the planting operation. For example, for trees this will include the digging of the hole, providing topsoil to the tree pit, planting the tree, staking, tying and mulching. By ensuring that all these items of work are included in the one unit price a simpler method of pricing is obtained than when these items are broken down separately for pricing. Normal practice among quantity surveyors however is to itemise and price each labour separately and in this case variations are possible down to each item, for example, more excavation, extra ties, etc. Similarly it is sometimes advantageous to have bills written in a manner which groups all the work related to one area e.g. 'north courtyard' or 'screen planting to car park') especially on large contracts. Major design alterations or omissions can then more readily be managed than if all paving and all planting is bulked together. Although this separation may be more difficult for the contractor to price, it does permit the use of special rates; these are reduced for bulk work in a simple area, and increased to cover difficulties of access to internal courtyards for example. It also helps the contractor with ordering materials and becomes essential on phased contracts.

12.4.3 Specification or description of work

All contracts using a bill of quantities must also incorporate a specification or description of work. This is usually divided into main sections following a system of lettered and numbered clauses.

General Conditions

This covers the preliminary aspects of the contract and sets out all the items of administration and overheads which must be allowed for in the contract pricing.

Materials

All materials to be used and the appropriate suppliers are specified and standards are laid down including reference to British Standards where they are applicable. Materials will include a detailed description of paving, grass seed mixtures, fertilisers, tree stakes and ties, and all other supplies which are needed for the particular contract.

Workmanship

Here should be described the specific methods of construction, planting, turfing, etc., to be used on the contract, with reference to applicable British Standards and Codes of Practice.

Maintenance and defects liability

This section must clarify the degree of maintenance to be included as part of the contract showing what work is expected in this respect both during the contract and after practical completion during the defects liability period to final hand over. It will also include clarification of the system of guarantees on materials and plants which may be written into the contract. The maintenance period may vary depending on the time of year the contract is done, but is usually 12 months. Two years is needed as a minimum for semi-mature trees and forestry.

Schedule of Rates, Materials and Labour

The specification should cover all the necessary items as briefly as possible. Long and complex documents may confuse the contractor and probably add to the price of tenders received. This demands a proper blend of common sense and business management. An elaborate specification for a small or simple job will do nothing to secure the client's proper needs. On the other hand a large project for a public authority requires a systematic specification especially when work may extend over a long period. At the end of such a document should be a schedule of rates for materials and labour.

12.5 Letting the contract

The two parties to the contract are the employer and the contractor and although the landscape architect will act as the agent of the client in all details and negotiations on the running of the contract, it is his clear duty to act fairly and impartially in enforcing reasonable standards of materials and workmanship, within the limits indicated in the contract. On difficult sites and in adverse weather conditions there may be occasions when he must exercise discretion and expect no more than is reasonable from this specialist contractor and here the landscape architect must be quite firm as the arbiter of what is reasonable if the client has different views.

12.5.1 Tenders

For competitive tenders a list of firms to be invited should be agreed with the client before the contractors are asked whether they wish to tender. Some authorities have approved lists of contractors or sub-contractors from which a selection can be made or agreed with the client. All government departments and most local authorities have regulations or standing orders which control invitation of tenders and sometimes it may be necessary to invite open tendering from all contractors who wish to submit a price. Selected lists of suitable tenderers are more usual. A firm indication of intention to tender should be obtained from each contractor on the agreed list before tender documents are despatched. Lists of possible tenderers can be obtained by consulting such organisations as the British Association of Landscape Industries, the British Association of Sportsground and Landscape Contractors and the National Association of Agricultural Contractors.

It is usual to obtain not less than three and not more than six competitive prices for a job, the latter number being on more important large contracts. Each tenderer will be sent a contract document in duplicate (at least) which will include the bill of quantities, and/or specification and working drawings. He will be asked to return one set of documents duly completed in a special envelope to be opened only at a specified date and time.

Some engineering consultants ask for several copies, triplicate or more, but this places an unreasonable administrative burden on the smaller contractor. Adequate time should be allowed for pricing; at least two full working weeks and often three or four. Tenders are often opened in the presence of the client.

12.5.2 Negotiated contract

In some instances, depending on the type of work, it is possible to arrange for a tender to be negotiated with one selected landscape contractor without inviting competitive prices. This usually occurs for private clients only and generally on high class schemes where a first rate contractor is selected on the basis of other work he has undertaken of a similar nature. Even in these circumstances bills of quantities and a specification must be used so that a simple and effective method is obtained for running a contract and checking the value of the work.

12.5.3 Contracts and sub-contracts

It is usual to arrange for the successful contractor and employer to enter into a formal agreement on a standard Landscape Institute form of contract*, but in many instances the employer (especially public bodies, corporations and large firms) has his own form of contract which would be used in place of the Landscape Institute one.

In some cases the landscape work is a sub-contract to a building contract and in these circumstances the R.I.B.A. nominated sub-contractor standard form or similar will be used. This tender form indicates that prices must allow for the $2\frac{1}{2}\%$ cash discount which the general contractor is entitled to receive on the value of all sub-contracts. The landscape contractor will then be a 'nominated sub-contractor', that is to say his employment will not have been decided upon by the general contractor himself. Alternatively it is possible to measure landscape work in the main bill and allow the general contractor to sub-contract or otherwise arrange for the execution of the work. This is a reasonable method for landscape work which includes a high proportion of earth moving, paving and details of a constructional nature; all items which may be somewhat beyond the experience and equipment of the average landscape contractor. For planting work this method is not satisfactory and the general contractor should be required to have the work done by a specialist.

The advantage of having the landscape work as a sub-contract is that its programming and dovetailing with the building work is under the direction of the general contractor who organises all trades on the site. However, care must be taken to ensure that the general contractor fully accepts this responsibility. Given the opportunity, he may attempt to disclaim the specialist skill needed for general organisation of landscape work, and unreasonably pass the entire burden of supervision to the landscape architect.

One disadvantage of this method is that the settlement of the final account of the building contract may have to be delayed until the defects liability period of the landscape sub-contract has expired which invariably is at a date much later than the end of the building defects liability period, although this can be an incentive for the general contractor to see that the work is properly programmed and completed on time. There are nevertheless a number of procedures by which this problem can be solved. Problems can also arise over payment as this will come to the landscape contractor through the main contractor instead of direct from the employer. When the main contractor is behind schedule he must cooperate with the landscape sub-contractor whose work is partly seasonal and cannot be reprogrammed easily, owing to the situation on planting seasons in particular.

It should be clearly stated that the successful tenderer is not permitted to sub-let any part of the work without the prior written agreement of the landscape architect.

12.5.4 Acceptance of tenders

It is usual for the lowest tender to be accepted, but if good reasons exist it may be desirable in rare instances to appoint the second lowest and the right for the employer to choose other than the lowest tender should clearly be stated in the general conditions of the specification. Acceptance or rejection of tenders should be decided upon without delay and the unsuccessful tenderers informed accordingly, and a contract signed by the successful firm.

From time to time problems of contract procedure arise. These may be of a minor nature (incorrectly addressed tenders for example) and no more than commonsense and ordinary fairness is necessary. More serious problems can arise and the checking and advice of an experienced quantity surveyor is invaluable in these circumstances. Exceptionally, however, serious problems may arise which call for discretion, careful judgment and scrupulous fairness.

* The Landscape Institute approved form of contract is now that of the Joint Council for Landscape Industries (J.C.L.I.), a form of contract prepared jointly by both trade and professional sides of the industry.

12.6 Consultations before and during contracts

12.6.1 Relationship with other professions

Although there are projects where the landscape architect is the only professional person employed, in most cases he is one of a team or group of consultants, such as town planners, architects, engineers, horticulturists, ecologists and foresters. It is essential at the beginning of every project to ensure that the limits of responsibility are clearly defined. In some cases for instance the landscape architect will be responsible for all the space between buildings while on other occasions he may design the soft landscape work only with the hard landscaping detailed by architects or engineers.

From the outset the method of working between members of a group of consultants must be decided to ensure efficient design and running of the contract. All the operations on site and production of drawings should be agreed between consultants to avoid conflict or overlapping of responsibility on drawings or in specifications. As a general working rule, ultimate project responsibility should rest with only one supervisory architect, landscape architect, engineer or other consultant. Specialist advice, negotiations and sub-contracts must be dealt with to channel information and instructions through this principal. On large projects or in the case of teams experienced in working together, this central responsibility may be little more than nominal, but it should clearly exist to be used in cases of doubt and difficulty.

12.6.2 Meetings

In exclusively landscape contracts the landscape architect will initiate regular site meetings, but where the landscape work is included as a sub-contract, landscape problems will be dealt with during the course of normal site meetings dealing with the main contract. All those expected to be present at a meeting should receive notification, ideally 3–4 weeks in advance. Where regular meetings are held (often monthly), reminders (and an agenda) should still be sent out. In all very major contracts the principal or the landscape architect supervising the contract should attend such meetings and not send an assistant.

Minutes of all meetings should be taken, but must be brief and to the point, recording all decisions but omitting full reports of lengthy discussions. These must be circulated to all those present and to others who are involved. As a result of some important meetings a brief report may need to be made to the client or other interested party not normally present or represented at site meetings.

12.6.3 Advisory work

Many large developers of land now engage landscape architects as consultants to advise on general policy and to assist with particular projects. Many afforestation, conservation, coastal, reclamation, road development, national and regional park, power production and distribution problems are now being tackled by national agencies with the advantage of such advice. Executive authority is not vested in the landscape architect, in fact no actual landscape contract may arise out of consultations, but by a process of formulating agreed land use policies, major decisions of land acquisition, design and management can be made, with due consideration having been given to overall landscape needs.

In the case of particular projects, of power production, New Towns, etc., a landscape architect may also be retained as a consultant to advise on policy and special problems. The authority may carry out substantial landscape works under its own technical staff on the basis of advice accepted.

Consultation procedures must be devised to suit each particular client and problem. Site meetings, committee procedures and public participation can be extensive, but regular attendance and prompt submission of reports are essential to establish confidence and to give the client a landscape service which will be respected and acted upon. Personal qualities are of primary importance but they must be backed by efficient office routine geared to match the scale and pace of each project. If the authority employs its own landscape staff their ability to adopt proper landscape policies, secure adequate financial provisions, and carry out effective work will usually be reinforced by the assistance of the consultant. Close collaboration here can be readily established.

12.7 Contract management and supervision

12.7.1 Control of work in progress

Where the landscape architect is retained to give a full service, site visits will be required regularly during the course of the contract. Although impromptu visits have advantages at times, it is often advisable for site visits to be arranged for a specific time, with the contractor, so that he can be on hand to answer queries or raise points needing immediate site decisions. It is very desirable, especially on large schemes, to have a competent clerk of works capable of supervising the landscape work. Unless this is the case the landscape architect is burdened with an unreasonable degree of day-to-day supervision.

Special arrangements must be made for landscape work which is a sub-contract. The landscape architect and the specialist contractor may have an informal working arrangement, acting directly and keeping the architect or general contractor fully informed. But formal contract responsibility for giving instructions will be that of the architect or engineer (on whose behalf the landscape architect is acting as a consultant). The formal instructions will be given direct to the general contractor who must then instruct his sub-contractor.

All site instructions should be confirmed in writing immediately on return to the office. It is essential to use some kind of standard instruction form (L.I. or R.I.B.A.) so that all communications to the contractor during the course of the contract are in a file of quick reference sheets which eliminate the need for looking through a correspondence file for information. Copies should also go to the quantity surveyor for pricing.

Landscape architect's instructions should clarify a point or tell a contractor to proceed with some particular portion of the work, not involving any alteration in the contract or the price of the contract. The issue of drawings should normally be with an instruction to proceed with the work on them.

Variation orders should instruct the contractor to make variations in the contract by omission, addition or substitution. The variations must refer where applicable to the original clause number in the bill of quantities. It is useful for office purposes to note on a file copy the reason for the variation and whether the client needs to be informed. All changes in the plans or specification should be confirmed in a variation order issued by the landscape architect and the pricing of the additions or omissions should be agreed at the same time, if not at bill rates. The use of variation orders is now often deprecated, all instructions being on one set of forms only.

If additions are made which cannot be based on the unit price in the tender, a price must be obtained for the work from the contractor and approved by the client, if necessary, before an instruction is given to proceed with the extra. This avoids disputes on prices of new items at the final account stage.

12.7.2 Certifying payments
During the course of the job the contractor will submit statements for the value of work done and the landscape architect, on receipt of his valuation form will make out a certificate for 90% of the amount (or 80% of materials on site), 10% being retained for the period of the contract.*

The contract will normally state that the employer must honour the certificate by paying the contractor within 21 days of the certification. In most cases half of the 10% retention is released at the point of practical completion or at the point when the limit of the retention fund is reached and half at the end of the defects liability period.

---

*The percentages quoted here relate to the conventional construction industry methods of contract payment in most common use. They have been varied in some respects in the J.C.L.I. form of contract.

12.7.3 Completion and hand-overs
At the time of practical completion, the site should be offered for inspection to the client or his representative, so that a clear understanding is reached on the contractor's responsibility for maintaining the scheme. If his contract allows for continued maintenance during the defects liability period then the inspection is to agree the start of that period, not hand-over. The final hand-over then takes place at the end of the clearance of faults at the end of the defects liability period. The final hand-over is most conveniently timed either in autumn or spring, owing to the seasonal nature of the work. However, on many sites it will be found that the hand-over is not a single clear-cut matter. The client, may for example, have to take over grassed areas after the contractor's first cuts, but will not necessarily take over planted areas at that time. This sort of arrangement should be avoided if at all possible. On large sites, particularly those associated with extensive building projects or housing schemes in which blocks are handed over stage by stage, there may be corresponding staged completions of landscape work. It is very important that all parties concerned, architect, general contractor, specialist contractor, client and his maintenance staff should be advised by the landscape architect, in writing, of the up-to-date division of maintenance responsibilities. In all cases the parcels for hand-over should be as large as possible and all elements of parcels should be complete.

An inspection must be held at the end of the defects liability period, at which point the contractor will be instructed to remedy the defects and replace dead plants where these failures are the result of his work. These remedial works and replacements will be done at the contractor's own expense and this fact must be clearly stated in the specification. Some additional replacements may be necessary at the client's expense, in certain circumstances. Once this work is done and the client has agreed to take over, all maintenance and replacement work is the sole responsibility of the owner, unless he retains the contractor on a separate after-care contract, which is a course of action seldom taken. The need for good thorough maintenance and after-care is not always fully appreciated by clients. Their attention should be drawn to this important aspect to ensure that the newly-planted scheme does not suffer from neglect after completion, resulting in large numbers of plant casualties and the gradual disintegration of the design concept (see also Chapter 11 – Conservation and Management).

12.7.4 Final account
If a file of instructions has been kept throughout the contract the final account will be a simple matter of pricing out the items on these forms. If it is a fixed priced contract, most of these items can be calculated by reference

to the unit price and schedule of rates for materials and labour contained in the tender and contract documents. Settlement of the final account is made easier if the variations have been priced as the job proceeds and are not all left to the end of the contract. The contractor should be asked to sign the final account when it has been agreed before the final certificate is issued.

12.8 Negotiations and legislation relevant to landscape architecture

12.8.1 Consultations with authorities

Consultations with statutory and local authorities are necessary on many commissions. On frequent occasions planning permission is granted for development, subject to a satisfactory landscape scheme being submitted for approval, prior to development commencing.

Normally, provided the client agrees, this should be discussed with the planning department concerned before a formal submission is made, in order that the planting scheme takes into account the particular reason for the request for landscape work in the planning consent. With such a condition applied to a consent it is often essential for the landscape proposals to be prepared for approval before any building takes place on the site.

12.8.2 The principal planning Acts

The Town and Country Planning Act, 1971, consolidated the original Town and Country Planning Act, 1947, with its many subsequent amending Acts. This consolidating Act has now been amended by the Town and Country Planning (Amendment) Act, 1972 and the Town and Country Amenities Act, 1974 in relation to Conservation Areas. These Acts establish a comprehensive control of land use in England and Wales. The 1947 Act firstly provided that all development taking place on land after 1 July 1948 must have planning permission. 'Development' is defined as 'the carrying out of building, engineering, mining or other operations in, on, over or under land, or the making of any material change in the use of any building or other land.'

There are some exceptions such as the General Development Order, 1973, which automatically grants permission for twenty-three classes of development.

Both in the 1947 Act and in delegated legislation under the Act, certain exemptions were made in order to reduce the administration burden of dealing with applications for all types of development which fell within the definition. Secondly the Act nominated county councils and county borough councils (as they then were) as local planning authorities with the functions of granting permissions, subject to permission for county councils to delegate this function to county district councils in certain circumstances. Thirdly, the Act made the Secretary of State for the Environment (in England and Wales) the chief policy-maker for land use and appeals from refusals of planning permission are heard by inspectors, on behalf of the Secretary of State, upon whose reports he gives his decisions. In certain cases the inspector himself now has delegated powers to make the decision.

Accordingly in relation to landscape and site layout work the importance of these Acts is that they require planning permission to be obtained in all cases except where it is automatically granted under the Act or subordinate legislation. Of particular interest is the power contained in the Acts to make Tree Preservation Orders, Building Preservation Orders and orders to compel the proper maintenance of waste land.

By the Town and Country Planning (Landscape Areas Special Development) Order, 1950, the automatic planning permission granted by delegated legislation to enable agricultural and forestry building and works to be carried out is made subject to a condition that notification of such a development is to be made to the local planning authority, who have fourteen days, in which to object after which time, if no such objection is made, the development can be carried out.

Under the Local Government Act, 1972, a new local government system came into being in April 1974, necessitating many adjustments to the body of planning law in these Acts and other statutes. The Town and Country Planning Acts of 1947 and 1971, plus their subsequent amending and consolidating acts, do not apply to Northern Ireland.

The corresponding relevant acts in Scotland were the Town and Country Planning (Scotland) Acts of 1947 and 1972. In the latter case all Scottish planning legislation was then consolidated in the one Act. In Scotland, appeals against refusals of planning permission are heard by a person known as a reporter, appointed by the Secretary of State for Scotland.

12.8.3 The Civic Amenities Act of 1967

This was an important piece of legislation in that it made it a duty of local authorities to identify and designate Conservation Areas, tightened up the procedures on Tree Preservation Orders and increased powers to dispose of abandoned vehicles and bulky refuse. Its main provisions have since been incorporated into the later consolidating planning acts especially the Town and Country Amenities Act, 1974. It did not apply to Northern Ireland but was applicable to Scotland and Wales.

12.8.4 Tree Preservation Orders

One result of the Town and Country Planning Act of 1947 was the statutory powers given to planning authorities to serve Tree Preservation Orders. The provisions were strengthened by the Civic Amenities Act of 1967 but this and the 1947 Act have been superseded by the Town and Country Planning Act, 1971, by the Town and Country Planning (Tree Preservation Order) Regulations, 1969, and by the Town and Country Amenities Act, 1974. Preservation Orders may sometimes be placed on newly planted trees if a special situation requires it and if new trees might otherwise be in danger of not surviving. Tree Preservation Orders cannot be placed on trees covered by a Forestry Commission dedication covenant. Automatic blanket Tree Preservation Orders now apply to all trees within a Conservation Area, regardless of the serving of an Order on Individual owners for specific trees.

Normally Orders are only served on trees in the property of private owners and cannot be served on trees on land owned by government departments, institutions, statutory bodies and nationalised industries. Although a local authority would not usually make an order in respect of trees on its own land it might acquire land affected by an existing order. Under Section 266 of the 1971 Act, orders were made possible on trees on Crown Land with the consent of the appropriate authority. Once an Order has been served on the owner of a property the specified trees (shown on plan and on a typed schedule) may not be cut down or lopped without the prior consent of the planning authority, although there are certain exemptions from obtaining such consent incorporated into the 1969 regulations. A fine can be imposed for non-compliance with the Orders which does not have such an exemption.

If a landscape architect or another professional person is involved in the planning of a scheme containing trees protected by Tree Preservation Orders, he will often find that a flexible attitude will be adopted by the planning authority and that some trees which inhibit the building layout can be removed if the final project will provide new trees sufficient in number and size to produce a reasonable degree of replacement for the loss.

Protected trees on land where a planning permission for a development is granted can be exempted from preservation even if the Order predates the planning application, if the planning application clearly indicates or implies the removal of the trees to make the development possible. Anyone served with a Tree Preservation Order may appeal to the Secretary of State for the Environment against confirmation of the Order.

12.8.5 The Forestry Acts 1919–67
The Forestry Act, 1919, established the Forestry Commission with the general duty of promoting the interests of forestry, the development of afforestation and the production and supply of timber in the United Kingdom. The Act empowered the Commissioners to make advances by way of grants or loans for the purpose of the afforestation or replanting of land, to establish or assist in the promotion of woodland industries, to collect and publish statistics relating to forestry, to promote and develop education in forestry, to carry out forestry research and experiments and to make, or aid in making, such enquiries as they consider to be necessary for the purpose of providing an adequate supply of timber in the United Kingdom.

The Forestry Act of 1945 changed the constitutional status of the Forestry Commission. Forestry policy became the direct responsibility of the Minister of Agriculture, Fisheries and Food and the Secretary of State for Scotland. The main functions of the Commissioners became subject to the direction of these ministers and the powers of the Commissioners to acquire land were transferred to them. The land vested in the Commissioners at the date of the Act was transferred to the ministers, who manage and use any land vested in or acquired by them which they have not placed at the disposal of the Commissioners. The land in the possession of the Commissioners at the date of the Act was to remain at the disposal of the Commissioners until the ministers directed otherwise. The Commissioners' powers under the Forestry Act of 1919, in respect of forestry operations, education, research and grants were unaffected.

The Forestry Act of 1947 provided for the dedication of land for forestry purposes, the enforcement of forestry dedication covenants (in England and Wales) and of dedication agreements (in Scotland) and empowered certain categories of owners to enter into such covenants or agreements.

The Forestry Act, 1951, dealt with the licensing of the felling of growing trees and made permanent the control, previously operated as a temporary measure, under *Defence Regulation No. 68*. The Forestry Commission took over this control in January 1950 from the Board of Trade. The Forestry Act, 1967, consolidated the various Forestry Acts from 1919 to 1963. In 1965 the forestry functions of the Ministry of Agriculture in Wales were transferred to the Secretary of State for Wales. The Secretary of State for Scotland remains responsible for forestry in Scotland.

12.8.6 Tree and woodland grants
The woodland dedication schemes, provide comprehensive assistance from the Forestry Commission to private owners of woodland. Planting and annual management grants are provided under the schemes. The original scheme ceased in June 1972 and an interim scheme of assistance closed in December 1973. A new scheme was introduced in October 1974 (Basis III Dedication) and grants were increased considerably in October 1977, with extra incentive grants for planting broadleaves. Also in

October 1977 the Forestry Commission introduced an entirely new Small Woods Scheme to encourage woods from a quarter to ten hectares in area. Under the Local Government Act, 1974, the Countryside Commission have powers to give financial aid to tree planting to public authorities and private individuals. High priority is now given to tree planting in Areas of Outstanding Natural Beauty, Green Belts and areas suffering from losses as a result of Dutch elm disease. The Countryside Commission for Scotland has similar powers.

12.8.7 National Parks Acts

The National Parks and Access to the Countryside Act, 1949, the Countryside Act, 1968, and subsequent Countryside Acts provide comprehensive legislation for National Parks and the countryside generally. The 1949 Act established the National Parks Commission with functions:

(a) For the preservation and enhancement of natural beauty in England and Wales, and particularly in the areas designated under the Act as National Parks or as areas of outstanding natural beauty.

(b) For encouraging the provision or improvement, for persons resorting to National Parks, of facilities for the enjoyment thereof and for the enjoyment of the opportunities for open-air recreation and the study of nature afforded thereby.

The 1968 Act established the Countryside Commission which assumed the functions of the National Parks Commission but had wider powers extending to the countryside in general. These functions:

'are to be exercised for the conservation and enhancement of the natural beauty and amenity of the countryside, and encouraging the provision and improvement, for persons resorting to the countryside and of open-air recreation in the countryside'.

A total of ten National Parks and thirty-two Areas of Outstanding Natural Beauty (A.O.N.B.s) have been designated together covering about 18% of the total area of England and Wales. Both the 1949 and the 1968 Acts were amended by the Local Government Act in 1972 (which changed the administration of National Parks) and by the Local Government Act 1974 (which altered the system of financing them).

The Amenity Lands Act (Northern Ireland), 1965, made provision for National Parks in that province. Scotland has a separate Countryside Commission set up under the Countryside/Scotland Act 1967 with similar powers and functions to the Countryside Commission for England and Wales. There are, however, no National Parks in Scotland so far.

The Peak and Lake District National Parks are each administered by Planning Boards. Responsibility for each of the remaining eight parks is vested in an executive committee of the county council (or councils) known as the National Park Committee. These authorities have the task of keeping fine landscape unspoilt whilst ensuring that people can get there to enjoy it. They work through the normal processes of planning control, but try to observe specially high standards. The two Park Planning Boards are the local planning authorities for this purpose.

No special administrative arrangements apply in A.O.N.B.s. Like National Parks, the A.O.N.B.s have been designated for their importance to the national landscape. In this respect they are not secondary to National Parks; they differ in that they are generally less suitable for recreation provision. The purpose of designation is to strengthen the power of the local authority to protect the landscape of the area through policies in the development plan and development control, and to enhance the landscape through positive action.

Under the 1949 Act, National Park authorities were empowered to provide accommodation and meals, camping sites and car parks, to improve waterways for amenity and to restrict traffic on the roads in conjunction with the Department of the Environment. All local planning authorities were empowered to plant trees and to restore and improve derelict land in their area. Under the 1968 Act local planning authorities were authorised to provide country parks, camping sites and picnic sites. The Countryside Commission was empowered to give financial assistance to any person (other than a public body but including the National Trust) in carrying out a project 'conducive to the attainment of any of the purposes' of either the 1949 or 1968 Act.

The 1949 Act enabled the local planning authority in a National Park or elsewhere to enter into access agreements with owners of areas of open country, or in default of agreement by the use of Access Orders to enable the public to enjoy these areas for recreation. A warden service may be established to assist visitors and to enforce bye-laws to ensure proper standards of behaviour. The Act also provided for a survey of public rights of way, for the settlement of disputes over such rights and for definitive maps of rights of way, subject to periodic revision. New rights of way may be created if necessary by compulsion. Paths may be diverted and obsolete paths closed. Subject to the approval of the Secretary of State for the Environment or the Secretary of State for Wales local authorities are responsible for carrying out the work of creating and maintaining new rights of way.

The 1949 Act also provided for the creation of long-distance footpaths and bridleways of which the Pennine Way is perhaps the best known.

Until March 1974 a number of specific grants were

payable towards expenditure incurred on defined projects or services in the countryside in general and National Parks in particular. They have been replaced since 1 April 1974 by incorporation of the relevant expenditure in connection with National Parks. In addition, Section 9 of the 1974 Act empowers the Countryside Commission to provide direct financial assistance towards expenditure which, in the Commission's opinion, is conducive to the attainment of any of the purposes of the 1949 or 1968 Acts; this expenditure may be incurred by a local authority, public body or private person.

Under Section 86 of the 1949 Act and Section 2 of the 1968 Act the Commission has a duty to provide or to assist in the provision of information services in the National Parks or in the countryside generally.

The Commission is required to prepare annual reports. These reports are available from H.M.S.O. and provide valuable accounts of progress. The Commission also publish many research reports, guides and information leaflets, a list of which is obtainable free of charge from their office.

12.8.8 Control of caravan and camp sites
Caravan sites are subject to control under the Caravan Sites and Control of Development Act, 1960, and the Public Health Act, 1936. Camping sites for tents etc. are controlled under the various consolidated Town and Country Planning Acts. In general, a person intending to operate a caravan site must apply for and obtain planning permission from the appropriate planning authority and a site operating licence from the local authority. This licence must then be prominently displayed on the site. Local authorities can themselves provide and operate caravan sites. The Mobile Homes Act, 1973, provides some security of tenure for those who live in caravans.

Planning permission and a site licence are not necessary if a caravan is used in conjunction with a dwelling house; if it is on the site for less than a period of twenty-eight days in a year and used only casually, if it is under the auspices of an approved recreational organisation; or if it is to be used in connection with building or agricultural operations or by travelling showmen.

The Secretary of State for the Environment is empowered to specify model standards for caravan sites. Those laid down in 1960 specified, for instance, the spacing between caravans, width of roads and footpaths and the minimum area to be allocated to recreational purposes, on permanent caravan sites. Similar but less demanding standards were set for holiday caravan sites in use regularly, except during the winter. Anyone undertaking work concerning caravan or camp sites should contact their local planning authority, the Department of the Environment or the Countryside Commission for the latest information on regulations which are applic-

able, especially as model standards are advisory rather than mandatory.

12.8.9 Reclamation of derelict land
There is no statutory definition of derelict, neglected or unsightly land but for grant purposes the Department of the Environment have adopted the following (Ministry of Housing and Local Government Circular 68/65). 'Derelict land means land so damaged by industrial or other development that it is incapable of beneficial use without reinstatement. This definition includes sites such as disused spoil heaps, worked out mineral excavations, abandoned industrial installations and land damaged by mining subsidence. It *excludes* land which may be regarded as derelict from natural causes such as marsh land and neglected woodland.'

The legislation at present mostly relevant to reclamation are section 8, Local Employment Act 1972, section 9, Local Government Act, 1966 and section 97 (1) (c) of the National Parks and Access to the Countryside Act, 1949. Grants for work on derelict, neglected or unsightly land carried out by local authority may be payable under the following provisions.

Act	Area to which Act applies	Rate of Grant
(a) Local Employment Act, 1972	Development areas, derelict land, clearance areas and intermediate areas	100%
(b) National Parks and Access to the Countryside Act, 1949, Section 97 (1) (c)	National Parks and Areas of Outstanding Natural Beauty	75% of work carried out under Section 6 (1) 1963
(c) Local Government Act, 1966	Elsewhere in England and Wales	50%

Development areas are defined in Statutory Instrument 1966/1032; details are available from the Department of Trade and Industry. Intermediate areas and derelict land clearance areas are specified in the Intermediate Areas Order, 1970 (S.I. 1970 No. 308), and the Derelict Clearance Area Order, 1970 (S.I. 1970 No. 309), respectively and as amended by the Intermediate Areas Order, 1971 (S.I. 1971 No. 329) and the Intermediate Areas and Derelict Land Clearance Order, 1972 (S.I. 1972 No. 421). As the procedures for making grant applications are varied from time to time it is advisable to obtain the relevant information from the Department of the Environment or one of its regional offices.

12.8.10 Agriculture Act, 1947

Under this Act, the National Agricultural Advisory Service was established. The free technical advice and information which it supplied was of considerable value to the landscape architect undertaking large-scale landscape surveys and dealing with landscape and planning problems in the countryside. In order to improve regional organisation, the Agricultural Development and Advisory Service came into being on 1 March 1971 replacing the National Agricultural Advisory Service. This new body combines the Ministry's professional, scientific and technical service. Some advice can be obtained free but a charge is made for services such as testing and analysis.

12.8.11 Recent legislation and taxation

The Health and Safety at Work Act, 1974, and the Control of Pollution Act, 1974, have a peripheral relevance to the subject of this chapter, the former mainly for the procedural improvements in the system of building control and the latter for its provisions regarding water, noise and atmospheric pollution.

Related to land use and planning applications, the Community Land Act, 1975, and the Development Land Tax Act, 1976, should be studied, particularly in relation to housing and commercial developments over a certain specified size.

Capital Transfer Tax is of importance in relation to forestry in particular as it can involve tax being demanded on the value of standing timber which has no actual commercial value until it is old enough to be felled. The tentatively proposed Wealth Tax, if introduced, would have even more severe consequences on standing timber in woodland and forestry areas. The proper legal and financial expert advice should be sought on these matters.

Value Added Tax is of importance on most landscape work. It is usually applicable to all landscape and planting work except that of a semi-engineering type (like playing fields) and that which forms part of a building contract. There are no exact criteria for its application in marginal cases and the decision rests between the contractor concerned and his local Customs and Excise Office.

Scottish Development Agency Act, 1975. This gives extensive powers in relation to landscape work in Scotland with respect to derelict land and rehabilitation.

Bibliography

Elements of Quantity Surveying, Willis, Crosby Lockwood.

Handbook of Architectural Practice and Management, Royal Institute of British Architects.

Metric Handbook Architects Journal, Architectural Press.

Specification (with section on landscape), Architectural Press.

Specification Writing for Architects and Surveyors, Willis, Crosby Lockwood.

Spon's Landscapes Handbook, edited by Derek Lovejoy and Partners, E. & F. N. Spon Limited.

Standard Method of Measurement, Royal Institution of Chartered Surveyors.

Standard Method of Measurement, Institution of Civil Engineers.

British Standards applicable to landscape work; many are available on various materials and of especial relevance is B.S. 4428:1969, *Recommendations for general landscape work*.

LI Standard instruction/variation forms and certificates are now available only from R.I.B.A. Publications Ltd.

JCLI Form of Contract also available only from R.I.B.A. Publications Ltd.

Appendix

A.1.1 Linear measure

CONVERSION TABLES

	Centimetres	Metres	Kilometres
1 inch	2·54	0·025	0·00002
1 foot	30·48	0·304	0·00030
1 yard	91·44	0·914	0·00091
1 mile	—	1609·344	1·60934

	Inch	Foot	Yard
1 centimetre	0·393	0·032	0·010
1 metre	39·370	3·280	1·903
1 kilometre	—	3280·8	1093·6

CONVERSION FACTORS

To convert	Multiply by
Metres to inches	39·37
Metres to feet	3·280
Metres to yards	1·093
Kilometres to miles	0·6214
Inches to metres	0·025
Feet to metres	0·304
Yards to metres	0·914
Miles to kilometres	1·609

A.1.2 Area

CONVERSION FACTORS

	Square metres	Hectares
1 square foot	0·093	—
1 square yard	0·836	—
1 acre	4046·860	0·405
1 square mile	—	258·999

	Square feet	Square yards	Acres
1 square metre	10·76	1·196	—
1 hectare	—	11959·9	2·471

A.1.2.1 Acres to square yards

Acres	Square yards	Acres	Square yards
0·005	24·2	0·20	968
0·01	48·4	0·207	1000
0·02	96·8	0·30	1452
0·021	100	0·40	1936
0·03	145·2	0·413	2000
0·04	193·6	0·50	2420
0·041	200	0·60	2904
0·05	242	0·619	3000
0·062	300	0·70	3388
0·083	400	0·80	3872
0·10	484	0·826	4000
0·103	500	1·0	4840

CONVERSION FACTORS

To convert	Multiply by
Square feet to square metres	0·093
Square yards to square metres	0·836
Acres to hectares	0·405
Square miles to hectares	258·9
Square metres to square feet	10·76
Square metres to square yards	1·196
Hectares to acres	2·471
Hectares to square miles	0·0039

NOTE
1. An acre is equivalent to a square of 208 ft 8 in side. A hectare is equivalent to a square of 100 m side.
2. Irish, Scottish and Welsh acres may occasionally be encountered. They vary in different parts of the British Isles from 3,240 sq yd to 9,780 sq yd.

A.1.3 Volume

CONVERSION TABLES

	Cubic metres	Litres	U.S. liquid pints	U.S. gallons
1 cubic foot	0·028	28·316	59·844	7·480
1 cubic yard	0·764	764·5	—	—
1 U.K. pint	—	0·568	1·201	0·150
1 U.K. gallon	0·0045	4·546	9·607	1·201

	Cubic feet	Cubic yards	U.K. pints	U.K. gallons
1 cubic metre	35·315	1·308	—	—
1 litre	0·035	—	1·760	0·220
1 U.S. liquid pint	0·017	—	0·833	0·104
1 U.S. gallon	0·134	—	6·661	0·833

CONVERSION FACTORS

To convert	Multiply by
Cubic inches to cubic centimetres	16·39
Cubic feet to cubic metres	0·028
Cubic yards to cubic metres	0·764
Cubic metres to cubic feet	35·315
Cubic metres to cubic yards	1·308
U.K. pints to U.S. liquid pints	1·201
U.K. gallons to U.S. gallons	1·201
U.K. pints to litres	0·568
U.K. gallons to litres	4·546
U.S. liquid pints to U.K. pints	0·833
U.S. gallons to U.K. gallons	0·833
U.S. liquid pints to litres	0·473
U.S. gallons to litres	3·785

NOTE

An Imperial Bushel is a dry measure equivalent to 8 U.K. gallons or 4 pecks, and contains 1·28 cubic feet (e.g. 10 in × 10 in × 22 in)

A.1.3.1 Rainfall

CONVERSION TABLES

Inches of rainfall	Gallons per acre	Cubic feet per acre	Tons per acre
1	22,635	3,630	101·1
2	45,270	7,260	202·2
3	67,905	10,890	303·3
4	90,539	14,520	404·4
5	113,174	18,150	505·5
10	226,348	36,300	1011·0

A.1.4 Weight

CONVERSION TABLES

	Kilo-gramme	Tonne	U.S. short cwt	U.S. short ton
1 lb	0·45	0·00045	0·01	0·0005
1 cwt	50·8	0·0508	1·12	0·056
1 ton	1,016	1·016	22·4	1·12

	Pound	Hundred-weight	Ton
1 tonne	2,204·62	19·684	0·984
1 kilogramme	2·205	0·020	—
1 U.S. short hundred-weight	100	0·893	0·045
1 U.S. short ton	2,000	17·857	0·893

CONVERSION FACTORS

To convert	Multiply by
Hundredweights to kilogrammes	50·8
Hundredweights to tonnes	0·051
Hundredweights to U.S. short hundredweights	1·12
Hundredweights to U.S. short tons	0·056
Tons to kilogrammes	1,016
Tons to tonnes	1·016
Tons to U.S. short hundredweights	22·4
Tons to U.S. short tons	1·12
Tonnes to hundredweights	19·684
Tonnes to tons	0·984
Tonnes to U.S. short hundredweights	22·046
Tonnes to U.S. short tons	1·102
U.S. short hundredweights to hundredweights	0·893
U.S. short hundredweights to tons	0·045
U.S. short hundredweights to kilogrammes	45·359
U.S. short hundredweights to tonnes	0·045
U.S. short tons to hundredweights	17·857
U.S. short tons to tons	0·893
U.S. short tons to kilogrammes	907·185
U.S. short tons to tonnes	0·907

A.1.4.1 Weight per unit area

CONVERSION TABLES

	Grammes per square metre	Kilogrammes per hectare
1 oz per sq yd	33·906	339·057
1 lb per acre	0·112	1·121

	Ounces per square yard	Pounds per acre
1 g per sq m	0·029	8·922
1 kg per hectare	0·0029	0·892

CONVERSION FACTORS

To convert	Multiply by
oz per sq yd to g per sq m	33·906
oz per sq yd to kg per hectare	339·057
lb per acre to g per sq m	0·112
lb per acre to kg per hectare	1·121
g per sq m to oz per sq yd	0·029
g per sq m to lb per acre	8·922
kg per hectare to oz per sq yd	0·003
kg per hectare to lb per acre	0·892

A.1.4.2 Weight per unit area

CONVERSION TABLE

Ounces per square yard	Pounds per acre	Hundredweights per acre	Tons per acre
$\frac{3}{8}$*	112	1	
$\frac{1}{2}$	151$\frac{1}{4}$	1$\frac{1}{3}$*	
$\frac{3}{4}$*	224	2	
1	302$\frac{1}{2}$	2$\frac{2}{3}$*	
1$\frac{1}{2}$*	448	4	
1$\frac{3}{4}$*	560	5	$\frac{1}{4}$
2	605	5$\frac{1}{2}$*	
2$\frac{1}{4}$*	672	6	
3*	896	8	
3$\frac{3}{4}$*	1,120	10	$\frac{1}{2}$
4	1,210	10$\frac{3}{4}$*	
7$\frac{1}{2}$*	2,240	20	1
15*	4,480	40	2
29*	8,960	80	4
60*	17,920	160	8
74*	22,400	200	10

* approximate

A.1.5 Temperature

CONVERSION TABLE

Fahrenheit	Centigrade	Fahrenheit	Centigrade
212*	100*	98·6†	37†
200	93·3	90	32·2
180	82·2	80	26·6
160	71·1	70	21·1
140	60	60	15·5
120	48·8	50	10
100	37·7	40	4·4
		32‡	0‡

* Boiling point   † Blood heat   ‡ Freezing point

CONVERSION FACTORS

To convert degrees Centigrade to degrees Fahrenheit multiply by $\frac{9}{5}$ and add 32.

To convert degrees Fahrenheit to degrees Centigrade subtract 32 and multiply by $\frac{5}{9}$.

A.1.6 Gradients

CONVERSION TABLE

Gradient	Angle	%
1 in 1	**45°**	**100**
1 in 1·732	**30°**	5
1 in 2	26° 34′	**50**
1 in 2·747	**20°**	
1 in 3	18° 26′	33$\frac{1}{3}$
1 in 4	14° 02′	**25**
1 in 5	11° 19′	**20**
1 in 5·671	**10°**	
1 in 10	5° 43′	**10**
1 in 11·430	**5**	
1 in 14·301	**4°**	
1 in 15	3° 49′	6$\frac{2}{3}$
1 in 19·081	**3°**	
1 in 20	2° 52′	**5**
1 in 28·65	**2°**	
1 in 40	1° 25′	2$\frac{1}{2}$
1 in 57·290	**1°**	
1 in 60	0° 57′	1$\frac{2}{3}$
1 in 80	0° 43′	1$\frac{1}{4}$
1 in 100	0° 34′	**1**
1 in 114·59	0° **30′**	
1 in 150	0° 23′	

NOTE

All gradients in this table are calculated 1/horizontal distance

A.1.7 Cost

CONVERSION TABLE

Cost per square yard (p)	Cost per acre (£)	Cost per square yard (p)	Cost per acre (£)
0·1	4·84	**5·00**	242
0·2	9·68	6·20*	**300**
0·25	12·10	7·50	363
0·3	14·52	8·26*	**400**
0·4	19·36		
0·5	24·20	**10·00**	484
0·52*	**25·00**	10·33*	**500**
		20·00	968
0·75	36·30	20·66*	**1,000**
		25·00	1,210
1·0	48·40	**30·00**	1,452
1·03*	**50·00**	**40·00**	1,936
2·0	96·80	41·32*	**2,000**
2·07*	**100·00**	**50·00**	2,420
2·5	121·00		
3·0	145·20	**75·00**	**3,630**
4·0	193·60		
4·13*	**200·00**	**100·00**	4,840

* approximate

A.2.1 Weights of Construction Materials

Material	Specific gravity	Weight per cubic foot (lb)
Granite	2·65	166
Marble	2·7	170
Portland stone	2·2	140
Slate	2·7	170
York stone	2·2	140
Brickwork	1·84	115
Concrete; lightweight	1·44	90
Concrete; precast	2·1	130
Concrete; reinforced	2·4	150
Lime	0·84	53
Plaster	0·8	50
Timber; hardwood	0·72	45
Timber; softwood	0·56	35
Cast iron	7·2	450
Steel	7·8	490
Bronze	8·2	510

A.2.1.1 Weights of soils

Material	Specific gravity	Weight per cubic yard (cwt)
Clay soil: compacted, dry	1·2–1·6	18–24
Clay soil: compacted, wet	>2·0	30
Clay soil: loose dry	1·7	25
Loam: *in situ*, dry	1·3	20
Loam: *in situ*, wet	1·9	29
Loam: loose dug	1·2	18
Sandy loam: *in situ*	1·5–1·6	22–24
Sandy loam: loose dug	1·5	22
Dry sand	1·5–1·75	22–26
Wet sand	1·75–2·0	26–30
Gravel	1·75	26
Chalk	2·0	30
Limestone	2·2	33
Marl	1·7	25
Sandstone	2·0	30
Shale	2·4	36

A.2.1.2 Water

1 Imperial gal = 10 lb = 0·16 cu ft = 4·54 l.
1 U.S. gal = 8·33 lb = 0·13 cu ft = 3·79 l.
1 ton of water = 36 cu ft
= 224 gal
1 ft head of water = 0·434 lb per sq in (p.s.i.)
1 lb per sq in (p.s.i.) = 2·3 ft head of water
1 atmosphere = 34 ft head of water
= 14·7 lb sq in (p.s.i.)
= 30 in of mercury (inHg)

$$\text{Water horsepower} = \frac{\text{gal per min} \times \text{total head in ft}}{3,300}$$

$$\text{Horsepower required to drive pumps} = \frac{\text{water hp} \times 100}{\text{efficiency percentage of motor or engine}}$$

A.2.2 Textural composition of soils

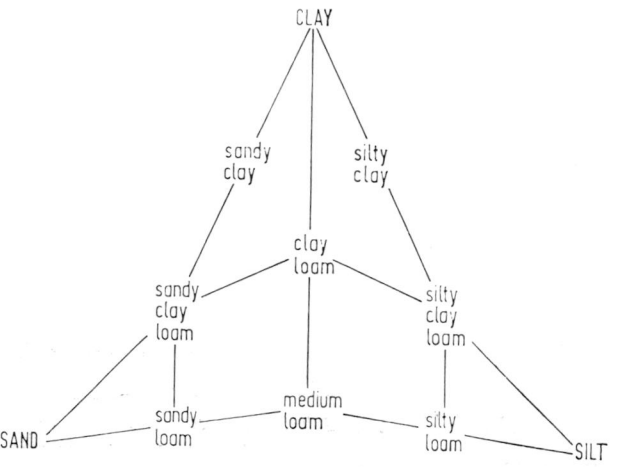

A.2.2.1 Soil: Hand test for texture

Work a handful of *moist* soil in the fingers:

If it is gritty and fails to soil the fingers	**Sand**
If it is gritty but soils the fingers and can be pressed roughly into a ball	**Sandy-loam**
If it is 'sticky', easily moulded in the fingers and quickly 'polished' by sliding between the finger and thumb	**Clay-loam**
If it is sticky, stiff and plastic enough to be rolled into long flexible 'worms'	**Clay**
If it is not sticky, nor can be polished, but feels 'silky' or 'soapy', and can be moulded but is not cohesive	**Silty-loam**
If it is neither gritty, sticky nor silky	**Medium-loam**

DEFINITIONS

Loam: a mixture of clay, sand and silt in fairly balanced proportions
Marl: a mixture of clay and chalk

A.2.2.2 Soil: Water holding capacity (expressed as a percentage of weight)

Coarse sandy soil	15–30
Light loam	22–34
Stiff clay	36–50
Sandy peat	53–60

A.2.2.3 Angle of repose of various soils

Firm earth (*in situ*)	50°
Loose earth or vegetable soil	28°
Firm clay	45°
Wet clay	16°
Dry sand	38°
Wet sand	22°

A.2.2.4 Constituents of soils (main constituents given as a percentage: according to Dr Voelcker)

	Organic matter	Clay	Sand	Lime	Potash	Phosphoric acid	Alkalies (incl. magnesia)
Fertile loam	4·38	18·09	76·16	1·37	0·49	0·12	—
Orchard soil (under turf)	11·70	48·39	35·95	1·54	0·91	0·08	—
Calcareous clayey soil	11·08	52·06	24·53	11·53	0·32	0·12	—
Heavy clay	4·87	72·29	9·26	1·15	0·06	1·37	—
Sterile sandy soil	5·36	4·57	89·82	0·25	—	(trace)	0·49

A.2.3 Principal constituents of manures (figures given are average gross percentages)

	Water	Organic matter	Nitrogen (or ammonia)	Phosphoric acid or phosphates	Potash	Lime	Magnesium
Farmyard manure	72·6	27·4	0·77	0·39	0·6		
Poultry manure (dried)	7		4	2·3	1·2		
Hoof and horn			12·5	1·0			
Dried blood			12·5				
Bone meal			3·7	22			
'Improved' blood, meat and bone meal			3	9	5		
Fish meal	14	50	4·5	9	5	12	
Wood ash				2·8	9	4·3	3·8
Sewage sludge (dried)	5–10		2·0	2·0			
Sewage sludge (activated)	5–10		6·0	3·0	0·5		
Spent mushroom beds			1·0	0·7	1·5		
Basic slag				15		45	
Guano (very variable)	5–20	7–40	2–14	40 av.	0·5–3·0	10–40	
Human faeces	77	20	1	1·1	0·3	0·6	0·5
Garden compost (av.)	10–15	10–20	0·8	0·45	1·45	1·25	0·3

254

A.2.3.1 Mixing of manures and fertilisers (Geehen's Chart)

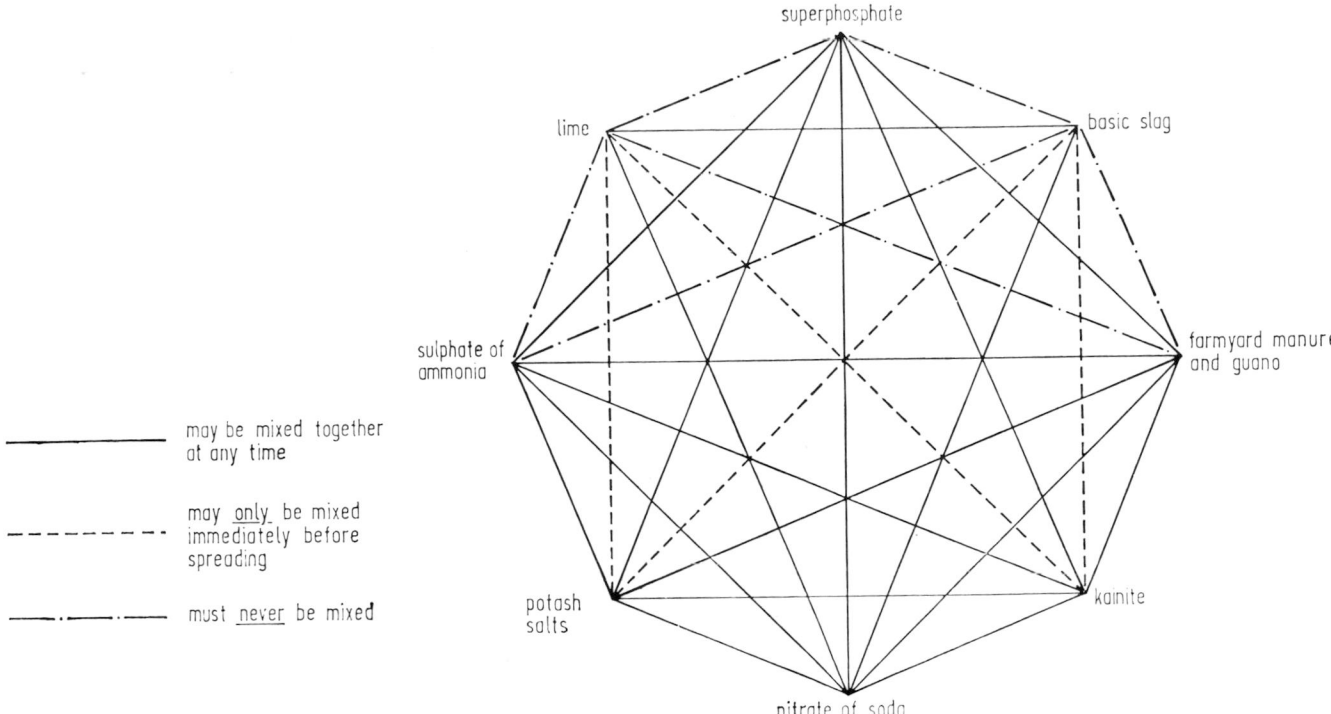

may be mixed together at any time

may only be mixed immediately before spreading

must never be mixed

A.2.4 Comparative rates of growth of trees

Heights given in the tables are approximate and show the likely growth in 20 years and 50 years of trees growing in *average* conditions in Britain. Slower rates of growth should be expected in difficult exposure or town conditions.

Expected height in 20 years	Expected height in 50 years
LESS THAN 6 M (APPROX. 20 FT)	LESS THAN 12 M (APPROX. 40 FT)
Arbutus	Arbutus
Almond	Almond
Japanese Cherry	Japanese Cherry
Cedar	
Crab Apple	Crab Apple
Catalpa	
	Eucalyptus
Gleditschia	Gleditschia
Hawthorn	Hawthorn
	Holly
Laburnum	Laburnum
Hornbeam	
Magnolia	Magnolia
Field Maple	Field Maple
Oak	
	Willow-leaf Pear
Plane	
Rowan	Rowan
Whitebeam	Whitebeam
Yew	Yew

Expected height in 20 years	Expected height in 50 years
6 M TO 12 M (APPROX. 20 TO 40 FT)	12 M TO 18 M (APPROX. 40 TO 60 FT)
Ailanthus	
Alder	Alder
Ash	Ash
Beech	Beech
Birch	
	Catalpa
	Cedar
Eucalyptus	
Horse Chestnut	Horse Chestnut
Red Chestnut	Red Chestnut
Sweet Chestnut	Sweet Chestnut
Lawsons Cypress	
Swamp Cypress	Swamp Cypress
English Elm	English Elm
Cornish Elm	Cornish Elm
Wych Elm	
Gean	
Gingko	
Holly	
	Hornbeam

255

Expected height in 20 years	Expected height in 50 years
6 M TO 12 M (APPROX. 20 TO 40 FT) Larch	12 M TO 18 M (APPROX. 40 TO 60 FT)
Lime	Lime
Silver Maple	Silver Maple
Oak	Oak
Scarlet Oak	Scarlet Oak
Holm Oak	Holm Oak
Turkey Oak	
Corsican Pine	
Scots Pine	Scots Pine
	Plane
Serbian Spruce	
Sycamore	
Walnut	Walnut
Willows	Willows
OVER 12 M (APPROX. 40 FT) Acacia	OVER 18 M (APPROX. 60 FT) Acacia
	Ailanthus
	Birch
	Lawsons Cypress
	Wych Elm
Noble Fir	Noble Fir
	Gingko
	Larch
	Turkey Oak
	Corsican Pine
Grey Poplar	
	Spruce
	Serbian Spruce
	Norway Spruce
	Sycamore
Thuya plicata	Thuya plicata
Tulip Tree	
Tsuga	
	Willows
White Willow	
Wellingtonia	
OVER 18 M (APPROX. 60 FT) Douglas Fir	OVER 24 M (SAY 80 FT) Douglas Fir
Giant Fir	Giant Fir
Black Poplar	Black Poplar
	Grey Poplar
Lombardy Poplar	Lombardy Poplar
Sitka Spruce	Sitka Spruce
	Tulip Tree
	Tsuga
	Wellingtonia
	White Willow

A.2.4.1 Plants which assist in indicating soil conditions

Sphagnum mosses	Wet, acid, peaty soil
Heather and ling Erica and Calluna spp.	Dry acid soil
Rushes and reeds Juncus and Carex spp.	Wet, poor (boggy) soil
Common (perennial creeping) stinging nettle – Urtica dioica	Potentially fertile soil
Chickweed Stellaria media	Potentially fertile soil
Canterbury bells Campanula glomerata	Chalky or limey soil
Thistle Carduus spp.	Waste ground
Sheep's sorrel Rumex acetosella	Poor, light, dry acid (sour) soil
Foxglove Digitalis purpurea	Dry, sandy or gravelly soil
Hoary plantain Plantago media	Dry, hard, stony, alkaline soil
Barren (wild) strawberry Potentilla fragaria	Dry, stony, barren soil
Common furze Ulex europaeus	Poor, infertile soil
Heath bedstraw Galium saxatile	Dry, light, acid soil
Silverweed Potentilla anserina	Damp places (profuse on clay)

A.2.4.2 Number of plants to the square metre

Distance apart* (mm)	Number per square metre†	Distance apart* (m)	Number per hectare
200	25·00	1·2	6,940
250	16·00	1·5	4,444
300	11·10	2	2,500
400	6·25	2·5	1,600
450	5·00	3	1,110
500	4·00	4	625
600	2·78	5	400
700	2·04	6	278
750	1·78	7	204
800	1·56	7·5	178
900	1·23	8	156
1,000	1·00	10	100

* In rows at the same distance apart.
† To 2 places of decimals.

A.2.4.3 Number of plants to the square yard (area)

Distance apart*	Number per square yard	Number per acre
6 in	36	174,240
9 in	16	77,440
12 in	9	43,560
15 in	$5\frac{4}{5}$	27,878
18 in	4	19,360
2 ft	$2\frac{1}{4}$	10,890
3 ft	1	4,840
4 ft	—	2,722
5 ft	—	1,742
6 ft	—	1,210
7 ft	—	889
8 ft	—	680
9 ft	—	537
10 ft	—	435
12 ft	—	302
14 ft	—	222
15 ft	—	193
20 ft	—	108
25 ft	—	70
30 ft	—	48
40 ft	—	27
50 ft	—	18

* In rows at the same distance apart.

A.3.1 British Standards applicable to landscape work

B.S.12–	Portland cement (ordinary and rapid-hardening)
Part 1: 1958	Imperial units
Part 2: 1971	Metric units
B.S. 65 and 540	Clay drain and sewer pipes including surface water pipes and fittings
Part 1: 1971	Pipes and fittings
Part 2: 1972	Flexible mechanical joints
B.S. 76: 1974	Tars for road purposes
B.S. 144: 1973	Coal tar creosote for the preservation of timber
B.S. 340: 1963	Precast concrete kerbs, channels, edgings and quadrants
B.S. 368: 1971	Precast concrete flags
B.S. 381C: 1964	Colours for specific purposes
B.S. 435: 1975	Dressed natural stone kerbs, channels, quadrants, and setts
B.S. 497: 1967	Cast manhole covers, road gully gratings and frames for drainage purposes
B.S. 539: 1971	Dimensions of fittings for use with clay drain and sewer pipes
B.S. 556–	Concrete cylindrical pipes and fittings including manholes, inspection chambers and street gullies
Part 1: 1966	Imperial units
Part 2: 1972	Metric units
B.S. 565: 1972	Glossary of terms relating to timber and woodwork
B.S. 594: 1973	Rolled asphalt (hot process) for roads and other paved areas
B.S. 743: 1970	Materials for damp-proof courses
B.S. 802: 1967	Tarmacadam with crushed rock or slag aggregate
B.S. 864: 1953 –	Capillary and compression tube fittings of copper and copper alloy
Part 2: 1971	Metric units
Part 3: 1975	Compression fittings for polyethylene pipes
B.S. 881, 589: 1974	Nomenclature of commercial timbers, including sources of supply
B.S. 882, 1201: 1965	Aggregates from natural sources for concrete (including granolithic)
Part 2: 1973	Metric units
B.S. 892: 1967	Glossary of highway engineering terms
B.S. 913: 1973	Wood preservation by means of pressure creosoting
B.S. 1010 –	Draw-off taps and stopvalves for water services (screwdown pattern)
Part 1: 1959	Imperial units
Part 2: 1973	Draw-off taps and above-ground stopvalves
B.S. 1014: 1975	Pigments for Portland cement and Portland cement products
B.S. 1185: 1963	Guards for underground stopvalves
B.S. 1192: 1969	Building drawing practice
B.S. 1194: 1969	Concrete porous pipes for under-drainage
B.S. 1196: 1971	Clayware field drain pipes
B.S. 1198–1200: 1955	Building sands from natural sources
B.S. 1217: 1975	Cast stone
B.S. 1222: 1945	Battery-operated electric fences
B.S. 1241: 1959	Tarmacadam and tar carpets (gravel aggregate)
B.S. 1242: 1960	Tarmacadam 'tarpaving' for footpaths, playgrounds and similar works
B.S. 1247: 1975	Manhole step irons
B.S. 1282: 1975	Guide to the choice, use and application of wood preservatives
B.S. 1286: 1974	Clay tiles for flooring
B.S. 1308: 1970	Concrete street lighting columns
B.S. 1377: 1975	Methods of testing soils for civil engineering purposes
B.S. 1426 and 3461: 1969	Surface boxes for gas and waterworks purposes
B.S. 1438: 1971	Media for biological percolating filters

B.S. 1446: 1973	*Mastic asphalt (natural rock asphalt fine aggregate) for roads and footways*	B.S. 1984: 1967	*Gravel aggregates for surface treatment (including surface dressings) on roads*
B.S. 1447: 1973	*Mastic asphalt (limestone fine aggregate) for roads and footways*	B.S. 2028,	
B.S. 1485: 1971	*Galvanised wire netting*	B.S. 1364: 1968	*Precast concrete blocks*
B.S. 1621: 1961	*Bitumen macadam with crushed rock or slag aggregate*	B.S. 2040: 1953	*Bitumen macadam with gravel aggregate*

B.S. 1446: 1973 *Mastic asphalt (natural rock asphalt fine aggregate) for roads and footways*
B.S. 1447: 1973 *Mastic asphalt (limestone fine aggregate) for roads and footways*
B.S. 1485: 1971 *Galvanised wire netting*
B.S. 1621: 1961 *Bitumen macadam with crushed rock or slag aggregate*
B.S. 1690: 1962 *Cold asphalt*
B.S. 1710: 1971 *Identification of pipelines*
B.S. 1716: 1963 *Cycle stands*
B.S. 1722 – *Fences*
  Part 1: 1972 *Chain link fences*
    Supplement No 1: 1974 Gates and gateposts used in conjunction with chain link fences
  Part 2: 1973 *Woven wire fences*
  Part 3: 1973 *Strained wire fences*
  Part 4: 1972 *Cleft chestnut pale fences*
  Part 5: 1972 *Close-boarded fences including oak pale fences*
  Part 6: 1972 *Wooden palisade fences*
  Part 7: 1972 *Wooden post and rail fences*
  Part 8: 1966 *Mild steel or wrought iron continuous bar fences*
  Part 9: 1963 *Mild steel or wrought iron unclimbable fences with round or square verticals and flat standards and horizontals*
  Part 10: 1972 *Anti-intruder chain link fences*
  Part 11: 1972 *Woven wood fences*
B.S. 1737: 1951 *Jointing materials and compounds for water, town gas and low-pressure steam installations*
B.S. 1740 – *Wrought steel pipe fittings (screwed BSP thread)*
  Part 1: 1971 *Metric units*
  Part 2: 1971 *Imperial units*
B.S. 1775: 1964 *Steel tubes for mechanical, structural and general engineering purposes*
B.S. 1788: 1964 *Street lighting lanterns for use with electric lamps*
B.S. 1831: 1969 *Recommended common names for pesticides*
B.S. 1840: 1960 *Steel columns for street lighting*
B.S. 1878: 1973 *Corrugated copper jointing strip for expansion joints for use in general building construction*
B.S. 1924: 1975 *Methods of test for stabilized soils*
B.S. 1926: 1962 *Ready-mixed concrete*
B.S. 1972: 1967 *Polythene pipe (Type 32) for cold water services*
B.S. 1973: 1970 *Polythene pipe (Type 32) for general purposes including chemical and food industry uses*

B.S. 1984: 1967 *Gravel aggregates for surface treatment (including surface dressings) on roads*
B.S. 2028,
B.S. 1364: 1968 *Precast concrete blocks*
B.S. 2040: 1953 *Bitumen macadam with gravel aggregate*
B.S. 2468: 1963 *Glossary of terms relating to agricultural machinery and implements*
B.S. 2484: 1961 *Cable covers, concrete and earthenware*
B.S. 2494 – *Rubber joint rings for gas mains, water mains and drainage purposes*
  Part 1: 1955 *Rubber joint rings for gas mains and water mains*
  Part 2: 1967 *Rubber joint rings for drainage purposes*
B.S. 2499: 1973 *Hot applied joint sealants for concrete pavements*
B.S. 2580: 1955 *Underground plug cocks for cold water services (Scottish type)*
B.S. 2760: 1973 *Pitch-impregnated fibre pipes and fittings for below and above-ground drainage*
B.S. 2787: 1956 *Glossary of terms for concrete and reinforced concrete*
B.S. 2847: 1957 *Glossary of terms for stone used in building*
B.S. 2871 – *Copper and copper alloys, tubes*
  Part 1: 1971 *Copper tubes for water, gas and sanitation*
  Part 2: 1972 *Tubes for general purposes*
B.S. 3049: 1973 *Pedestrian guard rails (metal)*
B.S. 3051: 1972 *Coal tar creosotes for wood preservation (other than creosotes to B.S. 144)*
B.S. 3148: 1959 *Tests for water for making concrete*
B.S. 3178 – *Playground equipment for parks*
  Part 1: 1959 *General requirements*
  Part 2A: 1959 *Special requirements for static equipment (except slides)*
  Part 2B: 1960 *Special requirements for slides*
  Part 3A: 1960 *Pendulum see-saws*
  Part 3B: 1962 *Plane swings*
  Part 3C: 1964 *Plank swings*
  Part 3D: 1964 *Swings*
  Part 3E: 1964 *Rocking boats*
  Part 3F: 1964 *Rocking horses*
  Part 4: 1965 *Rotating equipment*
B.S. 3191 – *Fixed playground equipment for schools*
  Part 1: 1959 *General requirements*
  Part 2: 1959 *Rope equipment*
  Part 3A: 1961 *Special requirements for steel tubular assault poles*

Part 3B: 1964   *Special requirements for steel tubular climbing apparatus*

Part 3C: 1964   *Special requirementss for frames for climbing ropes, rope ladders, hand rings and trapeze bars*

Part 3D: 1964   *Special requirements for steel tubular horizontal bars*

Part 3E: 1965   *Special requirements for steel horizontal ladders*

Part 3F: 1965   *Special requirements for steel parallel bars*

Part 3G: 1965   *Special requirements for steel window ladders*

B.S. 3251: 1960   *Hydrant indicator plates*

B.S. 3284: 1967   *Polythene pipe (Type 50) for cold water services*

B.S. 3416: 1975   *Black bitumen coating solutions for cold application*

B.S. 3445: 1961   *Field water troughs*

B.S. 3452: 1962   *Copper/chrome water-borne wood preservatives and their application*

B.S. 3453: 1962   *Fluoride / arsenate / chromate / dinitrophenol water-borne wood preservatives and their application*

B.S. 3470: 1975   *Field gates and posts*

B.S. 3505: 1968   *Unplasticized PVC pipe for cold water services*

B.S. 3506: 1969   *Unplasticized PVC pipe for industrial purposes*

B.S. 3589: 1963   *Glossary of general building terms*

B.S. 3656: 1973   *Asbestos-cement pipes, joints and fittings for sewerage and drainage*

B.S. 3690: 1970   *Bitumens for road purposes*

B.S. 3746: 1964   *PVC garden hose*

B.S. 3797: 1964   *Lightweight aggregates for concrete*

B.S. 3798: 1964   *Coping units (of clayware, unreinforced cast concrete, unreinforced cast stone, natural stone and slate)*

B.S. 3826: 1969   *Silicone-based water repellents for masonry*

B.S. 3867: 1969   *Outside diameters and pressure ratings of pipe of plastics materials*

B.S. 3882: 1965   *Recommendations and classification for top soil*

B.S. 3892: 1965   *Pulverized-fuel ash for use in concrete*

B.S. 3921: 1974   *Clay bricks and blocks*

B.S. 3936 –   *Nursery stock*

Part 1: 1965   *Trees and shrubs*

Part 2: 1966   *Roses*

Part 3: 1965   *Fruit*

Part 4: 1966   *Forest trees*

Part 5: 1967   *Poplars and willows for timber production*

Part 7: 1968   *Bedding plants grown in boxes or trays*

Part 9: 1968   *Bulbs, corms and tubers*

B.S. 3969: 1965   *Recommendations for turf for general landscape purposes*

B.S. 3975 –   *Glossary for landscape work*

Part 4: 1966   *Plant description*

Part 5: 1969   *Horticultural, arboricultural and forestry practice*

B.S. 3989: 1966   *Aluminium street lighting columns*

B.S. 3998: 1966   *Recommendations for tree work*

B.S. 4008: 1973   *Cattle grids on private roads*

B.S. 4043: 1966   *Recommendations for transplanting semi-mature trees*

B.S. 4072: 1974   *Wood preservation by means of water-borne copper/chrome/arsenic compositions*

B.S. 4092 –   *Domestic front entrance gates*

Part 1: 1966   *Metal gates*

Part 2: 1966   *Wooden gates*

B.S. 4101: 1967   *Concrete unreinforced tubes and fittings with ogee joints for surface water drainage*

B.S. 4102: 1971   *Steel wire for fences*

B.S. 4132: 1973   *Winkle clinker for landscape work*

B.S. 4147: 1973   *Hot applied bitumen based coatings for ferrous products*

B.S. 4156: 1967   *Peat*

B.S. 4164: 1967   *Coal tar based hot applied coating materials for protecting iron and steel, including suitable primers where required*

B.S. 4261: 1968   *Glossary of terms relating to timber preservation*

B.S. 4324: 1968   *Litter bins*

B.S. 4346 –   *Joints and fittings for use with unplasticized PVC pressure pipes*

Part 1: 1969   *Injection moulded unplasticized PVC fittings for solvent welding for use with pressure pipes, including potable water supply*

Part 2: 1970   *Mechanical joints and fittings principally of unplasticized PVC*

Part 3: 1974   *Solvent cements*

B.S. 4357: 1968   *Precast terrazzo units*

B.S. 4428: 1969   *Recommendations for general landscape operations (excluding hard surfaces)*

B.S. 4449: 1969   *Hot rolled steel bars for the reinforcement of concrete*

B.S. 4461: 1969   *Cold worked steel bars for the reinforcement of concrete*

B.S. 4466: 1969   *Bending dimensions and scheduling of bars for the reinforcement of concrete*

B.S. 4471 –   *Dimensions for softwood*

Part 1: 1969	Basic sections
Part 2: 1971	Small resawn sections
B.S. 4482: 1969	Hard drawn mild steel wire for the reinforcement of concrete
B.S. 4483: 1969	Steel fabric for the reinforcement of concrete
B.S. 4504 –	Flanges and bolting for pipes, valves and fittings. Metric series
Part 1: 1969	Ferrous
Part 2: 1974	Copper alloy and composite flanges
B.S. 4622: 1970	Grey iron pipes and fittings
B.S. 4625: 1970	Prestressed concrete pressure pipes (including fittings)
B.S. 4660: 1973	Unplasticized PVC underground drain pipe and fittings
B.S. 4721: 1971	Ready-mixed lime: sand for mortar
B.S. 4729: 1973	Shapes and dimensions of special bricks
B.S. 4772: 1971	Ductile iron pipes and fittings
B.S. 4800: 1972	Paint colours for building purposes
B.S. 4887: 1973	Mortar plasticizers
B.S. 4962: 1973	Performance requirements for plastic pipe for use as light sub-soil drains
B.S. 4978: 1973	Timber grades for structural use
B.S. 4991: 1974	Propylene copolymer pressure pipe
B.S. 5056: 1974	Copper naphthenate wood preservatives
B.S. 5075 –	Concrete admixtures
Part 1: 1974	Accelerating admixtures, retarding admixtures and water-reducing admixtures
B.S. 5178: 1975	Prestressed concrete pipes for sewerage and drainage
B.S. 5212: 1975	Cold poured joint sealants for concrete pavements
B.S. 5326: 1975	Recommendations for cultivation and planting of trees in the advanced nursery stock category

British Standard Codes of Practice applicable to landscape work

Building

C.P. 94: 1971	Demolition
C.P. 96 –	Access for the disabled to buildings
Part 1: 1967	General recommendations
C.P. 98: 1964	Preservative treatments for constructional timber
C.P. 99: 1962	Frost precautions for water services
C.P. 101: 1972	Foundations and substructures for non-industrial buildings of not more than four storeys
C.P. 102: 1973	Protection of buildings against water from the ground

C.P. 121 –	Walling
Part 1: 1973	Brick and block masonry
CP. 121.201: 1951	Masonry walls ashlared with natural stone or with cast stone
C.P. 121.202: 1951	Masonry. Rubble walls
C.P. 202: 1972	Tile flooring and slab flooring
C.P. 221: 1960	External rendered finishes
C.P. 231: 1966	Painting of buildings
C.P. 297: 1972	Precast concrete cladding (non-loadbearing)
C.P. 298: 1972	Natural stone cladding (non-loadbearing)
C.P. 301: 1971	Building drainage
C.P. 302: 1972	Small sewage treatment works
C.P. 302.200: 1949	Cesspools
C.P. 308: 1974	Drainage of roofs and paved areas
C.P. 310: 1965	Water supply
C.P. 402.101: 1952	Hydrant systems
C.P. 499 –	Metal railings and balustrades for use in buildings and their curtilages
Part 1: 1972	Institutional, administrative and residential buildings and stores

Electrical engineering

C.P. 1004 –	Road lighting
Part 1: 1973	General principles
Part 2: 1974	Lighting for traffic routes (Group A)
Part 3: 1969	Lighting for lightly trafficked roads and footways (Group B)
Part 4: 1967	Lighting for single-level road junctions, including roundabouts
Part 5: 1973	Lighting for grade-separated junctions
Part 6: 1967	Lighting for bridges and elevated roads (Group D)
Part 7: 1971	Lighting for underpasses and bridged roads
Part 8: 1967	Lighting for roads with special requirements (Group F)
Part 9: 1969	Lighting for town and city centres and areas of civic importance (Group G)
C.P. 1014: 1963	The protection of electrical power equipment against climatic conditions

Civil engineering

C.P. 2001: 1957	Site investigations
C.P. 2003: 1959	Earthworks
C.P. 2005: 1968	Sewerage

C.P. 2007 – *Design and construction of reinforced and prestressed concrete structures for the storage of water and other aqueous fluids*

Part 1: 1960 *Imperial units*
Part 2: 1970 *Metric units*

C.P. 2010 – *Pipelines*

Part 1: 1966 *Installation of pipelines in land*
Part 2: 1970 *Design and construction of steel pipelines in land*
Part 3: 1972 *Design and construction of iron pipelines in land*
Part 4: 1972 *Design and construction of asbestos cement pipelines in land*
Part 5: 1974 *Design and construction of prestressed concrete pressure pipelines in land*

D.D.17: 1972 *Basic range for the co-ordination of colours for building purposes*
D.D. 34: 1974 *Clay bricks with modular dimensions*
P.D. 6444 – *Recommendations for the co-ordination of dimensions in building*

Part 1: 1969 *Basic spaces for structure, external envelope and internal sub-division*
Supplement No. 1 1974 *Agricultural items*

These B.S.I. publications can be obtained from British Standards Institution, Sales Department, Newton House, 101 Pentonville Road, London N1 9ND.

Index

Numbers in bold type refer to plates or figures.

Readers are also referred to the chapter contents pages, which set out the contents of each chapter in considerable detail.